NIGHT FEVER 3

Hospitality Design

FRAME

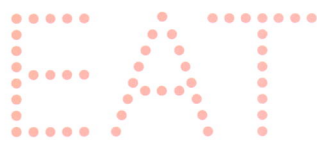

.HBC
UNIT-BERLIN
012

BARBICAN
FOODHALL &
LOUNGE
SHH
014

BOND & BROOK
D-RAW
018

BULLEREI
GIORGIO GULLOTTA
ARCHITEKTEN
024

BUON GRANDE ARIA
BROWNBAG LAB.
026

BURJ AL HAMAM
GM ARCHITECTS
030

CHARLIE
STUDIO NITZAN
COHEN
034

COCORO
STUDIO
GASCOIGNE
036

CORNELIA & CO
GCA ARQUITECTES
ASSOCIATS
042

DACAIO
SYNERGYHAMBURG
044

DE GUSTO
C+L STUDIO AND
COSTA GROUP
046

DN INNOVACIÓN
VERY SPACE
050

ETEN BIJ LIEVEN
LIEVEN MUSSCHOOT
058

GALOUPET
BLACKSHEEP
060

GIACOMO
PLAJER & FRANZ
STUDIO
064

GRAB THAI STREET
KITCHEN
MANSIKKAMÄKI+JOY
070

GRAND CAFÉ PEARL
BARZILEYE
CONCEPT & DESIGN
072

H3
MARCO SOUSA
SANTOS AND TOMÁS
AZEVEDO NEVES
076

HAIKU
IMAGINE NATIVE
078

HOLYFIELDS
IPPOLITO FLEITZ
GROUP
080

JAFFA\TEL AVIV
BK ARCHITECTURE
086

KOOZIE
BEERS|BRICKWORKS
090

KÜNSTLERHAUS-
FARM
STUDIO NITZAN
COHEN
096

KÜNSTLERHAUS-
GRILL
STUDIO NITZAN
COHEN
098

KUSH
AOO ARCHITECTURE
100

KWINT
SAQ ARCHITECTS
102

LES CAVISTES
BLAZYSGÉRARD
108

LOFT
NUCA STUDIO
110

MAZE
BATES SMART
114

MOMOFUKU SEIŌBO
LUCHETTI KRELLE
118

MOSI
SHH
122

MOTTO AM FLUSS
BEHF ARCHITECTS
124

PARK CAFÉ
MAURICE MENTJENS
128

PHILL
NUCA STUDIO
134

PROSOPA
360ID STUDIO
138

RENAISSANCE
GLENN SESTIG ARCHITECTS
140

SEERESTAURANT OLYMPIAPARK
CLEMENS BACHMANN ARCHITEKTEN
146

SPICE MARKET
CONCRETE ARCHITECTURAL ASSOCIATES
152

STUDIO EAST DINING
CARMODY GROARKE
158

SUSHI ABUSE
AOO ARCHITECTURE
162

THE FORGE
FFD
168

THE TASTINGS ROOM
STUDIO SKLIM
172

TINELLO
BRINKWORTH
178

TORI TORI
ROJKIND ARQUITECTOS AND ESRAWE STUDIO
180

UBON
RASHED ALFOUDARI
186

UDON
GIRBAU MATEU
188

VUE DE MONDE RIALTO
ELENBERG FRASER
190

WHAT HAPPENS WHEN
THE METRICS
194

WIENERWALD
IPPOLITO FLEITZ GROUP
198

YOSHINOYA
AS DESIGN SERVICE
204

ZIZZI
D-RAW
208

ZUIDERS PROEFLOKAAL
PUBBLIK
212

DRINK

ALLURE BY CIPRIANI
ORBIT DESIGN STUDIO
220

ARTHOUSE CAFÉ
JOEY HO DESIGN
224

ATELIER MECANIC
CORVIN CRISTIAN
228

BONBON CLUB
VLS INTERIOR ARCHITECTURE
230

BUCK AND BRECK
MOTORBERLIN.COM
234

CAFÉ FOAM
NOTE DESIGN STUDIO
238

CAFÉ SCHILDERS
PUBBLIK
244

CLUB 69
GLENN SESTIG ARCHITECTS
246

CLUB MUSÉE
PAROLIO & EUPHORIA LAB
250

CRISTINI
ANDREA LUPACCHINI ARCHITETTO
254

D'ESPRESSO
NEMAWORKSHOP
258

DA RE
ANDREA LUPACCHINI ARCHITETTO
260

DAS NEUE KUBITSCHECK
DESIGNLIGA
264

DE VORSTIN
BEERS|BRICKWORKS
268

DISHOOM POP-UP BEACH BAR
HONEST ENTERTAINMENT
270

DUYCKER CAFÉ
BEERS|BRICKWORKS
276

ELBGOLD
GIORGIO GULLOTTA ARCHITEKTEN
278

GINETTE
RAËD ABILLAMA ARCHITECTS
280

HAPPY VIP
CLOUD-9 INTERIOR DESIGN
284

HI/LO
WORKSHOP OF WONDERS
286

HOUSE OF THE PURPLE
...,STAAT CREATIVE AGENCY
292

HYDE
KINNEY CHAN & ASSOCIATES
300

KISMET
BLACKSHEEP
302

KLUCHI
ANTON GRECHKO,
PETER KOSTELOV
AND ALEXEY
ROZENBERG
304

KUFRA LOUNGE BAR
COLLIDANIEL-
ARCHITETTO
308

LA GAÎTÉ LYRIQUE
MANUELLE
GAUTRAND
ARCHITECTURE
314

LE FONOGRAF
ANDREA MANTELLO
ARCHITETTO
320

LOOKOUT CAFÉ
DESIGN SPIRITS
326

MELTINO BAR &
LOUNGE
LOFF
328

MOCHA MOJO
MANCINI
ENTERPRISES
334

MS CAFÉ
WUNDERTEAM
336

OZONE
WONDERWALL
342

PLAZA
AROMA
350

PONCELET CHEESE
BAR
GABRIEL CORCHERO
STUDIO
354

PROJECT
RAW DESIGN
358

SMITH&HSU
TEAHOUSE
CARSTEN
JÖRGENSEN
364

STARHILL
TEA SALON
DESIGN SPIRITS
366

TANJONG BEACH
CLUB
TAKENOUCHI WEBB
368

UNPLUGGED BAR
C4ID
INTERIEUR-
ARCHITECTEN
370

YOUDO STONE CAFÉ
LITTLE
374

YUCCA
DARIEL STUDIO
378

ZUMBO
LUCHETTI KRELLE
380

DRINK

SLEEP

25HOURS HOTEL ZURICH WEST
ALFREDO HÄBERLI
388

25HOURS HOTEL VIENNA
DREIMETA
392

25HOURS HOTEL HAMBURG HAFENCITY
STEPHEN WILLIAMS ASSOCIATES
398

CITY GARDEN HOTEL
IDA 14
406

COSMO HOTEL
DUKA DESIGN AND SEHW ARCHITEKTUR
410

EMPIRE HOTEL
AS DESIGN SERVICE
414

FORSTHAUS AM EISWOOG
NAUMANN. ARCHITEKTUR
418

GOLI+BOSI
STUDIO UP
424

HILTON PATTAYA
DEPARTMENT OF ARCHITECTURE
430

HOLIDAY INN
ROOMS
436

HOTEL ACTA MIMIC
EQUIP
440

HOTEL DA VILA
DUARTE CALDEIRA
446

HOTEL MISSONI
GRAVEN IMAGES
450

MANDARIN ORIENTAL HOTEL
PATRICIA URQUIOLA
454

MINT HOTEL
M+R INTERIOR ARCHITECTURE
462

MIURA
LABOR13
466

MOODS
VRTIŠKA·ŽÁK
472

NEW HOTEL
ESTUDIO CAMPANA
478

NHOW
KARIM RASHID
484

OPERA 02
COSTA GROUP
490

PURO HOTEL
BLACKSHEEP
494

QUOTEL
MODE:LINA
498

SANA
FRANCESC RIFÉ STUDIO
504

SCANDIC GRAND CENTRAL
KONCEPT STOCKHOLM
510

THE CLUB
MINISTRY OF DESIGN
514

THE MET HOTEL
ZEGE ARCHITECTS
518

THE MIRROR
GCA ARQUITECTES ASSOCIATS
524

THE NOLITAN
GRZYWINSKI+PONS
530

THE WATERHOUSE AT SOUTH BUND
NERI&HU DESIGN AND RESEARCH OFFICE
536

THE WEINMEISTER
RALF GRÜNDER
542

TOWN @ HOUSE STREET
SIMONE MICHELI
546

TULIP CITY
SPACE ARCHITECTS & DESIGNERS
552

W LONDON
CONCRETE ARCHITECTURAL ASSOCIATES
558

W RETREAT & SPA BALI
AB CONCEPT
566

YOTEL
ROCKWELL GROUP AND SOFTROOM
572

DESIGNER PROFILES
577

VENUE ADDRESSES
591

CREDITS
598

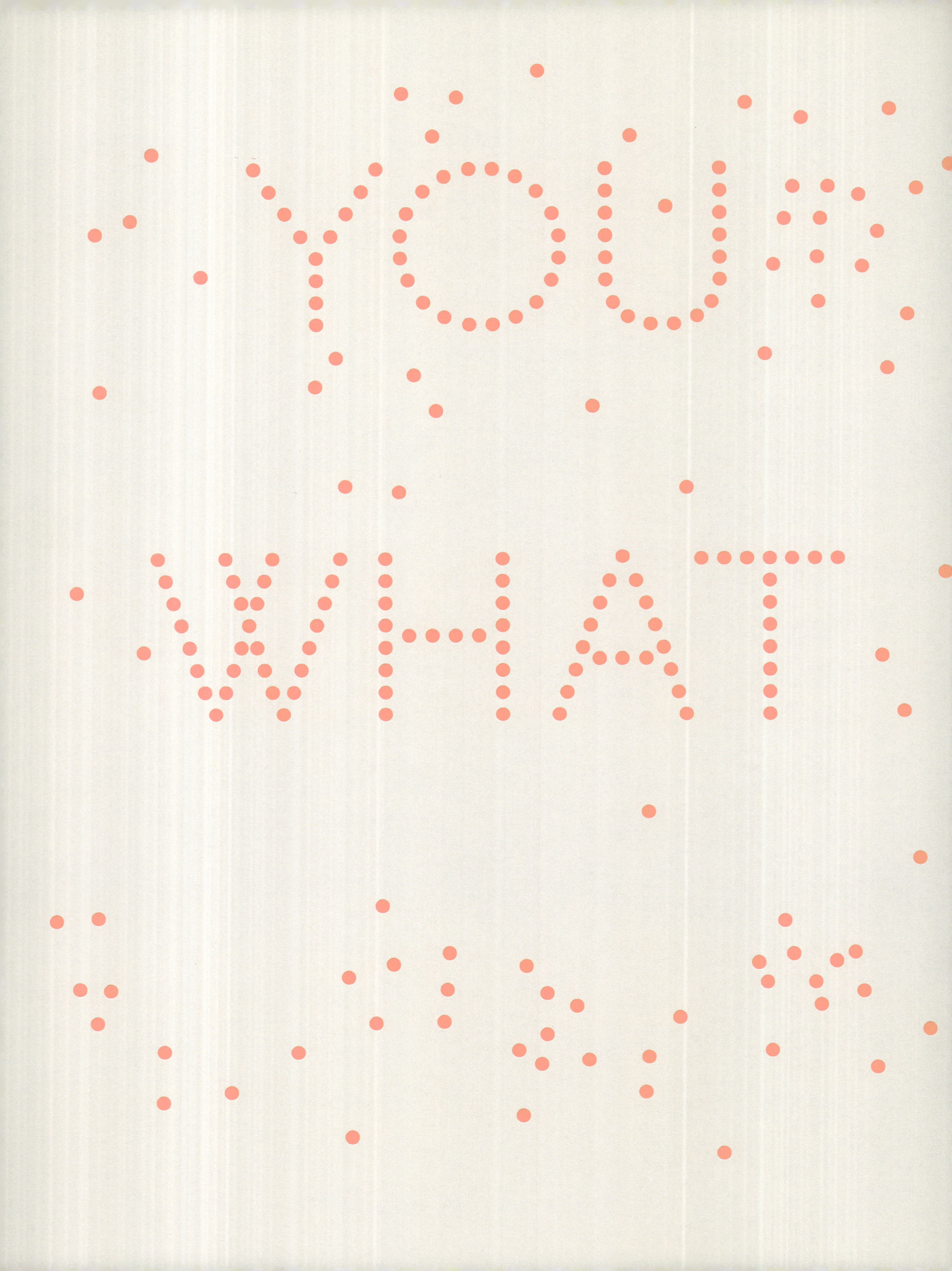

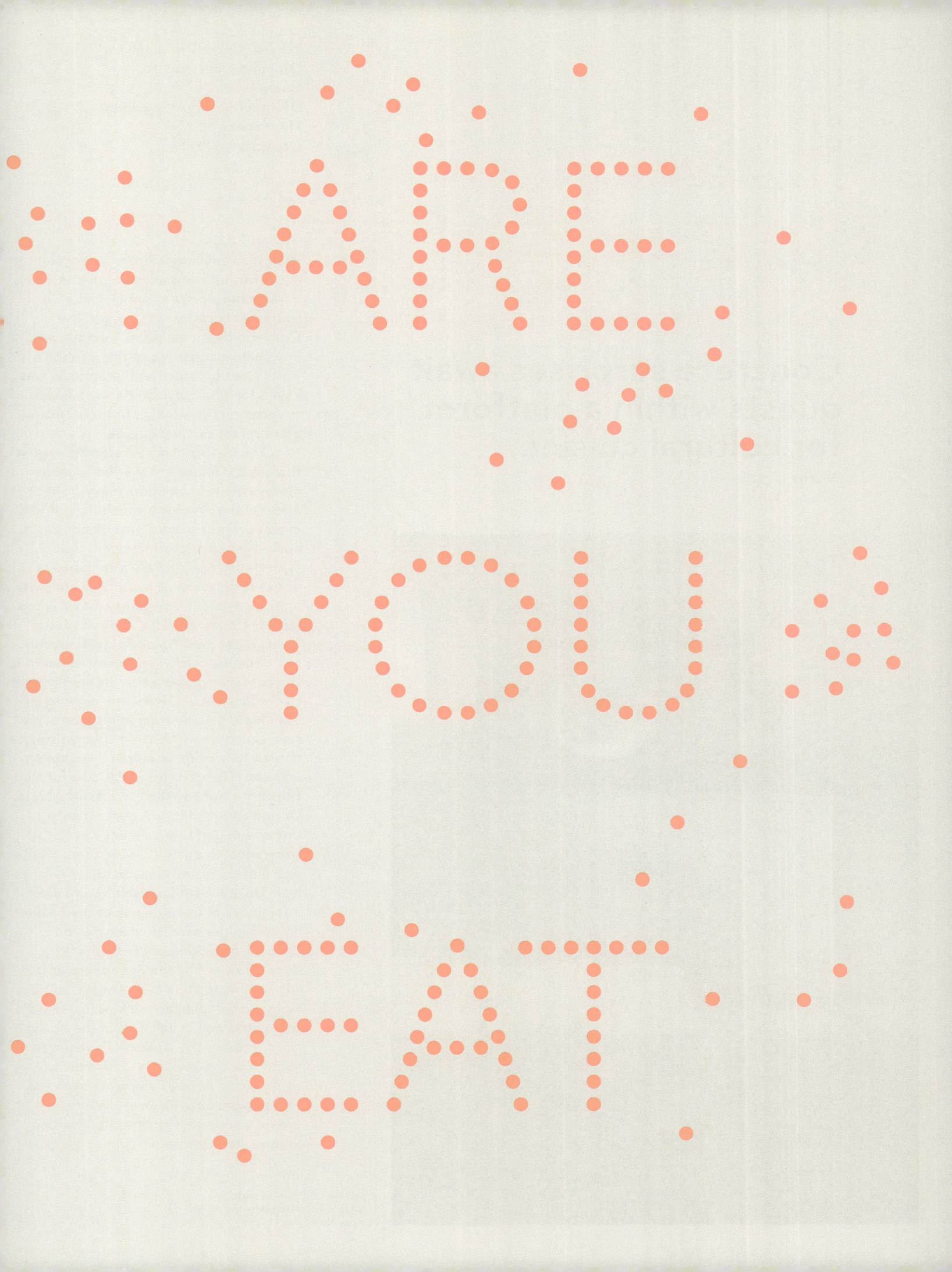

.HBC BY UNIT-BERLIN

Where Berlin, Germany
Opening October 2010
Client HaBeCe
Designer unit-berlin → p.590
Floor space 220 m²
Capacity 80 seats

Concrete surprises await guests within a platform for cultural cuisine.

Photos unit-berlin

With the redevelopment of its restaurant in the former Hungarian cultural institute on Alexanderplatz in Berlin, HaBeCe sought to breathe new life into the Communist-era building. A unique and imaginative approach to the location's history, architecture and geography was called for when unit-berlin was tasked to redesign the existing premises into a platform for cultural cuisine.

The concept was to radically expose the basic structure of the 1960s' multi-storey concrete building, playing with the materialities and form vocabulary already in place. This resulted in stark contrasts and a very special atmosphere that is typical of contemporary Berlin: glossy epoxy resin surfaces meet bare concrete, light blue velour upholstery meets wood veneer from the 1960s, and red plastic chairs meet gold-framed crystal mirrors.

One especially prominent element is the concrete-globe lamps created by unit-berlin for .HBC, which were inspired by the location's character and at the same time redefine it. The 12-kg spheres can be angled to provide spotlight illumination and can also actually swing – just for the fun of it – much to the surprise of guests. During an architecture performance one evening, this movement was so substantial that it left visible scars on the wall mirrors of the restaurant.

The pendant lampshades are also a reminder of the pinnacle of the Berlin TV tower, the base of which can be seen when looking out from the first floor window. The famous sphere at the top (265 m up), however, remains out of sight. To compensate for this loss, a gold geometric wall installation in the 'tower room' creates the illusion of a real-size section of the structure. The interior design incorporates elements from the restaurant's outside environment to create a very individual location with a unique atmosphere.

A palette of different muted colours is brightened by the coral red plastic chairs.

Panels with a metallic-gold coating create a geometric landscape that stretches up the wall behind the diners.

The cracks in the mirrors show evidence of a performance with swinging concrete lamps.

The concrete shell of the lampshades was cast in a mould with holes in the casing allowing for different hanging positions.

UNIT-BERLIN

The Barbican eateries feature bespoke lighting by .PSLAB and furniture designed by Helen Hughes and Stefan Bench.

Opposite The lacquered steel metal structure which houses the olive-lamp elements complements the raw nature of the space, with its concrete ceiling alcoves and Cradley brick paving stones.

BARBICAN FOODHALL & LOUNGE BY SHH

There's a whole lot to choose from in the eateries of this London exhibition centre.

Photos Gareth Gardner

Where London, United Kingdom
Opening September 2010
Clients Barbican Centre and Compass Leisure
Designer SHH → p.588
Floor space 700 m²
Capacity 442 seats

THE RACKS OF OLIVE-
JAR LIGHTING WERE
DESIGNED ESPECIALLY
FOR THE SPACE

The terrace features six SHH-designed 'urban tree' steel umbrella units with built-in planters and seating ledges.

A blue, upholstered Hans Wegner sofa complements the bold design of the upstairs Lounge restaurant.

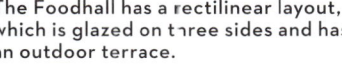
The Foodhall has a rectilinear layout, which is glazed on three sides and has an outdoor terrace.

The Barbican Centre is world-famous for its art exhibitions and performances, but its food and beverage offerings were not of the same standard. SHH was therefore commissioned to create two new dining spaces in the Centre, each fit for its own purpose, and to make the most of the location within this iconic building envelope.

The first space is Barbican Foodhall, a restaurant and shop with a range of deli-style products to take away or consume at its counter-top bars and deli tables. The design approach links the space to the architecture of the building itself by exposing the original concrete ceilings and using Cradley brick pavers, which not only brought the flooring back into line with the original treatment, but also linked it to the existing external walkways. The terrace features bespoke 'urban umbrella' installations made out of off-centre perforated aluminium disks. Internally, the space boasts striking feature areas, such as the racks of olive-jar lighting and chairs and tables designed especially for the space, and innovative recycled materials, including shelving made from old Belgian army storage boxes.

The second space is Barbican Lounge, a bar and restaurant. The first-floor Lounge has material links to its ground-floor sister, the Foodhall, but also boasts a very individual design treatment in striking colours, including peacock-blue banquette seating with red upholstered buttons, vintage 1960s' tables with Murano glass tops and a variety of free-standing furniture in blue with splashes of green and red. The bar, 14 m long, in black glass with a black mosaic bar front, continues through the glazing onto the outside terrace. The Lounge also features a timber wall enclosing the kitchen hot-pass and a peacock-green resin floor, specifically colour-matched to a photo taken in summer of the green water of the Barbican outdoor lake.

Opposite Other than the physical and logistical aspects of the huge bar, the challenge was to create an amazing centrepiece that wouldn't take over the space.

BOND & BROOK BY D-RAW

A pristine white space, decked-out in classic marble and shiny pewter.

Photos Richard Leeney

Where London, United Kingdom
Opening August 2010
Client Rhubarb
Designer d-raw → p.581
Floor space 250 m²
Capacity 90 seats

Behind the booth seating you can see the floor-to-ceiling glass 'fins' that can conceal the restaurant from the fashion floor.

High Ribbon stools by Nendo for Cappellini are used at the bar.

In the café section, Vitra's C1 chairs by Verner Panton are upholstered in a Kvadrat fabric.

In the bosom of London's extravagant Mayfair district, on the second floor of quintessential British department store Fenwick, is Bond & Brook: a surprisingly seductive multipurpose restaurant concept, central to the re-branding of the luxury retailer's prestigious London flagship. Conceived as a new take on retail hospitality, combining the fun, frivolous side of fashion with culinary excellence, the boutique-style restaurant concept was designed by interior specialists d-raw in collaboration with graphic branding agency Made Thought and hospitality consultancy A Private View.

Neatly occupying one corner of the store's contemporary fashion floor, an area reclaimed from its previous guise as a staff restaurant, the space now simultaneously hosts a daytime restaurant an informal café area and an opulent cocktail bar including a super-sized, sculpturally styled centrepiece bar wrapped in pewter.

Every aspect of the ultramodern design, from the architectural reframing of the space to the texture of the leather finishes on the banquettes, is bespoke. Lighting comes from a staggered arrangement of differently sized circular ceiling lights, casting soft beams that compound a sense of intimacy. Most prominently, a sweeping, peek-a-boo curtain of semi-reflective, floor-to-ceiling asymmetric glass 'fins' encircles the two store-facing sides of the restaurant, allowing the restaurant to be concealed from or opened up to the fashion floor at will. Other features include a decadent grey marble floor, a full fashion library of books, journals and magazines, and a 'champagne burst' chandelier, which rises above the cocktail bar as a visual echo of the restaurant's celebratory ambiance.

THE BOUTIQUE-STYLE RESTAURANT HAS A SURPRISINGLY SEDUCTIVE CONCEPT

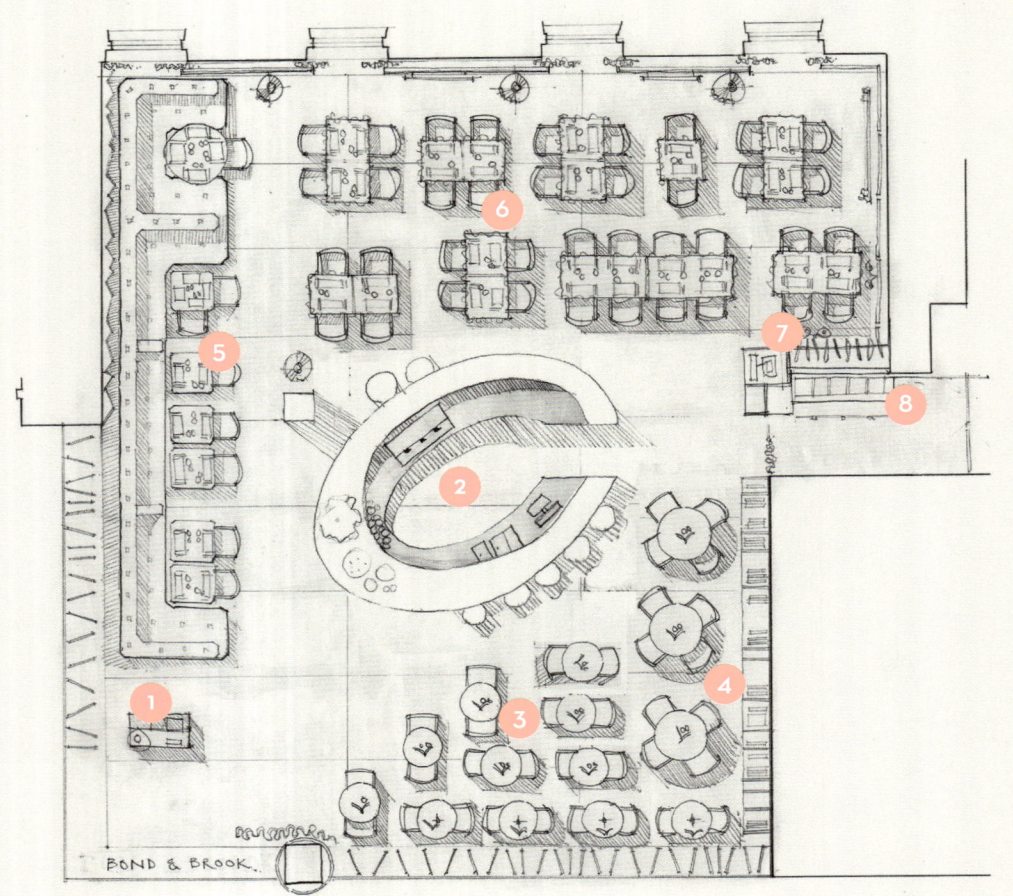

1. Welcome desk
2. Bar
3. Café seating
4. Library
5. Booth seating
6. Restaurant seating
7. Wardrobe
8. Waiter station

A SUPER-SIZED, SCULPTURALLY-STYLED CENTREPIECE BAR IS WRAPPED IN PEWTER

Initial sketch of the interior.

Initial sketches of the entrance elements.

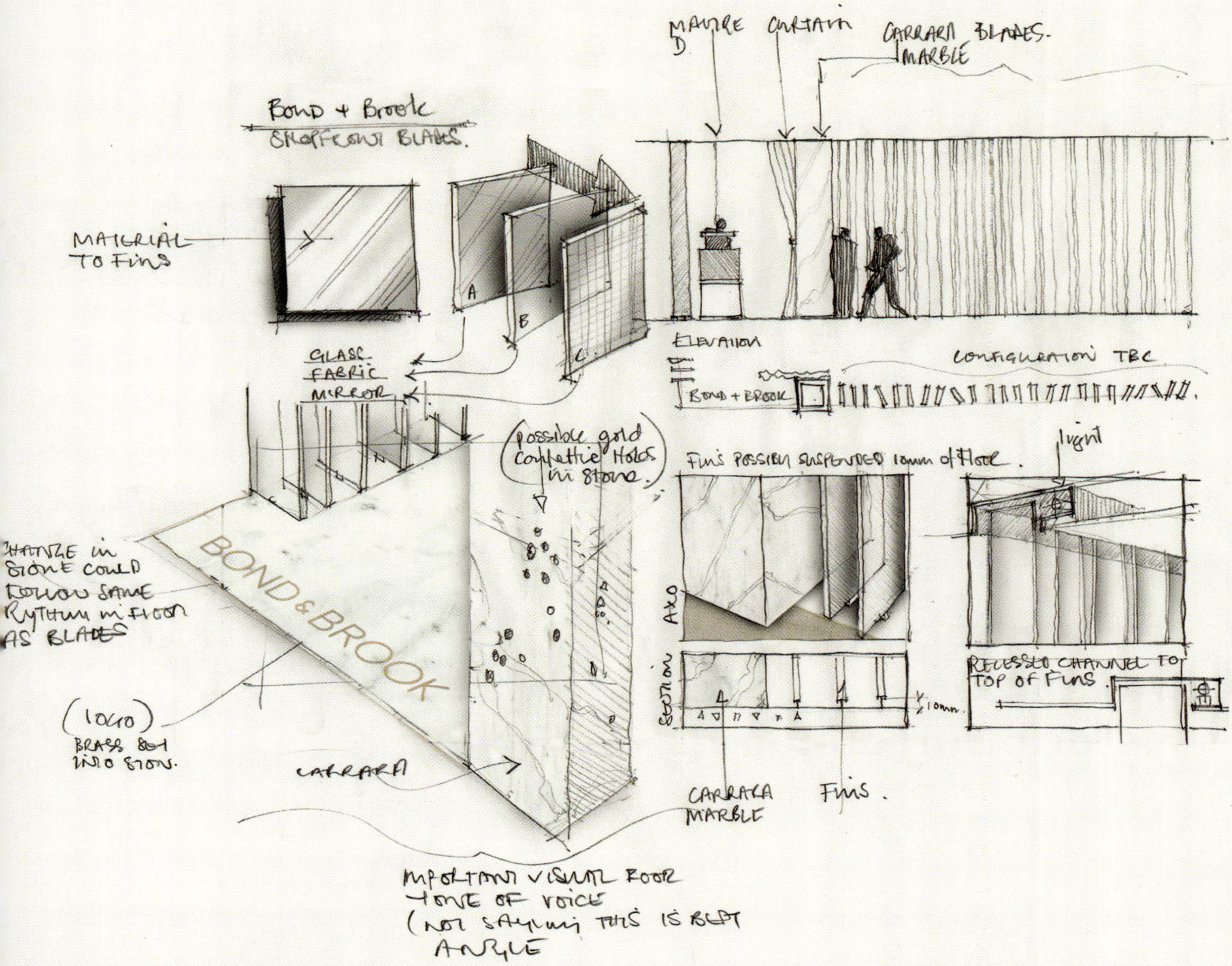

A sketch of the library wall.

A sketch of the booth seating.

BULLEREI BY GIORGIO GULLOTTA ARCHITEKTEN

Where Hamburg, Germany
Opening July 2010
Client Bullerei
Designer Giorgio Gullotta Architekten → p.583
Floor space 810 m²
Capacity 180 seats

A cosmopolitan eatery which blends in with its historic surroundings.

Photos Philipp Rathmer and Jochen Stüber

The Bullerei restaurant is located in the historic cattle-market halls right next to the meat-packing district in Hamburg, Germany. For many years these market halls sat idle, a blind spot in the quarter, until architect Giorgio Gullotta developed his vision for the venue: a place with great food, a quiet courtyard and well-lit office spaces. Tim Mälzer and Patrick Rüther were immediately inspired to join the project as future tenants; they wanted a new restaurant suitable for any time of the day, for all tastes and every circumstance. The challenge was to create a unique place in Hamburg that would easily blend into its historic surroundings.

The design is defined by the interaction between the historic structure and the new architecture. Thanks to the natural stone floors, walls of exposed brick only partially covered in plaster and walls lined with antique tiles, the charm of the historic cattle-market hall remains. The concept mixes design classics with simple objects. The tables in the restaurant are made of 200-year-old oak planks, which go well with the colourful upholstery of the lounge chairs and the framed benches clad in modern graffiti. This mix concept works equally well in the deli, where high-gloss wooden tables, made of ragtag remnants, are surrounded by a motley collection of old chairs. The main bar in the restaurant area is covered in deep-blue Art Nouveau tiles as a highlight and to contrast with the dark stone floors. The work of stage designer Kathrin Bade complements the overall design. She completed the rooms by contributing accessories like one-off pieces of furniture, tableware and decoration.

A huge terrace has been placed in front of the historical building.

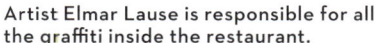

Upholstered chairs and benches can be seen on the right, while various wooden chairs were used in the left half of the restaurant.

Artist Elmar Lause is responsible for all the graffiti inside the restaurant.

Huge vintage industrial lamps have been hung above the bar at the deli.

GIORGIO GULLOTTA ARCHITEKTEN

Opposite The work of art adorning the wall is by Shoji Koyabu and includes mosaic-style squares of colour printed on blocks of glass.

Through the slatted wood façade customers can sneak a peek into the interior.

BUON GRANDE ARIA BY BROWNBAG LAB.

A warm wood-lined atmosphere at Osaka's hip riverfront.

Photos Nacása & Partners

Tables on the terrace with a perfect view of downtown Osaka are much sought after.

Where Osaka, Japan
Opening June 2011
Client Daiichi Kogyo
Designer brownbag lab. → p.580
Floor space 181 m²
Capacity 32 seats

BROWNBAG LAB. 027

Grey floor tiles pave the way for visitors heading to take a seat by the riverside.

Teak panelling wraps around the restaurant, lining walls, ceiling and floor.

'BECAUSE THE STREET IS VERY BUSY, I WANTED TO SUBTLY BLOCK THE VIEW FROM THE OUTSIDE'

In Kitahama, traditionally the financial hub and now the hip riverfront area of Osaka, owner Daiichi Kogyo opened his second Italian restaurant, Buon Grande Aria. Shingo Abe of brownbag lab. was asked to design the interior for an upscale dining experience.

Situated in a busy street between stone-clad office buildings, Abe choose wood as the restaurant's main material to create a striking contrast. To start with, he created an impressive wooden façade, in front of the normal façade, to subtly block out the busy street. The chequered pattern of the façade consists of a combination of roughly finished solid woods, including Paulownia, Norway Spruce, cypress and oak. Vertical wooden louvers are positioned in different ways: at eye level the header faces the street, while at the top and bottom the long side faces the street. Because of this, the interior cannot be seen from passing cars, but pedestrians can look inside and see this is a canal-side restaurant.

Inside, guests are welcomed into a warm atmosphere, created by the wooden floors, ceiling and walls. Guests can choose to dine at a private table or sit at the bar in front of the semi-open kitchen where they can watch the chefs cook their meal. The bar is made of wooden wine crates and framed photos of Italian scenery above the bar refer to the Italian cuisine. One colourful piece of art at one end of the restaurant brings the overall calm interior into balance.

BURJ AL HAMAM

Opposite The impressive cloaked chandeliers are a grand gesture that fits in with the dramatic height of the interior.

Where Doha, Qatar
Opening November 2009
Client UDC
Designer GM Architects → p.583
Floor space 300 m²
Capacity 200 guests

BURJ AL HAMAM BY GM ARCHITECTS

The luxury of a 19th-century palace in an ocean oasis.

Photos Fares Jammal

Alternating panes of dappled hand-blown glass have been inserted into a bronze metal framework behind the reception desk.

A dusty pink palette is repeated throughout the interior décor, from the materials and fabrics to the lighting and paintwork.

DRAPING TEXTURES ENVELOP THE ELEGANT SPACE

The custom-made armchairs are luxuriously upholstered in a soft felt fabric and bedecked with bejewelled buttons.

The design of restaurant Burj Al Hamam's new home at The Pearl-Qatar oozes the elegance and luxury of its location. On the glamorous Riviera-style man-made island in Qatar, Galal Mahmoud of GM Architects has created an interior décor with an atmosphere that is both classic and contemporary. The brand-new space is grand, having the look and feel of an old building that has been renovated with some of its original features kept intact, but of course this cannot be the case.

Inspired by traditional 19th-century Beirut palaces, the interior has a muted colour palette ranging from dusty pink to light grey, producing a sense of opulence and luxury. Imposing spherical columns coated in glistening gold and impressive chandeliers decorate the restaurant's capacious dining area, with large windows that take advantage of its prime waterfront location. Built originally as a two-storey space, the upper floor was removed to gain dramatic height and filled with six glass chandeliers 2-m high that were custom-designed in Italy, inspired by the Ottoman era, which influenced some Lebanese architecture.

Draping textures envelop the vast yet elegant space, softening the architecture. Dark-wood furniture and fittings sit alongside the coloured-glass surfaces, soft felt-upholstered lounge chairs and delicately patterned carpeting. Subtle blends of luxurious Middle Eastern details such as the hand-blown glass partitions and precious mother-of-pearl inlays contrast with contemporary minimalism.

Pearl-like droplets were incorporated into the chandeliers.

Lengths of chiffon fabric drape the vast windows of the restaurant.

CHARLIE BY STUDIO NITZAN COHEN

A Vietnamese vibe against a grey-washed Bavarian backdrop.

Photos Gerhardt Kellermann

Charlie is a Vietnamese restaurant located slightly off Munich's centre, in an area better known for its not-so-classy beer halls. Studio Nitzan Cohen was in charge of the project, which saw the original space – an outdated bar of Bavarian character with a slight 1970s' vibe that was dark, heavy and smoke-stained – completely transformed into a healthy, contemporary and vibrant eatery.

The primary challenge was financial, in that there was practically no money to work with, so the team opted to breathe new life into the run-down – but still functional – furnishings that were already there. The typical dark brown wood cladding was washed in a light-grey finish, a key colour in the design that was applied as a backdrop to the whole space. The shabby brown floor was treated with a dark grey industrial coating and the traditional Bavarian furniture was given a whole new character after a short sand-blasting session, with the bench seats reupholstered with a grey suede textile.

Strong colour accents helped bring the bar and canteen service areas back to life, with pink-hued tiles and yellow-painted walls behind the bar areas and bright-coloured plastic stools, all the way from a Vietnamese marketplace, dotted around the interior. The porcelain dishes in the restaurant come from Vietnam's largest porcelain producer and the original pressed aluminium lampshades, which hang over the individual tables creating an intimate atmosphere, are another marketplace find.

The exterior signage – like that of an old cinema – shows the restaurant's 'coming attractions'.

Where Munich, Germany
Opening September 2010
Client Charlie
Designer Studio Nitzan Cohen → p.589
Floor space 100 m²
Capacity 65 seats

The minimalist modernism of the interior has splashes of colour, like the pink tiles on the back wall.

The bar area is brightened by the lime-green plastic seats and the neon strip lighting.

The original stripped-back furniture was either left uncoated or painted grey.

STUDIO NITZAN COHEN

COCORO BY STUDIO GASCOIGNE

Opposite Concrete and Macrocarpa timber are the two main materials used in the interior.

Next spread At the 6-m long dining table, 16 guests can sit in black Pantone chairs.

A Japanese restaurant designed with minimal materials and simple lines.

Photos Patrick Reynolds

Cocoro is located in Auckland, New Zealand, in a concrete-walled former industrial space. The owners wanted to give their *dégustation* and Japanese tapas-style menu restaurant a modern, comfortable and natural environment and therefore called upon Studio Gascoigne to design it.

The name Cocoro, 'heart and soul' in Japanese, was chosen because it represents the owners' approach to food, service and ambiance, and this had to be reflected in the restaurant's interior design. The design team set out to design a space that reflects the best of Japanese design, using clean, natural, simple lines and minimal clutter.

The intimate décor includes woven charcoal- and chocolate-coloured carpets reminiscent of tatami matting. The ceiling is of exposed, sand-blasted concrete, partially lined with New Zealand native Macrocarpa timber battens with integrated LED down-lights, hiding sound-absorbing foam, which keeps the noise to a comfortable level. The same Macrocarpa timber battens are used to clad the rear wall, where a rectangular slot window affords a view into the kitchen. The up-lit, black, side walls have been printed with circular graphics derived from the restaurant's logo. The 6-m-long dining table in the middle of the room has been cut from a single tree and invites guests to dine side by side. All materials are recyclable. The result is a contemporary space, suitable for both lunch and dinner, which complements the menu with its simplicity, naturalness and authenticity.

Where Auckland, New Zealand
Opening September 2010
Client Coroco
Designer Studio Gascoigne → p.589
Floor space 125 m²
Capacity 40 seats

Part of the outdoor wall features the timber battens that are also seen inside.

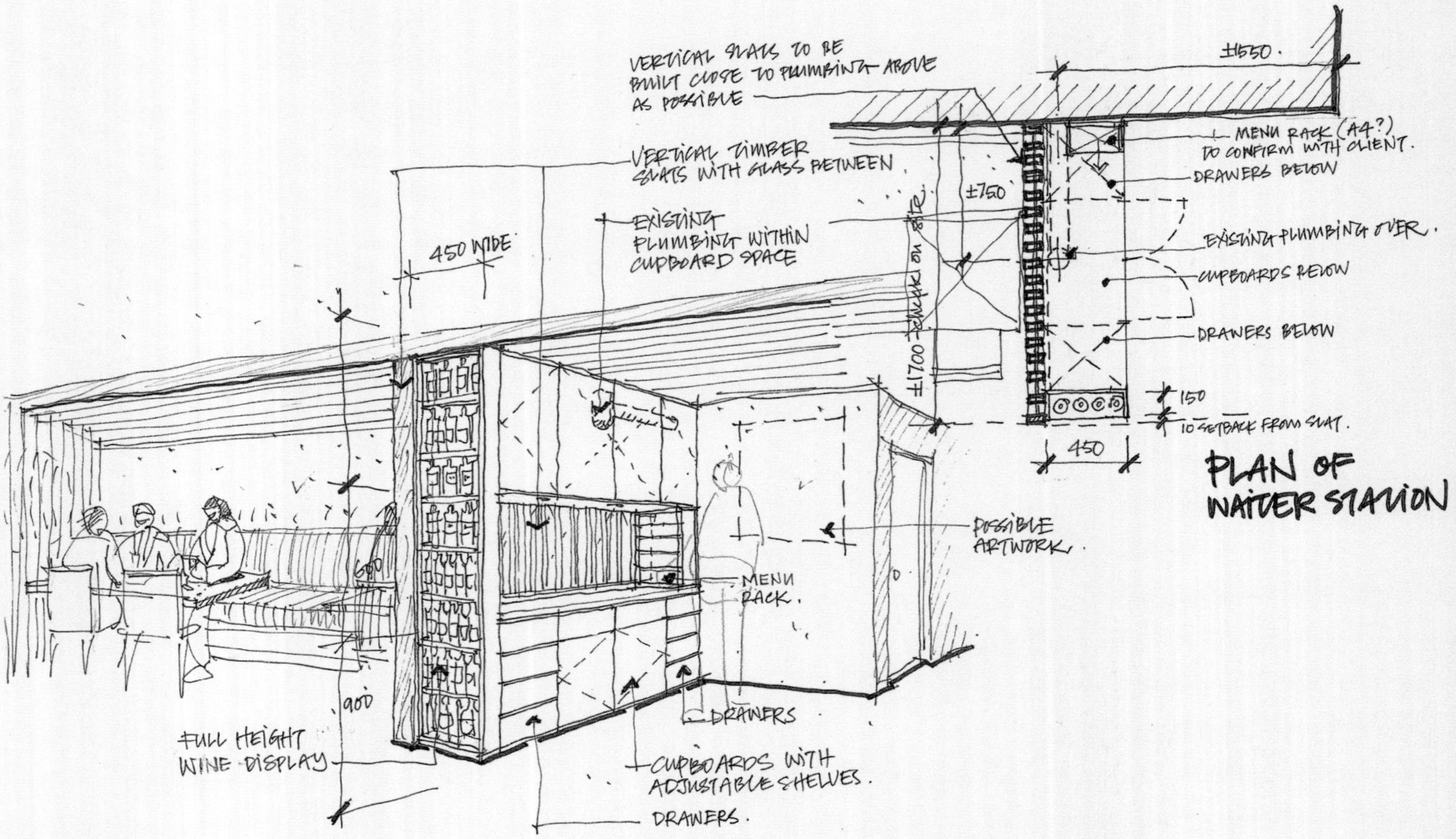

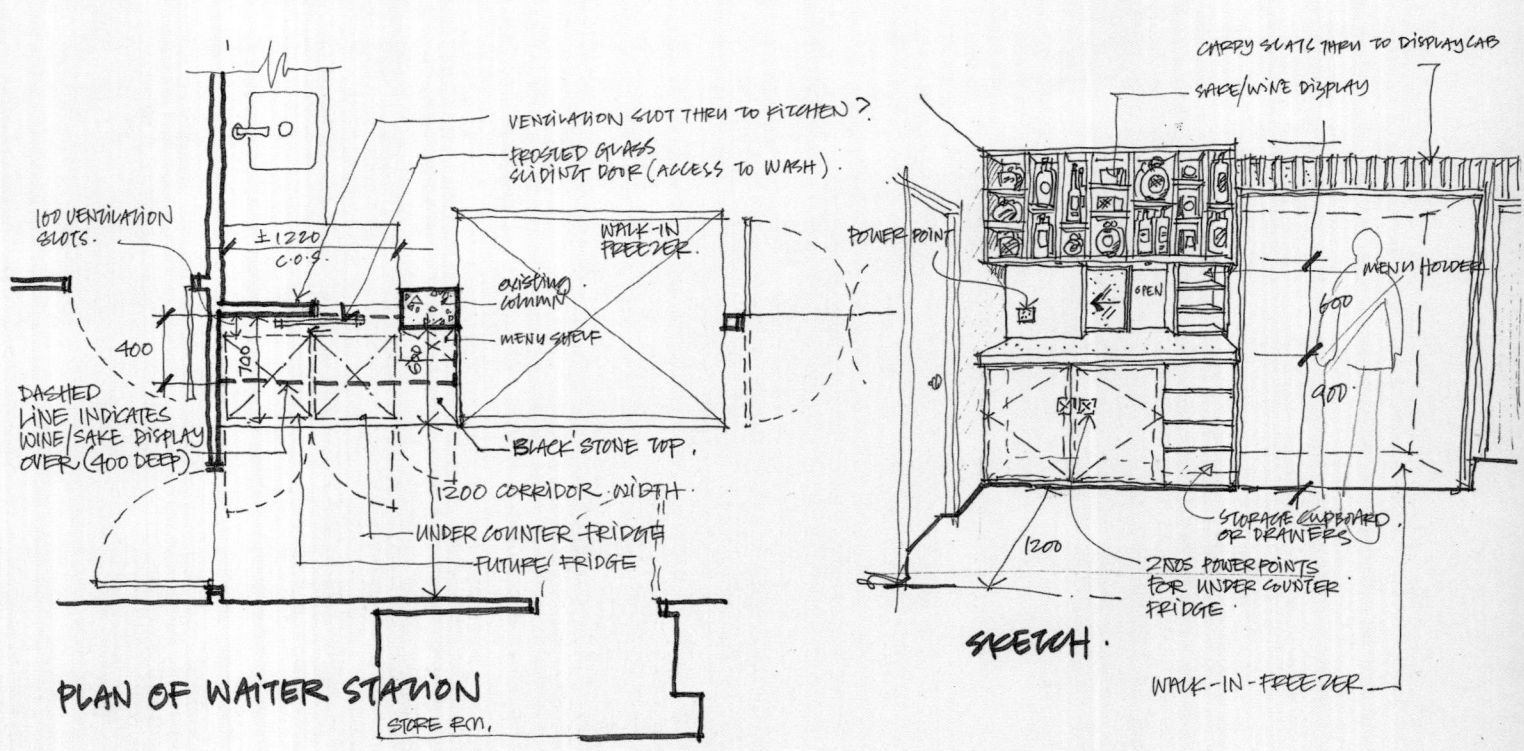

Initial sketches of the waiter station.

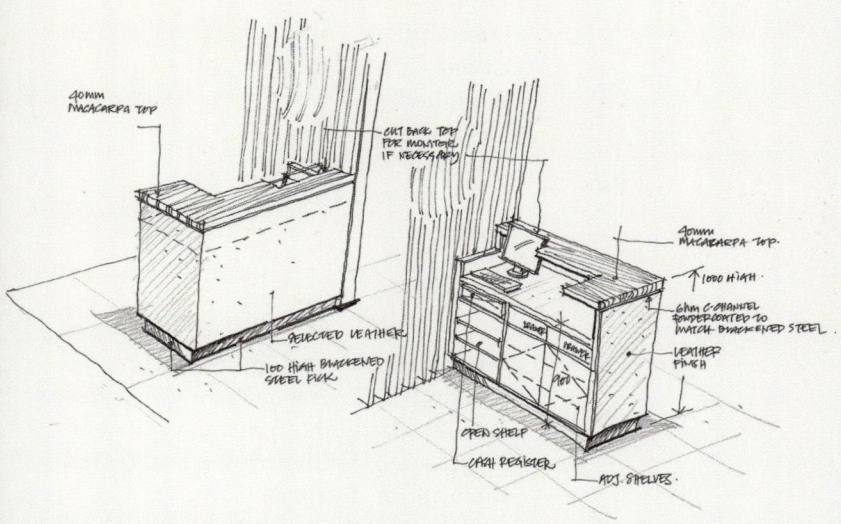

Sketch of the welcome desk.

THE 6-M-LONG DINING TABLE HAS BEEN CUT FROM A SINGLE TREE

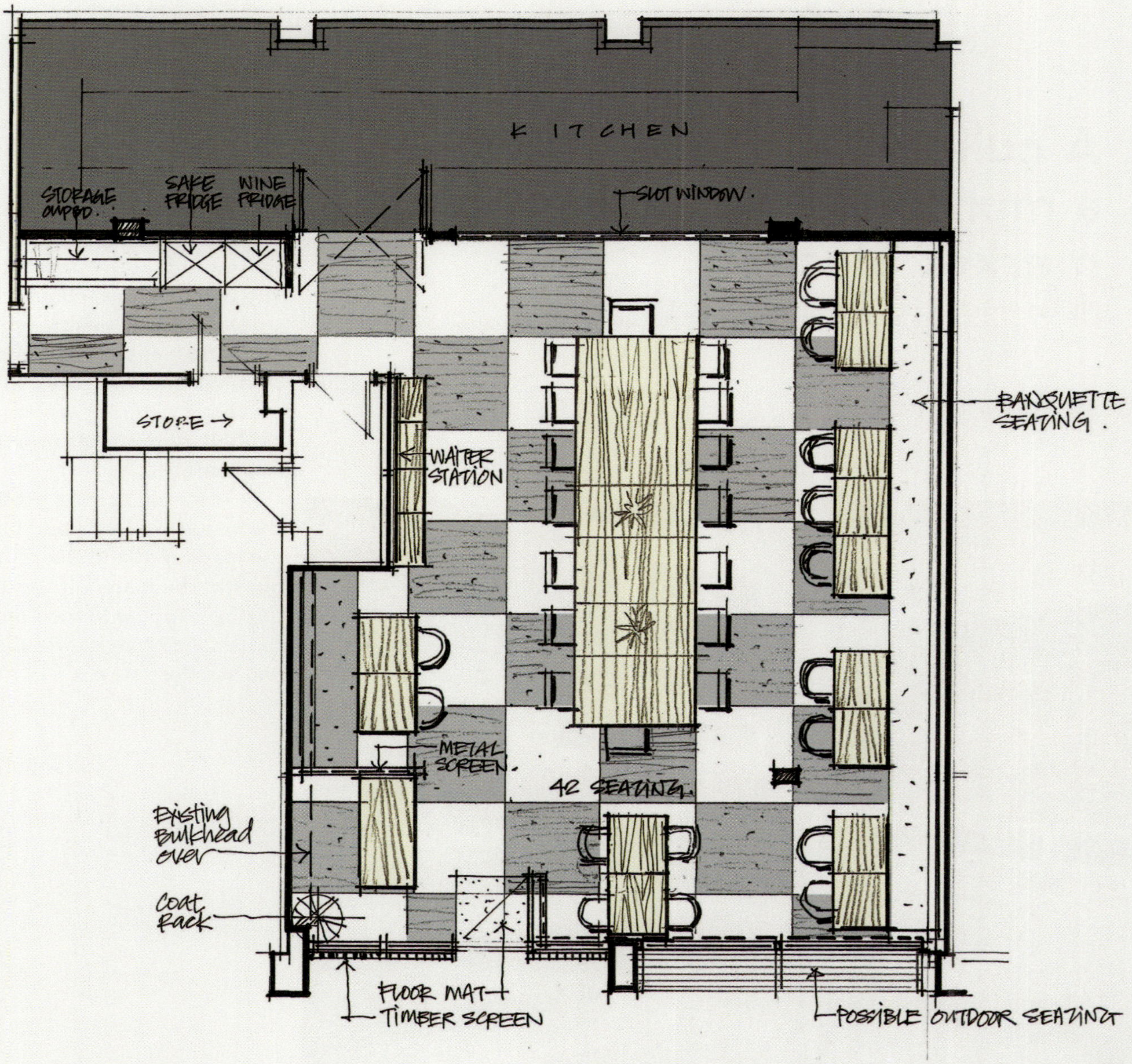

A sketch of the interior floor plan.

STUDIO GASCOIGNE

Where Barcelona, Spain
Opening November 2010
Client Copermine
Designer GCA arquitectes associats → p.5
Floor space 550 m²
Capacity 100 seats

CORNELIA & CO BY GCA ARQUITECTES ASSOCIATS

A culinary journey, which is a mixture of restaurant and market place.

Photos courtesy of Cornelia & Co

For her new Barcelona-based 'market-restaurant' Cornelia & Co, owner Carla Tarruella brought in designer Joseph Juanpere of GCA arquitectes to create the interior design.

A carefully chosen selection of products makes a visit to Cornelia & Co a great culinary journey. The venue is designed as a fresh-produce market: customers can stroll around the various areas dedicated to different delicacies, purchase the ingredients in the retail area or enjoy them in the restaurant area. The designers endeavoured to allow shopping and eating to interrelate, as activities do on the street or in a market square, because they did not want the interior design to pre-determine the guests' behaviour.

Two zones, both accessible from the street, take the customer towards a central spot at the end of the venue. The two walkways contain various shelving for the merchandise, a bar and tables with chairs and benches for eating or conversation. In the central spot, groups of different tables are surrounded by shelves; this is also where the kitchen is located.

The main colours used throughout the venue are white and black, to give the leading role to the products and the guests. The materials used – all of high quality – appear in their most natural form: solid Madeira wood, marble, iron and stainless steel.

Guests can pick their favourite foods at the daily picnic, the retail area of this venue.

The bar runs all the way from the front window to the back of the restaurant area.

The huge windows make it easy for passers-by to have a peek inside.

The large painting was made by owner Carla Tarruella.

GCA ARQUITECTES ASSOCIATS

Patterned wallpaper, dappled silver and dark glossy paint adorn the walls of the private dining area.

Where Hamburg, Germany
Opening October 2008
Client Kai Hollmann
Designer SynergyHamburg → p.589
Floor space 100 m²
Capacity 70 seats

DACAIO BY SYNERGY-HAMBURG

Tradition teamed with contemporary textures.

Photos Georgios Engonidis, Cyrus Saedi and Klaus Stemmler

The DaCaio bar and restaurant is situated in The George Hotel in a vibrant neighbourhood in Hamburg. The client commissioned Sibylle von Heyden of SynergyHamburg to create an interior that would add a touch of old-school elegance to this hip and fashionable quarter. Inspired by English-style membership clubs, the SynergyHamburg team created a handsome, spacious interior with a touch of tradition and a contemporary twist.

The primary design scheme components are coloured duos – black and white and gold and silver – contrasted and softened with warm dark woods and spots of colour. Heavier elements are skilfully balanced with craftsmanship and textured fabrics. Dark wood predominates in the floorboards and furniture. The bar and lounge invite guests to sink into the soft leather sofas and chairs or to prop themselves up by the custom-woodworked bar on elegant and classic tall stools. From here, a catwalk connects the bar to the restaurant, where guests will discover fine Italian cuisine, reinterpreted.

Lighting is a key feature throughout the interior, with Von Heyden pairing up modern strip lighting and delicate spotlights with oversized designer lampshades. In the bar area, placed on low side tables, these are teamed with retro-type spherical bases while the shades themselves have a tall and svelte design. In the dining area a long line of gold-lined shades illuminate the walkway between the tables, gracing the restaurant with a subdued ambiance. In the private dining area, above the spherical and oval tables, is another impressive lampshade with a lantern-like design.

Rich colours and textures predominate in the bar area.

Opposite Guests are welcomed with discrete elegance and Italian cordiality.

Opposite The architecture of the interior is sleek, linear and rigorous.

DE GUSTO BY C+L STUDIO AND COSTA GROUP

An experimental tasting theatre for pasta connoisseurs.

Photos Petro Savorelli

Near the entrance, the brand's name is carved into the oak-lined wall.

Where Lavezzola, Italy
Opening January 2010
Client Surgital Spa
Designers C+L Studio → p.580
and Costa Group → p.581
Floor space 230 m²
Capacity 60 seats

Surgital is an Italian company that is well-established in the deep-frozen fresh pasta sector. In 2010 it opened a brand-new tasting room at its headquarters in Lavezzola, in northern Italy. The De Gusto room is primarily a place where, once a product has been developed, it can be presented in a forum filled with atmosphere and technology. The idea behind the De Gusto concept was to create a meeting place for the best chefs, culinary connoisseurs and those who believe in the value of quality for the food sector. The client commissioned Costa Group to oversee the project, while the architectural aspect was developed and realized by C+L Studio. The brief for this new venture was to create a place with a strong identity in which, at the end of a visit of the manufacturing area, visitors (wholesalers, restaurateurs, retailers) can take part in the creation of experimental recipes, with an opportunity to taste them afterwards.

The architecture of the white interior is linear and rigorous, with simple lines and natural materials, such as oak-wood furnishings and veined white marble. The primary focus of the space is the central, open kitchen – akin to a theatre stage – with tiered seating at one end and, at the other, a more communal dining table. The kitchen is De Gusto's technological heart, with steel surfaces and professional equipment set within a slab of Calacatta marble. Surrounding the cooking area is a 15-m-long wooden counter and tall Scandinavian stools for those guests who want a seat close to the action.

An oak-clad wall behind the dining table facilitates a library of culinary literature.

The stairwell, with its linear and rigorous lines and oak wood material use, is in line with the restaurant concept.

From the tiered seating area, customers can get a full view of the gastronomic stage.

Opposite Plywood fixed onto a shaped-timber frame was used for the sculptural white walls.

DN INNOVACIÓN BY VERY SPACE

A lush décor with sweeping lines and metallic tones.

Photos Kuo Min Lee

Dramatic lighting complements the striking interior, including the Blum Suspension lamps by AXO Light.

Where Taipei, Taiwan
Opening October 2010
Client Daniel Negreira
Designer Very Space → p.590
Floor space 370 m²
Capacity 82 seats

VERY SPACE

A timber and light-steel framework forms the skeleton of the nautilus shell-inspired interior.

Metallic materials were used to upholster the custom-made chairs as well as the panels that sweep around the curvaceous walls.

At the very core of the interior is the Krug Champagne room with its shale-clad and black-mirrored walls.

A TRANQUIL YET MYSTERIOUS AND LUXURIOUS CELLAR IS AT THE CORE OF THE RESTAURANT

Next spread Reflective materials, such as metallic wallpaper and a mirrored ceiling, have been used in the light and airy dining area.

When chef Daniel Negreira opened a new restaurant in Taipei, he asked Very Space to design the interior. Negreira had one main stipulation: he wanted a private Krug Champagne room. The design team's idea was to create a tranquil yet mysterious and luxurious cellar-like VIP room at the core of the restaurant, unfolding the rest of the space like a pearly nautilus with its spiral shell.

'What interested us was not the VIP room itself, but the transitional spatial rituals between it and other spaces,' explains designer Louis Liu. 'I envisioned the enchantment that such a space could bring and how a representation of a space would define the narration and the interpretation itself. Throughout the restaurant, unique dimensions and different visual impacts are found and featured as a theatre play showing its own scenes and telling its own stories.'

The resulting 370-m² design mixes metallic wallpaper, artificial leather, mirrors and marble, as well as plywood, which formed the basis of the sculptural walls. These walls create partitions while flowing smoothly through the space.

The challenge of the project was to successfully translate the design idiom into an actual space. The result surpasses the original expectations: it integrates the most contrasting of elements such as transparent versus opaque, fluid versus concrete, and puts all the distinct materials into one space while maintaining a harmonious and balanced effect.

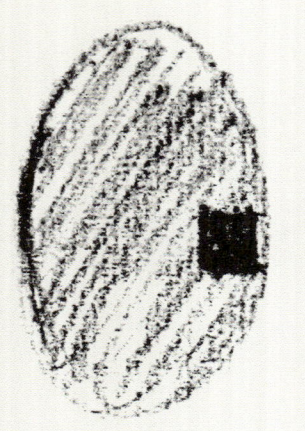

THE WALLS CREATE PARTITIONS FLOWING SMOOTHLY THROUGH THE SPACE

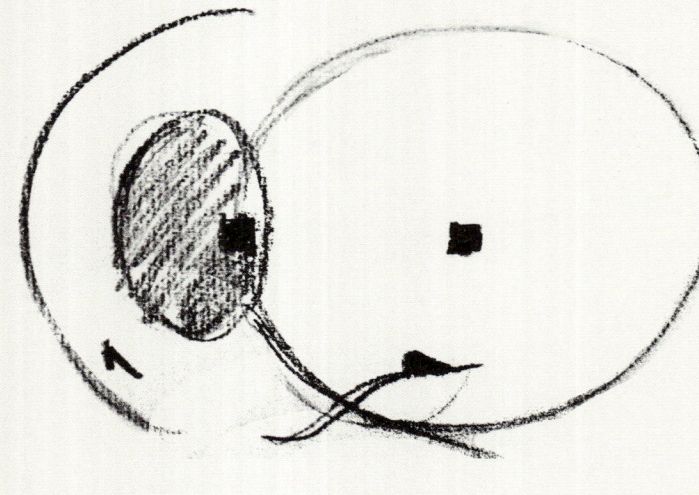

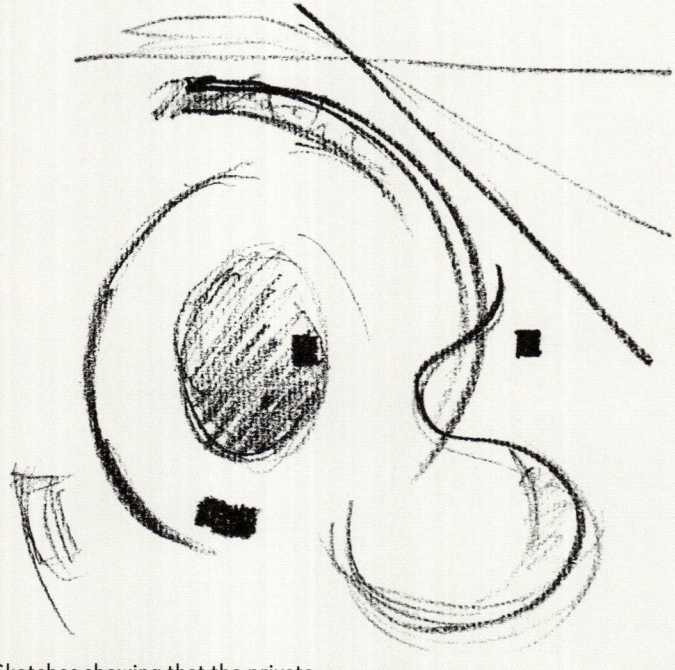

Sketches showing that the private VIP room was central to the interior concept.

Models of the sculptural partitions.

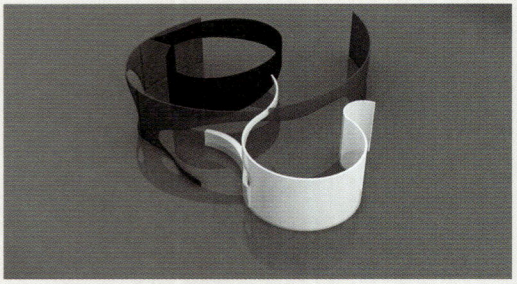

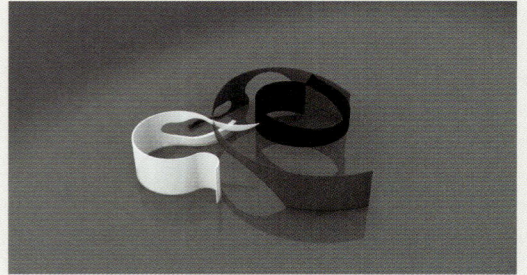

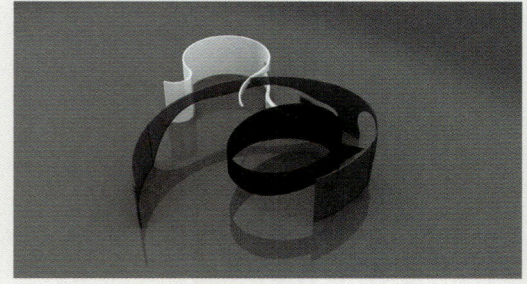

1. Lobby
2. Ascending corridor
3. Main dining area
4. Krug Champagne room
5. VIP room
6. Cellar
7. Kitchen
8. Storage
9. Office
10. Toilets

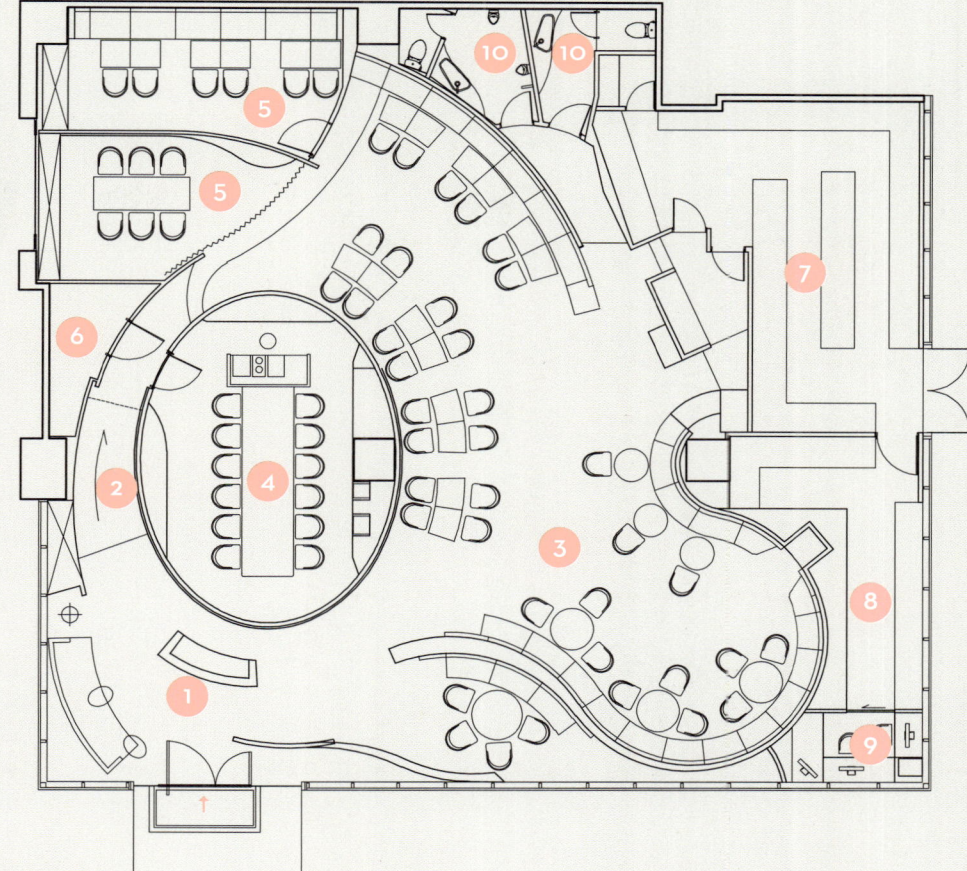

Drawings showing how the sculptural walls were built.

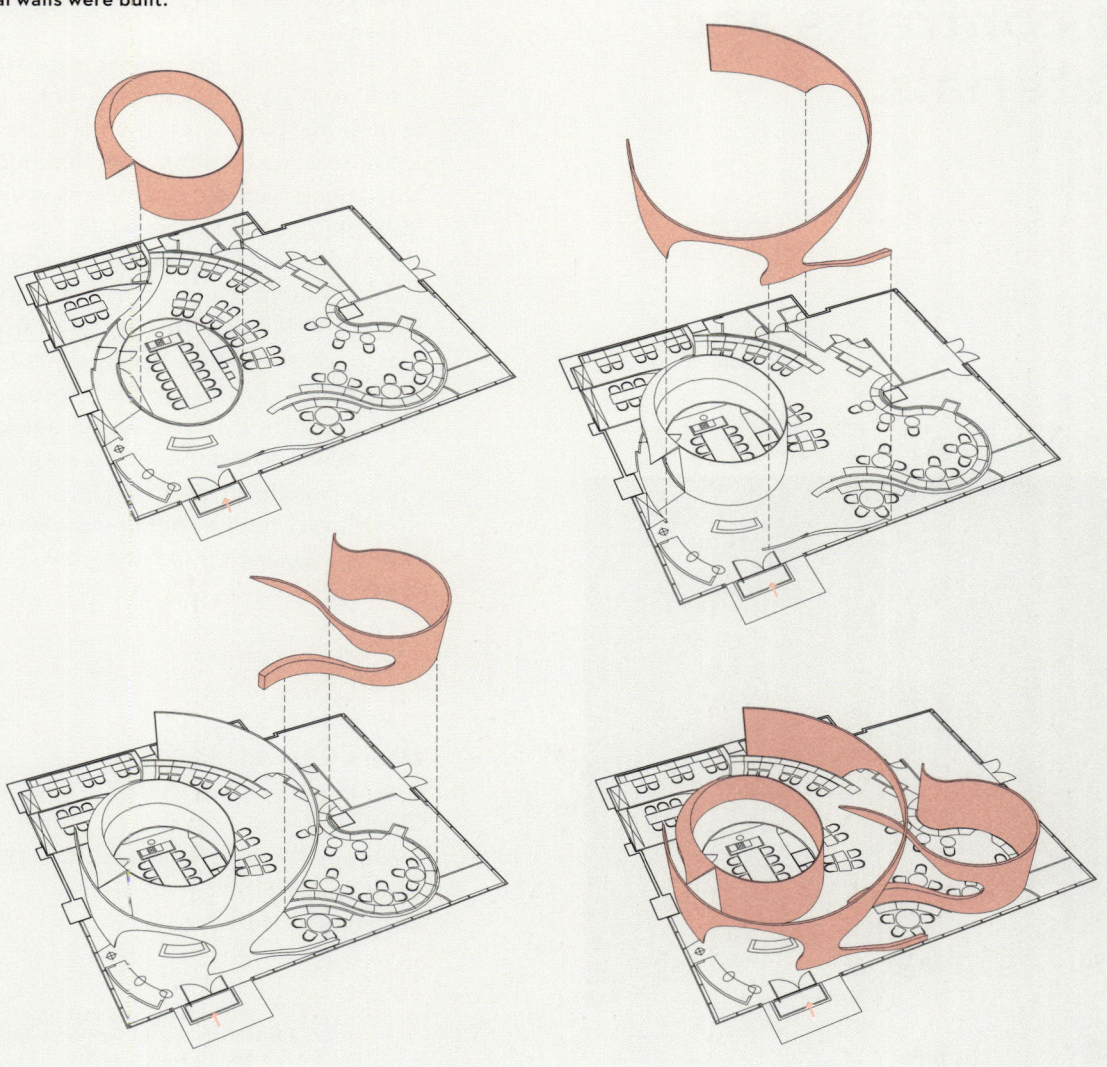

VERY SPACE 057

ETEN BIJ LIEVEN BY LIEVEN MUSSCHOOT

An eating space consisting of colour contrasts and mixed materials.

Photos Thomas De Bruyne

Lieven Vynck searched for a balance between old and new for his restaurant Eten bij Lieven (which translates to 'Dinner at Lieven's') in Bruges, Belgium. This delicate balance is oft-attempted, yet rarely well executed, so the challenge for designer Lieven Musschoot was to break this pattern.

Musschoot mixes reclaimed wooden furniture with contemporary touches with a deft touch, seamlessly marrying vintage and modern pieces to create something fresh and new. Musschoot's masterstroke is a 12-m wall, covered floor to ceiling in small stone and marble slabs by Dominique Desimpel in brown and off white colours. 'It's the most eye-catching element of Eten bij Lieven and stays with customers as they depart,' says Musschoot.

The rest of the interior is mostly black, with six tables in the front and several bar tables at the end of the restaurant, next to the open kitchen. The ceiling with old oak beams adds a rustic flair to the space, while Tom Dixon's elegantly sculpted Pipe Lights and Wever & Ducré lighting keep the space bright. The ground floor of the restaurant can seat 25 people, while the upstairs has a private dining room for ten. Here one finds furniture by 'scrapwood' designer Piet Hein Eek and the perfectly judged vintage touches really shine.

Musschoot has achieved a perfect harmony balancing old and new.

The 'living room' is upstairs, with a large table that offers space for a small party of people.

Where Bruges, Belgium
Opening May 2011
Client Lieven Vyncke
Designer Lieven Musschoot → p.584
Floor space 60 m²
Capacity 35 seats

Opposite A second seating area is located to the left of the stairs, next to the open-plan kitchen.

Where London, United Kingdom
Opening June 2011
Client AMS
Designer Blacksheep → p.579
Floor space 90 m²
Capacity 62 seats

The elevated ground-floor level provides extra ceiling space for the lower-floor dining area.

GALOUPET BY BLACKSHEEP

The taste of Provence in a palette of off-whites, silvers and golds.

Photos Paul Winch Furness and Nick Smith

Opposite The restaurant, located at the back of the shop, has a light and airy atmosphere.

Blacksheep designed the brass-edged coffee tables and all the seating elements on the lower level.

Natural daylight brightens up the basement thanks to the elongated window at street level.

Galoupet uses Enomatic wine dispensers to offer 36 wines and four different champagnes by the glass.

Opposite One wall in the private dining area is lined with antique mirrored panels, each framed with patinated brass borders.

Blacksheep was commissioned to create an intimate restaurant and lounge combined with a fine wine boutique showcasing wines from the client's Provençal vineyard, Chateau du Galoupet. The challenge for the design team was to provide a seamless integration between the two elements in the dark, narrow, compact space. They provided a wine shop at the front, leading through to a restaurant at the rear, while the lower floor houses the private dining room and lounge.

Blacksheep optimized light and the sense of space by installing a skylight above the dining room, four large bespoke glass floor plates in the shop, plus an all-glass surround on the staircase, allowing light to flow throughout the interior. In the wine shop, custom-made ridged glass display units edged in brass create a refined retail experience. Concealed ceiling lighting elements set in a swirl shape serve to guide the customer into the restaurant beyond.

In the restaurant the combination of pale oak flooring, angled wall mirrors and the restrained palette of off-whites, silvers and golds enhances a pared-back, minimalist sense of luxury, further reinforced by the pairing of Hans Wegner's Wishbone chairs with white leather button-backed banquettes. On the lower level this palette is reinforced in the private dining room with a leather-embossed wall, antique mirrors and a limestone-effect ceramic floor. The lounge is imbued with a more glamorous, evening feel, with darker tones of grey and luxurious textures in the form of a large brass-framed antique mirror, marbled black, white and gold wallpaper, graphite-grey faux-suede seating and patinated brass tables and stools. Galoupet allows the shopper and diner an unrivalled diversity of choice when it comes to enjoying wine.

GIACOMO

GIACOMO BY PLAJER & FRANZ STUDIO

Where Berlin, Germany
Opening November 2009
Client Giacomo Natural
Designer plajer & franz studio → p.587
Floor space 140 m²
Capacity 34 seats

A gourmet fast-food restaurant influenced by ancient Asian architecture.

Photos diephotodesigner.de (Ken Schluchtmann)

The elongated wall mirror reflects the individual spaces, which flow into each other.

Opposite Circular architectural motifs are a key feature in the light and airy interior.

A well-directed use of lighting cultivates an air of glamour for the gourmet fast-food.

Giacomo is a gourmet fast-food restaurant located in Berlin for which plajer & franz studio has created a concept influenced by ancient Asian architecture.

A spherical window akin to a circular 'moon gate' – a traditional architectural element in Chinese gardens – is incorporated into one of the side walls, lined with fringed curtains. The interior has a crisp, clean design that features a rich layering of horizontal planes of white and gold, underscored by a well-directed use of lighting. The stone floor tiles and painted ceiling envelop the space in gold-hued striations and, in between, strips of white and gold alternate. Intricate details can also be picked out, from the textured wallpaper to the gold stitching in the cushions, and from the circular patterns and shapes on the mirror to the pendant lampshades overhead. Part of the original stucco decoration has been exposed on the ceiling and, playfully integrating this historic reference into the overall design, an angular form flowing with the shape of the room has been cut out of the gold-painted drop ceiling to highlight this feature.

Contemporary lampshades hang beneath the original stucco ceiling decoration.

Glistening gold threads in the upholstery add to the rich ambiance.

Opposite The round window is inspired by the architecture of Chinese courtyards.

All functional aspects of a fast-food chain are incorporated in the service area at the front of the space, to guarantee a smooth workflow behind the counter, where the recessed bay is also painted gold. All finishes and colours are carefully tuned to the corporate image, resulting in a quality eatery with high brand recognition as well as a consistent design within the space.

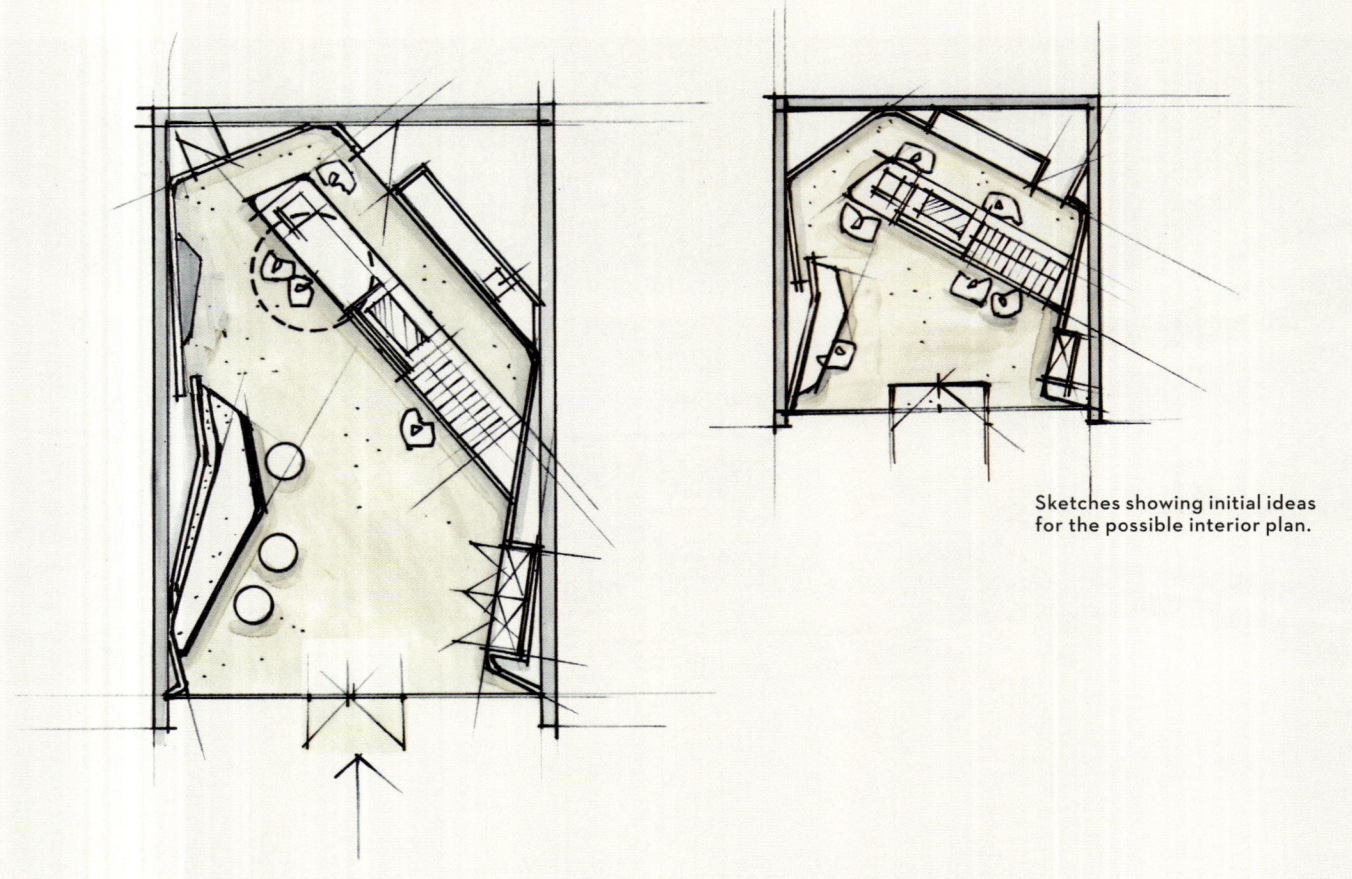

Sketches showing initial ideas for the possible interior plan.

Playing with the perspectives for the partition walls.

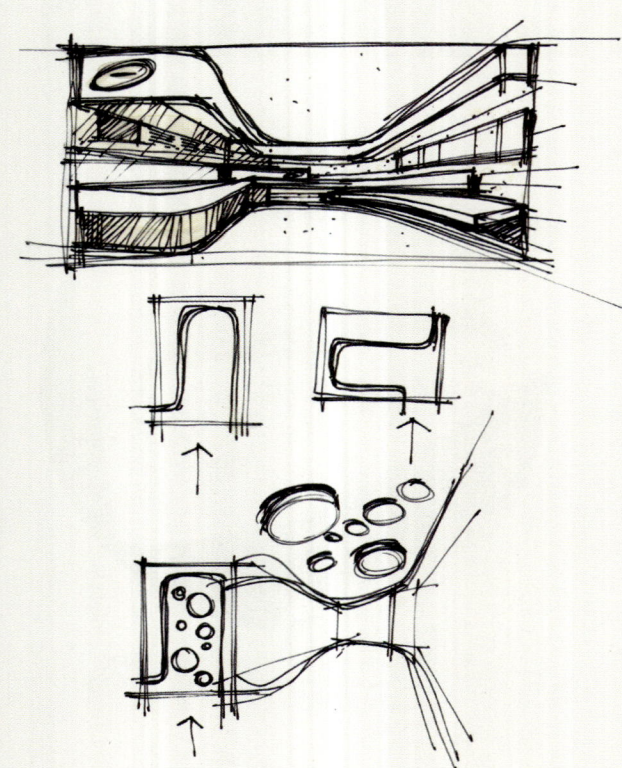

Initial sketch of the ceiling lights.

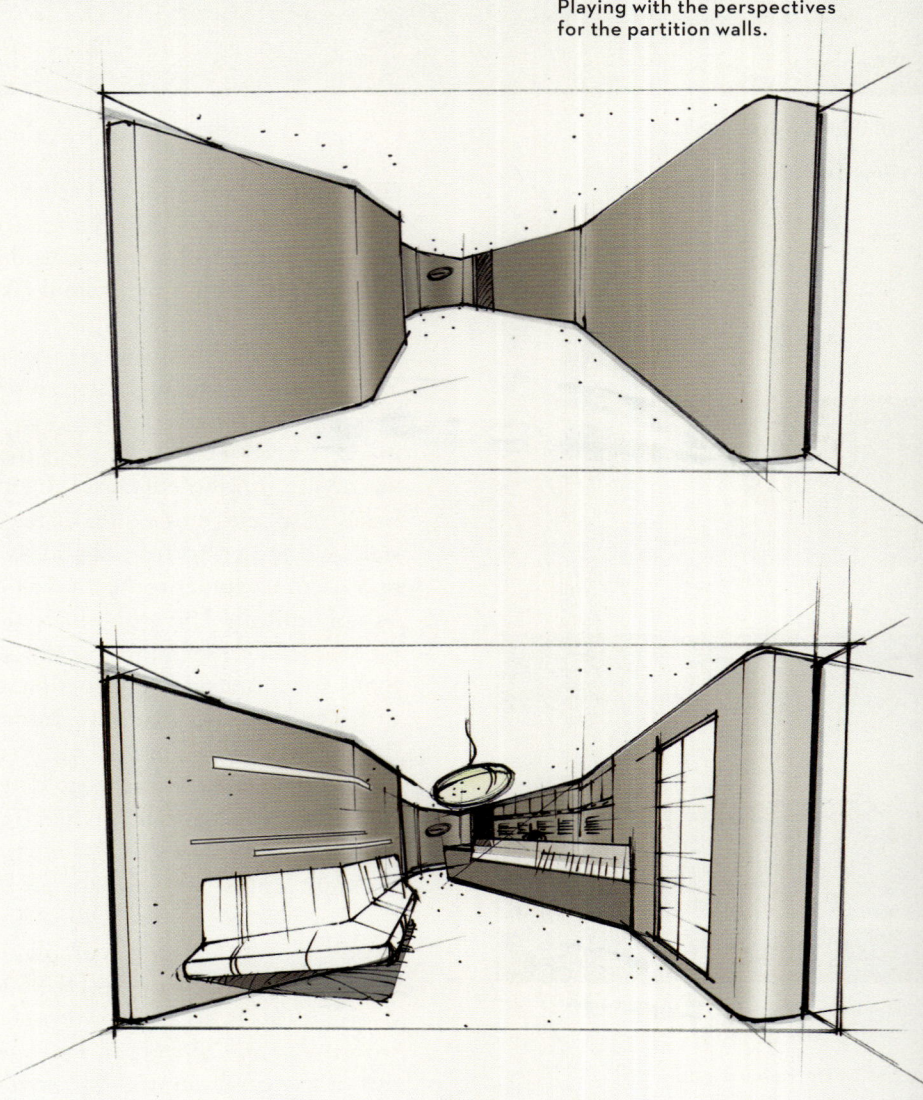

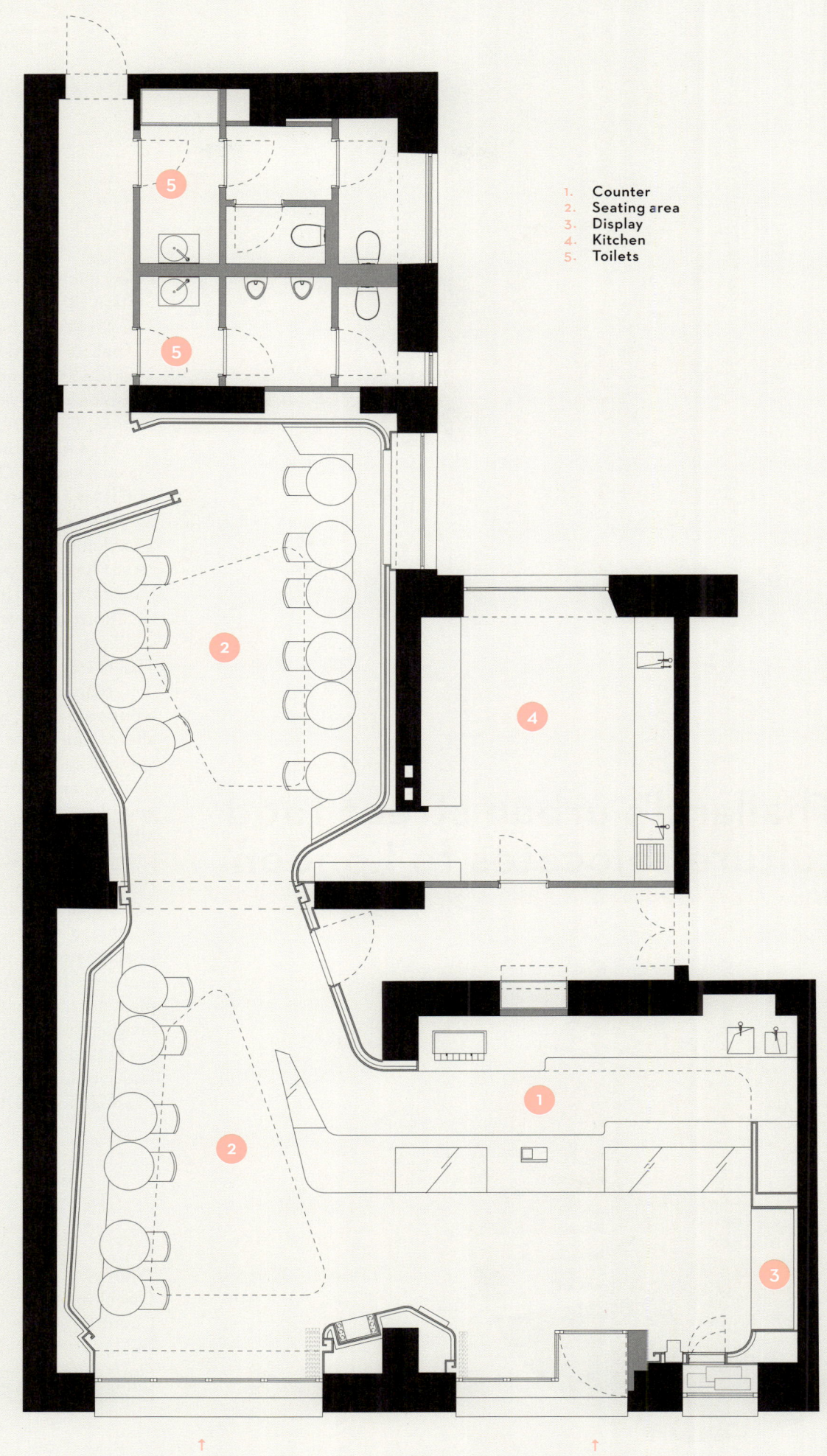

GRAB THAI STREET KITCHEN BY MANSIKKAMÄKI +JOY

Opposite The web of red and blue cables overhead echo the colours of the plastic stools and counter tray.

Thailand's urban street food culture relocates to London.

Photos Valerie Bennett

A few minutes' walk from Old Street Station sits the recently opened GRAB Thai Street Kitchen – a new concept in Thai cuisine. GRAB believes good Thai food does not have to be a once-in-a-blue-moon fine-dining experience. Instead, GRAB returns to the simplicity of Thailand's urban street food culture. Mansikkamäki+JOY, the creative directors of GRAB Thai Street Kitchen, designed an urban street atmosphere by translating affordable construction materials and street furniture into a clean and minimalist interior space. The brief was to create a recognizable brand and space that stands out from London's usually over-decorated Thai restaurants.

Menus hang off a wall of backlit wooden pallets, while corrugated metal sheets line some of the neighbouring vertical surfaces. Large globe light bulbs dangle haphazardly from a web of red and blue cables, creating an interior that, although minimalist, hints at the bustling scenes of Bangkok. The grab-and-go restaurant is the solution to the frantic schedules and lack of space in London – communal tables were made using the by-products of the restaurant's construction and are coupled with the iconic red plastic stools that are so integral to the image of urban street vending in Thailand. An easy-going atmosphere, raw design and simple materials allow the tasty food to speak for itself.

The choice of a red and blue colour scheme is evident in the menus positioned on the wood-clad wall.

Where London, United Kingdom
Opening May 2011
Client Grab Food
Designer Mansikkamäki+JOY → p.585
Floor space 50 m²
Capacity 22 seats

GRAND CAFÉ PEARL BY BARZILEYE CONCEPT & DESIGN

Where **The Hague, the Netherlands**
Opening **October 2010**
Client **Hilton Hotels**
Designer **Barzileye Concept & Design** → p.579
Floor space **245 m²**
Capacity **80 seats**

An elegant hotel restaurant decorated with Dutch classics.

Photos E-mage Victor van Leeuwen and Johan van Nispen tot Sevenaer

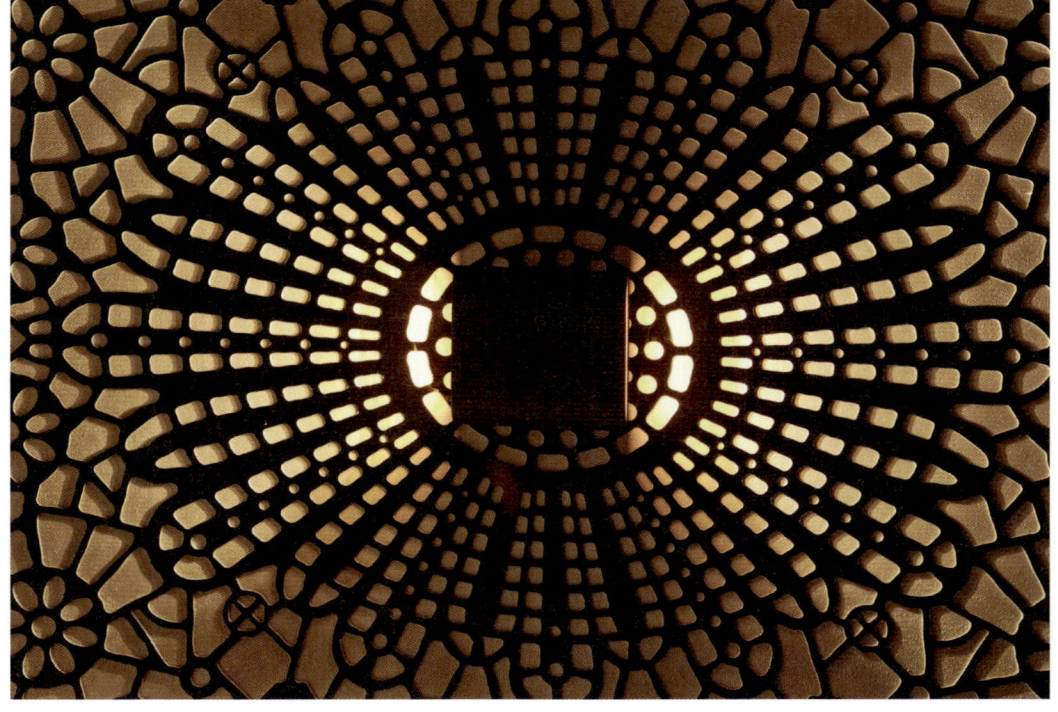

The wood panelling is laser-cut to resemble an old Dutch lace pattern.

Opposite A larger-than-life reproduction of Vermeer's famous work of art dominates the grand interior.

BARZILEYE CONCEPT & DESIGN

The sun shines through the window creating a colourful reflection on the black and white tiles.

The chandeliers were designed by Janne Kytannen and manufactured by 3D rapid prototyping.

For the design of the signature Grand Café for the new Hilton hotel in The Hague, Barzileye was commissioned to create not a typical 'hotel landscape' but an elegant meeting point – a place to meet friends and business partners alike, to have breakfast, stay for lunch or enjoy dinner. An additional requirement was to incorporate references to the local character of The Hague.

Inspired by the city's rich history, the Barzileye design team wanted the space to reflect the glory of the Dutch Golden Age, contrasting this with modern materials, techniques and atmospheric lighting. The interior is a continuous play of old with new, inspired by several themes, in particular the Dutch painter Johannes Vermeer and his *Girl with the Pearl Earring*, a large reproduction of which dominates the space. Printed on glass and forming an illuminated light box hung high on the wall behind the bar, it helps to emphasize the double height of the central space, along with the contemporary chandelier overhead. The designer considers lighting to be a crucial factor in design – and one often neglected in hotels – she asked Design Electro (DEP) to produce all the lighting solutions.

White-washed oak parquet have been laid in a traditional grid pattern on the floor, with dark wood panelling on the walls. On a number of the columns, the wood has been laser-cut in lace-like patterns, creating eye-catching and intricate wall decorations.

The café has an atmosphere of elegance, with a classic and neutral colour palette, except for the vibrant splashes of Delft blue. This colour is found in the custom-made chairs – luxuriously upholstered with a specially woven velvet produced in Italy – and in the tiles on the front of the bar counter, which have been given a modern twist by cutting each of the tiles into three pieces and laying them in a paving-pattern motif.

Contemporary conjugation of the cut Delft tiles creates a unique pattern on the counter front.

THE DESIGN TEAM WANTED THE SPACE TO REFLECT THE GLORY OF THE DUTCH GOLDEN AGE

BARZILEYE CONCEPT & DESIGN

A continuous, geometric 'skin' wraps around the walls, columns and room dividers.

Where Lisbon, Portugal
Opening February 2011
Client H3
Designers Marco Sousa Santos → p.585 and Tomás Azevedo Neves → p.590
Floor space 290 m²
Capacity 98 guests

H3 BY MARCO SOUSA SANTOS AND TOMÁS AZEVEDO NEVES

A gourmet burger restaurant with a geometric second skin.

Photos Fernando Guerra

The Portuguese fast-food chain H3 has numerous franchises across Lisbon and in other parts of Portugal, Brazil, Spain and Poland. The brand's hamburger restaurants offer fare that stands equidistant between fast food and gourmet dining, introducing the idea of 'not-so-fast food'. With the opening of a new restaurant in the centre of Lisbon's trendiest neighbourhood, the challenge for the design team was to bring the 'new hamburgology' to a more classical district of Portugal's capital city. The brief for transforming the 1970s' architecture into the new branded space stipulated that customers had to clearly identify with the corporate colours, which should be interwoven into the restaurant's concept.

The approach taken by H3 artistic director Luis Homem de Mello, along with architect Tomás Azevedo Neves and interior designer Marco Sousa Santos, was to develop a visual and graphic 'skin' for the existing space. The target audience is a young clientele that might grab a bite to eat before going clubbing, so a light and fresh space was created. Against a white backdrop, different jigsaw-like patterns line columns, walls and room dividers in bright colours such as yellow, pink and blue. The geometric detailing is systematic and evolutionary in nature and its connective detailing suggests a construction that develops and grows into the space, deforming itself and creating visual mutation dynamics around the restaurant.

The furniture, in contrast to the graphic geometry, is fluid and organic. Curved white tall stools are positioned by the windows beneath oversized lampshades. The central white tables have seats upholstered in the chain's corporate pink, and fluid forms continue overhead with large circular illumination in corporate blue and white.

The light and contemporary design appeals to the young clientele.

The structured shapes morph into a more haphazard design, while interconnecting like an evolutionary jigsaw.

MARCO SOUSA SANTOS AND TOMÁS AZEVEDO NEVES

HAIKU BY IMAGINE NATIVE

Where Shanghai, China
Opening August 2010
Client Haiku Restaurant Group
Designer Imagine Native → p.584
Floor space 320 m²
Capacity 95 seats

Origami-clad walls provide distinctive reliefs in a restaurant serving up Asian cuisine.

Photos Kingkay Architectural Photography

The new Haiku restaurant is located in the open courtyard of the recently completed Shanghai International Finance Centre (IFC). The client wanted to introduce new and fun design elements into its venue, while combining them with design elements from other Haiku restaurants.

The design team used the concept of origami as the major driving force behind the design. The restaurant space is divided into zones: a sushi bar, a cocktail bar, two main dining areas, booth seating and tatami rooms. Each zone is characterized by an origami-like feature, each made of different materials, such as perforated aluminium composite panels, translucent stone slabs and linen fabrics. Different lighting effects give the zones their own spatial character. Three of the zones are united by a suspended ceiling of origami that runs like a ribbon through the entire venue, creating a spatial transition across the restaurant. To contrast with the origami features, the designers used more natural materials, often seen in other Haiku restaurants, such as timber wall panels, pebbles and wood flooring as a backdrop for the more extravagant walls and ceiling. This juxtaposition of materials enhances the sleekness of the origami features while evoking the concepts of other Haiku restaurants. •

The suspended ceiling zigzags through the restaurant and is partly covered with wallpaper.

The custom-designed tables have the same zigzag line as the ceiling structure.

Curved stainless steel panels in different widths cover the tatami rooms.

This view of the restaurant shows the juxtaposed use of materials.

IMAGINE NATIVE

The bar counter is crafted from dark-stained oak with a black leather-clad front.

HOLYFIELDS BY IPPOLITO FLEITZ GROUP

A high-end restaurant experience at good value for money.

Photos Zooey Braun

Where Frankfurt, Germany
Opening November 2010
Client Holyfields Restaurant
Designer Ippolito Fleitz Group → p.584
Floor space 459 m²
Capacity 113 seats

Opposite The illuminated ceiling element, designed by pfarré lighting, is positioned above the host counter to designate it as the pivotal point of the room.

Guests can enter their order at one of the six touch-screen terminals.

Holyfields, a wholly new restaurant chain concept, commissioned Ippolito Fleitz Group to develop a modular, scalable space system with a distinctive look and feel. The new brand promises a high-end restaurant experience at good value for money, while respecting today's need for simplicity and speed.

Holyfields offers a unique, vibrant yet cosy setting, based on a highly differentiated haptic environment. The guest is guided through the space with precise choreography. He is greeted by a white host counter supported on a multitude of different table legs. To the immediate right, terminals with large touch screens set in white steel-plate casing await your order. Their four sturdy legs conjure up a whole spectrum of associations, from waiting staff ready to proffer their services to antique furniture.

The dining room contains a variety of seating; four tiers are staggered in height from the front windows to the rear wall. A band of 'normal' wooden tables creates a classic restaurant setting immediately adjacent to the windows. Specially designed pendant luminaires add a touch of intimacy here. The next tier consists of a row of white tables with upholstered benches on a slightly raised dark-wood plinth with a gently lowered ceiling above. A net of taut rubber laces separates the individual booths without impeding the view across the space. The third tier offers guests a seat at a long bleached oak bar table. Finally, four white six-seat tables are aligned with the rear wall, which is clad in dark wooden slats. Capacious U-shaped enclosures provide a final parenthesis to the space. The far wall of the venue accommodates the food counter, prominently encompassed by a floor-to-ceiling copper wall. In front of this backdrop stands a broad stainless steel counter where guests can pick up their order.

With its innovative food concept, Holyfields sets new accents in system gastronomy for a discerning urban clientele. It satisfies the need for fast and great-value food, as well as providing a visual and atmospheric dining experience.

The front surface of the food counter is printed with the folds of an imaginary white tablecloth.

The printed animal motifs on the white-tiled wall behind the bar recall antique engravings.

TOUCH-SCREEN TECHNOLOGY TAKES YOUR ORDER

A specially commissioned acoustic ceiling with geometrically patterned holes guarantees good acoustics.

A sketch of the floor pattern with its floral motif.

A detailed sketch of an eagle used at the rear wall of the bar.

Initial renderings of the interior concept.

HOLYFIELDS SETS NEW ACCENTS IN SYSTEM GASTRONOMY FOR A DISCERNING URBAN CLIENTELE

1. Host counter
2. Order terminals
3. Bar
4. Seating area
5. Lounge
6. Food counter
7. Take-away
8. Kitchen
9. Office
10. Toilets

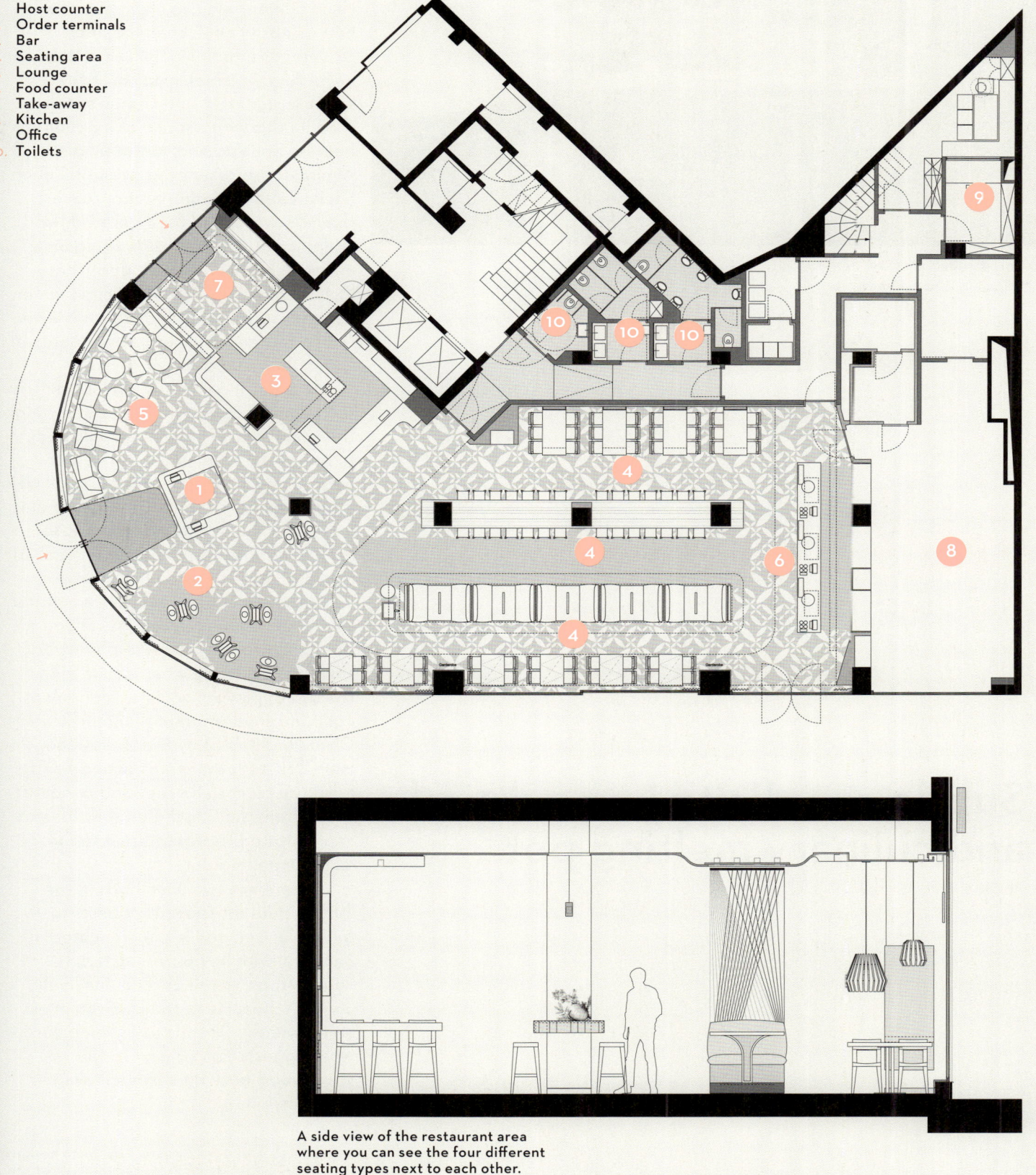

A side view of the restaurant area where you can see the four different seating types next to each other.

IPPOLITO FLEITZ GROUP

Different types of bar stools are used at the dining bar.

Where Tel Aviv, Israel
Opening November 2011
Clients Haim and Sigal Cohen
Designer BK Architecture → p.579
Floor space 350 m²
Capacity 117 seats

JAFFA\TEL AVIV BY BK ARCHITECTURE

Subtle simplicity in a cultural and culinary melting pot.

Photos Amit Geron

Haim Cohen, widely known as Israel's first celebrity chef, commissioned BK Architecture to design his new restaurant in Tel Aviv. In Israel, many culinary traditions coexist, and Cohen's menu reflects this with a touch of ingenuity, bearing honesty and subtle simplicity. Aiming to represent the spirit of Cohen's kitchen and mirroring his approach, the BK team opted for a pared-down and uncomplicated design using local materials with a raw aesthetic. These include basic ingredients such as water, cement, aggregates and steel, vis-à-vis the restaurant's culinary components of water, flour and olive oil.

A natural colour palette arises from the exposed concrete walls that envelop the space, which have been polished to reveal the true nature of the stone aggregates. Hanging from the back wall is a patchwork of worn Turkish carpets, a design aspect with a dual purpose. Practically, the carpets dampen acoustic levels while each piece has its own history and a story to tell, like a cultural kaleidoscope that evokes the charm of the historic city. Natural poplar wood shutters facing the west façade allow the sun to play a magical symphony of light and shadow upon the interior walls. Chairs and tables by Dutch designer Piet Hein Eek, together with second-hand furniture pieces and recycled pendant lamps from the Czech Republic, bestow sophisticated representation to the cultural melting pot.

There are two main hubs in the long restaurant space for guests to gather: at one end is the elongated bar area, with its poured terrazzo countertops, at the other is the lively, open kitchen. Here, the large stainless steel counter extends as a dining bar where guests can sit next to the large wood-burning stove and watch the 'show'. •

Opposite Furniture by Dutch designer Piet Hein Eek is used throughout the restaurant, accompanied by a few second-hand pieces.

Guests who sit at one of the four high tables that project from the bar have a nice view of the premises.

THE CONCEPT REPRESENTS THE SPIRIT OF THE KITCHEN

The patchwork of Turkish carpets, each with its own story, evokes the flair of old Jaffa where multicultural traditions live side by side.

The façade of this double-height restaurant consists of floor-to-ceiling windows, covered with shutters at the top.

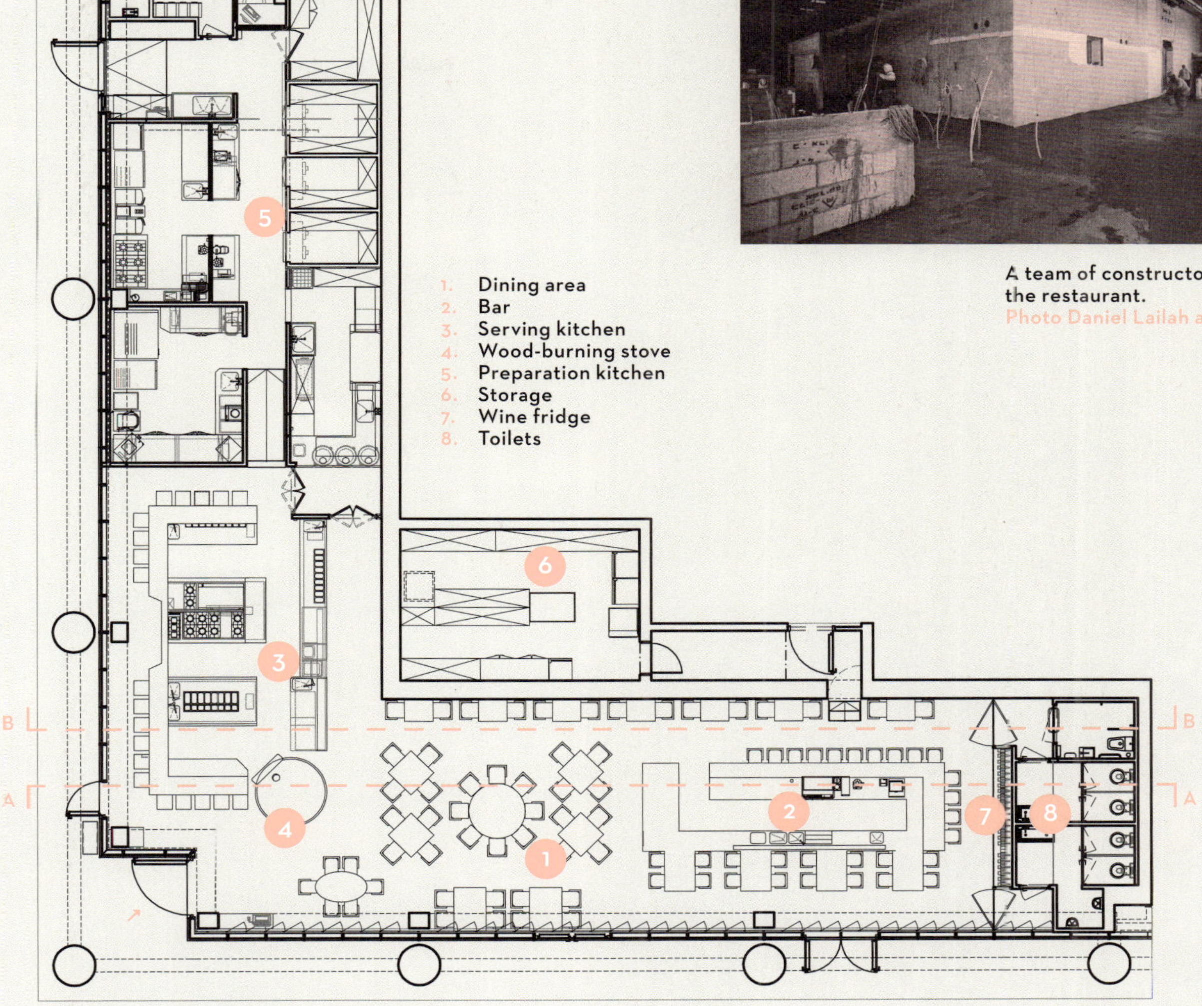

1. Dining area
2. Bar
3. Serving kitchen
4. Wood-burning stove
5. Preparation kitchen
6. Storage
7. Wine fridge
8. Toilets

A team of constructors is working on the restaurant.
Photo Daniel Lailah and Amit Farber

Section AA

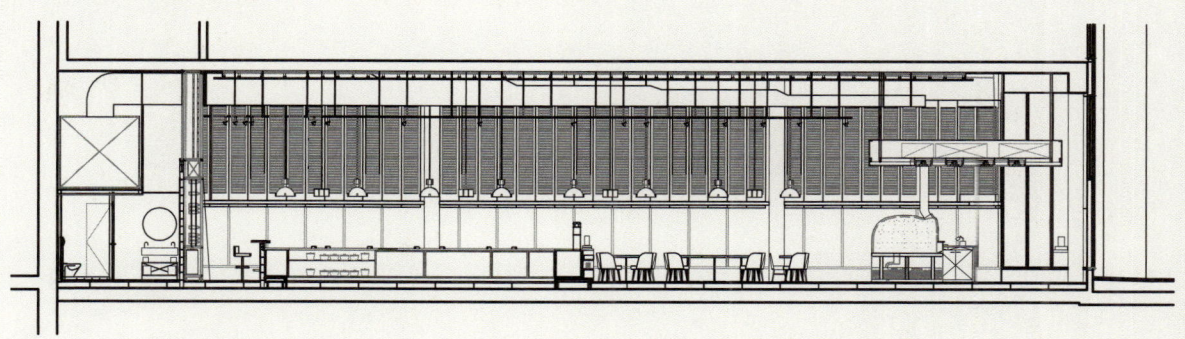

Section BB

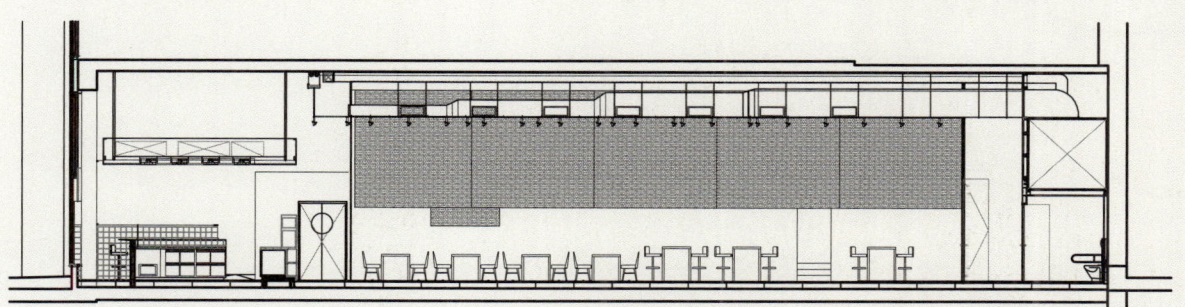

Wood panelling and a split-level layout give the space a loft-style aesthetic.

Where Oss, the Netherlands
Opening March 2011
Client Pierre Vink
Designer Beers|Brickworks → p.579
Floor space 350 m²
Capacity 98 seats (inside), 50 seats (outside)

KOOZIE BY BEERS|BRICKWORKS

A restaurant which oozes craftsmanship in a loft-style interior.

Photos Colinda Boeren

A cluster of lamps with copper lampshades illuminates the mid-floor level.

Opposite One wall is drilled with holes into which wine bottles can be slotted, or out of which light can pour.

Overhead hangs a white wooden frame decorated with a print found on an old ceiling.

Spectacular views, the use of raw materials to contrast with copper, and different atmospheres on each level: this was exactly what Beers|Brickworks had in mind for the new restaurant Koozie.

The best investment of this project is the new façade, positioned 80 cm in front of the old one, creating a huge space 6-m high. It opens up the characteristic split-level layout. Although each level has a different atmosphere, the correct use of the walls and open spaces between each level makes the restaurant a coherent whole.

At the entrance, a two-storey wine rack serves as a showcase for the wine concept that defines Koozie. The clapboard wall of wine bottles covers the right wall of the venue from floor to ceiling, crossing each level of the restaurant. Indirect lighting shines through the perforations when bottles are taken out. The wall in the centre of Koozie is rough, made of wood and sloppily painted white. A striking contrast with the other materials, it lends the restaurant freshness. Cookbooks, cooking materials and ingredients are displayed here – storage turned inside out.

In the middle level of the restaurant the open kitchen, covered with mosaic, acts as a living painting. The owners' passion for beautiful wines and ingredients is visually emphasized by the lifesize prints and the wine list on blackboard walls.

Thanks to the materials selected by Beers|Brickworks, Koozie will age well, becoming even more beautiful over time.

Walls are decorated with culinary connotations.

COOKBOOKS AND INGREDIENTS ARE DISPLAYED - STORAGE TURNED INSIDE OUT

There are structured arrays of blue lamps lighting up the top-level dining area.

Opposite The towering custom-designed wine rack is a showstopper.

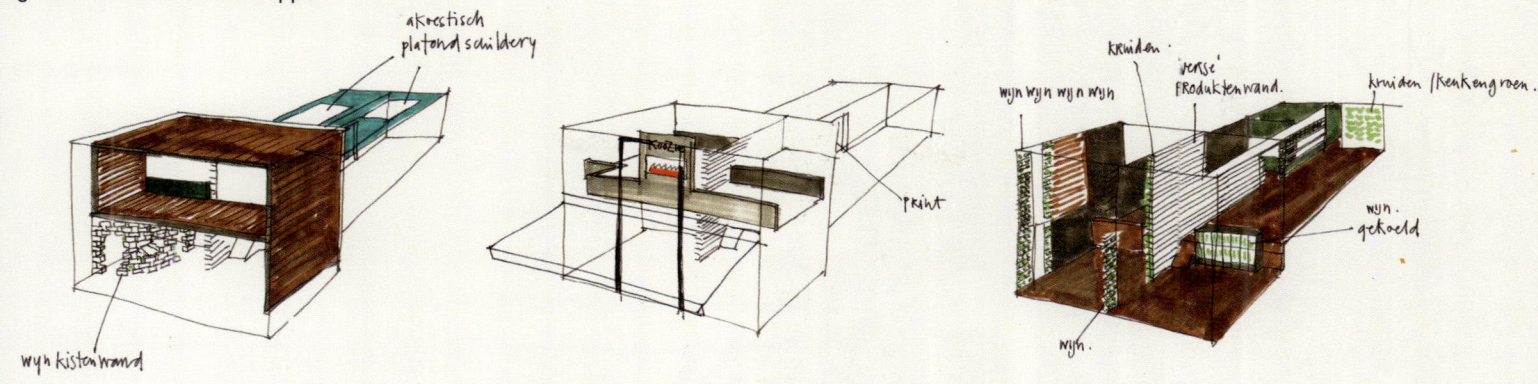

Initial sketches showing the development of the design concept.

A TWO-STOREY WINE RACK DEFINES THE DESIGN CONCEPT

Section AA

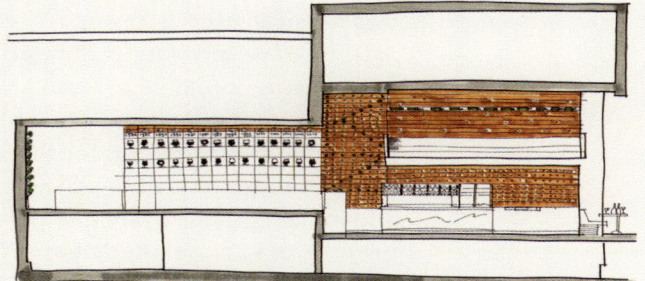

Section BB

Section CC

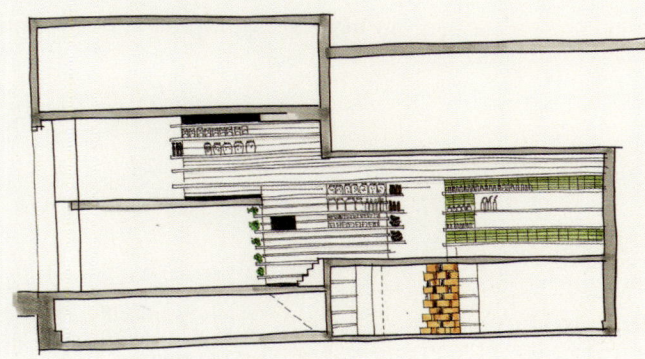

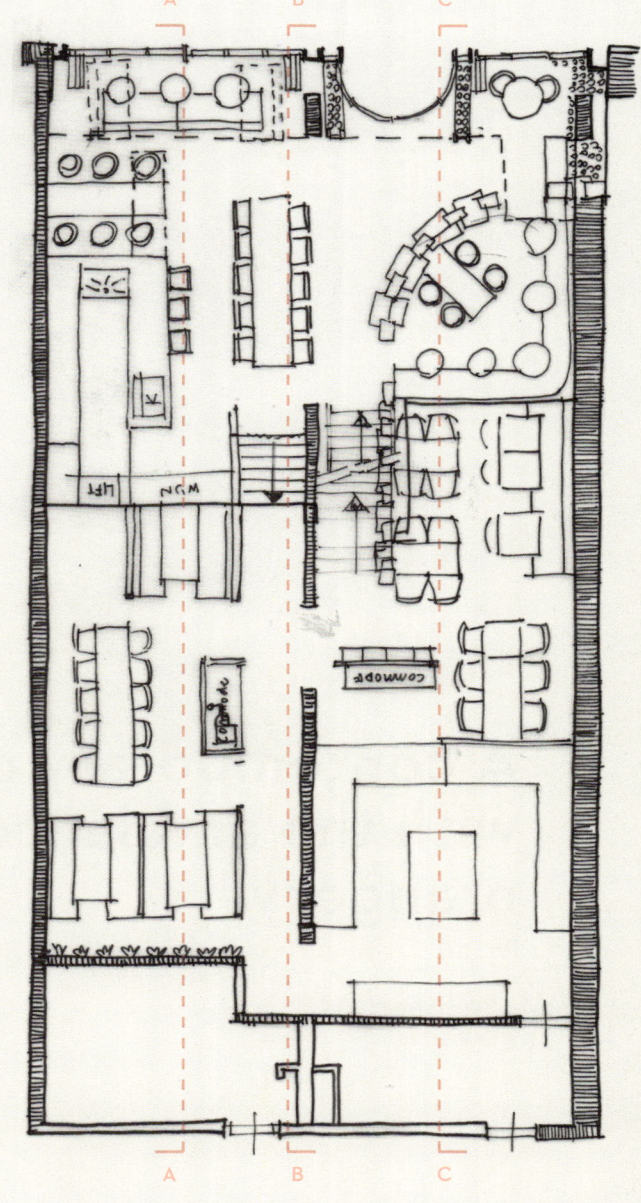

BEERS | BRICKWORKS   095

Contemporary furnishings contrast with the neoclassical décor at one end of the restaurant.

The delicate lamp stems that emerge from the counter seem too thin to support the bespoke lollipop shades.

Where Munich, Germany
Opening April 2010
Client Künstlerhaus Gastronomie
Designer Studio Nitzan Cohen → p.589
Floor space 220 m²
Capacity 120 seats (inside), 120 seats (outside)

Located in the very heart of Munich is the recently renovated Künstlerhaus (artists' house), a grand building with curved gables and two lower wings enclosing a courtyard in front of it. Studio Nitzan Cohen designed the ground-floor vegan restaurant Farm to have the ambiance of an orangery, in part created by the existing architecture of the building and the fact that the restaurant extends onto the large terrace.

The challenge was to integrate a contemporary concept within the neoclassical interior, many of the core aspects of which were protected by a preservation ordinance. Metallic chairs dating from the 1900s were all hand-painted in burgundy red for the seating in the baroque-style tile-walled section, and in pale yellow, white and grey in the brighter area positioned nearer the full glass doors leading to the garden terrace.

The design team's main focus was to create special pieces of furniture and extensive object families that featured a clean, modern design. These include a number of custom-designed interior elements, each of which is mobile, such as the oversized rolling plant pots, trellises for climbing plants and orange trees designed as room dividers and specialized waiter trolleys. These all incorporate a white metal tubing design, which is also featured in the bespoke 'lollipop' light fittings derived from iconic garden lamps. The disproportionally thin stem supporting the globe gives the lights a fragility and personality akin to plants growing tall or – in the case of the wall lights illuminating the individual side tables – drooping from the weight of a flower head.

KÜNSTLERHAUS-FARM BY STUDIO NITZAN COHEN

A contemporary concept with the ambiance of an orangery.

Photos Gerhardt Kellermann and Myrzik and Jarisch

Opposite top and bottom Wooden tabletops and different coloured Tolix chairs distinguish the dining area close to the terrace.

STUDIO NITZAN COHEN

KÜNSTLERHAUS-GRILL BY STUDIO NITZAN COHEN

Opposite The transparent walk-in wine room has three different temperature zones.

A culinary contrast in a neoclassical interior.

Photos Myrzik and Jarisch

Concurrently with the commission for the ground-floor vegan restaurant in the recently renovated neoclassical Künstlerhaus in Munich, Studio Nitzan Cohen was also commissioned to design the first-floor restaurant. The Grill, specializing in grilled meat dishes, is in stark contrast to its downstairs neighbour, not only in its culinary tastes but also in its interior décor.

The design team has imbued the restaurant with a noble elegance by creating a dark, sleek space with subdued lighting and bespoke brass fittings. It is furnished with upholstered wooden chairs, elongated sofas and oversized black mirrors, with the layout inspired by open-plan office cubicles. The sofas are used to confine and at the same time define – and divide – the space, with each wood-lined 'cubical' area given its own fabric and colour, ranging from dark plum and rich brown to charcoal grey, with the textiles specially crafted by a local weaving company.

As in any good brasserie, there is an extensive wine selection available to complement the range of fare on offer. The wine is housed not in a cellar but in a glass-walled wine room integrated alongside the restaurant, which functionally connects the bar and the kitchen areas and makes for a visual centrepiece at the heart of the space. There is also a VIP dining room for customers who want extra privacy, and an urban roof terrace that opens up the space and gives guests a view of the courtyard and surrounding architecture.

Where Munich, Germany
Opening April 2010
Client Künstlerhaus Gastronomie
Designer Studio Nitzan Cohen → p.589
Floor space 220 m²
Capacity 120 seats (inside), 80 seats (outside)

The dark wood furniture was custom-designed for the restaurant.

Blackened spotlights enhance the atmosphere within the dark, sleek interior.

Fabric panels line the walls in the dining area, giving it a warm and cosy atmosphere.

Where **Shanghai, China**
Opening **August 2011**
Clients **Gilles Bini-Zinou and Frank Steffe**
Designer **AOO Architecture → p.578**
Floor space **68 m²**
Capacity **18 seats**

KUSH BY AOO ARCHITECTURE

The food is the star – the design must complement it.

Photos courtesy of AOO Architecture

Kush shares the same clients and is housed in the same industrial building as the Japanese restaurant Sushi Abuse. Kush serves healthy, simple vegetarian food, which is surprisingly under-represented in Shanghai. 'The food is the star – the design must complement it and provide the serenity our client envisioned,' says Sacha Silva of AOO Architecture. 'The client wanted the design to provide a more relaxing experience, somewhere to escape the bustle that is Shanghai life.'

Kush is a compact space, and off-site deliveries are a big part of its business model, yet the seeds for what a full restaurant could be had to be created here. The biggest challenge therefore was to decide what feeling and configuration the seating should have in order for people to feel they were in a restaurant rather than eating in a corridor. So the seating area really had to have its own sense of place. Upon entering, guests see a semi-open kitchen and a long service and display counter, and tucked away in the back, seating for just 18 people. To create a cocoon feeling, the designers chose to use padding on the walls, which contributes to the atmosphere along with the nooks for bookshelves and the compact banquette seating. ●

The built-in seating has a plywood construction covered in oak veneer.

Opposite The main island counter is made of solid oak with a white marble worktop.

KWINT BY SAQ ARCHITECTS

Where Brussels, Belgium
Opening January 2010
Client Square and GL-events
Designer SAQ architects → p.588
Floor space 250 m²
Capacity 72 seats (inside), 72 seats (outside)

A modern metallic sculpture sits alongside diners in a historic setting.

Photos Dave Bruel

Located in the centre of Brussels, in the Mont des Arts or Kunstberg, the city's museum quarter, Kwint serves as a central meeting place for the Brussels Square Conference Centre. The arcades in which the restaurant is housed were renovated with due respect to their architectural heritage. In breathing new life into this ensemble, SAQ has made a minimal intervention: the unique atmosphere has been created with a limited number of elements.

The length of the space is emphasized both by the padded side wall and by the sculpture hovering over the dining tables. This 30-m-long sculpture is an Arne Quinze creation, erupting from the bar at the end of the room almost like a living, articulated organism and giving the customers seated below a sense of protection, intensifying the idea of gathering.

Not only does the upholstered wall function as a perfect acoustic absorber for the diners' conversations, it conceals all the essential service elements and infrastructure: the heating and ventilation system, the electrical installations, but also access to adjacent spaces like the kitchen, toilets and lounge. The wall features an irregular pattern of dots that seems formed by the shadow of the moving sculpture.

One colour prevails: the glossy copper of the sculpture's skin and of the crackled surface of the side-wall openings interacts magnificently with the natural light pouring through the ample front windows. On summer days, these accordion windows are opened up, making the view of the ancient centre of Brussels below an intrinsic component of the setting. •

The customers' ambient conversations are absorbed by the soft, padded walls.

Opposite The sculpture stretches up and over the diners, from one end of the restaurant to the other.

SAQ ARCHITECTS

Opposite Contemporary art mingles with fine dining.

Previous spread Although the textures are contrasting, there is a complementary colour palette linking the historic archways, the metallic sculpture and the padded walls.

NEW LIFE WAS BREATHED INTO A HISTORIC BUILDING WHILST RESPECTING ITS ARCHITECTURAL HERITAGE

Models showing how the sculpture concept was developed.

1. Dining area
2. Bar
3. Wine bar
4. Lounge
5. Kitchen
6. Storage
7. Toilets

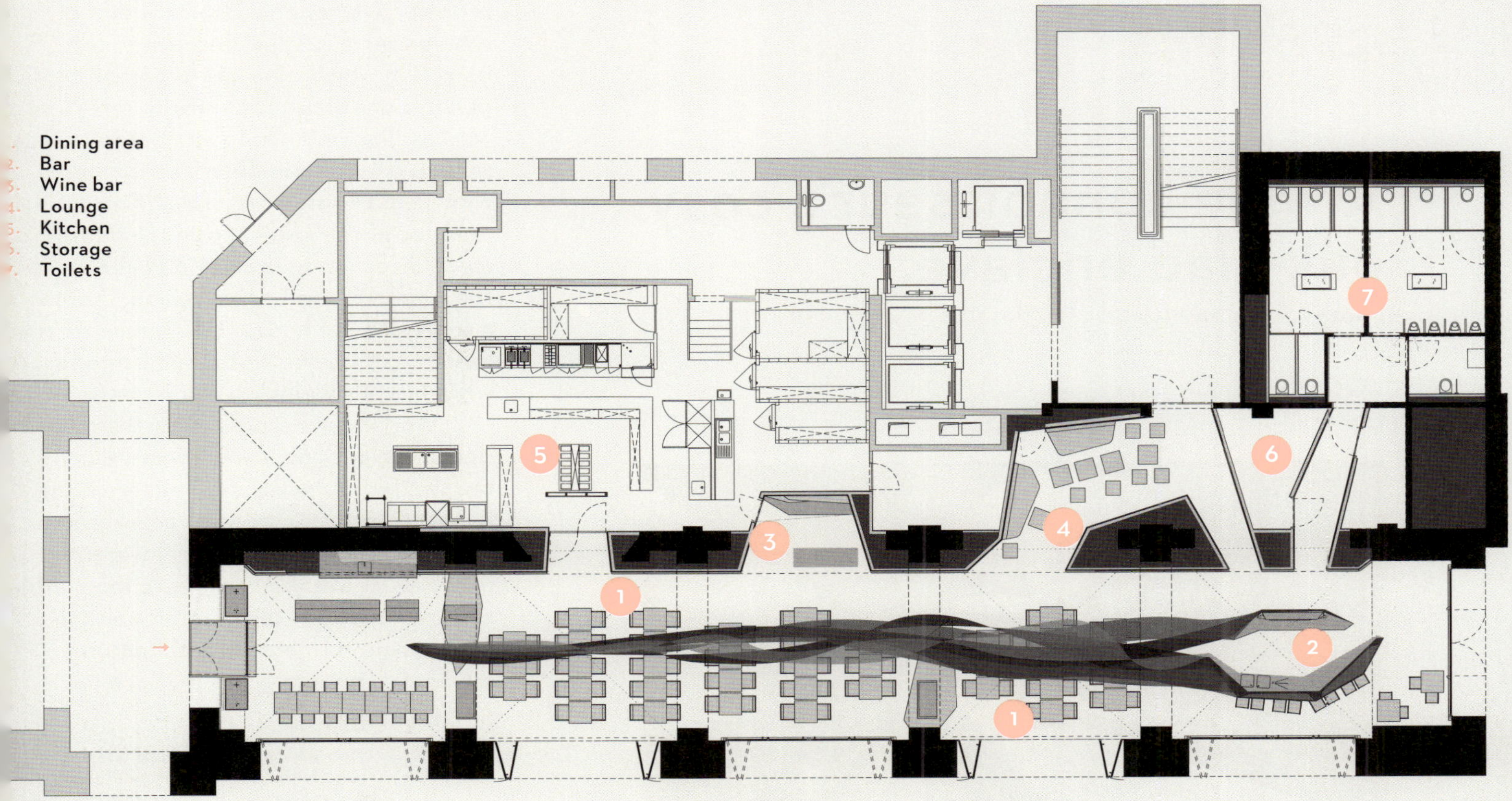

SAQ ARCHITECTS

The building in which the restaurant is located was originally designed by distinguished Montreal architect Joseph Venne.

Where Montreal, Canada
Opening January 2010
Clients Robert Herrera and Maud Séguin
Designer blazysgérard → p.579
Floor space 140 m²
Capacity 70 seats

LES CAVISTES
BLAZYSGERARD

A wine connoisseur's cosy oak-clad enclave.

Photos Steve Montpetit

Les Cavistes is a restaurant in Montreal designed by blazysgérard. The team fulfilled a very specific brief from its client, a discerning duo with both business acumen and extensive experience as restaurateurs. Both are avid wine amateurs and wanted to create a bold and unique character-driven restaurant concept around the full-bodied nectar.

Translated as 'the cellars', the boutique restaurant's name fits well with its vision: it is a place for guests to discover select wines accompanied by bistro-inspired meals. Guests are to be inspired, seduced and even educated by the wine list in this venue, which is on a quest to become a 'Montreal Classic' that will age gracefully as its distinctive character develops. To realize this, the design team chose a concept of *de rigueur* and quiet sophistication. A distinctive material choice is that of oak veneer, a subtle reference to the barrels in which wine has been aged for generations around the world. A rhythm was instilled in the long and narrow space, reflected in the use of strict alignments with all of the architectural and structural features of the space. From the flooring's metal insertion to the oak panelling and the design of the backlit ceiling, there is a succession of horizontal alignments that helps organize the restaurant's interior while visually widening its perception.

Working in harmony with the neutral décor, the lighting is a key feature in the design. Illumination comes from the backlit translucent acrylic ceiling over the main dining area and the oversized cylinders above the bar, where the marble and metal used in the counter – and in other made-to-measure architectural elements – help to give the space its noble notes.

Opposite top Oiled wood flooring is used in the dining room, while matt and glossy two-tone ceramic tiles have been laid in the bar area.

Opposite bottom The restaurant is furnished with black and chrome dining chairs and bar stools.

BLAZYSGÉRARD

Black pencil-like pendant lamps by Davide Groppi illuminate the restaurant.

LOFT BY NUCA STUDIO

A modern restaurant and lounge with an old industrial memory.

Photos Nicu Ilfoveanu

Historic aspects are revealed in some areas, with exposed brick being a recurring feature.

Where Bucharest, Romania
Opening October 2010
Designer Nuca Studio → p.586
Floor space 680 m²
Capacity 130 seats

In the heart of Bucharest, a printing house built in 1919 was transformed into a mixed-use facility including residential, office and commercial spaces. On the ground floor of the old building, between the fully restored walls of a 680-m² space, you can find Loft, a restaurant and lounge aimed at both 'gourmet cuisine' enthusiasts and cool party people.

Designed by Nuca Studio, the high-tech kitchen that caters for the 130 seats is separated from the main space, but the drinks are in plain sight behind a 12-m-long Corian bar. Parallel to the bar, a linear black sofa serves as the starting point – and more often the end point – of the evening. Above this lounge area hangs a big white chandelier; this lighting piece is the signature statement of the owners. The polygonal decorative ceiling is the supporting act for the chandelier connecting its solitary presence with the bar's abundant display of drinks. The glamorous tone becomes more subdued towards the table area.

The materials used for the restaurant zone make references to the old features and functions of the building: exposed brick walls, large wooden planks as dividers and stainless steel mirrors try to capture a small part of its old industrial legacy. Special attention was given to the lighting scheme. The lights on the tables feature dimmable incandescent bulbs, but the rest of the lighting uses RGB LED light, working on nine separate channels. This system permits a wide range of lighting scenarios allowing the look of the entire space to evolve over the course of the evening or from one day to another.

Opposite The overhead installation, made of plastered aluminium bond and foam, is like a canopy over the dining area.

A computer sketch of the ceiling structure.

Initial renderings of the interior concept.

1. Entrance hall
2. Bar
3. Lounge area
4. Restaurant area
5. Kitchen
6. Toilets

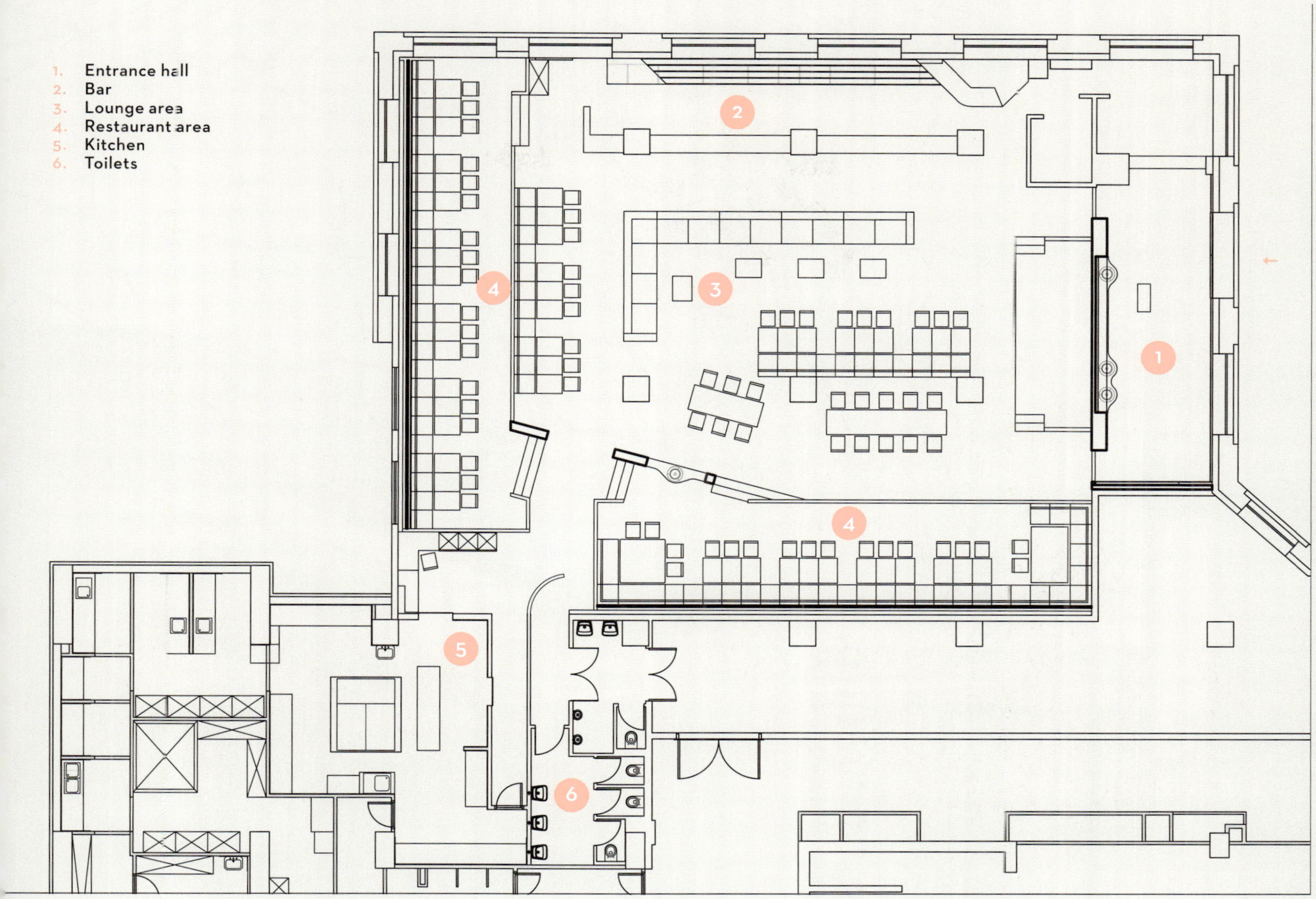

Constructors trying to get the ceiling structure in place.

A member of the design team working on the brick walls that will remain visible at the restaurant.

Opposite A wall relief by David Band made of birch tree branches evokes the image of an ivy-clad wall as it travels 60 m around the space.

MAZE BY BATES SMART

A restaurant which is sophisticated and has boutique aesthetics.

Photos Shannon McGrath

Splashes of aqua blue and vibrant green are apparent in the tiles behind the counter.

The white ladles hanging over the serving counter are like an art installation.

Where Melbourne, Australia
Opening March 2010
Clients Crown Limited and Gordon Ramsay Holdings
Designer Bates Smart → p.579
Floor space 1345 m²
Capacity 300 seats

BATES SMART

Maze, a Gordon Ramsay restaurant, is located at the Crown Metropol hotel in Melbourne and offers an appealing variety of dining experiences. The design team of Bates Smart wanted the restaurant to exude both the sophistication of Ramsay's brand and the boutique aesthetic of the Metropol.

Highly crafted woodwork, carefully selected objects and custom-designed light fittings, furniture and floor coverings are found at every turn. Collaboration with artisans, craftsmen and textile designers has allowed Bates Smart to create unique and memorable signature elements.

Guests have a choice of spaces: first they encounter a communal high table and adjacent long bar featuring crafted charcoal, turquoise and platinum mosaic tiles and a marble top. The adjacent cocktail bar is an intimate box-like folly with shuttered panels guests can open to view the lobby below or close for privacy. The *à la carte* restaurant is defined by its soaring glass volume and the banquette seating enclosing it. A boldly patterned, vibrant and contemporary carpet, like a flower bed, adds a strong accent to an otherwise neutral palette of taupes, charcoals and earth tones. Oversized light fittings hover above the dining room, beacons to passers-by in the street below. Two dramatic basket-like pavilions of hand-woven wicker form a private dining room seating twelve and a unique Sommelier Experience enclosure. The Maze grill celebrates a vibrant combination of raw steel, rough-cut slate and rustic thick-glazed tiles in deep emerald, creating a bold and robust backdrop to the dynamic action in the kitchen.

Creating intimacy within this vast architectural space was the key challenge. Inspired by the Maze concept, Bates Smart has crafted the interior as a journey of intrigue and discovery. Like an evocative landscape, the dining experiences unfold before the visitor to create an earthy and sensuous interior. A single design imbues the whole space, but each 'room' has its own distinctive ambiance.

Allegro pendant lampshades by Foscarini illuminate the dining tables.

The woven wicker screens were designed by Bates Smart and manufactured by Design Sense.

Bespoke carpets were designed by Bates Smart in association with NIBA Rugs.

CREATING INTIMACY WITHIN A VAST ARCHITECTURAL SPACE WAS THE KEY CHALLENGE

Opposite An intimate private dining area can be created by lowering the blinds.

Discreet lighting integrated into the metal finish overhead pools light on the dark timber counter, highlighting the diner's position and the dishes that are served.

MOMOFUKU SEIŌBO BY LUCHETTI KRELLE

A serene, dark and moody restaurant with a palette of rich, yet restrained materials.

Photos Murray Fredericks

Where Sydney, Australia
Opening October 2011
Client Momofuku
Designer Luchetti Krelle → p.585
Floor space 240 m²
Capacity 36 seats

LUCHETTI KRELLE   119

With the blinds up, the restaurant has an open plan dining area.

SIMPLICITY AND ATTENTION TO DETAIL ARE AT THE CORE OF THE DESIGN

The brief that the design team of Luchetti Krelle received for the Momofuku seiōbo restaurant, set within Sydney's new casino complex 'The Star', was to create a space that reflected the Momofuku ethos, with simplicity and attention to detail at the core of the design. The kitchen is its heart, and the chefs at work the main focus of the intimate 36-seat restaurant.

The restaurant is protected from the bright lights of its busy address with a rigid, vertical black steel front. The regularly spaced steel sections give the façade dynamism across its entire length, revealing flickers of light and activity from the interior to passers-by. A bronze peach pinpoints the entry. Guests step into a serene, dark and moody space with a palette of rich, yet restrained materials. An open working bar horizontally clad in dark stained Tasmanian oak with a large, purpose-built wine refrigerator faces the entrance.

Luchetti Krelle has designed flexibility into the small, narrow dining space, allowing patrons to dine at individual tables, adaptable to large or small groups, with operable blinds that are architecturally lit to divide the space and create further intimacy. At the edge of this dining space is the counter, a shining hub of activity under a reflective bronze metal bulkhead. Here guests can engage with the chefs' work. The counter and bar are both set on board-form concrete, lit to accentuate their position and importance in the room. The room's slate flooring is reminiscent of two Momofuku restaurants in New York and, along with an expansive, smooth concrete-rendered wall, provides a restrained backdrop for the dining experience. A Momofuku-commissioned work of art by photographer Damien Bennett dresses the concrete wall. Deep, dark blue ripples soothe and remind patrons of their Sydney context.

Passers-by can peek through the powder-coated steel façade to get a glimpse of the restaurant.

Guests are greeted at the welcome desk.

LUCHETTI KRELLE

MOSI BY SHH

A night out at the Manchester museum.

Photos Alastair Lever

Where Manchester, United Kingdom
Opening September 2010
Clients MOSI and Compass Leisure
Designer SHH → p.588
Floor space 460 m²
Capacity 208 seats

As part of an overall refurbishment of Manchester's Museum of Science & Industry (MOSI), SHH was asked to create the visitors' restaurant. The huge space is divided in two, with one part located in the Museum's original 19th-century building and the second in an extension built in 1990. The 19th-century space, which guests enter first, accommodates the servery, kitchen and seating. The second serves as an overspill area and is specially intended for school groups and families with young children.

Depending on the time of year, the restaurant can be either very quiet or enormously busy, with huge usage peaks during school holidays. The design responded to this with robust and flexible furniture. The overspill area in particular needed to be adaptable, as its secondary function is a corporate event space.

The 19th-century warehouse section had exposed brickwork walls, original timber ceiling lining and exposed steel beams, along with new galvanized steel ventilation ductwork. SHH took its lead from these existing elements. Bespoke, vibrant-green steel work benches were designed as servery counters, as unapologetically large-scale industrial references. Varied types of seating are provided, with robust and cost-effective Formica-topped tables for smaller groups and long tables and bench seats for larger groups. Vinyl floor tiles with the appearance of concrete further emphasize the industrial aesthetic.

The main feature of the light, bright overspill space was a specially commissioned graphic illustration along one wall, providing a playful riff on standard industrial components. White tables with red and black chairs were arranged around a central cluster of interlocking seating – deliberately lightweight, communal and easy to move for events. •

A variety of contemporary furniture is placed against the industrial-style backdrop, including the white Formica tables and benches by James Burleigh.

The spillover area features bright and easily reconfigurable lightweight foam bench seats and coloured stools.

The vast space is illuminated by Kao strip lights and Nur pendants (by Artemide).

The casual, elegant and custom-made restaurant furnishings have been handcrafted with a maritime sensibility.

Opposite The Stockholm suspension lamp by Omikron Design, with its yellow interior, hangs above the bar.

MOTTO AM FLUSS BY BEHF ARCHITECTS

An Austrian restaurant pays homage to Venice of the 1950s.

Photos Bruno Klomfar and Yvonne Oswald

Where Vienna, Austria
Opening July 2010
Client Motto Group
Designer BEHF Architects → p.579
Floor space 745 m²
Capacity 268 seats (inside), 126 seats (outside)

The interior of the landing bridge is dominated by a high-tech diagonal steel tube structure.

The dynamic interior is reflected in the various mirrors positioned in the angular walls.

The huge terrace of the restaurant can seat up to 126 guests, who all can enjoy a great city view.

THE CHARM OF THE CAFÉ UNFOLDS LIKE A GATHERING IN MOTHER'S KITCHEN

The diverse functions and sophisticated atmospheric needs of the Vienna-based restaurant Motto am Fluss, spread over two levels, pay homage to the Venice of the 1950s. With its soft elegant forms, reminiscent of the early Italian industrial design that developed under the influence of the American way of life in the early 1950s, Motto am Fluss plays to the gallery: Venice's long and opulent celebrations are definitely in keeping with Vienna's lifestyle.

Situated along the banks of the Danube Canal, Vienna's inner city defines true cosmopolitan city life with its pulsating traffic streams and flows of people. From the upper deck of the restaurant the view of the canal and city skyline is breathtaking. Sitting in the lightweight, seemingly woven metal furniture, guests can enjoy the sun in comfort. On the same level, facing inwards, the charm of the café unfolds like a gathering in mother's kitchen.

Artfully patterned tile flooring and walls are paired with back-illuminated cherry-wood racks and gleaming black table tops in the restaurant on the lower level. A sense of comfort and cosiness is created by the shiny black velvet-upholstered furniture. An elegantly styled brass clock above the kitchen entrance evokes the culture of travel.

PARK CAFÉ

Opposite One large table was created as the balustrade of the restaurant area.

The multicoloured kitchen is constructed from a pile of jutting-out wooden beams.

PARK CAFÉ BY MAURICE MENTJENS

A walk in the park, in the usually grey world of the airport lounge.

Photos Arjen Schmitz

Where Schiphol, the Netherlands
Opening May 2011
Client Amsterdam Airport Schiphol
Designer Maurice Mentjens → p.585
Floor space 2750 m²
Capacity 350 guests

The real tree trunks that dot the 'park' were provided by Kunstboomkunst.

CUSTOMERS CAN RELAX BENEATH THE SHADE OF THE 'MOTHER TREE'

Lacquered parquet in several shades of semi-transparent green is used throughout.

The wall elements consist of large photographic reproductions of famous parks from around the world.

The world's only airport rooftop terrace.

Butterfly light projections flutter around the seating area.

A green haven greets travellers at Schiphol Airport, where Maurice Mentjens has transformed a concrete environment into a natural, playful and relaxing space. Working closely with the Schiphol team, Mentjens has landscaped an indoor 'city park' concept that also extends outside onto the roof terrace, the first in any airport anywhere in the world.

Trees and greenery predominate in the café's interior design, with the kitchen built of beams piled one on top of the other, reminiscent of a log cabin or perhaps of the follies occasionally found in public spaces. A central aspect to the design is the series of trees dotted around the space, which – undeterred by the ceiling – seem to grow ever upwards. The trunks are real, but the crowns of the trees are made of artificial leaves. As is the custom in historic parks, there is also a well-established 'mother tree', the large trunk of a 130-year-old beech tree. In the simulated shelter of the shade of the trees, customers can relax on bespoke furniture consisting of landscape benches, tree-trunk seats and slatted benches. Integrated into the floor design are five large circles in various tints of green that indicate the different functional zones, such as the kiosks that would have stood in city parks of old, selling magazines, newspapers, flowers and souvenirs.

A special aspect is the integration of sustainable materials and design solutions. In order to further reinforce the park-like concept, virtual butterflies flutter and fly around above the picnic island and the walls feature *trompe-l'oeil* decoration, creating the illusion of a relatively far-off panorama. Complemented by other 'mixed reality' elements, the result is a playful atmosphere in the various green micro-environments.

MAURICE MENTJENS

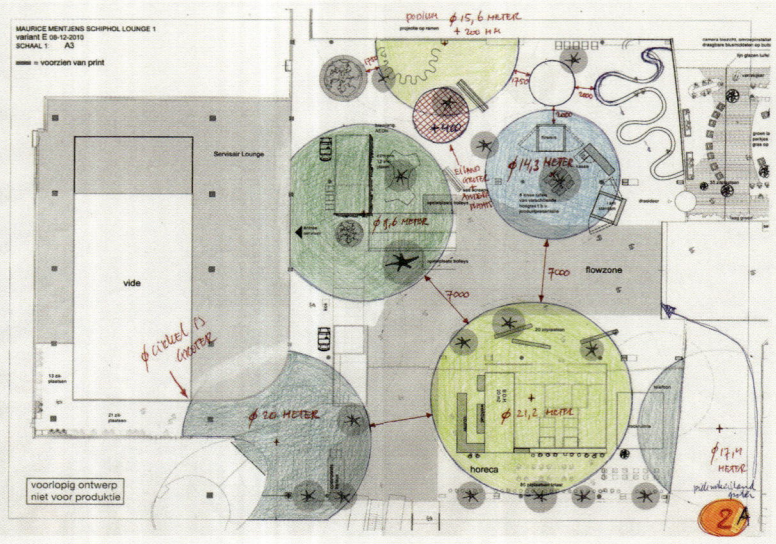
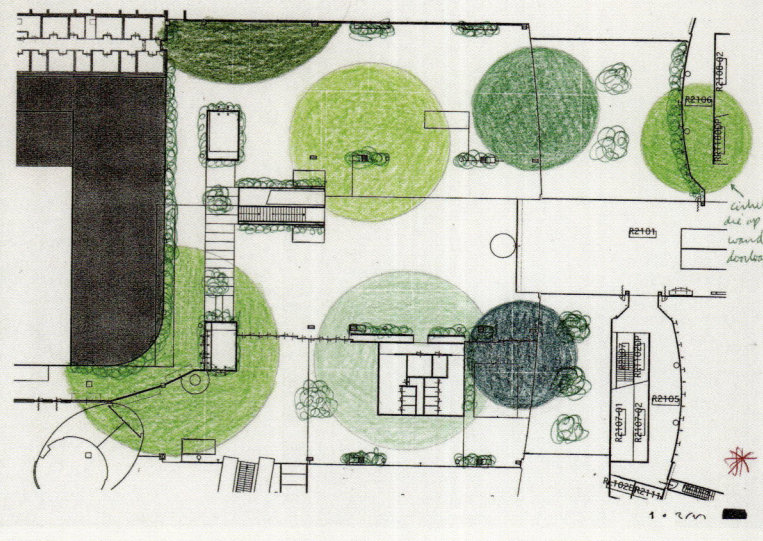
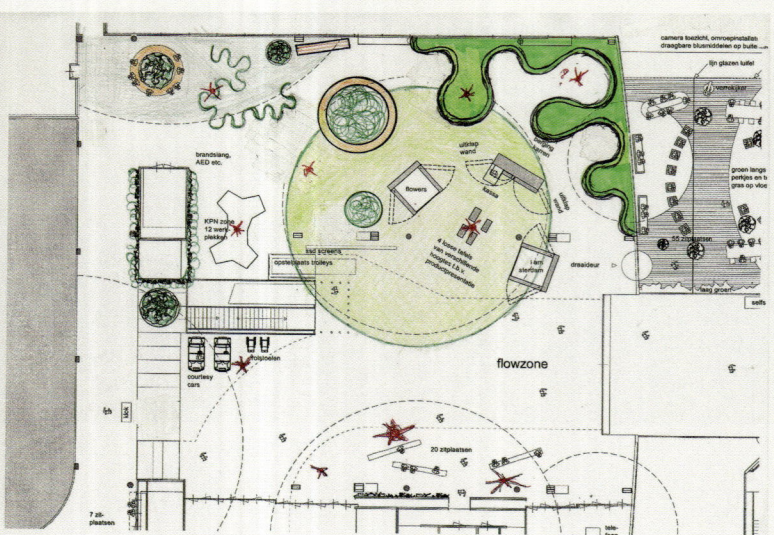

Sketches showing the development of the floor plan ideas for the Park Café.

VIRTUAL BUTTERFLIES FLUTTER ABOVE THE PICNIC ISLAND

The balustrade is replaced by one long, high table with four trees integrated in it.

Airport 'city park' floor plan

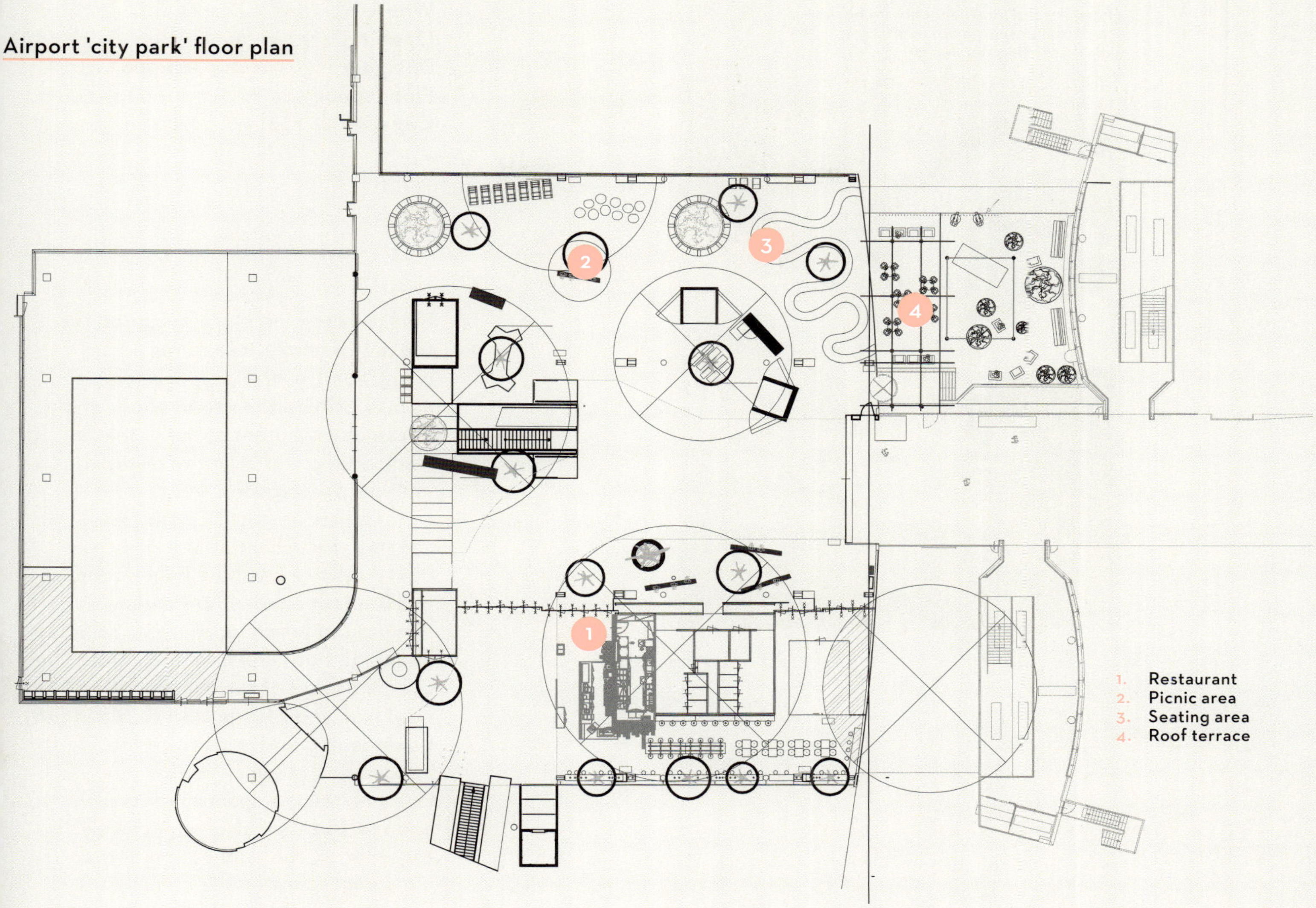

1. Restaurant
2. Picnic area
3. Seating area
4. Roof terrace

Restaurant floor plan

1. Dining area
2. Tree
3. Cash desk
4. Service area
5. Kitchen
6. Storage

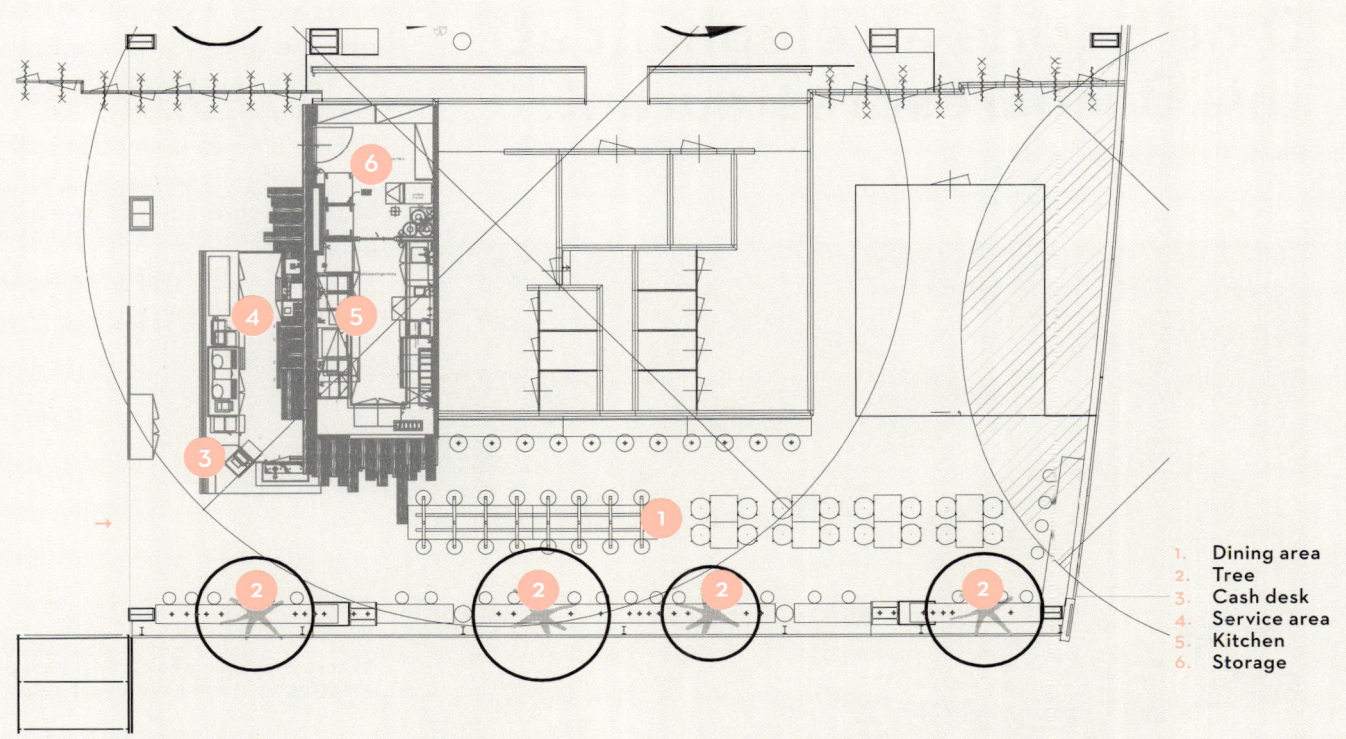

Imagery and interconnectivity between the distinct spaces are important aspects within the design.

Where Bucharest, Romania
Opening September 2011
Designer Nuca Studio → p.586
Floor space 587 m²
Capacity 96 seats

PHILL BY NUCA STUDIO

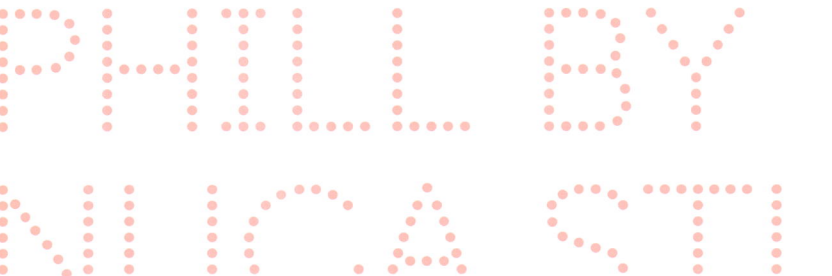

Dine beside an elephant at this Bucharest restaurant.

Photos Cosmin Dragomir

Phill is a meeting place designed for the entire family. It features a playground, a multipurpose room and a small café on the ground floor and a gourmet restaurant at the first level. Nuca Studio was asked to design this multipurpose space.

The list of specific activities seemed discordant at first glance – how does one combine haute cuisine, a restaurant atmosphere and a playground for children? In an effort to appeal to both children and adults, the overall design draws its inspiration from vinyl toys and Manga culture, aiming to be engaging and to capture the imagination of every visitor.

Each of the spaces has its own agenda, but they also work closely together, so the connection of the individual spaces is very important. In order to link these different rooms, the walls are perforated by circular openings, creating colourfully framed views between the rooms, allowing parents to keep an eye on their children. Special attention was paid to the design of the stairs. A 4-m-tall elephant stands over the central staircase and appears to be listening to music from a painted-on mp3 player and headphones. Upstairs, the dining area is an open space directly linked with the lobby. And with the use of the coloured carpet and Eames' Plastic Side Chairs, this 'adult' area is just as colourful as the playground, but in a sophisticated way. ●

A contemporary and colourful concept is incorporated in the restaurant décor.

Opposite The white elephant in the room elicits interesting responses from customers, adults and children alike.

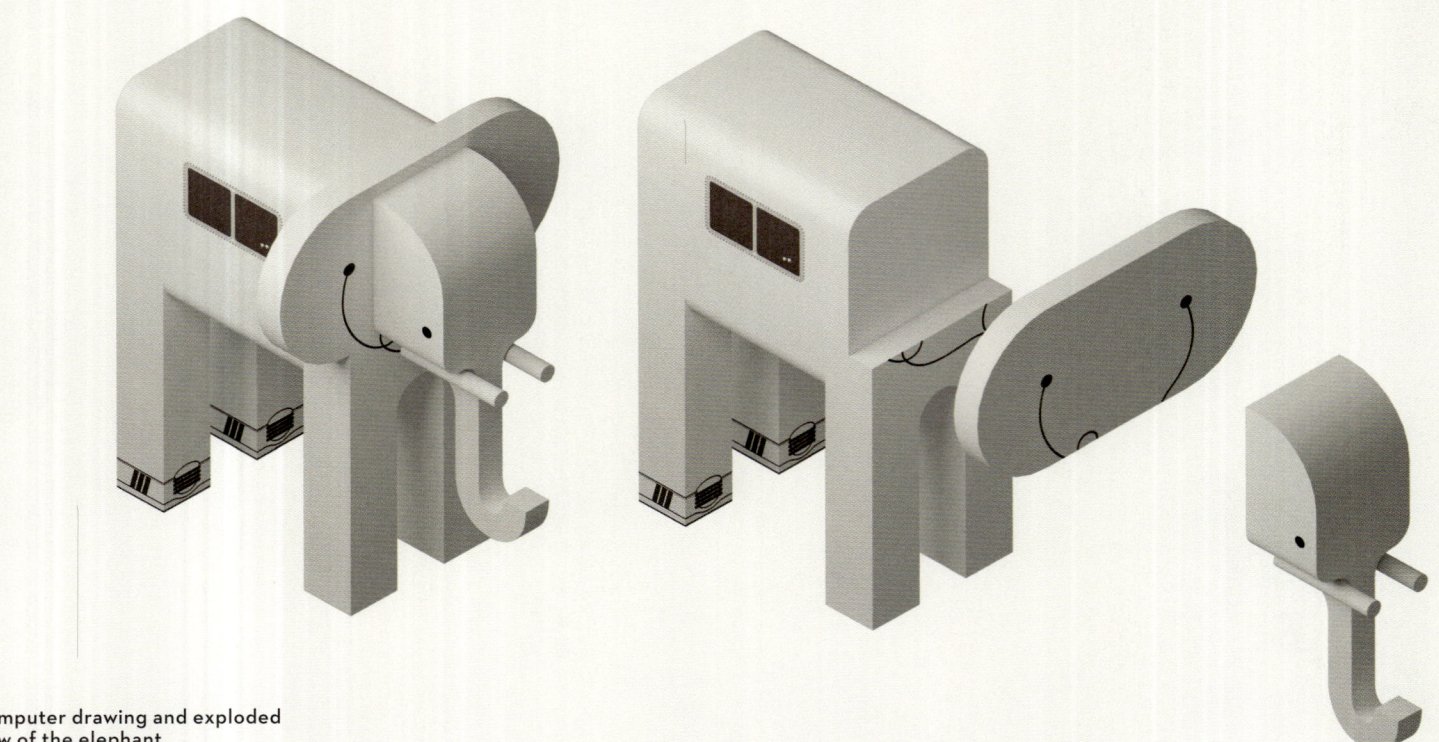

Computer drawing and exploded view of the elephant.

The 4-m-tall elephant was transported to the site by truck and assembled by a team of constructors.

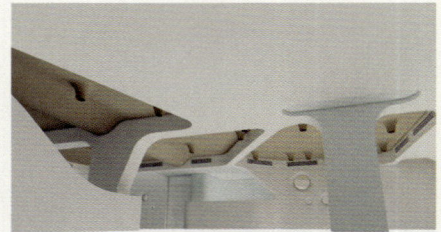

Renderings of the ceiling plan.

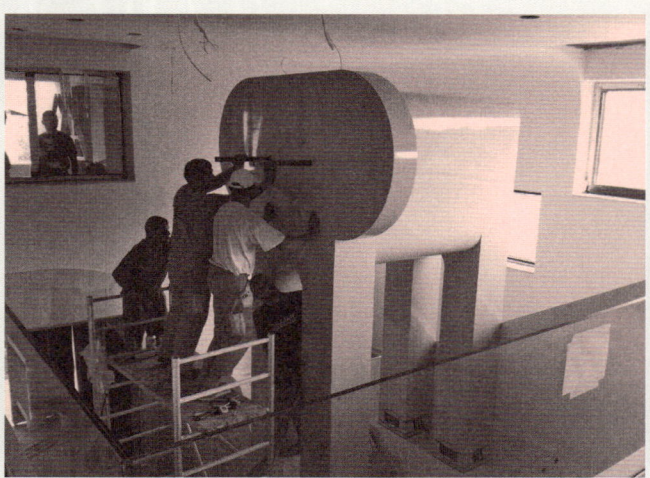
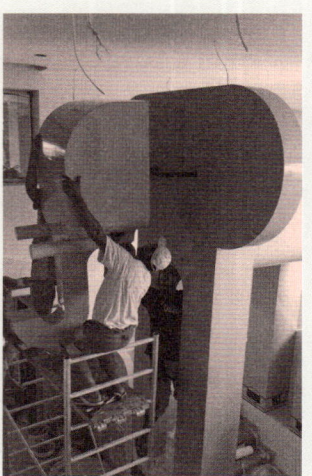

Ground floor

1. Lobby
2. Reception
3. Playground
4. Café
5. Multipurpose room
6. Dining area
7. Kitchen
8. Storage
9. Toilets

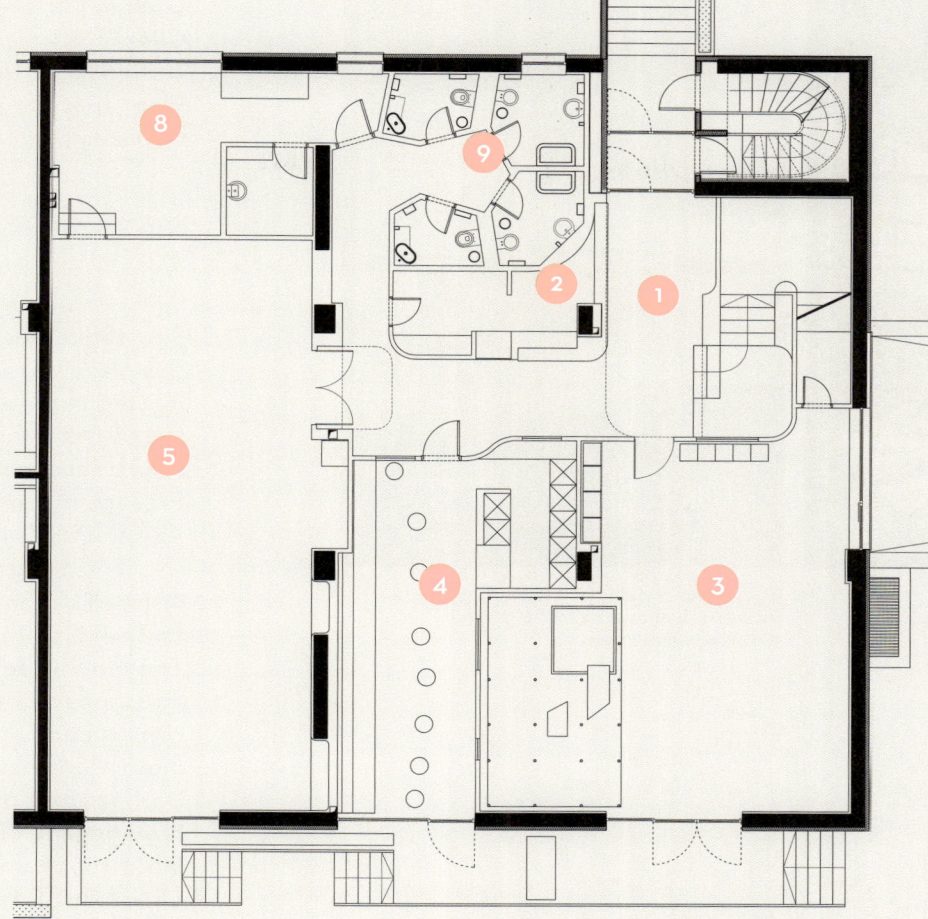

First floor

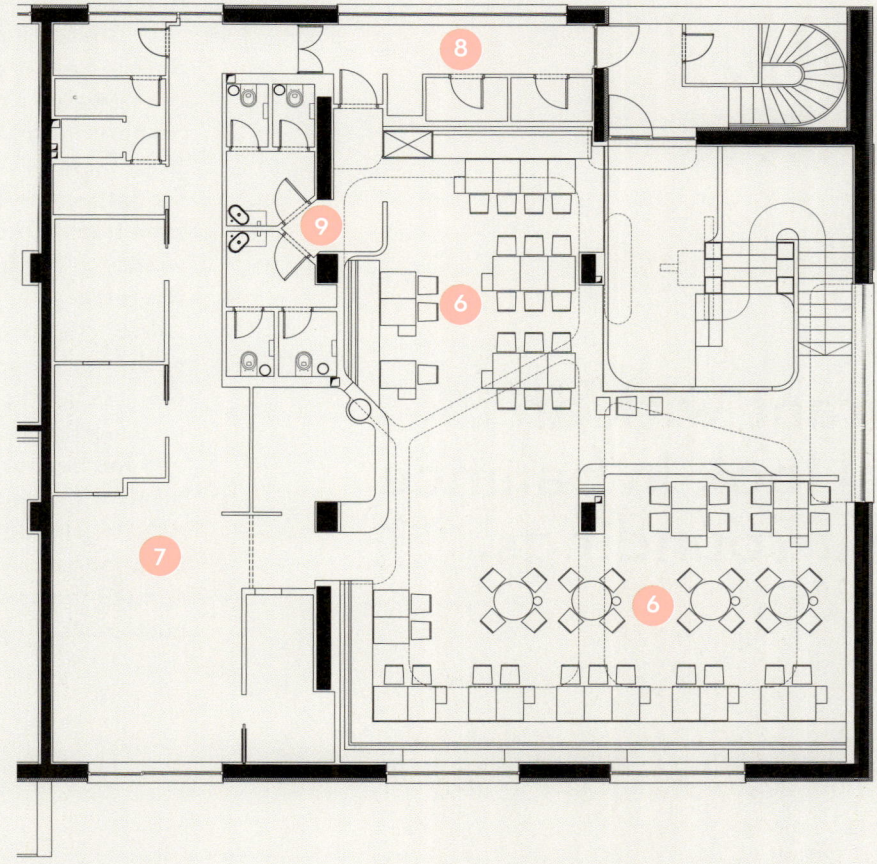

The raw industrial interior is illuminated by modern Moooi lamps.

The muted metallic palette is brightened by a splash of orange in the graphic detailing on the walls.

PROSOPA BY 360ID STUDIO

A restaurant with an industrial look in balance with its surroundings.

Photos Vangelis Paterakis

Where Athens, Greece
Opening March 2010
Client Prosopa restaurant
Designer 360id studio → p.578
Floor space 179 m²
Capacity 92 seats

Situated opposite the railroad tracks, this place was originally a glass factory located in the area of Rouf, one of the places to be in Athens. It was refurbished and converted into the Prosopa restaurant by interior designer Alexandros Tsikordanos of 360id studio.

The design for Prosopa was inspired by the faces (*prosopa* means faces in Greek) of the potential clients. The graphic design on the walls, with messages and symbols like 'under construction', create a link between the interior and exterior of the restaurant. Both façades of the old glass factory have been left relatively untouched. The industrial character of the façade has been transferred into the interior through the 360id studio's design approach. The materials used, such as steel, screed cement flooring, wood and brick, combine to create the overall industrial feel.

The restaurant is divided into two double-height spaces, which along with the revealed air ducts and vents and timber roof make reference to the former glass factory. While guests enjoy their food, they can enjoy the view of the train tracks through two large industrial windows. The bar, which is the heart of the restaurant, is positioned in its main space. The second space is at the back of the restaurant and is connected to the first by a corridor with exposed brickwork. The selection of furniture and the bespoke light fittings blend nicely with the main materials and colour palette. The design style of the restaurant is harmoniously balanced with the artistic style of the area and the potential customers. ●

Opposite The eatery is furnished with dining chairs by Stefano Giovannoni for Magis and Tio bar stools by Massproductions.

Opposite Large columns, circular and square, are spread throughout the double-height restaurant.

RENAISSANCE BY GLENN SESTIG ARCHITECTS

A restaurant concept that combines fine dining with fashion.

Photos Jean Pierre Gabriel

Where Antwerp, Belgium
Opening September 2010
Client Su Prano
Designer Glenn Sestig Architects → p.583
Floor space 140 m²
Capacity 60 seats

From the restaurant you can look into the fashion store, which is under the same roof.

In late 2010, Renaissance, a multi-brand store cum restaurant, opened its doors in a building formerly occupied by ModeNatie, on the Nationalestraat in Antwerp. The client specifically asked architect Glenn Sestig for a futuristic interior in this building with a triangular floor plan, to contrast with the classic style of its exterior.

An airy and relaxed atmosphere was created by making use of the existing shapes of the edifice. Without being overtly cold or intellectual, the design succeeds thanks to the use of panels of contrasting colours and materials hanging from the ceiling. The panelling also facilitates visitor traffic and provides privacy within the sizable volumes and high ceilings. Throughout the restaurant the design team chose to use neutral tones of white, black, bronze glass and wood.

The restaurant and the shop cohabitate without imposing on each other. You can shop without eating and eat without shopping. The selection of tables and chairs allows you to have a quick bite or choose to linger for a few hours. Sestig combined custom-designed tables with commercially available quality pieces on the market: chairs from Zeitraum. The use of white Carrara marble throughout the space serves as a discreet reminder of the Italian menu.

Sweeping lines and a monochrome décor provide a striking backdrop for the designer collections and also underscore the architecture of this beautiful building.

NEUTRAL TONES OF WHITE, BLACK, BRONZE GLASS AND WOOD PREDOMINATE

The Morph barstools by Zeitraum are executed in American walnut and leather.

The washbasins in the toilets are made of white Carrera marble, which is used throughout the interior.

Opposite Bronze glass panels hang from the ceiling above the bar.

Side elevation   **Front elevation**

The rounded façade of the old building.

YOU CAN SHOP WITHOUT EATING AND EAT WITHOUT SHOPPING

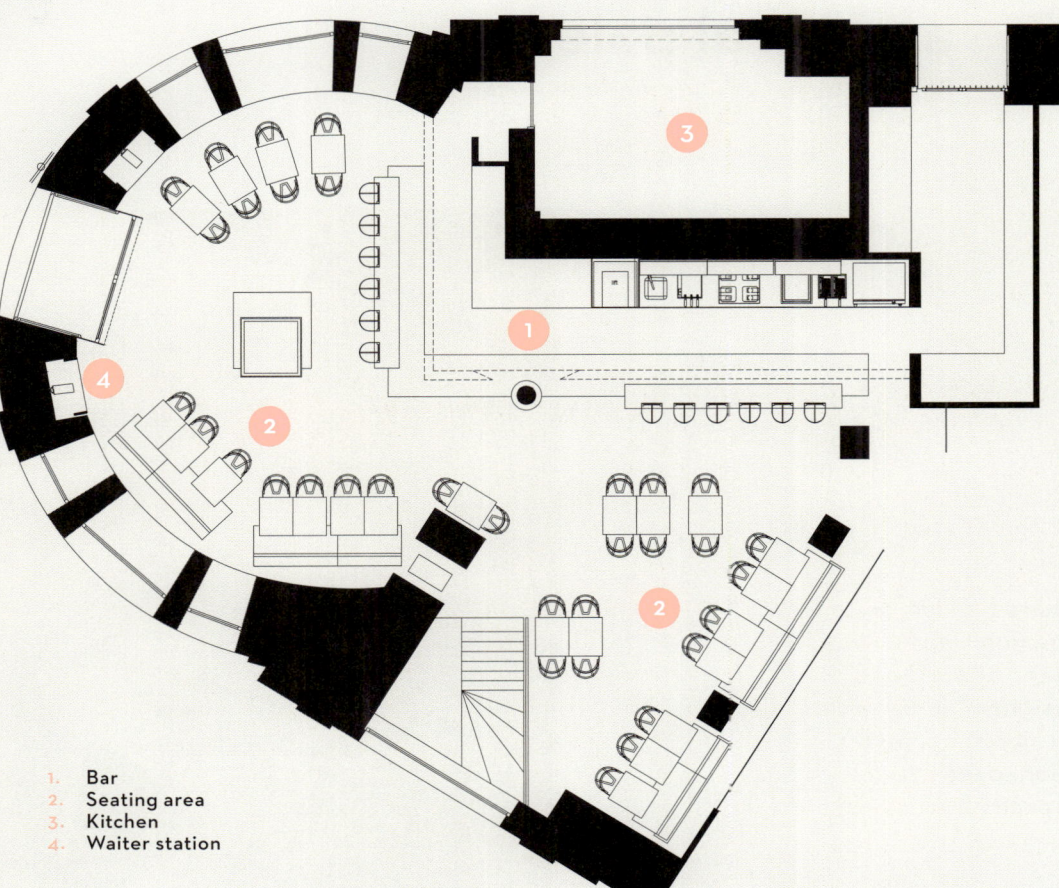

1. Bar
2. Seating area
3. Kitchen
4. Waiter station

Opposite The chairs in the restaurant are, just like the barstools, by Zeitraum.

GLENN SESTIG ARCHITECTS

SEERESTAURANT OLYMPIAPARK BY CLEMENS BACHMANN ARCHITEKTEN

A simple space with a natural palette.

Photos Clemens Bachmann Architekten

Opposite Following the 'stacked' concept, the bar area has stackable Miura stools by Konstantin Grcic.

The Olympic Park communications tower – a Munich landmark – is depicted on the wall.

Where Munich, Germany
Opening December 2011
Client Arena One
Designer Clemens Bachmann Architekten → p.580
Floor space 450 m²
Capacity 200 guests

CLEMENS BACHMANN ARCHITEKTEN

Linking the interior to the park surrounds was an important aspect of the design concept.

Clemens Bachmann Architekten was responsible for giving the existing restaurant in the middle of the Olympic Park in Munich a completely new look. What was called for was a venue that was open and flexible and that had a contemporary atmosphere. The design team decided to give the space the look and feel of a market hall and, as a consequence of working within a small budget, chose to work with wooden pallets as a key design element to zone different areas in the restaurant.

The original interior design – straight out of the 1980s – was stripped away, giving the designers a blank canvas to work on. The existing suspended ceiling was removed and the main room was opened up to a height of 5 m, with all technical equipment left visible under the rough concrete ceiling. Overhead, the surfaces were painted black and the walls that wrap around the space were decorated in a taupe hue. Parquet tiles were laid on the floor, tying in with the pale-coloured palette that extends throughout the interior. Natural wood is also seen in the tables, benches and low stools, which were chosen to contrast with the massive surfaces of the surrounding walls, as well as in the serving counter. The wooden block design of the furniture also reflects the structure of the untreated pallet systems. Stacked on top of each other, these are used as movable shelving units and underline the design concept of improvisation and simplicity.

Connecting the interior to the outside terrace are big sliding doors. Customers can also get a view of the surrounding park when seated inside the restaurant – both literally, through the full-height glass façade, and figuratively, thanks to a modern installation running the length of one wall made up of wooden panels that have been printed with pixelated motifs of the Olympic Park.

Stacked pallet systems are utilized as shelving units.

THE DESIGN CONCEPT IS ONE OF IMPROVISATION AND SIMPLICITY

The art work on wooden boards is printed as a pixelated image.

CLEMENS BACHMANN ARCHITEKTEN

Opposite Felt fabric in natural browns and beiges is fitted atop the wooden benches.

Models of the interior that use squares of cardboard to represent the stacks of storage pallets.

Two pixelated images, with views of the stadium, which are used in the interior.

WOODEN PALLETS ARE A KEY DESIGN ELEMENT

1. Bar
2. Cash desk
3. Seating area
4. Children's corner
5. Lounge area
6. Open kitchen
7. Main kitchen

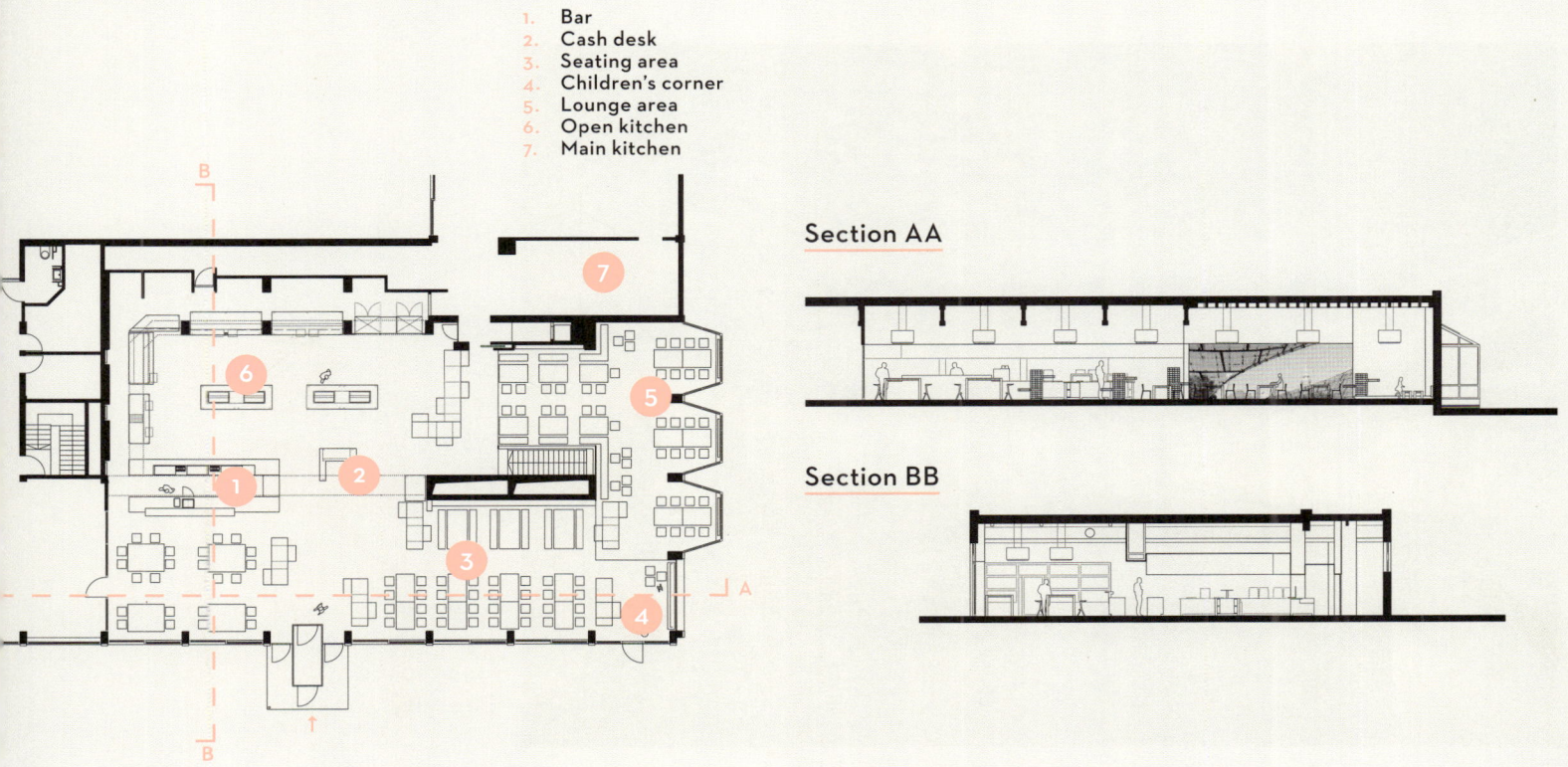

Section AA

Section BB

CLEMENS BACHMANN ARCHITEKTEN

SPICE MARKET BY CONCRETE ARCHITECTURAL ASSOCIATES

A gold-tinged spice cabinet offering a medley of Asian-inspired cuisine.

Photos Ewout Huibers for Concrete

Opposite The cage-like staircase was manufactured by Smederij van Rijn and has a balustrade of brass tubes, with black powder-coated handrails and a central spine.

The interior is richly decked-out with dark wooden furniture and metallic brass fittings.

Where London, United Kingdom
Opening February 2011
Clients Culinary Concepts, McAleer & Rushe Group and Starwood Hotels & Resorts
Designer Concrete Architectural Associates → p.581
Floor space 530 m²
Capacity 220 seats

CONCRETE ARCHITECTURAL ASSOCIATES

MONUMENTAL BRASS LANTERNS CAST A SOFT, WARM GLOW ACROSS THE SPACE

Seating is provided in the bespoke seating booths and on Duna dining chairs by Arper, upholstered in red Kvadrat fabric.

On London's Leicester Square is the Spice Market restaurant, a contemporary walk-in spice cabinet that tantalizes the taste buds with its medley of Asian-inspired cuisine. The client commissioned Concrete Architectural Associates to create an interior that would harmoniously complement the food on offer. The team chose to base its concept on a spice cabinet, one that is two floors high and 24 m long, revealing every ingredient the chef might need to create the distinguished Spice Market dishes.

The restaurant's façade is completely transparent on three sides, and showcases the wall of spices, which is enticingly visible from the street. The interior is an eclectic mix of dark wood, gold mesh sliding screens, brass screen lanterns, Jatoba hardwood flooring and 600 custom-designed 'wok lamps'. The two-level space is connected by a grand 'birdcage' spiral staircase and a central void in the mezzanine floor, transporting the buzz from the kitchen into the entire space. There is a wide variety of seating options for guests, whether in the cocktail bar, the sushi bar and lounge on the ground floor or the main restaurant area around the open kitchen on the upper level.

The atmosphere in the gold-tinged space is luxurious, enhanced by the bespoke lighting – the monumental brass lanterns with laser-cut patterns cast a soft, warm glow across the space and shed a decorative light throughout the restaurant area. Another distinctive lighting design is the seemingly endless sea of wok lamps that line both the lower and upper level ceilings.

The brass screens with laser-cut panels are backlit to give the impression of monumental lanterns.

CONCRETE ARCHITECTURAL ASSOCIATES

Mezzanine

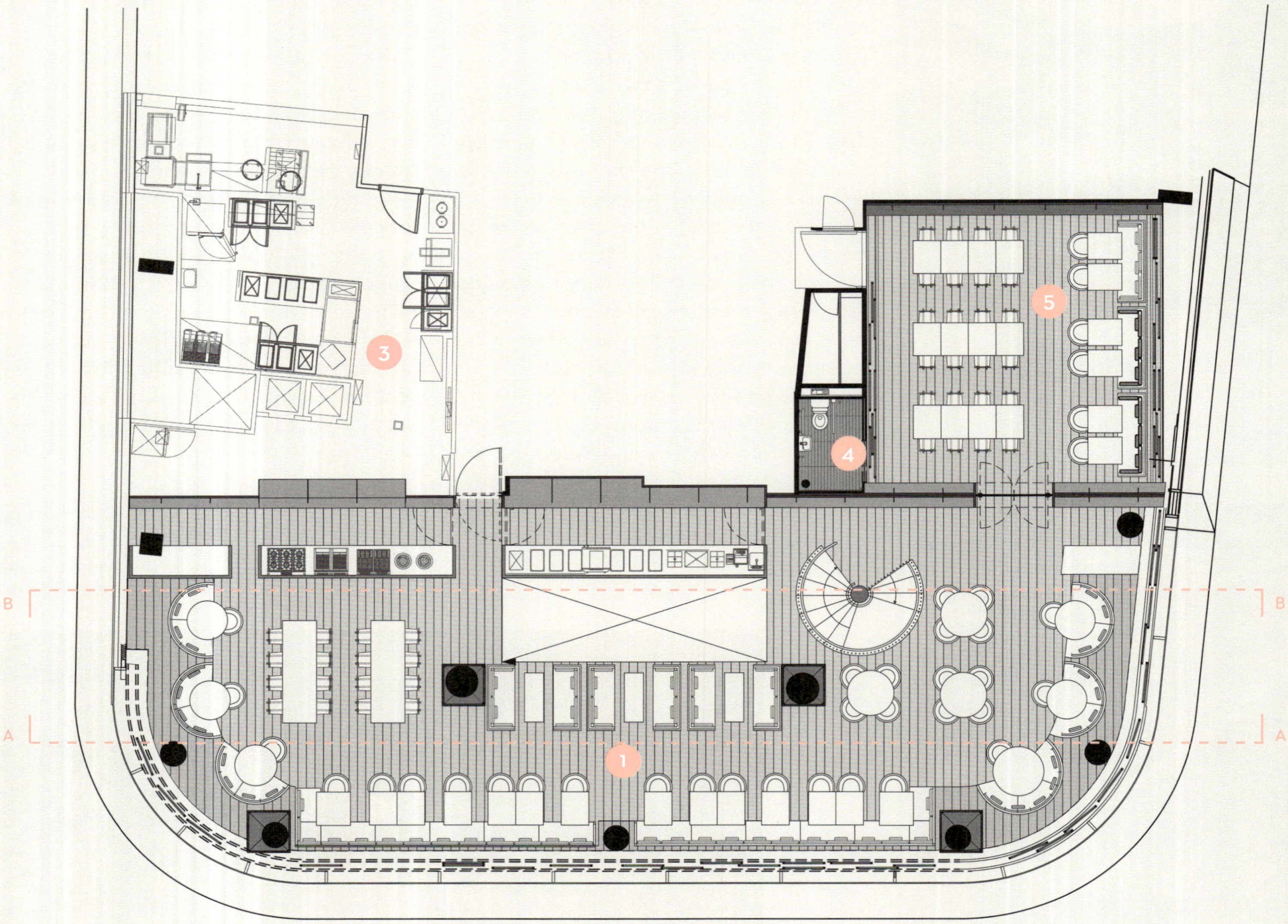

Section AA

156 SPICE MARKET

Ground floor

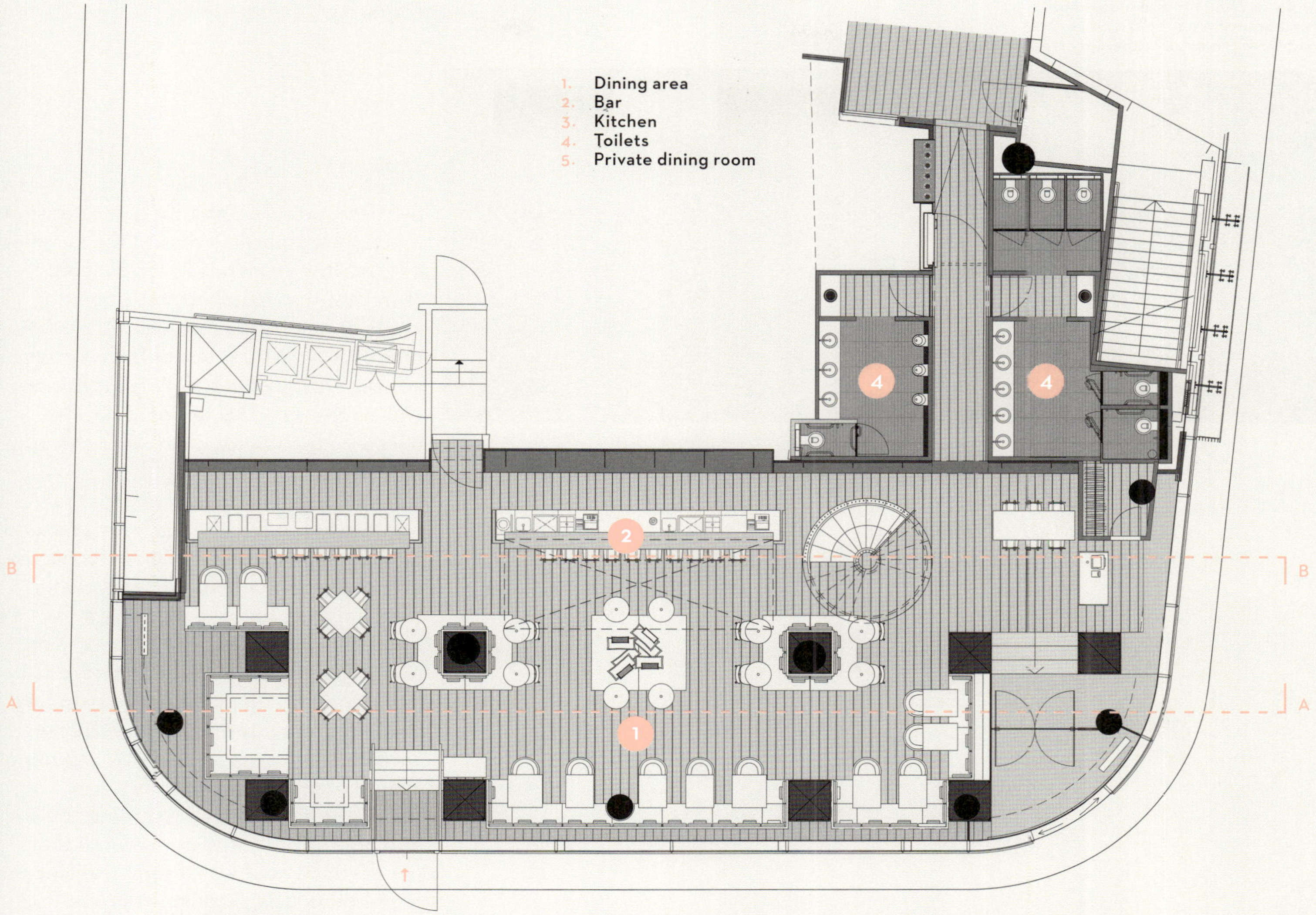

1. Dining area
2. Bar
3. Kitchen
4. Toilets
5. Private dining room

Section BB

CONCRETE ARCHITECTURAL ASSOCIATES

Where London, United Kingdom
Opening June 2010
Client Bistrotheque/Westfield
Designer Carmody Groarke → p.580
Floor space 800 m²
Capacity 140 seats

The different heights and lengths of the restaurant's elongated aspects are evident from the external perspective.

STUDIO EAST DINING BY CARMODY GROARKE

Dramatic rooftop dining with an Olympic panorama in East London.

Photos Luke Hayes

When Carmody Groarke was approached by restaurateurs Bistrotheque to design a temporary pavilion during the summer of 2010, the team opted for an iconic structure that matched the stunning views of its rooftop location. The pavilion's character was born out of Bistrotheque's concept for a unique dining experience as well as the spectacular location with a view of the Olympic site over the edge of a parapet.

The team realized a design that was deliberately industrial in spatial and structural character and unselfconscious in the choice of economic, recyclable materials. On top of a 35-m-high multistorey car park within an existing building site of Westfield Stratford City development, the lightweight structure made use of materials borrowed from the surrounding construction site, including scaffolding boards and poles, and reclaimed timber used to create the walls and floors. The cladding material that encased the roof was a semi-translucent membrane, using industrial-grade heat-retractable polyethylene that was 100 per cent recycled, as were all the other materials following the closure of the restaurant after its short three-week life span.

The front-of-house was arranged into a series of interlocking, narrow timber-lined spaces that had a radiating internal arrangement that accommodated the pragmatic requirements of running a kitchen. The interior was illuminated by industrial light installations suspended from the high ceilings tilted towards the key views at the end of the elongated edifices. The large dining area was broken into a cluster of timber rooms with long, galley-like tables proportioned to the scale of each space, allowing the guests to connect in a unique, communal dining experience.

Opposite A charmingly simple yet raw aesthetic was instilled in the temporary space.

CARMODY GROARKE

Site plan indicating the directional views afforded from the restaurant's elevated location.

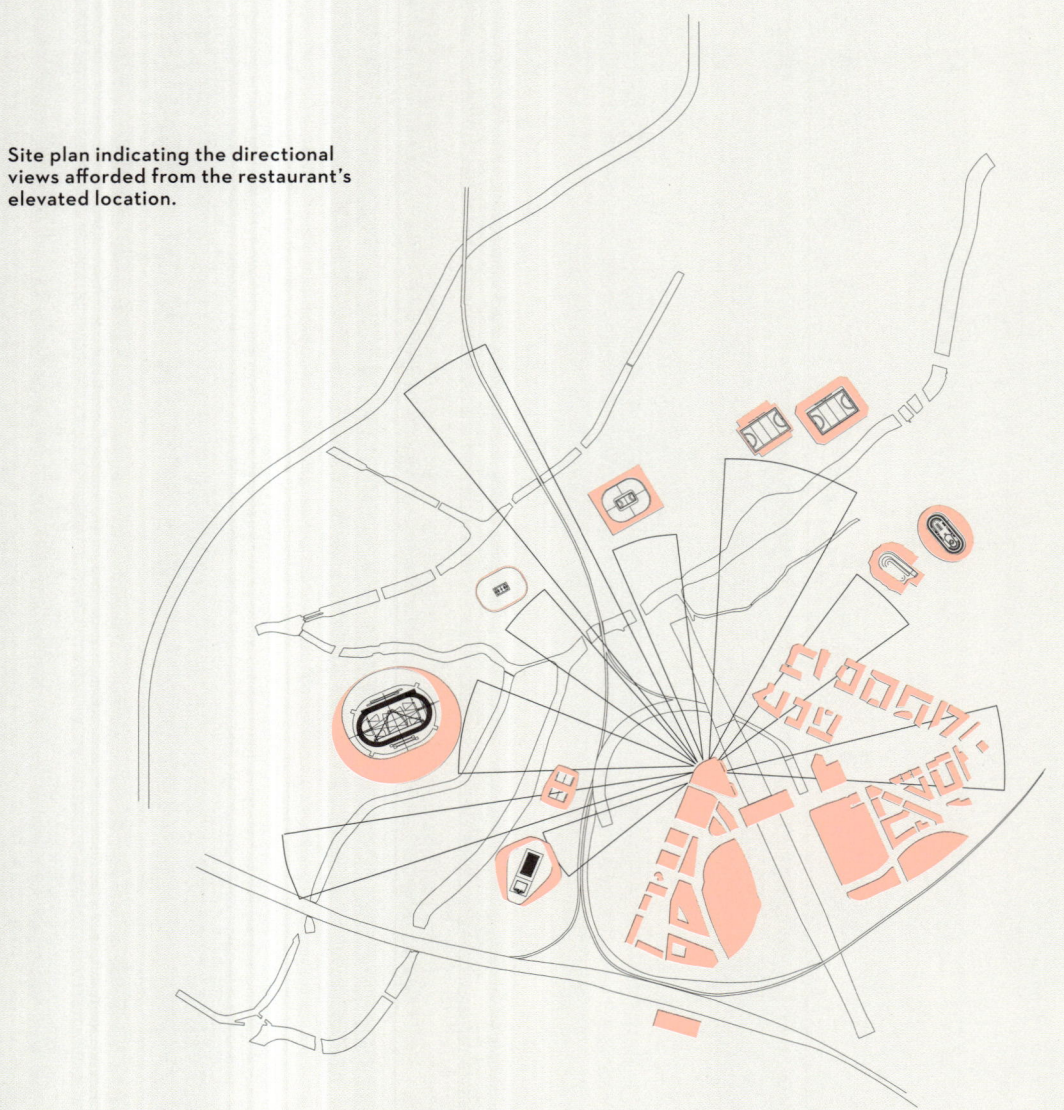

Model of the restaurant (top) and final building (bottom) showing the close vicinity to the Olympic site.

AN ICONIC STRUCTURE TO MATCH THE STUNNING VIEWS OF ITS ROOFTOP LOCATION

Section AA

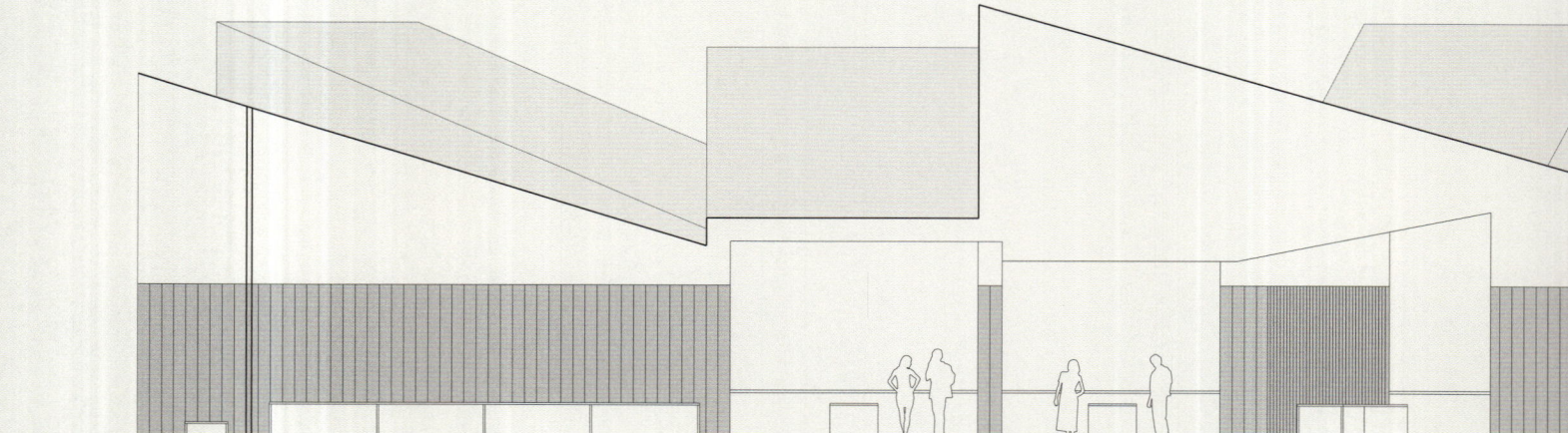

160   STUDIO EAST DINING

1. Dining area
2. Bar
3. Kitchen
4. Cloakroom
5. Exhibition area
6. Toilets

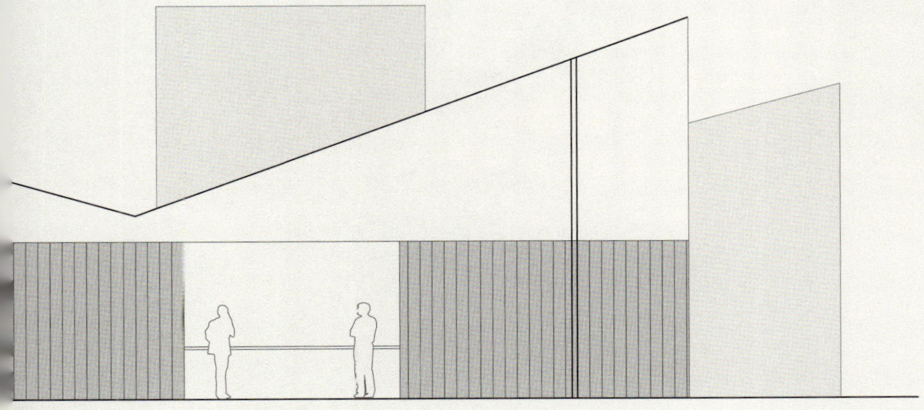

Section BB

CARMODY GROARKE

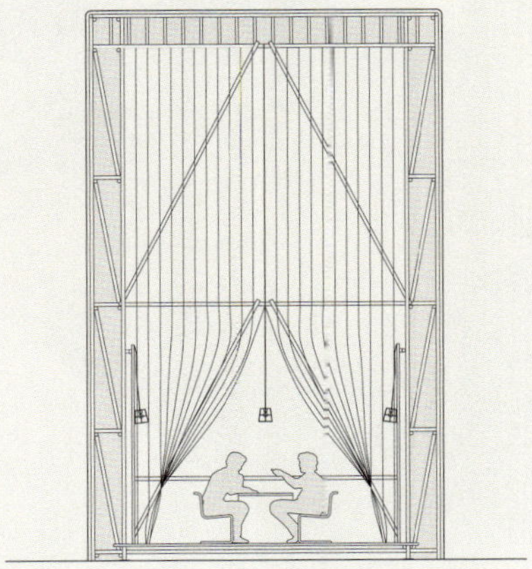

Where Shanghai, China
Opening August 2011
Clients Gilles Bini-Zinou and Frank Steffen
Designer AOO Architecture → p.578
Floor space 258 m²
Capacity 90 seats

The floor is laid with hexagonal grey ceramic tiles.

SUSHI ABUSE BY AOO ARCHITECTURE

A sustainable sushi restaurant with a healthy interior.

Photos courtesy of AOO Architecture

Opposite A simple geometric aesthetic is an underlying theme within the design team's concept.

Bamboo is used for the fixtures and fittings, as well as the decorative wall elements.

A raised concrete floor runs beneath the length of the feature dining table.

With its raw and natural décor, the interior is a delightful mix of textures and tones.

A solid slab of white-grained marble forms a low tabletop in the private dining area.

Two experienced restaurateurs opened the first sustainable sushi restaurant in Shanghai. Sushi Abuse only uses sustainable ingredients and serves no fish that is close to extinction. It was no surprise the owners hired AOO Architecture for the interior design of this venue, as the latter are known for their sustainable interior design solutions.

Designing a Japanese restaurant has been a dream of AOO for many years, so their ideas came quickly. They wanted to play with geometry, patterns and breaking away from what has become the 'standard' look of many Japanese restaurants in Shanghai.

Upon entering, guests are immediately welcomed by the bamboo panelling on the walls, cut to create a classic geometric pattern but blown up to a larger scale so that it can really be felt and captures the eye. Guests can sit at one of the tables, choose a spot at the bar, or go to the first floor, which accommodates most of the seating. Walking up the stairs guests can easily see that all the surfaces in the restaurant constantly alternate from smooth to textured. The warm elements in the space are exclusively done in bamboo panelling, contrasting with exposed concrete, brick and smooth ceramic tiles. On the first floor, one high table runs the entire length of the room, seating over 35 people on either leather bar stools or benches with bamboo panelling. An alcove with a traditional Japanese 'sunken' dining area offers a more private dining experience for small groups. AOO succeeded in creating a restaurant that captures a specific type of playfulness while clearly remaining a Japanese restaurant.

ALL THE SURFACES IN THE RESTAURANT CONSTANTLY ALTERNATE FROM SMOOTH TO TEXTURED

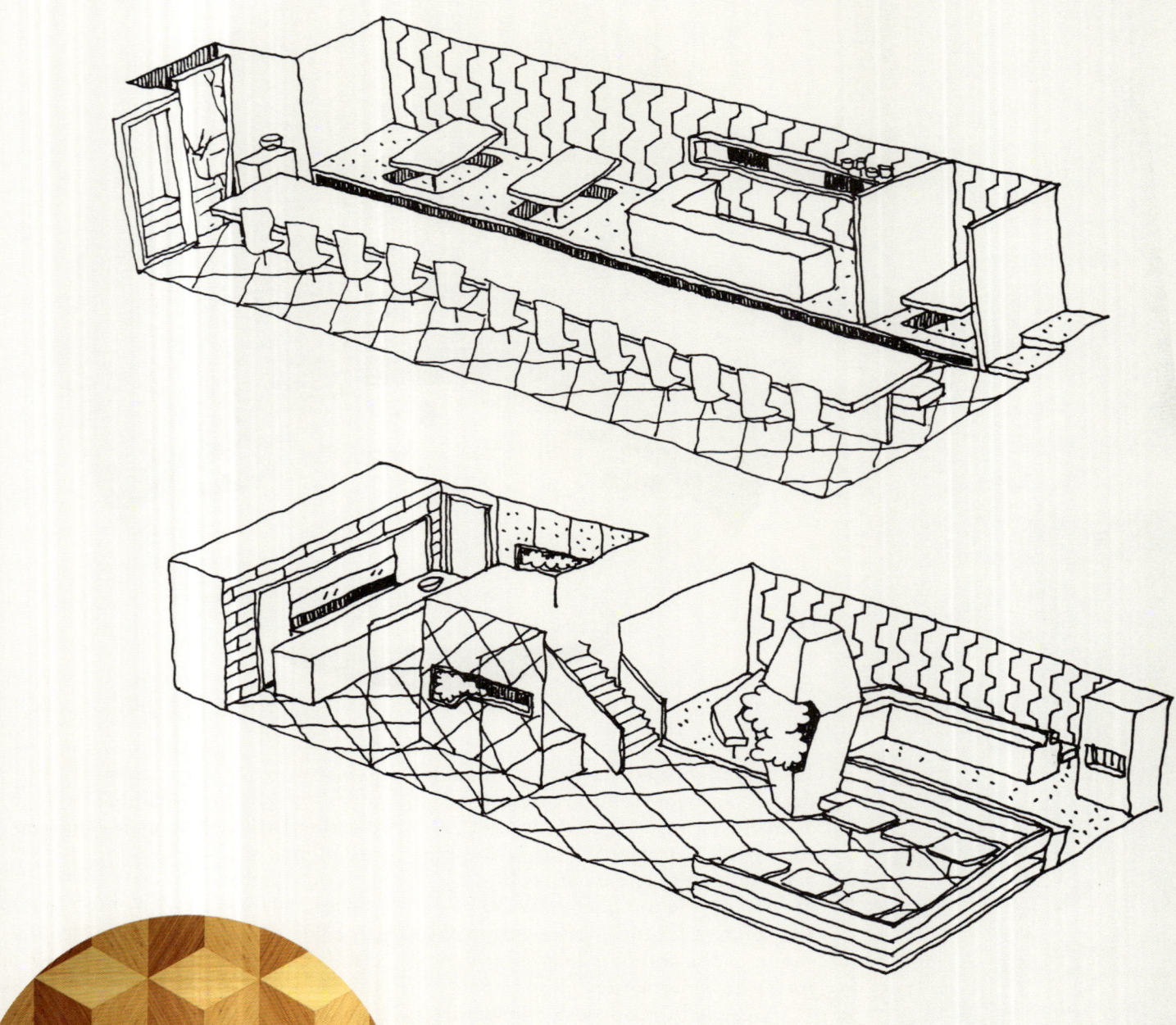

Initial sketches of the layout for the two-storey interior.

Three different bamboo types were used to create the geometric pattern.

'WE WANTED TO CREATE SOMETHING VERY FUN AND NEVER SEEN BEFORE IN SHANGHAI'

Elevation first floor

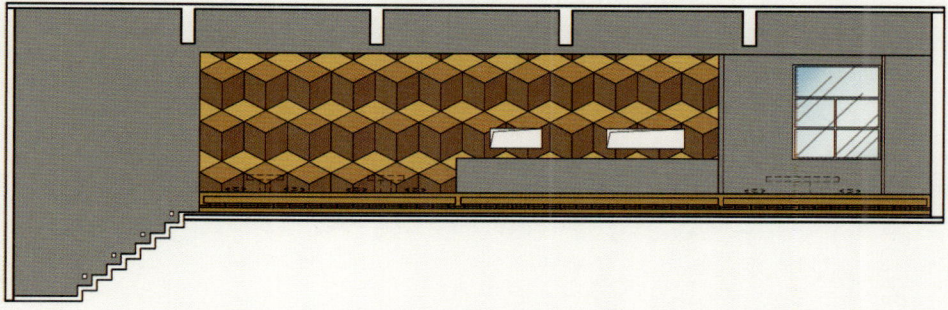

Elevation ground floor

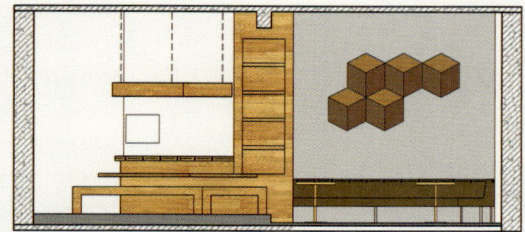

1. Seating area
2. Open kitchen
3. Bar
4. Private dining
5. Kitchen
6. Wardrobe
7. Toilets

First floor

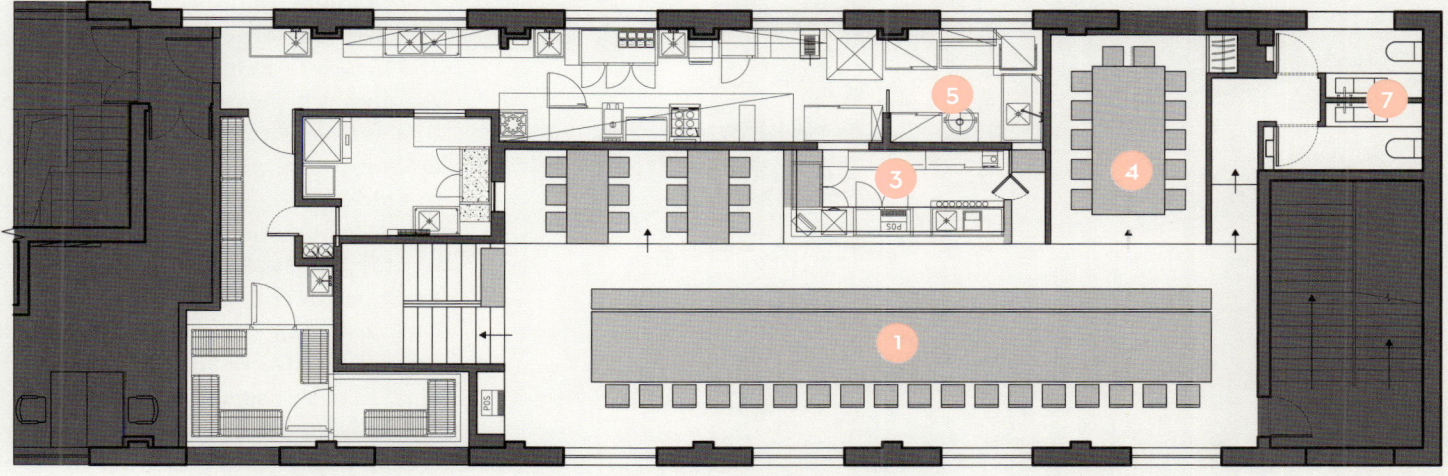

Ground floor

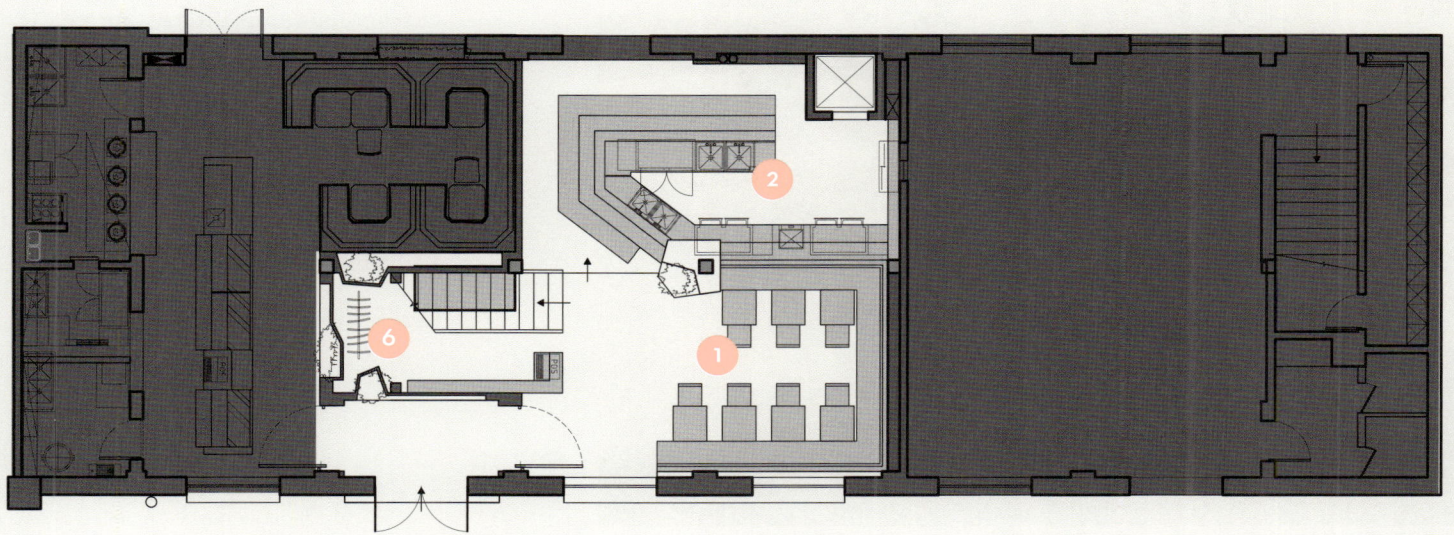

THE FORGE BY FFD

Where Miami, United States
Opening March 2010
Client Shareef Malnik
Designer FFD → p.582
Floor space 600 m²
Capacity 192 seats

Opulence abounds in this restaurant with a regal pedigree.

Photos Simon Hare

The Murano-glass chandelier from the 1930s has maintained its place in the restaurant.

The Forge is a restaurant in Miami with a regal pedigree that dates back to the Roaring Twenties. A recent renovation by François Frossard, founder of FFD, now sees the restaurant's décor infused with decadent glamour, whimsy and mystique, pairing contradiction with tradition. The Forge was a monumental design challenge, a 'redux' of a cherished venue already famed for its impeccable design. For this project, Frossard created a template of vibrant optimism, aiming to make the interior a good deal brighter than it used to be, as well as warmer, fresher and livelier.

Inspired by the psychology of the venue's traditionally opulent environment, the design concept was to make the Forge feel like an elegant and luxurious home. To that end, the restaurant is divided into various rooms that seamlessly blend yet have their own unique, plush personalities. It's a mix of the old and the new, of warm and cold tones. Wood and mirrors are accented by stainless steel and chrome detailing. Walls are decorated in a mix of gold lamé wallpaper, ash wood panelling, intricately carved woodwork and colourful stained glass. Lavish chandeliers illuminate the space, from the contemporary white crystal design of the main dining area to the lavish lilac Murano-glass designs in the bar.

An eclectic mix of furniture, custom-made for the restaurant, adds to the extravagant atmosphere. Low-slung white leather couches and high-backed leather chairs sit alongside hand-etched glass and monumental wooden table tops. There are spectacular surprises at every turn and Frossard has ensured that by working in so many intricate details there is always something new for guests to discover. ●

Opposite Stained glass overhead lamps light up the lavish dining space.

The shiny stainless steel bar counter echoes the silver-leaf domed ceiling above the lilac chandeliers.

Oversized white leather chairs give the private dining room an Alice in Wonderland air.

THE FORGE

1. Reception
2. Main dining room
3. Back dining room
4. Bar
5. Kitchen
6. Private dining room
7. Library
8. Terrace
9. Toilets

THE DESIGN CONCEPT WAS TO MAKE THE FORGE FEEL LIKE A LUXURIOUS HOME

Renderings depicting different views in The Forge.

Through the porthole windows on the back wall, customers can peek into the kitchen.

Where	Singapore, Singapore
Opening	July 2011
Client	Envis Group
Designer	Studio SKLIM → p.589
Floor space	137 m²
Capacity	64 seats (inside), 20 seats (outside)

THE TASTINGS ROOM BY STUDIO SKLIM

A sophisticated Singapore bistro with sleek geometric volumes and a yin-yang balance.

Photos Jeremy San

The Tastings Room offers French/Italian bistro cuisine and a wine cellar under one roof in the heart of Singapore's Central Business District. Studio SKLIM was commissioned to create an overall spatial experience that seamlessly merged the somewhat opposing aesthetics of being sophisticated yet affordable.

The design concept for the wine bar and bistro involved black geometric volumes sandwiched between two layers of industrial aesthetics: exposed ceiling and screed concrete floor. The rectangular space was crafted with a basic U-shaped layout, from the wine storage at one end, the various seating areas and kitchen at the other, with a bar in a central position between these along the opposite wall. The chiselled shape of the long bar counter is that of an angular black volume, distorted and then sliced in two along the middle, so that a floating tapered structure rises above it. This overhead unit has both form and functionality in that it houses a giant light fixture while simultaneously accommodating the bar's wine-glass racks. The outer skin of these volumes is a series of black diagonal tiles, which also line the walls of the restaurant, providing a sleek, textured layer that wraps around the space.

The bistro has several distinct seating areas, from the custom-made booths along the walls, above which more projecting volumes provide overhead illumination, to the central area with its solid-oak table tops, cast-iron stands and individual brass lamp shades above. There are also two private dining rooms – one entirely white, the other black – creating a visually opposing reflection when the partition between them is opened, providing an Asian yin-yang balance to an essentially European gastronomic experience.

Opposite The tapering central bar profile was a creative solution to the shopping mall's regulation for all interior works to be kept away from the building's glass frontage.

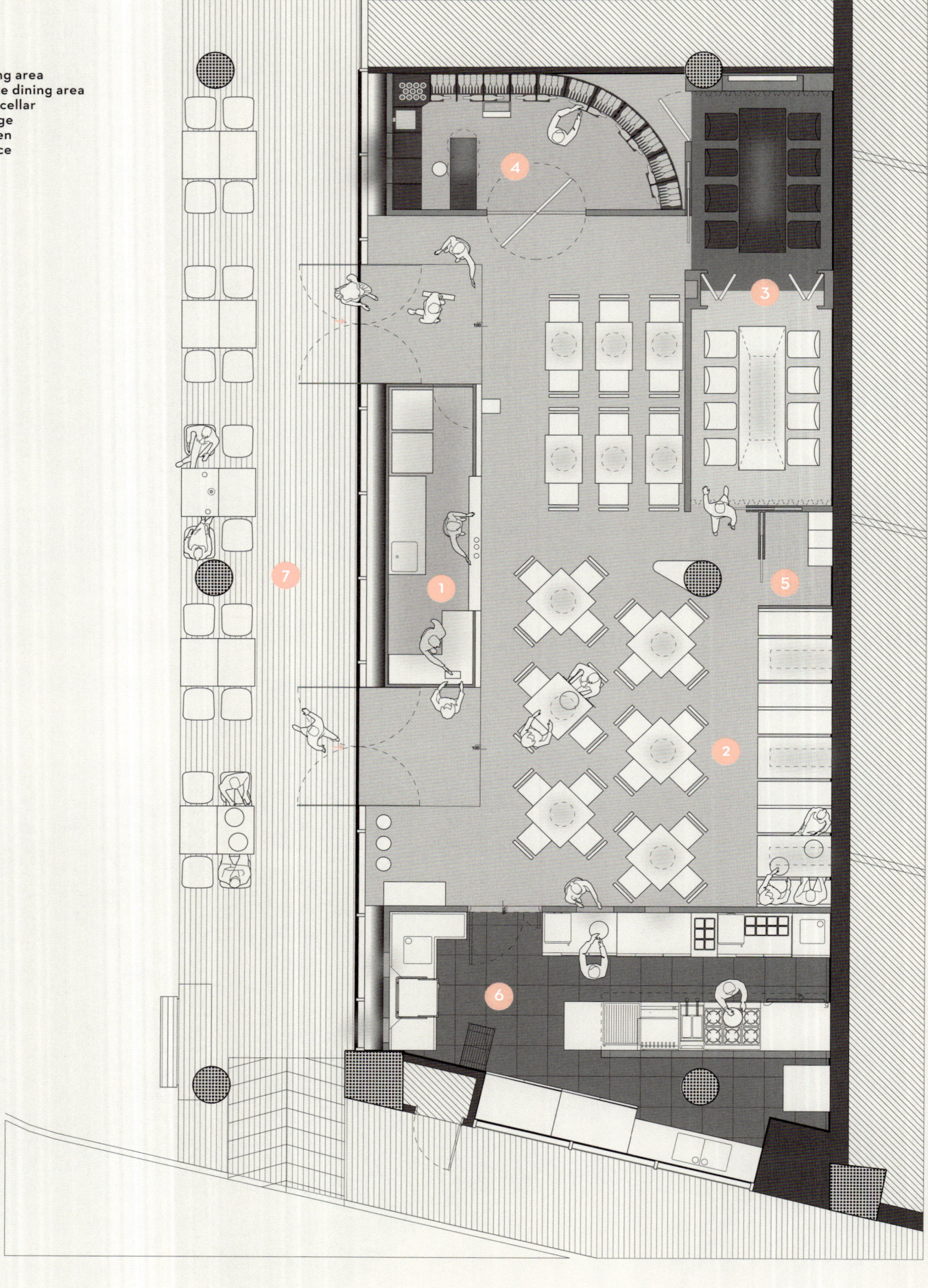

1. Bar
2. Seating area
3. Private dining area
4. Wine cellar
5. Storage
6. Kitchen
7. Terrace

Previous spread A total of 1200 individual pieces of plastic laminate on plywood substrate were used to form the 300 x 300 mm diagonal wall tiles.

BLACK GEOMETRIC VOLUMES ARE SANDWICHED BETWEEN TWO LAYERS OF INDUSTRIAL AESTHETICS

Sketches of the programmatic composition of the restaurant. Seen here the area is divided into three areas namely Wine, Bistro and shared spaces of Wine/Bistro.

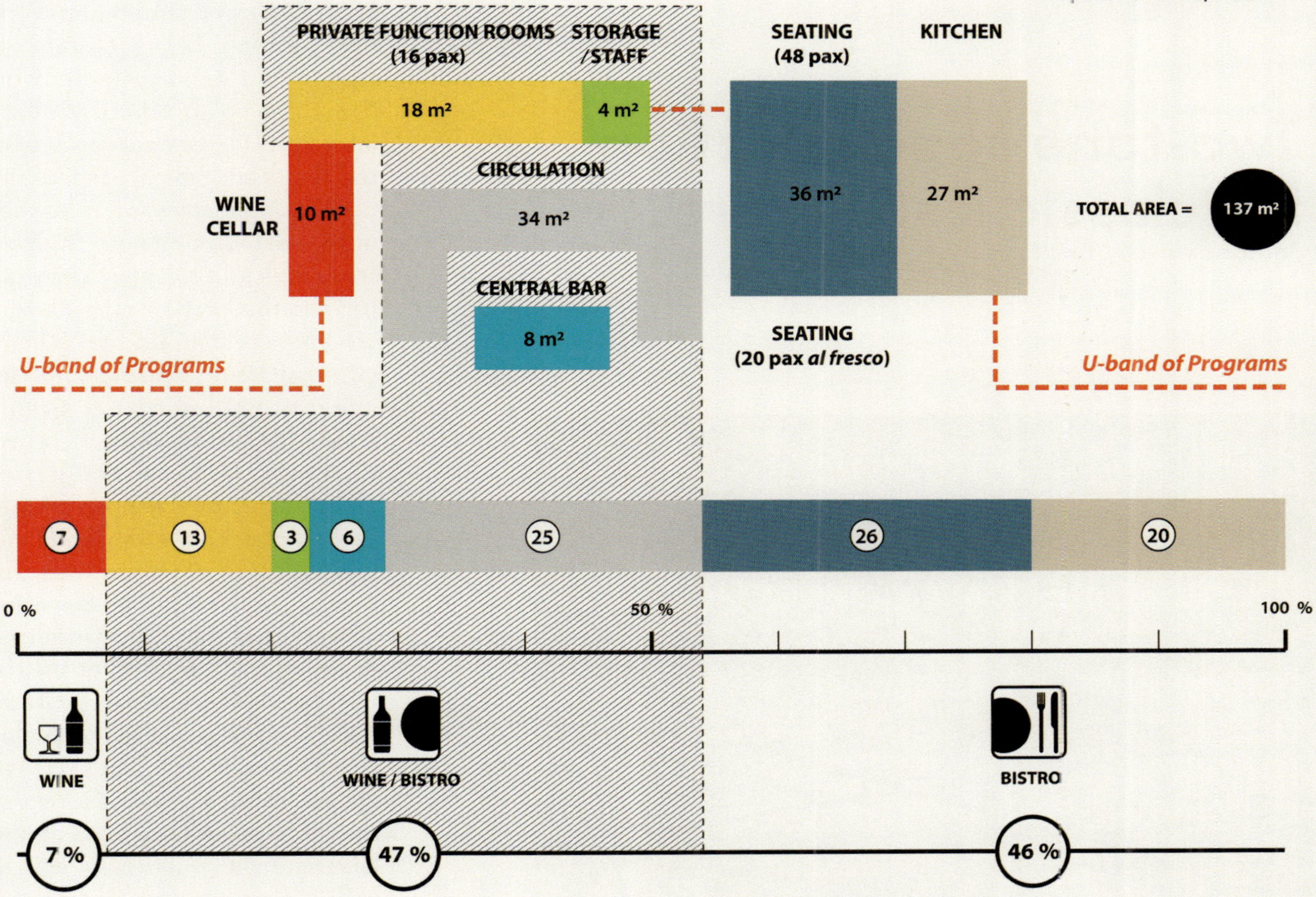

PRIVATE FUNCTION ROOMS (16 pax) — 18 m²
STORAGE / STAFF — 4 m²
SEATING (48 pax) — 36 m²
KITCHEN — 27 m²
TOTAL AREA = 137 m²
WINE CELLAR — 10 m²
CIRCULATION — 34 m²
CENTRAL BAR — 8 m²
SEATING (20 pax al fresco)

U-band of Programs

| 7 | 13 | 3 | 6 | 25 | 26 | 20 |

0 %   50 %   100 %

WINE — 7 %
WINE / BISTRO — 47 %
BISTRO — 46 %

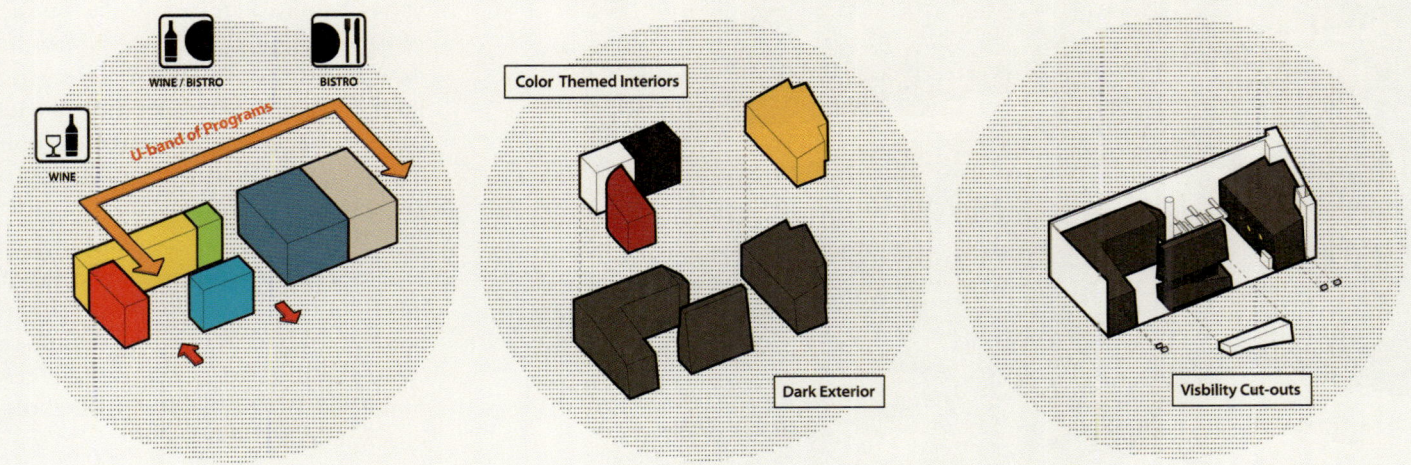

Color Themed Interiors · Dark Exterior · Visibility Cut-outs

STUDIO SKLIM

TINELLO BY BRINKWORTH

Where London, United Kingdom
Opening September 2010
Clients Massimiliano Sali and Federico Sali
Designer Brinkworth → p.580
Floor space 135 m²
Capacity 76 seats

Two-tone sophistication for classic Italian fare.

Photos Louise Melchior

Italian brothers Max and Federico Sali commissioned Brinkworth to design their first restaurant, situated on London's Pimlico Road. The restaurant serves Italian food 'as your mother would make it' and the Sali brothers wanted the interior of the restaurant to compliment the rustic and homely feel of the food.

Taking inspiration from the definition of the restaurant name, Tinello – which translates as a relaxed family dining space beyond the kitchen – the design team has created a restaurant that is inviting and informal. Using materials with inherent integrity, Brinkworth has given Tinello a sense of history, with the exposed brickwork, rustic oak flooring and brass and bronze metal fittings creating the feeling of a long-established venue. The sophisticated simplicity of the material palette remains true to the original character of the Victorian terrace while ensuring the longevity of the design.

Furnished with timber Thonet dining chairs and tables dressed in elegant white linen, Brinkworth also installed rich chocolate brown leather covered sofas that help create a relaxed atmosphere. Classic Italian pull-down table lamps in bronze hover over each table, creating warm, intimate dining spaces and enhancing the effect of the feature brass-conduit pendant lamps that anchor the room. Brinkworth installed wine racks at street level as well as in the basement; downstairs, guests find a cellar stocked floor to ceiling with wine bottles, while upstairs antique glass and Georgian diamond wire create a glamorous, sparkling focal point.

From the awning-covered glass façade and the bronze fretwork-adorned lobby to the special lighting, Brinkworth has succeeded in creating an appealing dining space that perfectly reflects the Tinello ideal of relaxed informal dining in comfort and style.

Conduit-type lighting runs across the ceiling in the basement dining area.

Guests are seated comfortably on Thonet 404 dining chairs, designed by Stefan Diez.

The wall of exposed red brick has rounded corner details made of Staffordshire blue brick.

Screens with a fret-cut brass pattern were sandwiched between two glass panes, framed in brass.

TORI TORI BY ROJKIND ARQUITECTOS AND ESRAWE STUDIO

Where Mexico City, Mexico
Opening September 2011
Client Dr. Kumoto
Designers rojkind arquitectos → p.588
and Esrawe Studio → p.582
Floor space 627 m²
Capacity 173 seats

A lattice-clad temple for sushi lovers.

Photos Paul Rivera

An organic laser-cut skin envelops the original structure of the building.

Opposite A wall of fresh green plant life towers over guests seated in the tea room.

ROJKIND ARQUITECTOS AND ESRAWE STUDIO

When the owner of the well-established Japanese restaurant Tori Tori was looking to relocate to a bigger premises in the same area of Mexico City, rojkind arquitectos and Esrawe Studio teamed up to make it happen. The restaurant is located in the Polanco district, an area which has undergone zoning changes so that private houses have been converted into restaurants or offices, often with the original exterior preserved. Tori Tori's new abode was to be dramatically different.

The design teams collaborated to totally transform the space from the inside out, restructuring and renovating the house, stripping the residential interior and removing all familiar features to produce an entirely different environment. The client wanted the design to be oriented towards a Japanese interpretation, while at the same time having its own personal expression, which was contemporary and cosmopolitan. The striking organic façade encases the building in a lattice structure that climbs up the exterior, mimicking the natural ivy on the retaining walls surrounding the terrace. Made up of two self-supporting layers of steel-cut plates, the exterior pattern filters light and shadows into the interior space, creating an atmosphere enriched by the spectrum of subtle changes.

On entering the restaurant, customers may initially have the feeling that they are stepping onto an indoor terrace, where eating and drinking is embraced by natural vegetation and wooden planks extend across the floor like patio decking. Each room has its own atmosphere and displays a clear relationship between form and function, thanks to the custom-made furnishings that provide a direct orientation through each space. There is the dark-marble sake bar, two relaxed dining areas – where the external lattice-work is visible – and the wood-clad tea room, which has an actual indoor terrace at the far end, complete with a double-height wall of green foliage and skylight overhead.

Opposite top The contrast in ceiling heights is emphasized by the surrounding walls and ceiling all being clad in wooden planks.

Opposite bottom Smooth surfaces envelop the sake bar with its marble surrounds.

Even in the heart of the building, natural vegetation can still be seen through the glass walls.

The criss-crossing steel bilayer is illuminated with coloured LED lights.

ROJKIND ARQUITECTOS AND ESRAWE STUDIO

Exploded view of the building.

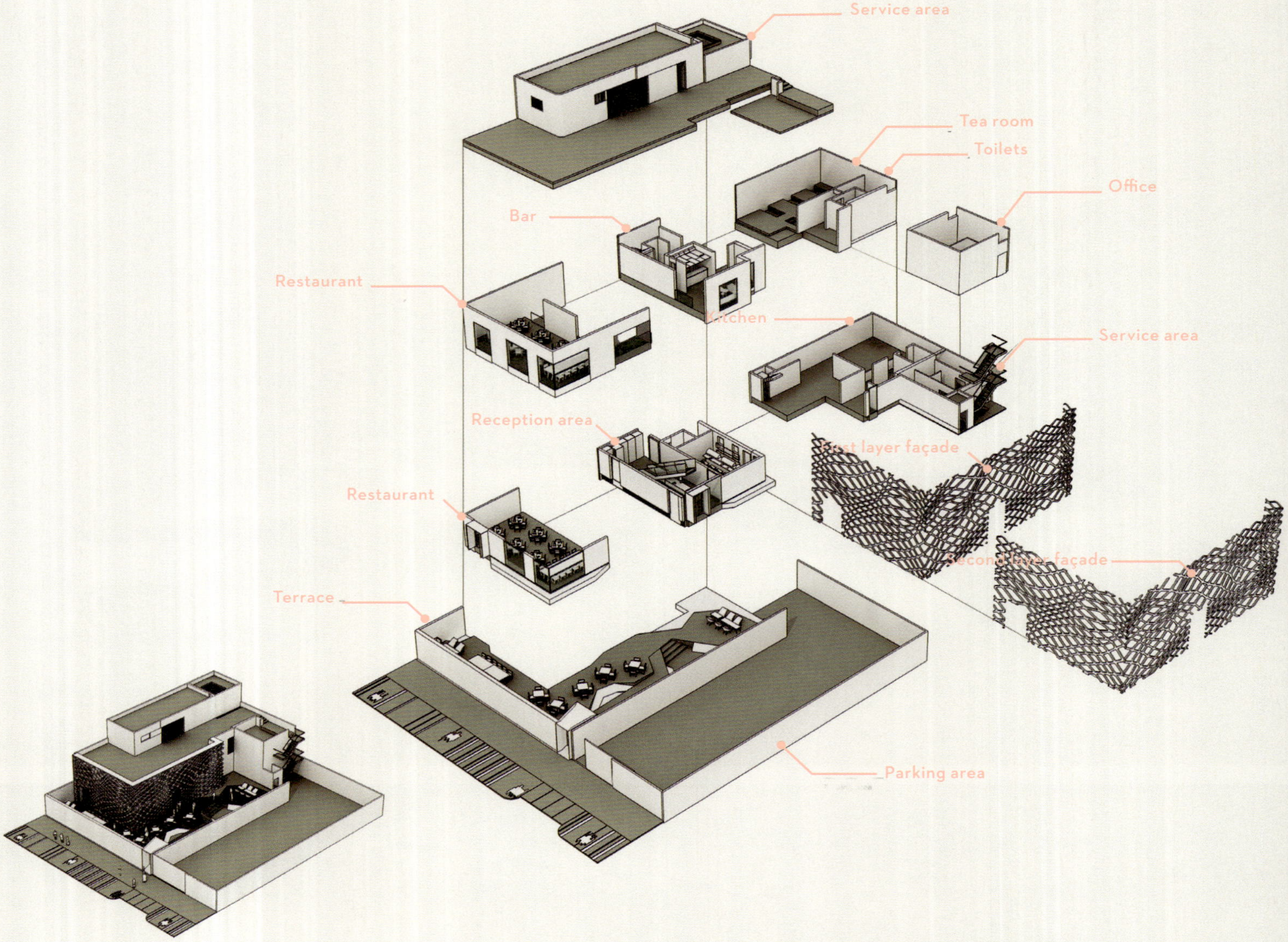

Rendering showing a slice of daily life in the Japanese restaurant.

184 TORI TORI

Second floor

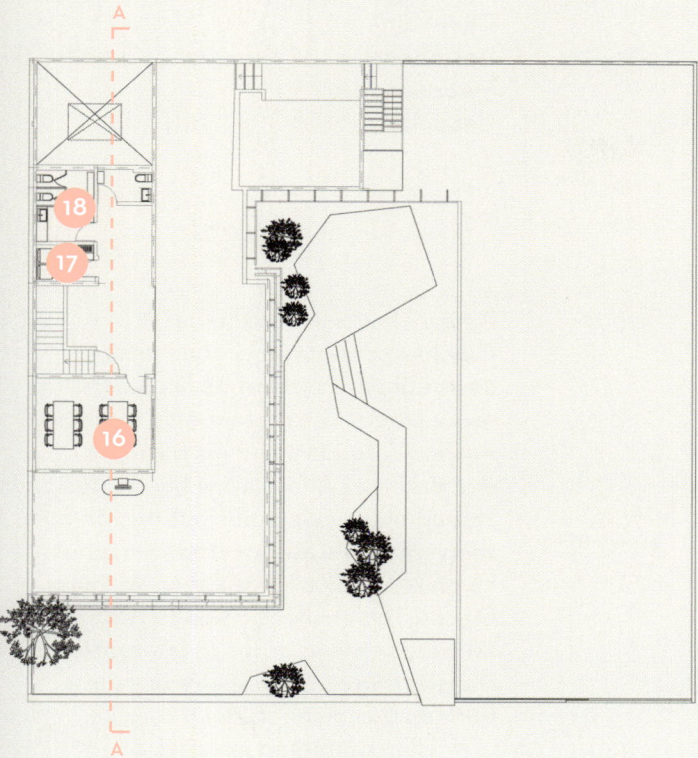

First floor

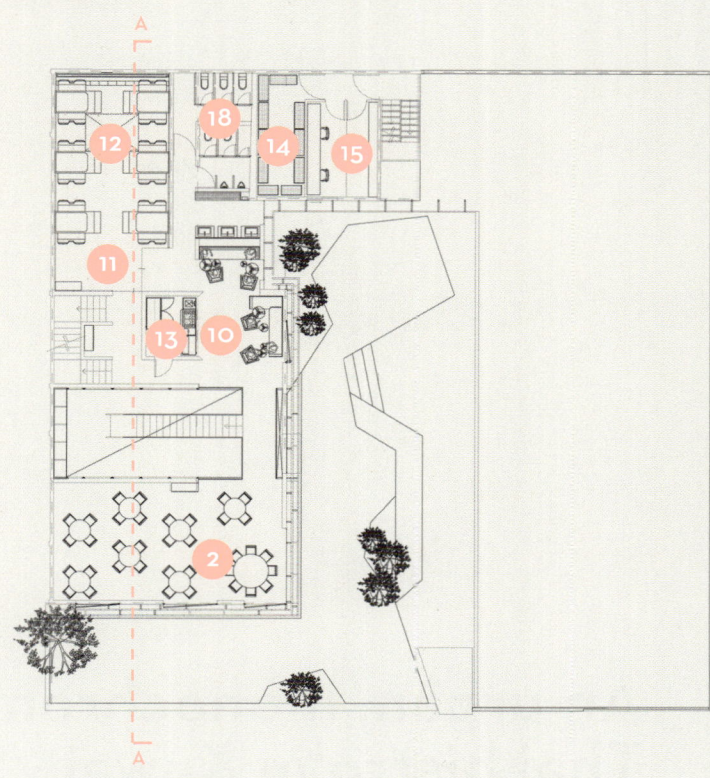

Ground floor

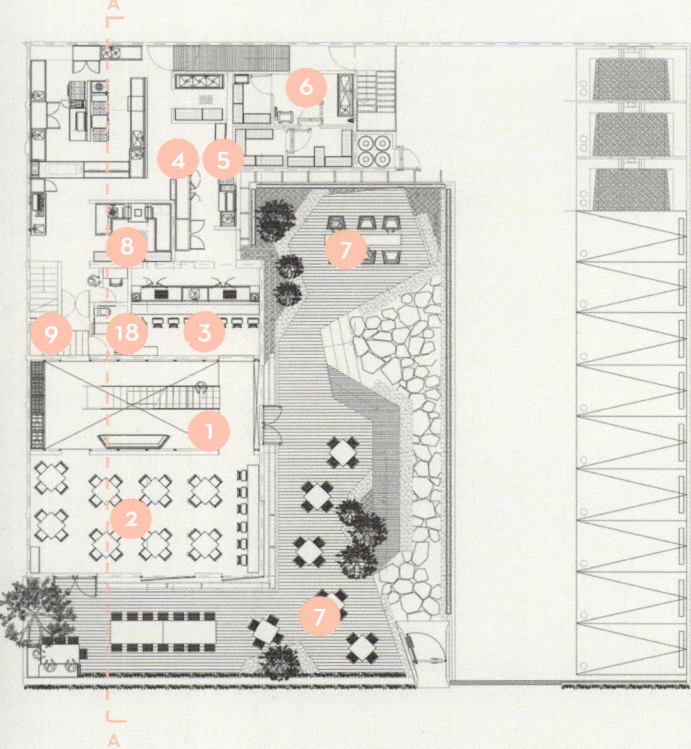

1. Reception area
2. Dining area
3. Sake bar
4. Kitchen
5. Sushi kitchen
6. Refrigeration area
7. Terrace
8. Cashier
9. Cloakroom
10. Bar
11. Tea room
12. Tea room terrace
13. Service area
14. Storage
15. Office
16. Staff room
17. Laundry
18. Toilets

South elevation

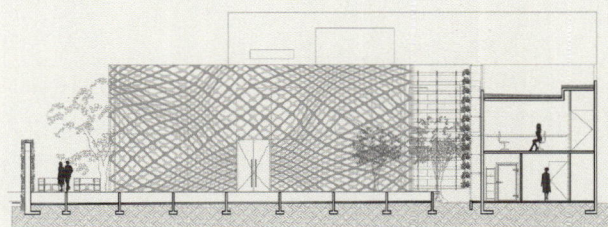

Section AA

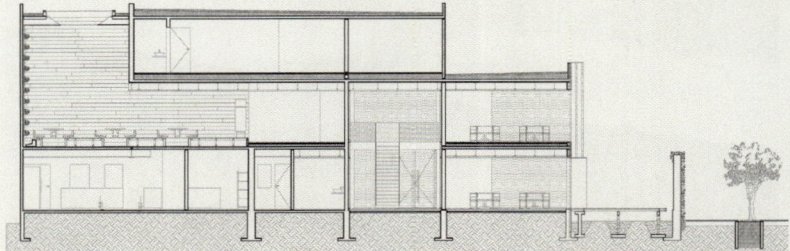

UBON BY RASHED ALFOUDARI

Where Kuwait City, Kuwait
Opening January 2012
Client Ubon
Designer Rashed Alfoudari → p.587
Floor space 60 m²
Capacity 28 seats

An urban, monochromatic Thai bistro in Kuwait.

Photos Rashed Alfoudari

A new Thai bistro in the heart of Kuwait City has connotations of an urban aesthetic, born out of its like-sounding name Ubon. The restaurant's owners, Rashed Alfoudari and his partners, decided that Alfoudari, who is a designer, should produce an efficient design for the venue which is located in the busy commercial district of Fahad Al Salim Street. The challenge was to rework the interior space in order to integrate with the existing structural elements in a harmonious manner.

The completed space is a contemporary, monochromatic hub decorated with dark burnt-wood panels and infused with golden copper elements that reflect the Asian influence of the bistro. From the street, customers can grasp the essence of the design thanks to the full-glass façade. On entering – through a door with the same dark wooden planks used in the panelling on the walls – there is a raw feel to the space, which has exposed concrete flooring treated with a matt water sealer. Black leather benches line the side walls, with white marble-top tables positioned alongside to delineate the seating areas. There is a noticeable vertical pattern in the bistro's design aspects; to tie in with this, concrete has been laid in strips up the restroom walls, imprinted with linear wood planks. There is also an ultramodern faucet fixture suspended above the centre of the sink that, along with the standalone basin, has an off-white concrete-coloured hue.

Back in the dining area, large pendant lampshades above the tables add an organic touch. Their curved design adds a softness to the structured space. The golden glow of the inner textured surface is also relevant, as gold is a colour often associated with ornamentation in Thai culture.

The lampshades (Beat Lights by Tom Dixon) are lined with hand-beaten brass with a patinated black exterior.

Opposite The burnt-wood planks used for the entrance and the interior walls have a protection layer coating them.

The basement level has a different look and feel than the ground-floor level.

Where Madrid, Spain
Opening May 2010
Client Udon
Designer Girbau Mateu → p.583
Floor space 210 m²
Capacity 75 seats

UDON BY GIRBAU MATEU

A chain restaurant inspired by the finesse of Japanese culture.

Text Sarah Martín Pearson
Photos Cristobal Roves

Unlike other chain restaurants, Udon is not one to clone its décor, instead interpreting each installation individually by adapting its global space identity to the unique features of each establishment. Its first Madrid eatery, in the buzzing Chueca area, is an example. Architect studio Girbau Mateu is behind the original Udon noodle restaurant space concept, inspired by the finesse of Japanese culture, which transpires from its culinary speciality, and turning the purity of lines and a monochrome scheme into features of its identity.

The Udon Chueca restaurant is divided into two levels, each with its own outstanding features. At street level, the dining area's main focal point is a succession of wavy slats which seem to float overhead like a cloud, made from computer-generated, organically shaped, white Alucobond panels. This aesthetic element improves the space's acoustic qualities while concealing the lighting fixtures between the slats. Downstairs, the walls are clad with a layer of metallic curtains, indirectly illuminated by fixtures concealed within the recessed ceiling, achieving an effect of faux transparency and suspension that help soften the boundaries of an otherwise enclosed space. Other elements, such as the white Corian communal tables and their overhead custom-built, linear xenon lighting fixtures, together with the Rietveld-inspired black, zigzagging stools establish the usual style pattern followed by all Udon eateries, becoming its brand identity. A play on visual perspectives, transparencies and reflections lend this project environmental comfort within the abstract originality of its design, while at the same time meeting all the functional needs required by a chain restaurant like Udon. •

Medio Design and LaN were responsible for the implementation of the wavy ceiling.

Opposite Red is used as an accent colour on both the walls and in the restaurant's logo.

VUE DE MONDE RIALTO

VUE DE MONDE RIALTO BY ELENBERG FRASER

Where Melbourne, Australia
Opening July 2011
Client Shannon Bennett
Designer Elenberg Fraser → p.582
Floor space 1200 m²
Capacity 48 seats (dining room), 26 seats (chef's table), 160 seats (function room)

An elevated antipodean outpost of molecular gastronomy.

Photos Dianna Snape

The hanging light sculptures are by Emma Lashmer.

Opposite top Hovering over the bar is a cloud-like art installation by Michaela Dwyer.

Opposite bottom The restaurant has a dark décor with atmospheric lighting. The neon artwork is by Joseph Kosuth.

ELENBERG FRASER 191

The path to the restaurant is lined with stainless steel pins.

The open kitchen creates intrigue for customers as they can watch their culinary delights being prepared.

THE CONCEPT CONNECTS TO AN ABSTRACT LOCAL LANDSCAPE

Corrugated curved walls shimmer in the darkness.

When acclaimed Australian chef Shannon Bennett decided to relocate his renowned restaurant to a dramatic location at the top of Melbourne's Rialto Tower, he commissioned Elenberg Fraser to produce an interior that is a celebration of Australiana, encapsulating the wonder of its contradictions by featuring both wildness and sophistication. The concept connects to an abstract local landscape, in particular that of Melbourne and its waterways. The Yarra River, the reeds, the billabong, Australian animals and insects are all referenced as inspiration and can be seen in the many individual art and design pieces used to decorate the sleek interior.

The guests' journey begins on stepping out of the lift on the 55th floor into the sumptuous yet pared-back space. From here there are two paths: one leads to the bar area, with its monolith of locally-sourced rough black basalt, the top polished to a mirror finish; the other leads to the restaurant, with its black-painted walls and dark wood parquet with sweeping views across the city and beyond. On the back wall, a neon art piece by conceptual artist Joseph Kosuth – interpreting one of Charles Darwin's sketches – forms a stunning backdrop for the dining room, sparsely furnished with tables and chairs covered in stretched black leather and clusters of light sculptures overhead, like hovering fireflies.

Off to the side, slabs of veined white marble delineate the open kitchen and a pathway to the private dining rooms can be found. Shiny corrugated chrome sheets feature throughout the space lining the walkway walls, as well as the unique wet areas that offer visitors the ultimate estuarine experience with waterfalls of 'e-water' running over their hands into the black steel pools of the basins.

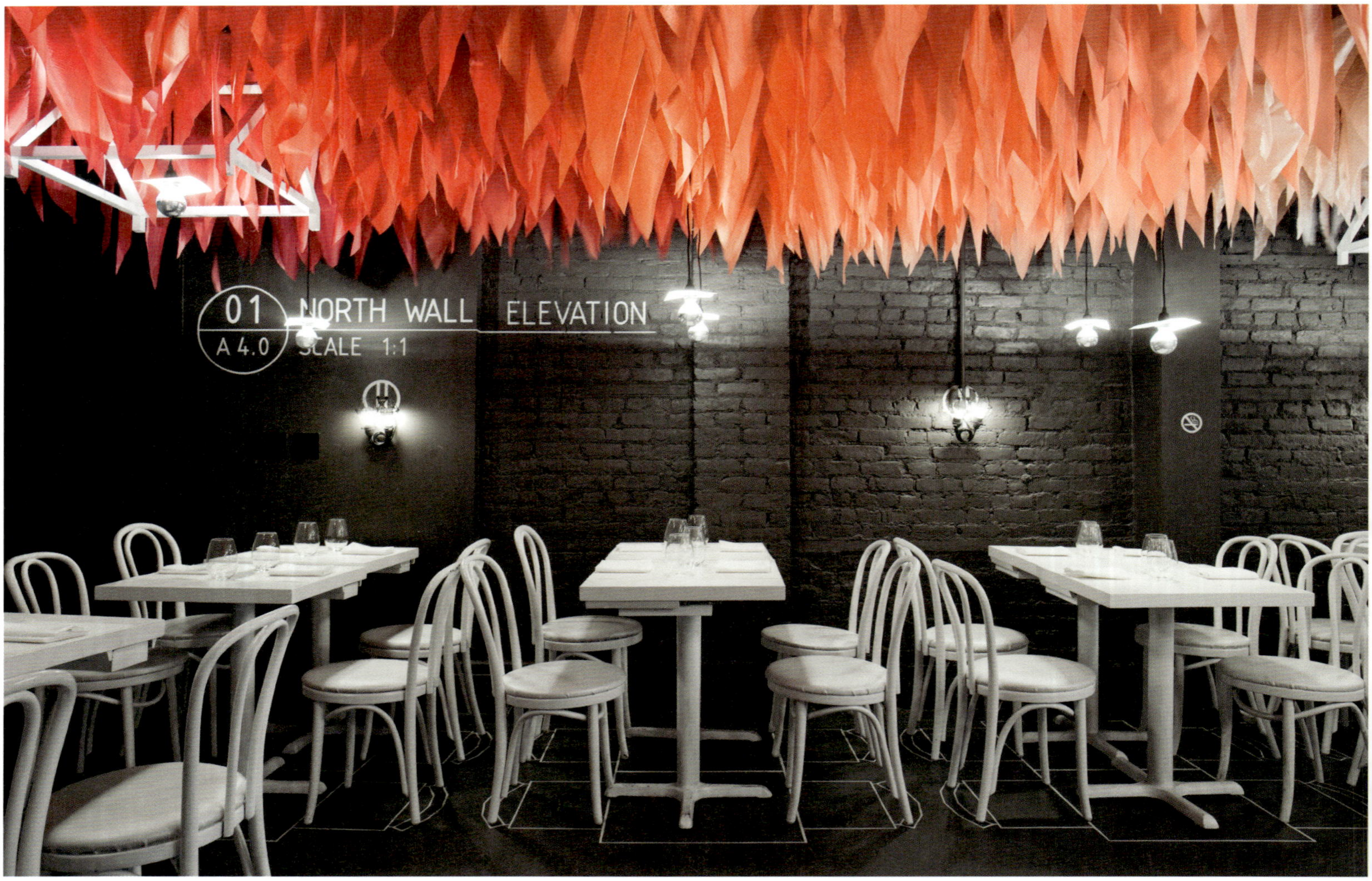
01
A 4.0
NORTH WALL ELEVATION
SCALE 1:1

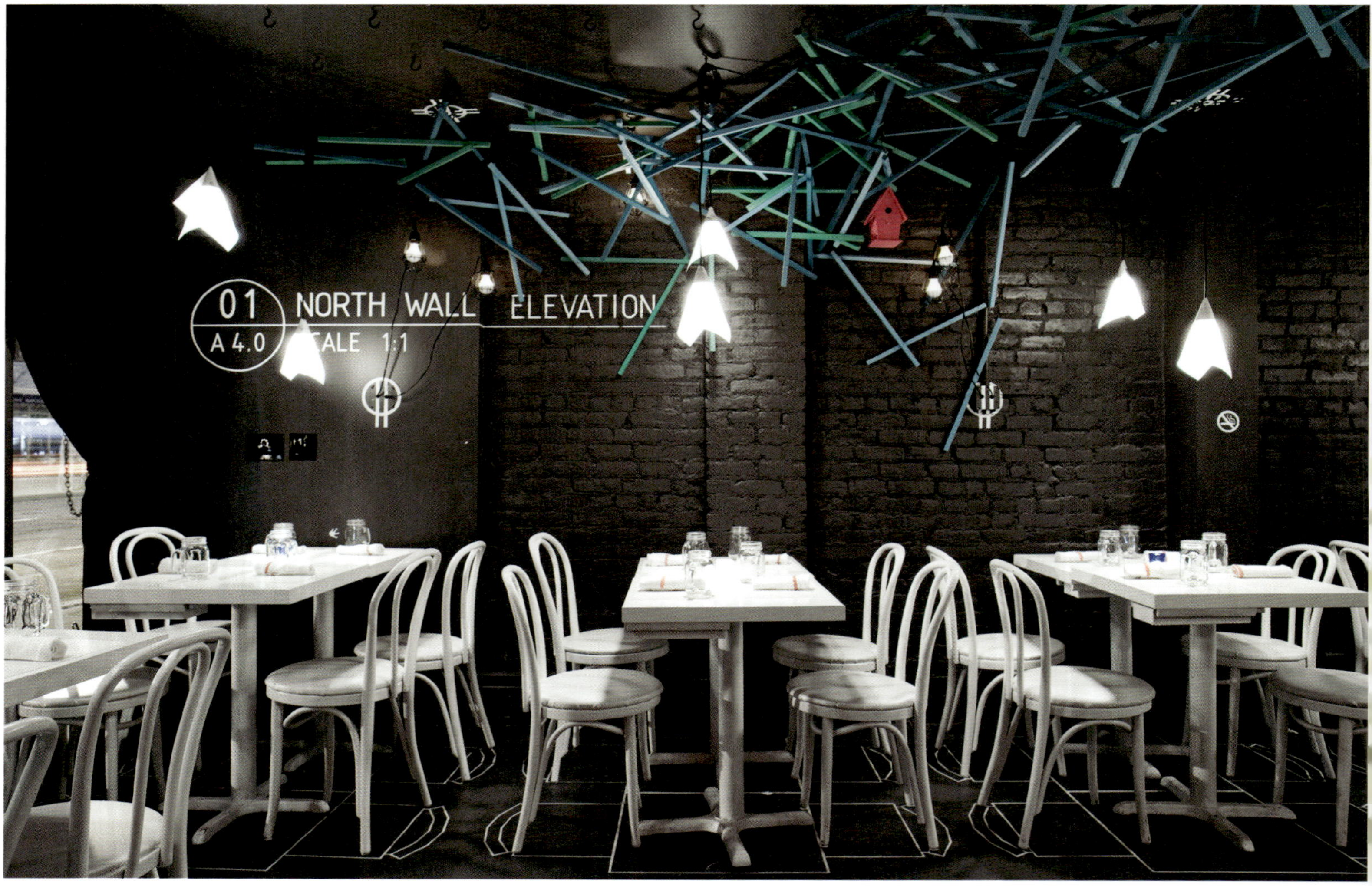
01
A 4.0
NORTH WALL ELEVATION
SCALE 1:1

For Jazz, parallel layers of thread were suspended from the ceiling to represent stringed instruments.

WHAT HAPPENS WHEN BY THE METRICS

A temporary 'work in progress' restaurant where the concept changed each month.

Photos Felix de Voss

Opposite top For Valentine's Day, fabric was cut into triangles and hung from the grid of hooks.

Opposite bottom A fantastical forest theme was installed for Where the Wild Things Are, with bird houses on the wall nestled beneath green 'pine needles' suspended from the ceiling.

Where New York, United States
Opening January 2011
Client John Fraser
Designer The Metrics → p.589
Floor space 110 m²
Capacity 60 seats

THE METRICS

Snowy white fixtures delineated the Nordic spatial concept.

METRICS DESIGNED SIX DIFFERENT INTERIORS FOR SIX DIFFERENT THEMES

The Silk Road space had intricately-cut square panels acting as room dividers, hung around light fixtures creating a play of light and shadow.

What Happens When was a creative collaboration initiated by chef John Fraser who wanted to create a temporary restaurant that would change concepts each month in order to explore what a dining experience could be. Metrics principal Elle Kunnos de Voss was asked to design the restaurant's monthly interior and spatial changes.

The design concept was 'work in progress' transparency, to reflect the project's changing and experimental nature. The actual architectural drawings were projected onto the floor, walls and ceiling on a 1:1 scale, inviting guests into the design process. The ceiling was covered with a grid of hooks to keep the space flexible and for easy reconfiguration of the lighting. Metrics designed six different interiors for six themes.

For Nordic, the spatial concept was a monochromatic landscape of deconstructed volumes and fixtures, with a pared-down aesthetic. White lines defined volumes within the space, in archetypal house and ladder shapes in distorted perspective.

For Valentine's Day, a fabric installation lowered the ceiling by 45 cm and made the space more intimate, with one big stroke of hot pink fading into deep purple.

For Where the Wild Things Are, the interior design concept played with scale, defining the space with an installation of oversized pine needles creating movement across the ceiling and stretching to the floor in some places to act as room dividers.

Garden Party was inspired by Renoir's painting *Luncheon of the Boating Party* and designed around a few significant elements and colouring from the Renoir painting to re-create an intimate 19th-century experience. An awning-like architectural stroke across the room, 8 m long, framed the dining settings in warm spring tones to re-create the painting's communal, intimate feeling.

For Jazz, Metrics used 2800 m of string to create different volumes throughout the space, creating a visual cadence from the entrance to the back, visually and spatially communication the rhythm and contrasts of jazz music. The light fixtures, in basic geometric shapes in bright colours, were inspired by jazz instruments.

For Silk Road the designer, using patterns inspired by regions spanning from Turkey to China, created a maze of screens made of 30 x 30 cm cardboard panels. The panels were hung in formations from the ceiling hooks, with Turkish patterns at the entrance all the way east through the space to the Chinese patterns at the back.

The atmosphere for the Garden Party setting was established by the colourful canopy overhead, creating an interplay between interior and exterior.

THE METRICS 197

Opposite Different-sized pendant lamps hang over the tables at varying heights.

WIENERWALD BY IPPOLITO FLEITZ GROUP

A fresh décor with quirky aspects is the focus of a fast-food outlet in Munich.

Photos Zooey Braun

Forest images in different shades of green are used on the windows.

Where Munich, Germany
Opening May 2010
Client Wienerwald
Designer Ippolito Fleitz Group → p.584
Floor space 125 m²
Capacity 21 seats (inside), 20 seats (outside)

Friedrich Jahn opened the first Wienerwald fast-food restaurant in 1955. His grandchildren, currently in charge, commissioned Ippolito Fleitz Group to develop a new corporate architecture for the chain. As they were changing Wienerwald's culinary selection, the new visual presence had to match the new menu. Chicken remains the main staple of the menu, but salads have been introduced to move the fast-food chain into the arena of fresh and healthy foods.

Materials and colours reflect the concepts of 'fresh' and 'natural', expressed in materials such as wood, leather and textiles, as well as in the dominant green tones that complement the fresh white. Gold is used as an accent colour, conjuring up associations of quality as well as the crisp, gold-coloured skin of the Wienerwald grilled chicken.

The space has been organized to guide customers efficiently. Upon entering the guest is led towards a frontally positioned counter, presented as a clearly structured, monolithic unit. In front of the counter is a service station with a white solid surface and standing on golden chicken legs, offering sauces, condiments and cutlery. Green instructions and Wienerwald chickens set into the rustic wood floor help the customer navigate.

The dining area offers a range of seating options: white, solid-surface, high bar tables are available for customers in a hurry, while opposite an elongated seating group upholstered in brown imitation leather is an echo of the traditional Wienerwald seating niches. Overlapping, rough-sawn oak panels on the rear wall allude to the forest theme. Round mirrors printed with the outlines of tree and forest motifs are set into this wall. A display of dining plates on the wall is dedicated to the company's long tradition and show a photograph of the first Wienerwald restaurant. Traditional elements of the brand have been incorporated and translated into modern spatial elements with an exciting twist. •

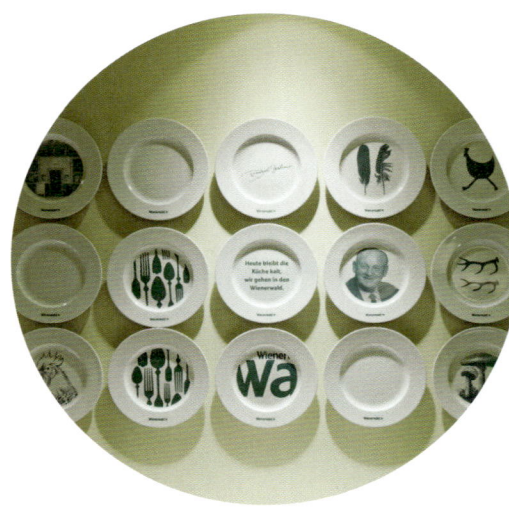

A display of dining plates on the wall shows the history of the Wienerwald brand in 14 motifs.

The pendent lamps are sheathed in a roughly woven fabric.

The chopping station is in the middle of the counter; salads are chopped under the guests' watchful eyes.

DOMINANT GREEN TONES UNDERLIE A FRESH AND NATURAL DESIGN CONCEPT

A WALL DISPLAY IS DEDICATED TO THE COMPANY'S LONG TRADITION

A detailed drawing of the custom-designed wallpaper with forest motif.

Sketch of the round mirrors, printed with the outlines of tree and forest motifs.

Heute bleibt die Küche kalt, wir gehen in den Wienerwald.

A sketch of the display of dining plates.

Front elevation

1. Counter
2. Service station
3. Seating area
4. Kitchen
5. Office
6. Toilets
7. Terrace

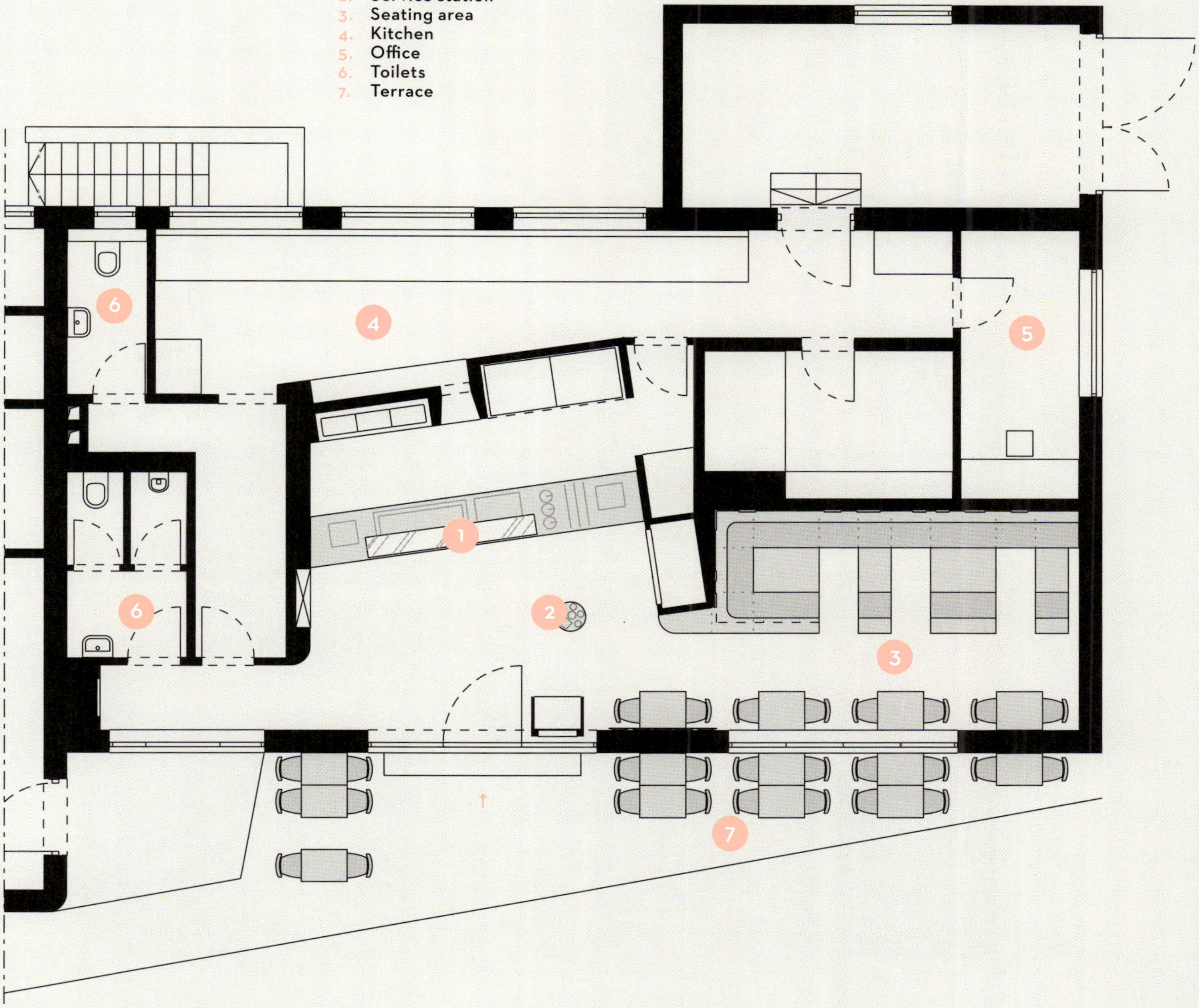

Opposite Diners are seated within the yellow house framework.

YOSHINOYA BY AS DESIGN SERVICE

A fast-food outlet where the concept of 'home' is used as the core design element.

Photos Sum Sing

The window around the pick-up point is painted a corporate orange colour.

Where Hong Kong, Hong Kong
Opening July 2011
Client Yoshinoya Fast Food
Designer AS Design Service → p.579
Floor space 123 m²
Capacity 80 seats

The menu wall incorporates an interactive screen.

Positioned in a rapidly growing market, fast-food outlets often target the younger generation; the Yoshinoya fast-food chain is no exception. AS Design Service was asked to design its latest restaurant in Hong Kong.

The design team wanted to use a direct and simple interpretation to demonstrate the brand image as innovative, clear and young. Using the concept of 'home' as the core design element to present the brand image as energetic and warm, the designers implemented the shape of a house, which customers can easily associate with the new image. A column structure in bright yellow was designed in the shape of a house, as were the lampshades hanging above the dining tables. The kitchen is concealed from the guests by a long, glossy white wall and can be glimpsed through the house-shaped counter only where guests pick up their orders.

The designers used bright yellow and orange to appeal to the young crowd. The orange triangle patterns on the walls were inspired by Japanese origami. It makes the 'home' vibrant and creates a relaxing and lively environment for dining.

THE DESIGNERS USED BRIGHT YELLOW AND ORANGE TO APPEAL TO THE YOUNG CROWD

A smaller version of the yellow house framework can be seen in the bespoke lampshades.

Opposite Customers place their orders on entering the restaurant.

AS DESIGN SERVICE

Opposite A ceramic 'vine', created by artist James Riglers, creeps up the tree.

Seven bench tables with white curved table lamps brighten up one side of the restaurant.

ZIZZI BY D-RAW

A restaurant incorporating its own Italian piazza, with a steel sculptured tree and ceramic vine.

Photos Richard Leeney

Through the double-height glass façade, passers-by can get a good glimpse of the special features inside.

Where London, United Kingdom
Opening November 2010
Client Zizzi
Designer d-raw → p.581
Floor space 427 m²
Capacity 114 seats (inside), 60 seats (outside)

Situated in a recently completed office building designed by famous Italian architect Renzo Piano, the challenge was to formulate a set of design components that would channel an authentic yet fresh understanding of the location, in the process presenting the restaurant as a new and exciting destination.

Mirroring the architectural cityscape of Piano's development, the d-raw design team–responsible for the interior design of the venue – created an authentic Italian piazza. A 6-m-high steel 'tree' unfolds within the restaurant, creating a canopy above the sofa seating area offering a localized 'intimate' moment of relaxation. A double-volume log wall at the back of the open kitchen ties the restaurant to Zizzi's visual DNA and pays homage to a traditional Italian dining experience and Zizzi's core offering, pizza.

Maintaining the transparency of the location, all services are located in a blackboard-painted cube next to the kitchen. Artist Camille Roussea created a large-scale, hand-drawn illustrated map on this blackboard wall, offering a visual journey through the history of St Giles.

Taking its cue from the enormous ceramic panels of Piano's architecture, d-raw worked with ceramic artist James Rigler to develop bespoke ceramic details, producing the hand-cast buttons in the central sofa, a ceramic 'vine' that creeps up the tree and, most strikingly, the beautiful white glazed chef's table tops. •

LED lights attached to each branch of the sculpture tree create a blue radiance.

Fresh Italian ingredients hang above the counter of the open-plan kitchen.

The chef's table stands out because of its white ceramic tabletop.

ZUIDERS PROEFLOKAAL

Opposite A variety of surface treatments help to create an authentic interior.

Where Uden, the Netherlands
Opening December 2010
Client Dick van Zutven
Designer Pubblik → p.587
Floor space 115 m²
Capacity 60 seats

ZUIDERS PROEFLOKAAL BY PUBBLIK

A Dutch eatery inspired by bars of the Basque region.

Photos Jim Ellam

The café has a charming, rustic appeal.

Old chopping boards of various sizes have been hung on the walls.

BLACK STEEL PIPES WITH MEAT HOOKS DISPLAY ORIGINAL BUTCHER TOOLS

Concrete flooring, brick, aluminium pipework and wooden planks are a selection of the surface textures visible in the eatery.

Beat pendant lamps by Tom Dixon illuminate the dining area and the serving counter.

The mission of Zuiders Proeflokaal is to present the simplicity and unique character of Basque food and hospitality. The owners were inspired by the bars of the Basque region on a trip to Spain: a culinary world that features a prominent position for pintxos displayed on the bar, served on small platters and eaten standing up. Pubblik extended and translated this concept into a light, fresh and sunny interior with bright yellow accents.

Using a palette of natural materials such as oak timber, a brick wall, leather benches and a concrete floor, Pubblik gave Zuiders Proeflokaal a warm and authentic feel. In an effort to suggest the look of a traditional butcher shop without being too literal, the walls at the small bar in the restaurant area are covered in uneven white tiles and the bar top is made of end-grain wood, like a butcher block. Black steel pipes with meat hooks throughout the restaurant display original butcher's tools, Spanish hams and old chopping boards with the specialties written on them. The back wall of the venue features shelving bearing Spanish olive oil cans, food packaging and traditional brown crockery.

The main bar is divided in two: guests can select their pintxos at the short side of the bar and sit down and enjoy a drink along the long side. The existing columns are covered in white plaster and horizontally connected to create space sections and avoid a straight, white surface. The special ceiling treatment makes the bar area a real eye-catcher: untreated old roof slats were reused and diffused light filters through the gaps to simulate an attic.

In order to unify the concept, Pubblik was also tasked with the design of the venue's graphic elements. The use of craft paper and large striking price numbers was inspired by large market signs. ●

PUBBLIK

ALLURE BY CIPRIANI

Where **Abu Dhabi, United Arab Emirates**
Opening **October 2010**
Client **Cipriani Group**
Designer **Orbit Design Studio** → p.586
Floor space **1100 m²**
Capacity **800 guests**

The luxury club towers like a beacon over the luxury yachts.

ALLURE BY CIPRIANI BY ORBIT DESIGN STUDIO

An ultramodern and dynamic club with exuberant elegance.

Photos Owen Raggett

Opposite An impressive colour-changing, illuminated, segmented skin stretches overhead.

The interior has an open plan, nautically inspired seating area and semi-secluded VIP booths.

AS WELL AS BEING UNFORGETTABLE THE INTERIOR HAD TO REFLECT THE CLUB'S LOCATION

The geometric contours that line the bar counter are made of MDF panels clad in mirrored stainless steel in a bronze colour.

For legendary restaurateurs Cipriani Group's first venture in the Middle East, a bold statement of intent was required. Bearing in mind Cipriani's strong brand integrity of refined exclusivity and its location at Abu Dhabi's exclusive new Yacht Club overlooking the Formula 1 race track, this was a project that had to appeal to the highest end of the international luxury crowd.

Orbit Design Studio met and exceeded all expectations with a striking design. As well as being unforgettable, the interior had to reflect the club's island location and its views of the luxury yachts. So, inside, units of bench seating, placed around the main floor and upholstered in white leather, are designed to resemble the living quarters of a luxury yacht. For the VIP seating areas, the challenge was to create the sort of intimate feel experienced in a private room, but without actually obscuring – or excluding – the guests. The answer was to build special structures, something like giant lampshades, suspended above each booth (pods), effectively giving each one its own ceiling while leaving it open at the sides. Made of steel frames clad in white MDF, each structure contains adjustable lighting and speakers and is fringed with a glittering curtain of metal beads. The final touch for VIPs is their own elevator. All this has combined to put Allure firmly at the top level of luxury clubs.

Perhaps the most distinctive element of the scheme is a feature made of tessellated triangular panels, which rises from behind the main DJ booth and continues across the ceiling. Each panel is made of a triangular MDF frame covered with translucent vinyl and backlit by coloured LEDs, which pulse in time to the music. It was one of the most challenging elements of the project. It was difficult to incorporate the new design elements with the existing mechanical and electrical equipment on the building's curved ceiling. The solution involved constructing the new ceiling in multiple parts, forming a flexible structure around existing duct work and making it a feature of the unusual space. To add yet another level of glamour, the designers created fractal, diamond-shaped walls finished with pink gold leaf and distinctive bronze cladding.

The monochrome bar stools and chairs by Konstantin Grcic also feature triangular surfaces and facets.

Opposite Vertical, geometric installations fill the void in the interior.

ARTHOUSE CAFÉ BY JOEY HO DESIGN

A futuristic setting in an arty space.

Photos Yong Chang Wu

Where Hangzhou, China
Opening November 2010
Client Shufa Hengye
Designer Joey Ho Design → p.584
Floor space 93 m²
Capacity 25 seats

The designers chose to use the same wood for the floor as for the installations.

THE INTERIOR DESIGN CONCEPT IS ONE OF SPATIALITY INSPIRED BY GEOMETRY

Arthouse Café is located on the top floor of a three-storey gallery totalling 278 m². Serving coffee in the daytime and alcohol at night, Arthouse Café provides a new dynamic ambiance within the exhibition building.

Joey Ho Design based the interior design on the concept of spatiality and, inspired by geometry, created a dynamic form for the static interior space. The concept is manifested by placing three-dimensional triangles around the entire sitting area. Slight changes in simple lines construct the café's unique character, bringing each visitor into a new geometric context.

With minimal use of such materials as timber, marble, glass and Corian, this space was constructed with basic components for building a new landscape. It aims to stimulate each visitor's unique and complex perception.

Introducing a simple triangular form in various dimensions creates a mass that tends to dematerialize through movement. This design attempts to break the boundary between traditionally distinct elements like the wall, floor and ceiling, hence enabling communication between the interior and its users. •

Left and opposite Some of the triangular openings are contained within wood-lined recesses, while others have thick wooden frames.

A mishmash of found furniture fits in with the muted palette and raw décor.

Where **Bucharest, Romania**
Opening **January 2011**
Client **Atelier Mecanic**
Designer **Corvin Cristian** → p.584
Floor space **70 m²**
Capacity **50 guests**

ATELIER MECANIC BY CORVIN CRISTIAN

A Romanian bar made of factory relics and salvaged leftovers.

Photos Cosmin Dragomir

Atelier Mecanic is a bar in Bucharest, located in a part of the city known as the Old Town. The client's brief only called for the creation of a space that would attract a cool crowd, so designer Corvin Cristian was completely free to determine his own interior concept. He now had the chance to bring his collection of vintage Romanian industrial products back to life. He wanted to reinstate some of Romania's heritage that had been stripped out of the city since the country's revolution in 1989. At that time, factories were perceived as a symbol of communism and demolished, so that 50 years of industrialization vanished in a flash.

The design team, made up of Corvin Cristian and collaborating architect Serban Rosca, wanted to bring a local flavour back to the city's bar scene, instilling the atmosphere of a place that might have once been a focal point of the Old Town. The designers used a mechanic's workshop as their inspiration, because the area used to have lots of small repair shops of all kinds. The 70-m² space, with its muted colour palette of greyish tones, has an industrial feel due to the choice of materials, from factory relics to salvaged leftovers. This aspect is also immediately clear to passers-by, as the bar's name on the façade is spelled out in workshop implements. Inside, along the left-hand wall, an original oak beam is integrated into the bar counter, extended at the front end to make an interesting seating arrangement. The space is uncluttered, with select vintage pieces of furniture lining the walls, positioned under retro hinged lamps. Acting as a divider down the centre of the space, a red-iron structural beam has been left uncovered in the gypsum board ceiling, allowing customers to catch glimpses of the original rafters. •

Among the industrial salvaged fittings are Jieldé lamps that light up the bar area.

An old switchboard has been placed on the copper-plated counter at one end of the bar, an interesting touch that intrigues the customers.

The raised booths and the numerous dance floors have randomized geometric shapes.

Opposite Dynamic coloured lighting lies at the heart of the design concept.

BONBON CLUB BY VLS INTERIOR ARCHITECTURE

A glamorous and modern interior for a reconstructed Estonian club.

Photos Ville Lausmäe

Where Tallinn, Estonia
Opening November 2011
Client Andres Peets
Designer VLS Interior Architecture → p.5
Floor space 397 m²
Capacity 350 guests

VLS INTERIOR ARCHITECTURE

A streak of vibrant cerise light demarcates the DJ booth.

232 BONBON CLUB

ABOVE THE BENCHES, TRIANGULAR LIGHTING PANELS CREATE A MORE INTIMATE FEEL

Tiny gold triangles are clustered on the ceiling above the bar, mimicking the main lighting aspects in the rest of the club.

The eye-catching architectural lighting used overhead consists of custom-made RGB-lighting panels.

The Bonbon Club has been the crème-de-la-crème of Estonia's nightclub scene for nine years, and in 2011 it was completely revamped. Since this is a partying venue for the elite, the brief the client gave VLS Interior Architecture was to create a brand-new interior with a glamorous atmosphere, fused with modernity. A rather important aspect was to maintain the inviting and friendly appeal to its loyal clientele and to therefore not transform the club in such a way that it would pull in an entirely different target audience.

The visual design is structural and straightforward, not associated with any specific style. The idea was for the design to be adjustable and – in its use of material and colour – as neutral and interpretable as possible. Hence the use of RGB lighting, giving the club different moods and colour adaptability as needed, according to the specific event or moment.

The lounge seating in the main room had to be integrated into the central area of the club in front of the dance floor, so that the VIPs – who buy their seats for the night – can be in the middle of the club life rather than on the outskirts, so that they can see and be seen. The custom-made benches are angular in shape and wrapped around one another. Above the benches, triangular lighting panels create a more intimate feel. The floor is raised towards the back of the main room to improve visibility and openness for all guests, whether seated or standing. The rear walls are covered with mirrors and faux-leather.

The design team kept the plan as open as possible to allow guests to move in a wide circle. The greatest challenge was to create a modern interior that would meet the approval of regular customers while appealing to new ones.

BUCK AND BRECK BY MOTORBERLIN.COM

Where Berlin, Germany
Opening December 2010
Clients Gonçalo de Sousa Monteiro and Holger Groll
Designer motorberlin.com → p.586
Floor space 92 m²
Capacity 20 guests

Get up close and personal with the bartender of a Berlin-based cocktail bar.

Photos Katja Hiendlmayer

In 2010, bartender Gonçalo de Sousa Monteiro and his partner Holger Groll commissioned Ingo Strobel to create an intimate atmosphere for his new Berlin cocktail bar, Buck and Breck. It needed to appeal to connoisseurs of quality cocktails and have as much panache as the late 19th century – the founding era of the cocktail – from which its name originates (the bar is named after 1860s US president James 'Buck' Buchanan and vice-president John C. 'Breck' Breckinridge).

Strobel, working with Marko Coric (C Plus Architects) on the construction, created a luxurious dark space dominated by a central island around which customers can congregate and get up close to watch the cocktails being created. The large black table has a textured surface covered with black Forbo Walton Crocodiles linoleum, which contrasts with the metal-lined sunken niches where the bottles and cocktail shakers are stored. A band of plasterboard runs around the walls of the main room just below the ceiling. It houses indirect lighting and is covered with a fresco showing poisonous plants in the dark. The reflecting bays in the walls are coloured gold, as are as the insides of the huge, custom-made lampshades above the bar. This arrangement of pendant lamps is an eye-catching aspect and counter-balances the huge table to a certain extent. From the street, Buck and Breck is not identified by a conventional sign. The façade window features changing installations curated by artist Theo Ligthart, aimed at luring visitors inside, where a calm, intimate retreat awaits. When the bar opened three oversized letters are set in a well-lit gallery window, forming the word 'bar'.

The motorberlin.com team created a bar that is as unique and intriguing as the often-changing art installations in the façade window.

The large central worktop allows customers to become an integral part of the mixologist's workspace, as if they have been invited into his home.

Textured dark surfaces feature in the interior.

Dark wood chairs at the central bar counter.

Initial sketches of the bar and the interior.

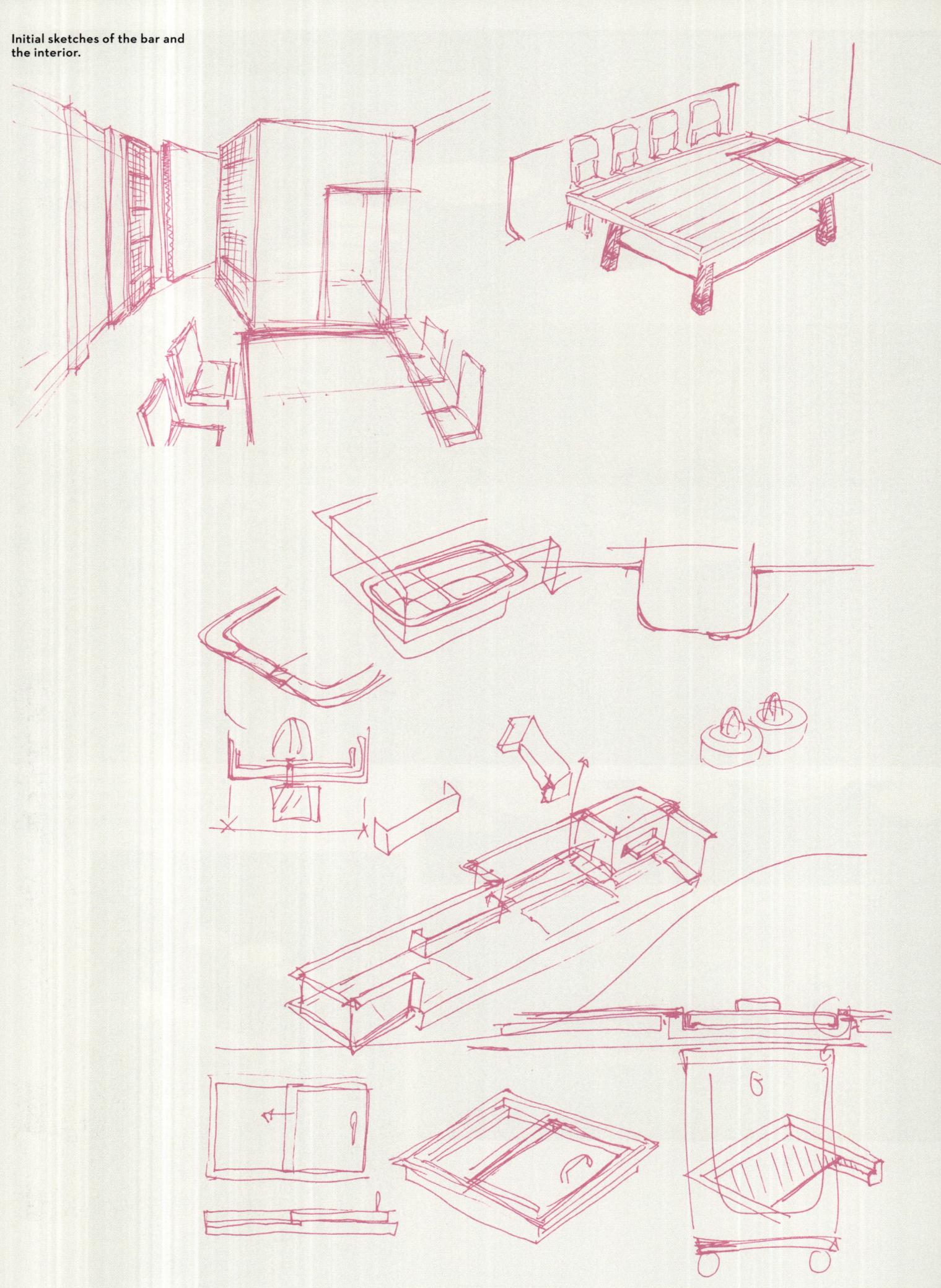

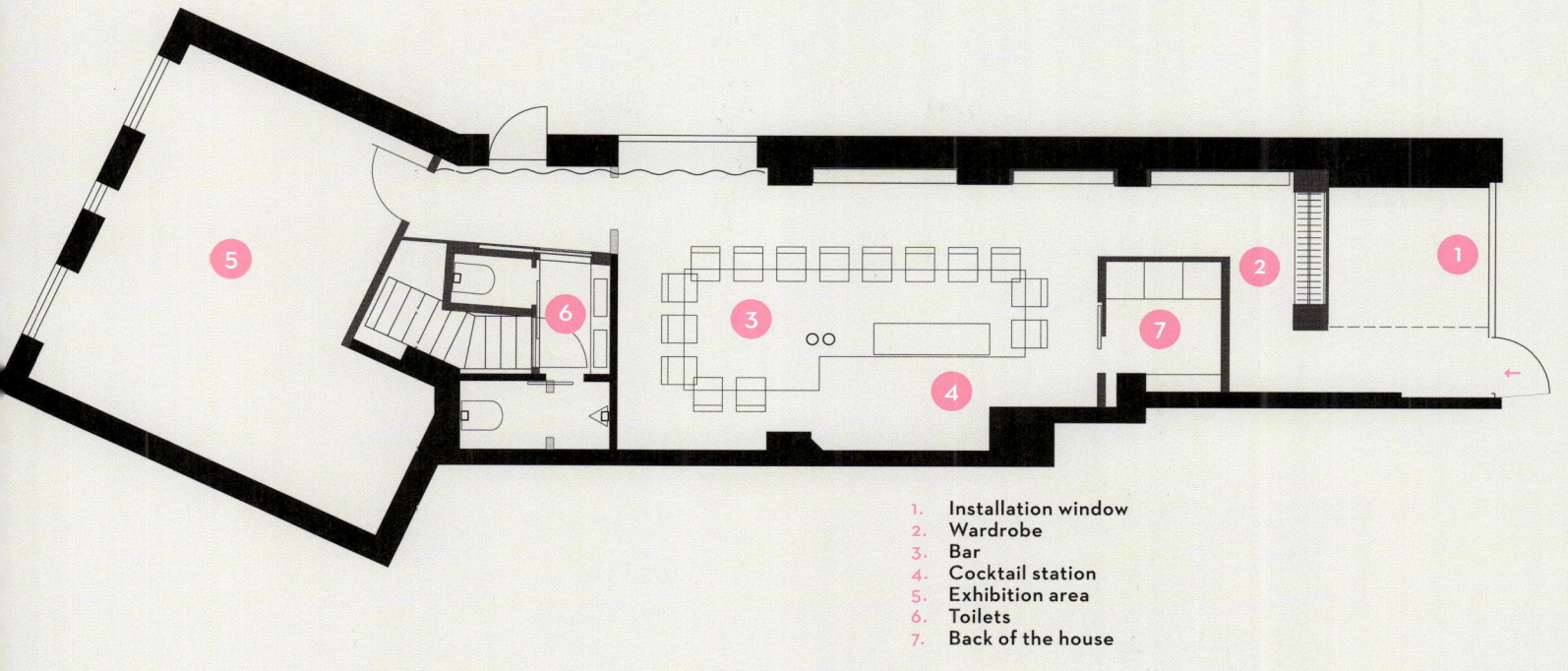

1. Installation window
2. Wardrobe
3. Bar
4. Cocktail station
5. Exhibition area
6. Toilets
7. Back of the house

BUCK AND BRECK NEEDED TO APPEAL TO CONNOISSEURS OF QUALITY COCKTAILS

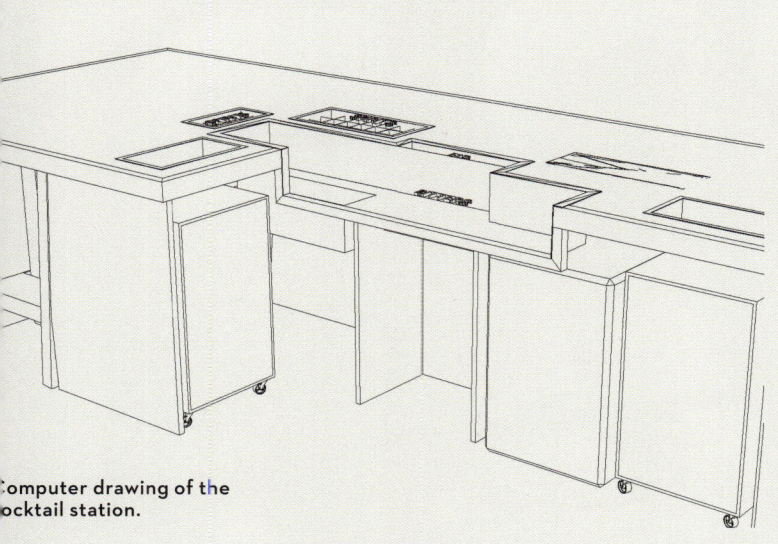

Computer drawing of the cocktail station.

Initial drawings of the plasterboard fresco.

One room, with a pink floor and black lampshades and furniture, is partitioned with red curtains, reminiscent of a bullfighter's cape.

Opposite Light-coloured wood, smooth grey and vivid pink create a palette that is repeated in the three rooms of the café.

CAFÉ FOAM BY NOTE DESIGN STUDIO

Spanish temperament meets Scandinavian cool in a Stockholm café.

Photos Stefano Barozzi

Where Stockholm, Sweden
Opening January 2010
Client Michael Toutoungi
Designer Note Design Studio → p.586
Floor space 180 m²
Capacity 70 seats

THE OWNER WANTED A PLACE THAT GUESTS WOULD EITHER LOVE OR HATE

Note Design Studio designed the new Café Foam in Sweden's capital, Stockholm. The owner of the café, Michael Toutoungi, asked the designers to create a place that guests would either love or hate – as long as no one was indifferent to the new design. The design team began searching for extremes in which passion and hate were equally present. Their angle on the project became the complexity around bullfighting as a phenomenon, as they were fascinated by the dance of the bull and the matador. This duel, along with the materials and colours of the arena, were the inspiration for the design of Café Foam. The design team allowed Spanish temperament to meet Scandinavian coolness.

Note Design chose to preserve certain well-known elements from the previous interior to make regulars feel right at home; they also created a vivid environment that makes meetings easier, protects the integrity of the customers and enhances the eating experience. The venue is divided into three areas. Guests enter a bar area where the main colour is grey. Here the designers used concrete flooring, grey painted walls and ceiling, and only high tables and bar stools. A second area is completely hued in fuchsia pink, with low black lounge chairs and tables. The third room has wooden walls, floor and ceiling and furniture similar to the lounge furniture of the second area, but now upholstered in grey tones. Although each room has a different look and feel based on the use of colour and material, they are interconnected by the fact that the designers have partially extended the colour palette of adjacent rooms, creating fluid transitions from space to space. The glass lamps used throughout the café were designed especially for this project and hand-blown at the Kosta glassworks. •

Five different colours of hand-blown glass were used for the pendant lights.

The bar has a counter made of natural wood.

The different wall treatments create a contrast, forming junctions of diagonal lines.

NOTE DESIGN STUDIO

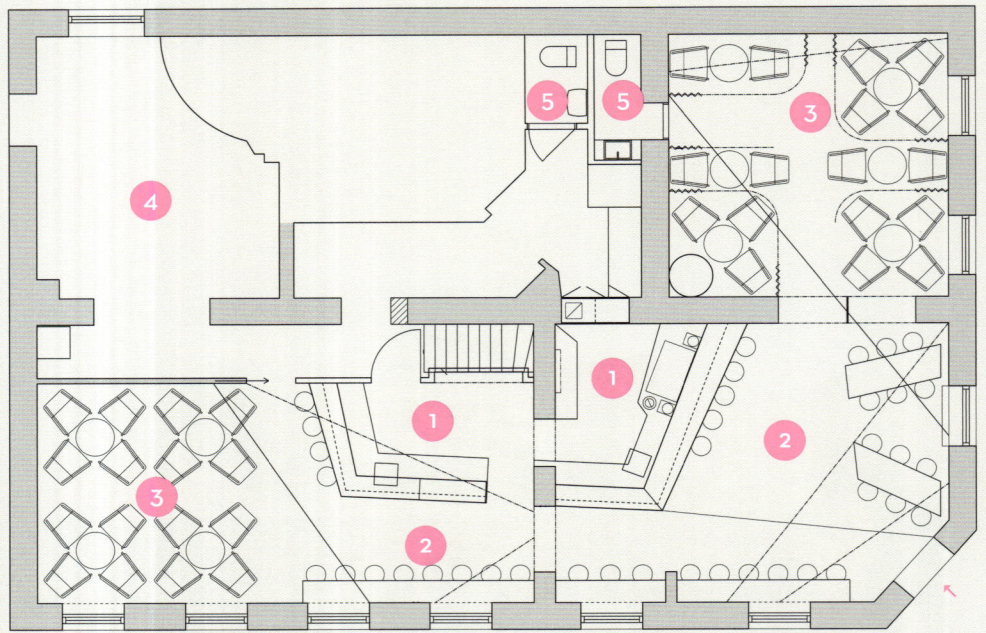

1. Bar
2. Bar seating
3. Lounge seating
4. Back of the house
5. Toilets

BULLFIGHTING, ALONG WITH THE MATERIALS AND COLOURS OF THE ARENA, SERVED AS INSPIRATION

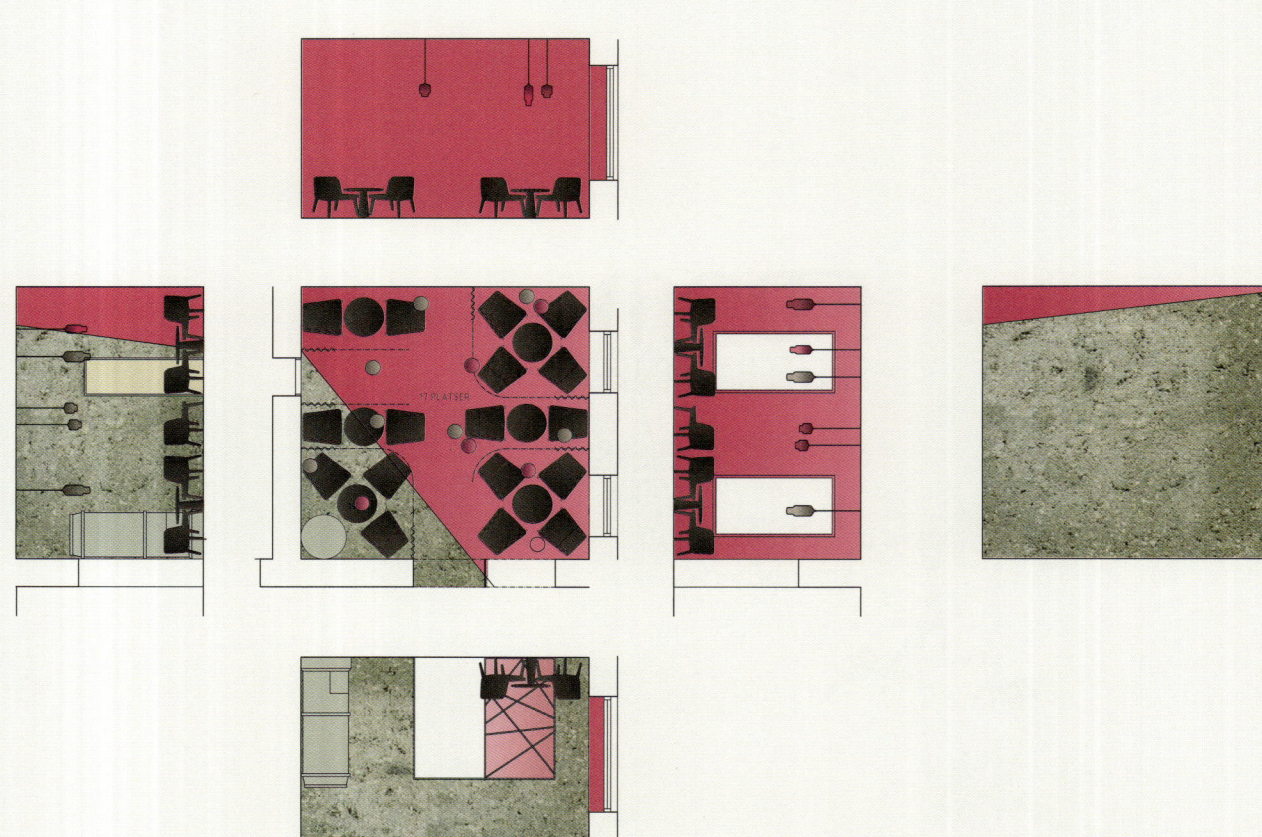

242　　CAFÉ FOAM

Below and opposite bottom
Drawing showing the colour scheme of the floor, walls and ceiling of the three spaces.

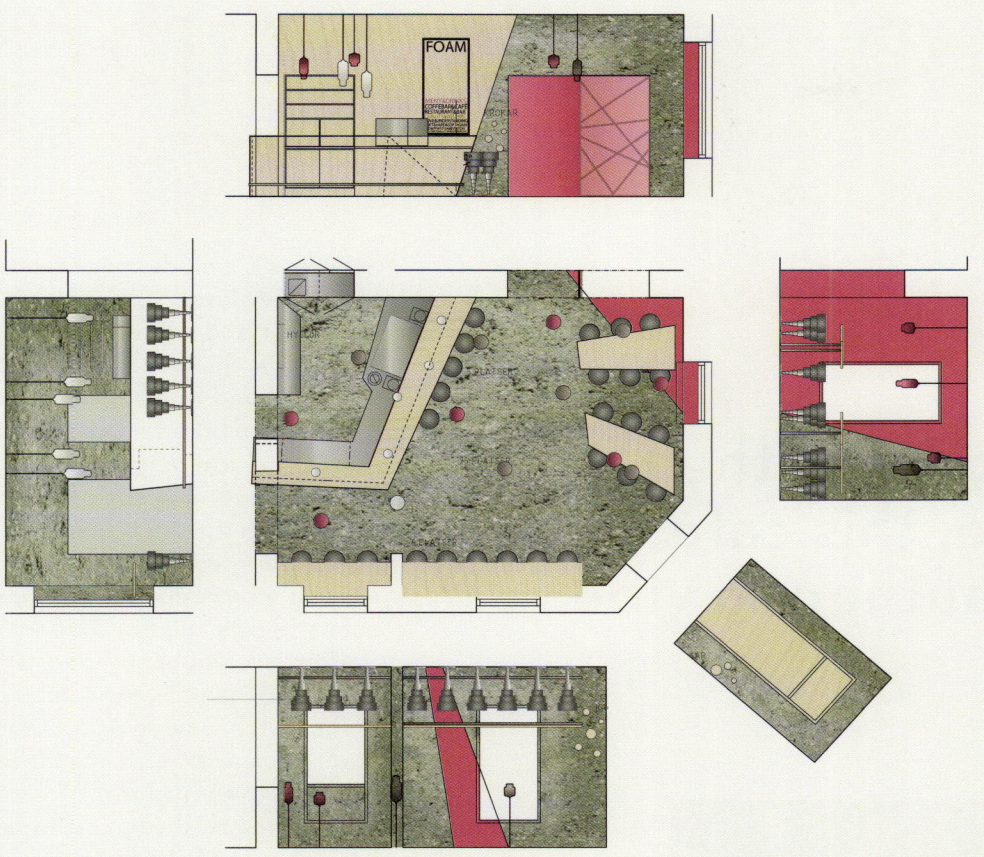

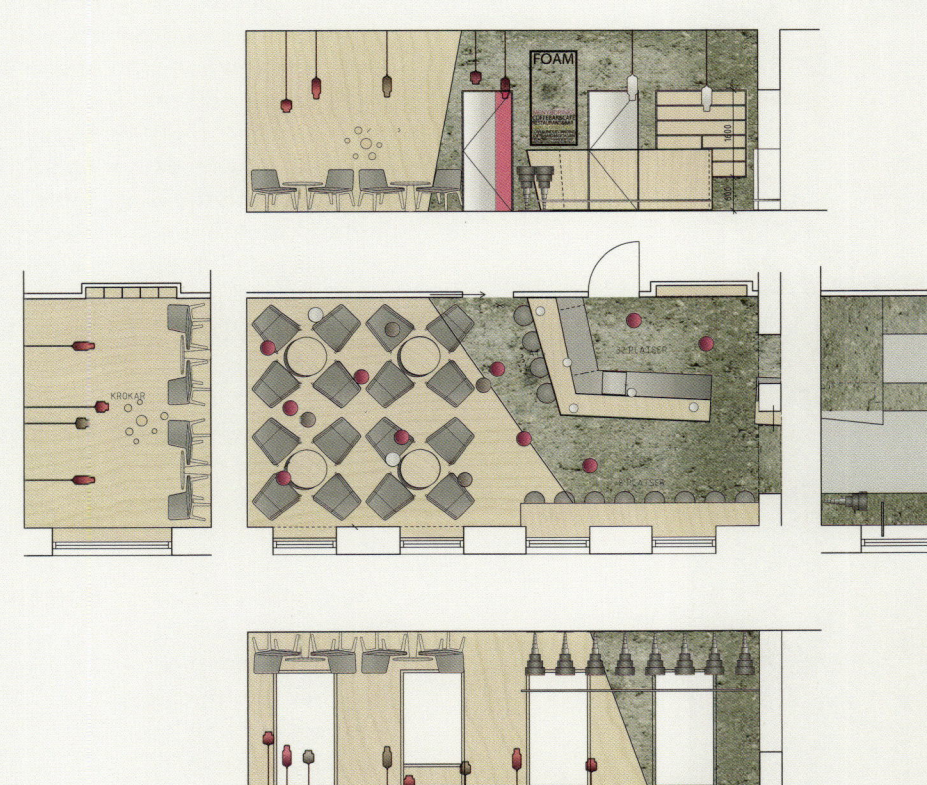

NOTE DESIGN STUDIO

Opposite The design focuses on those aspects of the project that give Café Schilders a timeless atmosphere.

CAFÉ SCHILDERS BY PUBBLIK

Evoking artists of the Dutch Golden Age, this café exudes an authentic vibe.

Photos courtesy of Pubblik

Schilders is a modern interpretation of a typical Amsterdam neighbourhood café: accessible and unpretentious. Designed by Pubblik, the team's aim was to create a space imbued with a timeless atmosphere featuring an urban touch that feels familiar to local patrons.

The first thing customers notice on entering the small space is a large portrait printed on a wooden panel, which is a reproduction of a work by painter Ferdinand Bol. This is a nod to this Amsterdam neighbourhood, where all the streets are named after famed painters of the Dutch Golden Age – which is also how the café got its name (*schilder* is the Dutch word for painter).

For the relatively small space, Pubblik opted for simplicity, but with a surprising mix of materials. A blend of contemporary, (re)used and handmade materials generates a unique air with a lively and informal vibe. Materials range from fine dark-wood panelling to black metro tiles, antique mirrors, a brass surface on the bar counter and bright green colour accents. The second-hand chairs and bar stools were given a new lease on life with leather upholstery and, combined with the brass table tops, give a modern twist to the low seating area. The ceiling is highlighted with a structured array of metal pendant lamps, in a similar green colour. Decades ago, the building used to be a butcher shop, and an old butcher block is incorporated at one end of the bar, providing a balance between authentic and new. •

The wooden stepladder at the end of the bar is for staff only and provides access to the custom-made beer barrels stored overhead.

Where Amsterdam, the Netherlands
Opening July 2011
Client Robbert Ros
Designer Pubblik → p.587
Floor space 70 m²
Capacity 48 seats

The club's logo was designed in the same colours as the beautiful façade.

Where Ghent, Belgium
Opening March 2011
Client Club 69
Designer Glenn Sestig Architects → p.583
Floor space 69 m²
Capacity 200 guests

CLUB 69 BY GLENN SESTIG ARCHITECTS

A neon pink and purple modern club space juxtaposed with vintage sporting elements.

Photos Jean Pierre Gabriel

'Don't stop the party!' When it comes to clubs, Glenn Sestig Architects are dead serious. Do not ask early-nighters to design a club. Regulars of after-parties during fashion week, Ibiza Indian summers and Miami Design Week, they like to dance and know what it takes to lure people onto the dance floor.

For this fifth club Glen Sestig Architects designed, the challenge lay in its size, rather limited in floor space: this was about making a packed club look roomy and an empty club look packed. The new owners wanted to give their Club 69 a totally new look, but how to go about it with only 69 m² to work your magic on? Given the music the designers like to dance to as inspiration, the obvious answer lay in the lighting and colours. The LED lighting moving in colour and rhythm with the music gives the whole space more volume and encourages people to let loose. Mirrors on the columns supporting the ceiling accentuate this digital display of lines and give a sense of infinity.

Acoustics are equally high on the priority list for a club, and here Glenn Sestig Architects made use of white wood/wool cement boards for the top end of the walls and kept a wooden floor. Added touches, not seen before in a club, are the natural leather vintage gym accessories to lean and sit on, providing a nice contrast to the contemporary atmosphere in both texture and shape. With their worn-out appearance they exude an appeal crucial to a club – a feel-good factor, a familiarity. Needless to say, this will be the starting point for many parties to remember! •

Opposite Columns and beams have been covered by mirrors to make the small club look bigger.

CLUB 69

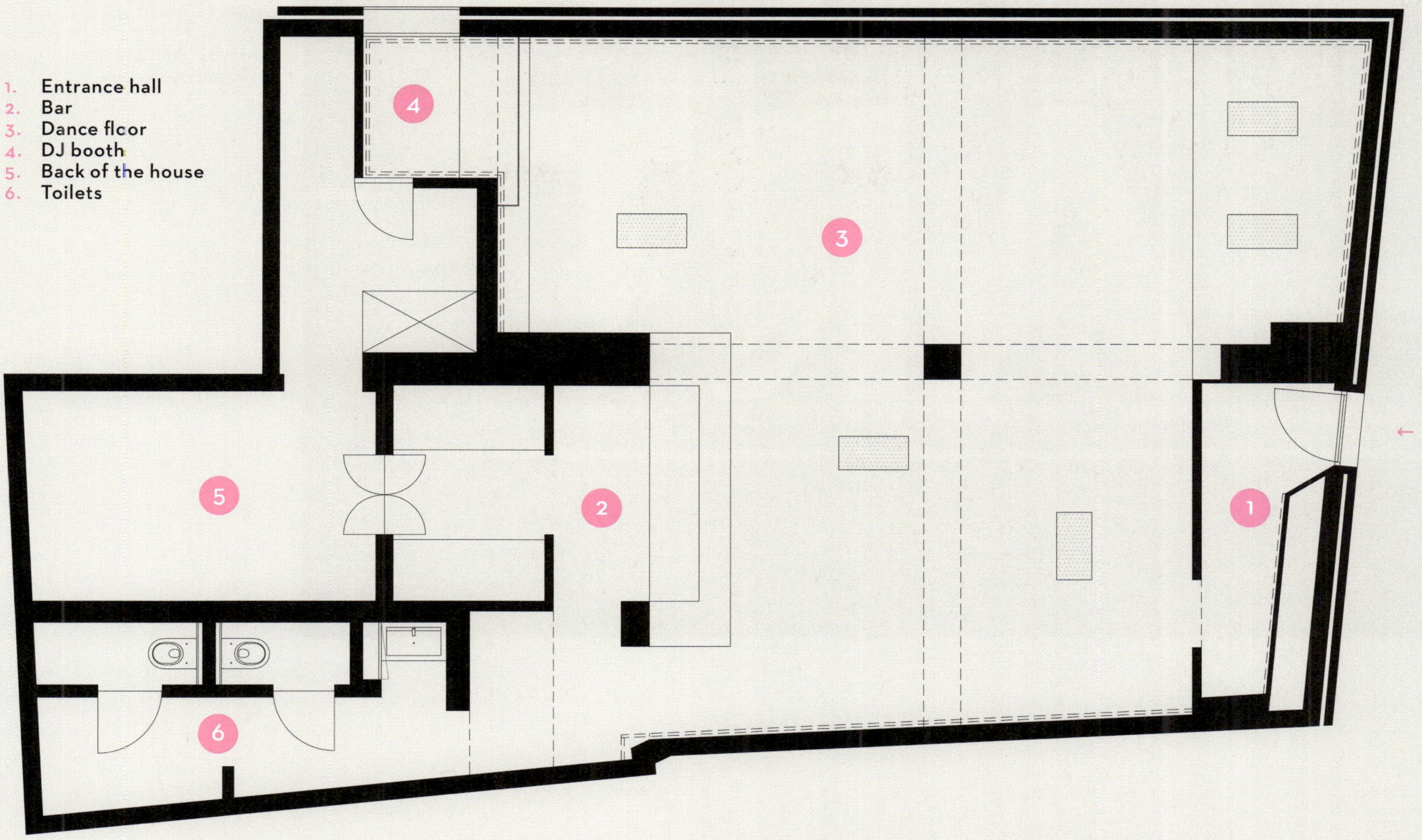

1. Entrance hall
2. Bar
3. Dance floor
4. DJ booth
5. Back of the house
6. Toilets

THE CHALLENGE WAS ABOUT MAKING A PACKED CLUB LOOK ROOMY AND AN EMPTY CLUB LOOK PACKED

A computer rendering of the interior seen from the DJ booth.

Opposite top A view of the DJ booth.

Opposite bottom Vintage gym pommel horse benches are the only 'furniture pieces' in the club.

A detailed image of the wood/wool cement boards used for better acoustics.

GLENN SESTIG ARCHITECTS

If clubbers have any doubts about the art on the walls being real, a lighting installation also spells it out.

Opposite The furniture is custom designed by Parolio.

CLUB MUSÉE BY PAROLIO & EUPHORIA LAB

A vibrant space for clubbing amid arty backdrops.

Photos Maria Primo

Where Madrid, Spain
Opening December 2010
Client Club Musée
Designer Parolio & Euphoria Lab → p.587
Floor space 400 m²
Capacity 300 guests

The brief for Club Musée – a newcomer in the competitive nightlife of Madrid – was to create a club and multi-use space with an international and powerful identity. That was the goal set by owners Fernando Nicolas and Jacobo Dominguez and their associates when Parolio & Euphoria Lab was commissioned to take on the project.

Parolio produced a concept and branding identity that merges the added cultural value of an art gallery with the exciting and colourful universe of the club scene. The result is a stimulating mix of streamlined interior design, dramatic structures and art. All the custom-made furniture items have been treated as sculptures, upholstered in multiple fabrics to create a 'colour block' patchwork effect. In the VIP room, and in the seating alcoves, the artwork is printed on fabric that decorates the cushioned walls and padded panelling. The hues of the sofas give the impression that they are an extension of the large photographs and works of art that envelop the space. Elsewhere, columns and surfaces are covered in black glass and mirrors in geometric shapes with illuminated borders.

Photography, video installations and illustrations by the designer as well as such renowned artists as Paco Peregrín, Robert Bartholot and Glenn Hillario are on display in the club, making it a complete cultural experience. On the dance floor, a floating DJ table is completed by an installation of 3-m-wide LED tubes on the wall and an illumination of geometric shapes overhead. •

Behind the DJ LED tubes, more often found lighting up aquariums, emanate a blue glow.

The way the mirrored walls are positioned gives the club a kaleidoscopic perspective.

Dramatic colour structures and art illuminate the space.

THE COLOURS ARE AN EXTENSION OF THE WORKS OF ART THAT ENVELOP THE SPACE

PAROLIO & EUPHORIA LAB

Opposite The sleek, solid and elegant Corian counter was treated as a monolithic object in the design process.

CRISTINI BY ANDREA LUPACCHINI ARCHITETTO

Contemporary décor for a bar with a chameleon-like character.

Photos Francesco Galli

Functional and visually attractive, the layered panels weave pathways overhead.

Where Albano Laziale, Italy
Opening March 2010
Client Andrea Cristini
Designer Andrea Lupacchini Architetto → p.578
Floor space 65 m²
Capacity 10 seats (inside), 16 seats (outside)

In a suburb 25 km to the southeast of Rome, Andrea Lupacchini was commissioned to rework a 65-m space in the town of Albano Laziale. There has been a family-run hospitality business at this location for many years and the new owners wanted it transformed into a contemporary space with a chameleon-like character – it needed to accommodate everything from early-morning breakfast to lunch and afternoon gelato, right through to late-night drinks at the bar. To create a unique architectural identity, the designers opted for organic forms that intersect overhead, hovering in space to visually expand its perception thanks to the reflective materials used.

Surfaces are wrapped in layers of crisp white Corian and positioned against walls and ceilings painted the colour of dark chocolate. The opaque choice of colour functions as a warm and homogeneous background and sets a theatrical backdrop, from which the architectural elements emerge like actors illuminated by spotlights. The white polished surfaces are developed in horizontal and vertical alignments, morphing from the geometric bar counter on one side, up and over the ceiling and down the other side, forming shelving and seating elements along the way. The panels sweep overhead, discretely concealing pipe work and overlapping at junctions to form functional voids where pendant lights can be snugly positioned.

The shiny surfaces create a three-dimensional décor that has an elegance and lightness that visually expands the small space. Furnished with white tables and white leather seats, there is also a dark wooden platform positioned in front of the bar. When the glass doors of the façade are fully opened, the bar space is extended in a seamless continuity between inside and out.

Curving Corian shelves are recessed into the white panels or affixed to the chocolate-coloured walls.

View from the back of the bar, showing how the terrace area opens onto the street.

WHITE POLISHED SURFACES
WRAP AROUND THE SPACE

ANDREA LUPACCHINI ARCHITETTO

D'ESPRESSO BY NEMAWORKSHOP

A small café that twists perception.

Opposite Visual perspectives are shifted, with the 'floor' ending up on the wall behind the leather-clad couch.

Located on Madison Avenue, the espresso bar conceptually and literally turns a normal room sideways, creating a striking identity for the emerging brand. The client approached nemaworkshop with the aim of building a unique espresso brand and developing a creative environment that connects to its location on Madison Avenue near Grand Central Station.

Inspired by the Bryant Park Library nearby, nemaworkshop designed a bar that is straightforward in a simple twisted way – take a library and turn it on its side. The book-lined shelves become the floor and ceilings, and the wood floor ends up on one wall, while the pendants protrude sideways from the opposite wall. To produce the bookshelves on the floor, the space was lined with sepia-toned full-size photographs of books printed on custom tiles. The custom tiles run along the floor, up the 4.5 m back wall and across the ceiling. The frosted glass wall behind the service counter illuminates the space and the wall directly opposite is clad in dark brown herringbone parquet flooring.

The thrust of this concept finds expression in the lighting and materiality, and ultimately the space gives definition to the emerging brand. •

The glass façade gives passers-by a clear view of the seemingly book-laden floor, wall and ceiling.

Where New York, United States
Opening September 2010
Client D'espresso
Designer nemaworkshop → p.586
Floor space 40 m²
Capacity 12 seats

DA RE BY ANDREA LUPACCHINI ARCHITETTO

Where Rome, Italy
Opening September 2011
Client Re Lu Ve
Designer Andrea Lupacchini Architetto → p.578
Floor space 60 m²
Capacity 10 guests

Artisan meets royalty in an Italian ice cream bar.

Photos Francesco Galli

A simple illuminated façade is sufficient to entice customers inside.

Opposite Natural colours and materials are combined in this tasteful décor.

Opposite A series of original black-and-white photos depicting local architecture, characters and culture are displayed on the side wall.

The hand-written menu board details delicious ice-cream recipes, some of which are 50 years old.

CINNAMON, LIQUORICE AND CHOCOLATE CHIPS MIRROR THE INTERIOR'S COLOUR PALETTE

When in Rome, what could be better than eating gelato fit for a king? Ice cream bar Da Re – which translated from Italian means 'the king's' – was established by its owners as a place for customers to delight in an artisanal product of the highest quality, aiming to offer the best ice cream in the city. Andrea Lupacchini was commissioned to realize an interior for this *gelateria* that would stay true to the original architecture of the building, dating back to the early 20th century, and that is warm and welcoming, with a homely atmosphere.

The first steps involved revealing the true personality of the building, stripping back the plasterwork and restoring the space so that its original brickwork was laid bare. With this natural envelope in place, Lupacchini proceeded to integrate the space with some core design elements. A key feature is the use of natural materials, such as the hexagonal slate tiles on the floor and the whitewashed wooden planks that line the counter front, all of which complement the exposed bricks. Solid colours and interesting shapes give texture to the small space. All the furniture and fittings are made of epoxy power-coated steel painted anthracite grey. A rich, dark chocolate colour coats the back wall, which to one side discretely houses a refrigerator for cakes and desserts behind a double-fronted door, and to the other has recessed alcoves containing precious vases inside which are some of the natural ingredients used in the ice cream – cinnamon, liquorice and chocolate chips – which also mirror the interior's colour palette.

Lighting is an important aspect, with dimmable spotlights around the perimeter highlighting the contrast between the surfaces of the chocolate-brown and brick walls. Overhead, large steel pendant lampshades of differing dimensions have been painted glossy white. Suspended at different heights through holes cut into the ceiling, they have been installed as a distinctive visual detail to appear as upside-down 'cups', representing the various sizes of ice cream cones available for the customers' favourite gelato favours. •

ANDREA LUPACCHINI ARCHITETTO

DAS NEUE KUBITSCHECK BY DESIGNLIGA

Where **Munich, Germany**
Opening **June 2010**
Client **Armin Stegbauer**
Designer **Designliga → p.581**
Floor space **65 m²**
Capacity **16 seats (inside), 12 seats (outside)**

Give back that gateau, granny.

Photos Pascal Gambarte

Contemporary cakes are at the core of this chilled out and equally contemporary café.

Opposite The interior is furnished with simple benches along with designer chairs and light fittings.

Creativity mixes with classic ingredients to conjure up some tasty treats for customers.

The hall towards the toilets is as colourful as the main café area.

Opposite The Persian carpets remind guests of the previous tenants of the space.

German studio Designliga created the new interior and branding for this patisserie owned by a Munich punk on a crusade against doilies. The client's brief was to revamp the confectioner's tradition for the modern age, but not without taking on board some endearing aspects of Germany's confectionery culture.

The venue is located in Munich's Westend, a district steeped in history that houses a cross section of social classes, coexisting in mutual understanding and respect. One of the main goals was to create a place that feels as if it has always been there. Designliga had to find a way to integrate it into the district: to pay homage to the multicultural location a mixture of different furniture pieces was used. Two long benches divide the café in two, each with a different look.

The design team decided to keep some of the elements that refer to the previous tenants – a men's Islamic association. The men met every evening and played chess and backgammon in a space that was covered in Persian carpets. The carpets stayed and a chess board is integrated into one of the tables; guests can even buy chocolate chess figures to play a game.

As one of the tasks was to retain some of the old confectionery culture, the design team used wooden panels to cover the counter, as a reference to old bakeries. The most striking part of the design is the jumble of boxes displaying cakes, mounted on the wall above the serving counter. The white wooden cubicles refer to an explosion of flour coming from the kitchen area, which is right behind the counter. But it is also an explosion of creativity from the kitchen, showcasing the results of that creativity – the real cakes.

Besides the interior design Designliga was also responsible for the corporate design, in line with the company's new slogan: 'Fuck the Cake Mix.' •

DESIGNLIGA

Solid colours, a striped counter front and a floral fabric panel hanging from one wall form part of the playful décor in this pop venue.

Where **Hilversum, the Netherlands**
Opening **September 2010**
Client **De Vorstin**
Designer **Beers|Brickworks** → **p.579**
Floor space **265 m²**
Capacity **300 guests**

DE VORSTIN BY BEERS| BRICKWORKS

A Dutch high-tech edifice with a warm and traditional atmosphere.

Photos Colinda Boeren

De Vorstin is a pop music venue, but one built as an architectural structure full of character rather than a square box. The building, designed by de Architekten Cie., is high-tech, with a lot of glass and steel and no right angles. The brief for the interior design – by design team Beers|Brickworks – was to give this high-tech edifice a warm, contemporary bar with a traditional atmosphere.

The concept Beers|Brickworks came up with was high-tech versus low-tech, with a swathe of warm, brown materials as its most striking element. The swathe goes through several phases, starting with three seats, moving across the dance floor, onto the podium, turning into a large bench, going back to the floor and ending in another bench in front of an enormous wall print. Wood and leather alternate in this path, with a beautiful leather floor as an extraordinary detail – which also provides great acoustics.

The benches invite guests to sit in an informal atmosphere on different levels, as in an amphitheatre. The back functions as a bar table, creating an area for drinking and talking. The bar is made of wooden laths with LED lights behind them. The shades above the bar mimic the building's exterior. The speaker lamps were custom-designed by Beers|Brickworks, creating an atmosphere reminiscent of listening to old LPs in an attic bedroom. Brown velour curtains can be drawn across the glass façades, so that special lighting can still be used for performances on summer evenings. The venue's logo is projected onto the curtains, providing a special effect. •

A light installation incorporates a number of music speakers.

Opposite top The stepped-style seating has been crafted to afford visitors the best view of the stage when a band is playing.

Opposite bottom The large print of a photo by Mark Janssen adorns one wall and adds to the vibrant atmosphere.

BEERS|BRICKWORKS

DISHOOM POP-UP BEACH BAR BY HONEST ENTERTAINMENT

Opposite With some paint and a creative reuse of plastic and bottle tops, a bright and cheerful interior was realized.

An Indian-inspired pop-up beach bar, creating a colourful oasis in the heart of London.

Photos James Bedford and Sim Canetty-Clarke

Sunset painted palettes created a splash of sunshine across the concrete clad Queen Elizabeth Hall.

Where London, United Kingdom
Opening May 2011
Client Dishoom
Designer Honest Entertainment → p.583
Floor space 160 m²
Capacity 92 guests

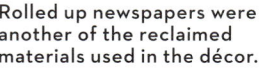

Rolled up newspapers were another of the reclaimed materials used in the décor.

Dishoom is an Indian restaurant based in Covent Garden inspired by the faded elegance of Bombay's 19th-century cafés. In 2011, its owners commissioned Honest Entertainment to take its ramshackle Bombay vibes, in the form of a pop-up beach bar, to London's South Bank for five months over the summer. The brief called for a flavour of the real Bombay as well as a colourful and lively counterpoint to the concrete modernist architecture that dominates one of London's principal art districts.

The team began the project by delving into the Hindi language, where they discovered the word *jugaad*, meaning 'making do', 'reusing' or 'creative improvisation'. This provided a springboard to address many specific aspects of the brief: positioning the brand as cool, forward-thinking, knowledgeable, fun and 'owned' by its people. By channelling an ever-increasing awareness and desire for sustainable design, it also gave Dishoom a valuable PR story. Most of the materials used for the design were recycled, found or second-hand, and were reinvented and up-cycled to create a welcoming and homely vibe.

Guests entered the beach bar via an arched walkway festooned with an array of multicoloured, used carrier bags, with reclaimed timber railway sleepers lovingly restored and used to make up exterior tables and benches. Dymo tags and clues throughout the space told the story of the origins of the re-fashioned materials: a wall constructed from tightly rolled newspapers, plastic bottles recycled and pressed to make coloured psychedelic bar fascia, 'junk' rescued from skips and street corners reinvented to produce textural intrigue on the walls. A patchwork of old freight pallets were given a sunset scenic painted wash to create a unique exterior cladding against the grey urban backdrop of the Queen Elizabeth Hall.

The bar was all about fun, as this moustache clock indicates.

A POP-UP BEACH BAR WITH BOMBAY VIBES

Opposite top Recycled glass jam jars with filament bulbs were hung over the dining tables.

Opposite bottom Pallets painted white surround the kitchen area.

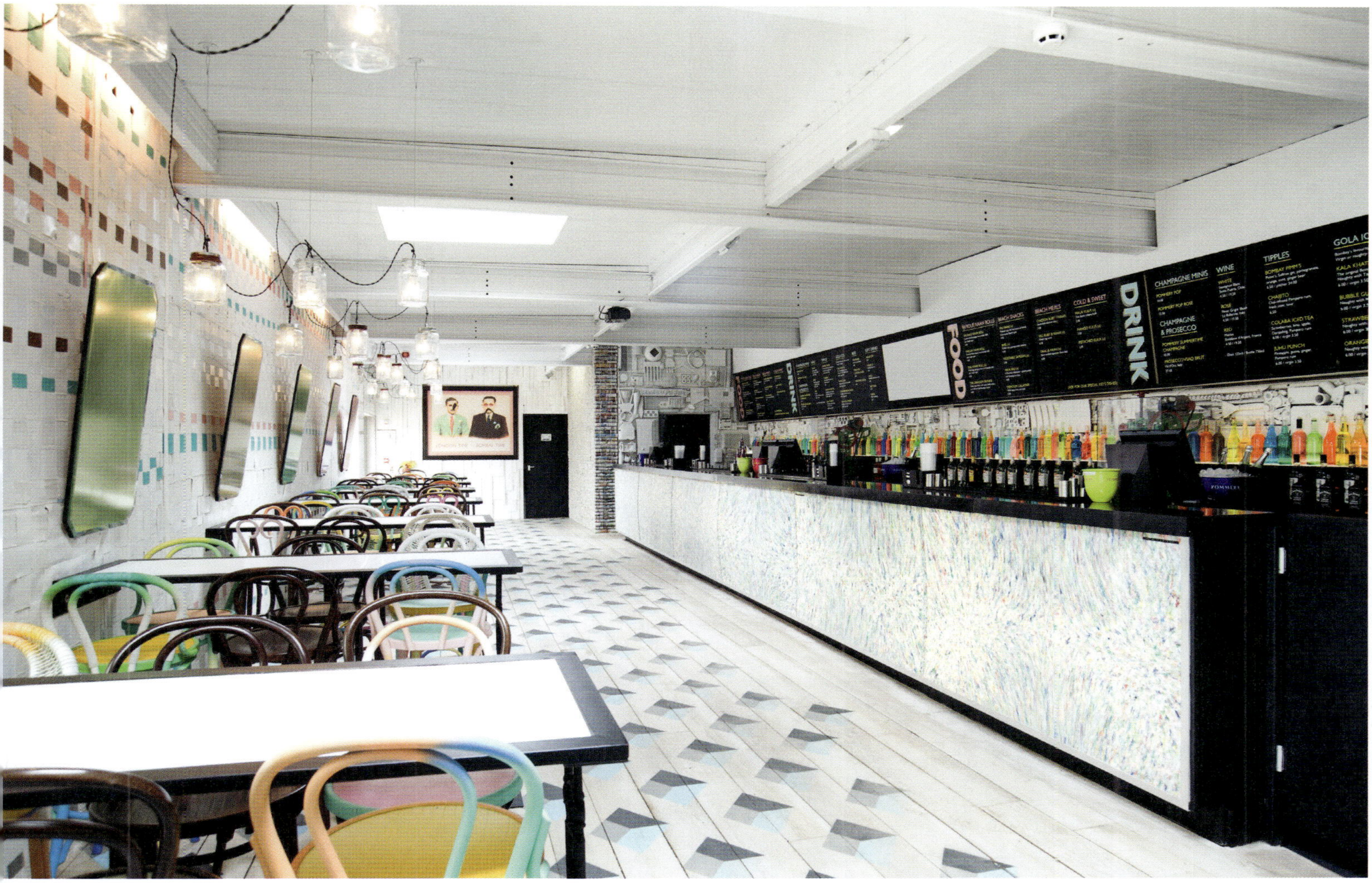
FOOD
DRINK
CHAMPAGNE MINIS
WINE
TIPPLES

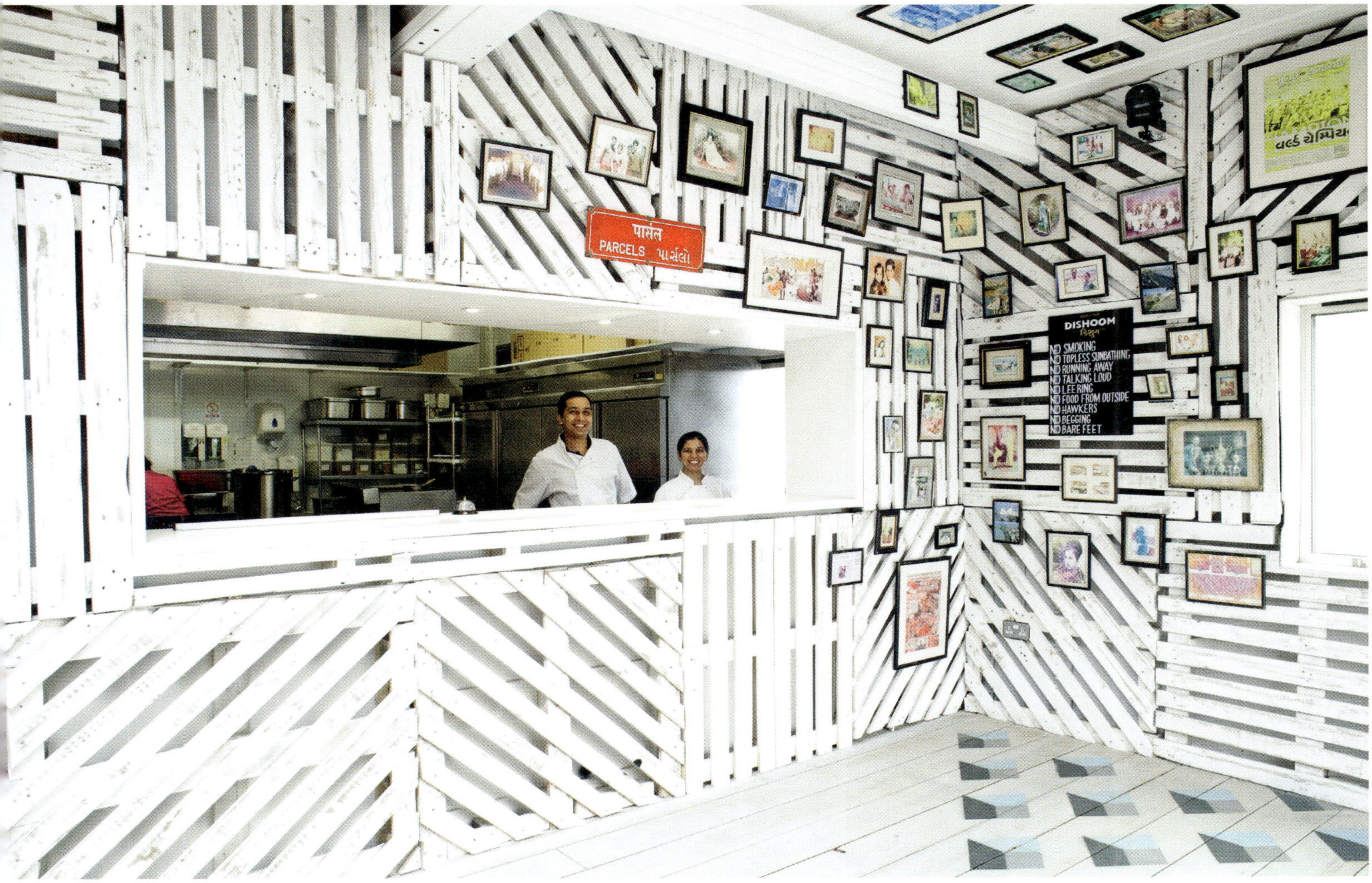
पार्सल
PARCELS પાર્સલો
DISHOOM
NO SMOKING
NO TOPLESS SUNBATHING
NO RUNNING AWAY
NO TALKING LOUD
NO LEERING
NO FOOD FROM OUTSIDE
NO HAWKERS
NO BEGGING
NO BARE FEET

Side view

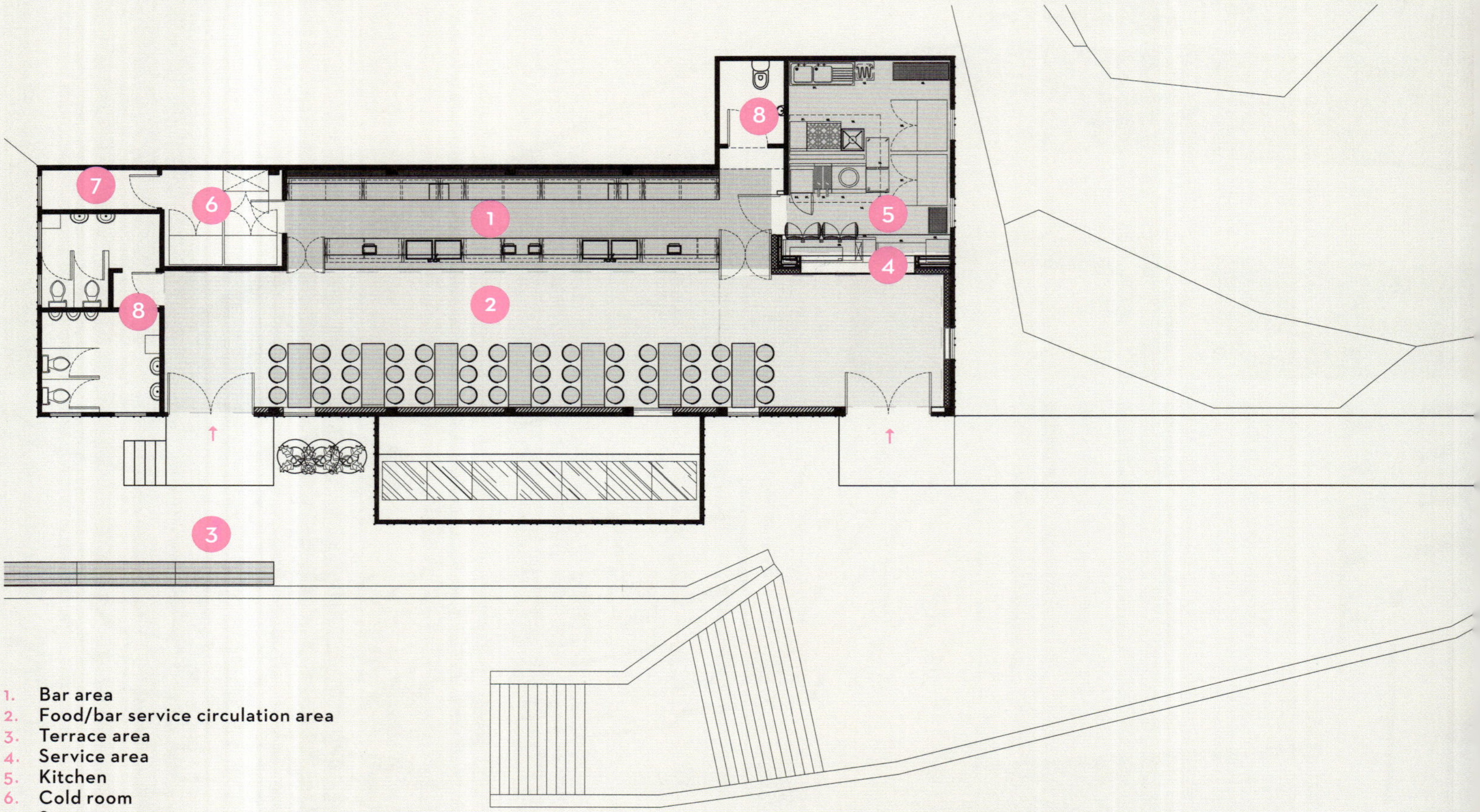

1. Bar area
2. Food/bar service circulation area
3. Terrace area
4. Service area
5. Kitchen
6. Cold room
7. Storage
8. Toilets

THE CORE CONCEPT WAS JUGAAD, MEANING 'MAKING DO' IN HINDI

Above and left Honest's in-house visual of the pop-up bar exterior, indicating some of the fun and games visitors were going to be involved in.

Close-up of the woven panel made of colourful ribbons.

DUYCKER CAFÉ BY BEERS|BRICKWORKS

Where Hoofddorp, the Netherlands
Opening January 2011
Client Podium Duycker
Designer Beers|Brickworks → p.579
Floor space 150 m²
Capacity 140 guests

A cool and poppy café which fits right in with the next door music hall.

Photos Colinda Boeren

Hoofddorp's culture square, which combines the local theatre, music venues, cultural centre and library, had no space allocated to a café. Impossible, thought the director of the Duycker music hall, and he asked Beers|Brickworks to convert a passage connecting the library and the music halls. The passage, never meant to house a bar, is genuinely unique. The dimensions of the space – 14 m high and very narrow – while spectacular, also challenged the designers in terms of creating an intimate, cosy atmosphere.

The lower part of the wall, up to 3 m, is clad with wooden slats, laid horizontally. Above this, black fabrics like velvet and smooth and crushed satin are combined into an oversized patchwork. Lamps dribble down from the ceiling. All of this creates an invisible added layer, giving the space a more human scale. The slats vary in width and thickness, turning into a display unit for bottles stored on their sides behind the bar. Above the bar, the designers made an installation with a larger version of the shades of the lamps that hang from the ceiling.

In front of the bar is a platform that serves as a lounge. The bench and stools are upholstered in denim and a picture of a frenzied crowd decorates the wall. Bar tables connect the lounge area with the bar area. The combination of wooden slats, black fabric, poster lamps, contemporary chandeliers and denim give the café a tough, cool and poppy feel, fitting right in with the music halls next door. •

The high ceiling is emphasized by an eye-catching contemporary chandelier, with pendant lights hanging from draped electrical wires.

Opposite Illuminating the bar area are tubular-shaped lamps, of a similar design albeit larger and aligned in a more orderly manner than those hanging high above.

BEERS|BRICKWORKS

ELBGOLD BY GIORGIO GULLOTTA ARCHITEKTEN

Where **Hamburg, Germany**
Opening **October 2010**
Client **Elbgold Röstkaffee**
Designer **Giorgio Gullotta Architekten** → p.583
Floor space **400 m²**
Capacity **30 seats**

Rustic charm abounds in this Hamburg coffee roasting facility and café.

Photos *Jochen Stüber*

Hamburg, a major trading centre for raw coffee, presented the perfect setting for a roasting facility. The owners of the Elbgold coffee brand found the ideal place to indulge their passion for coffee at the Schanzen-Höfe, next to the meat-packing district. The increasing demand of customers led to a combination of roasting facility, shop and café. Architect Giorgio Gullotta was asked to design the interior; the challenge in this project was creating a harmonious blend between the roasting business and a cosy café.

The focus of the overall concept was a compact, material-oriented space with high recognition value. In addition to the business activities, the 400-m² site provides sufficient space for special events and seminars. Visitors get a chance to witness the coffee-roasting process inside a charming historic factory building. A sliding divider made of woven Corten steel separates the café and shop area from the production facilities. A total of twelve custom-made coffee silos at one end of the venue allow guests to select the Arabica bean of their choice. The combination of luxurious materials such as oiled oak and gold-lacquer surfaces creates a fascinating contrast to the existing industrial architecture. Solid Italian wood furniture by Riva 1920 is combined with individual artisan pieces. To match the antique 1930s' 'Probat' roaster, the Gullotta team installed vintage French industrial factory lights. The Elbgold venue's interior was designed as painstakingly and lovingly as they treat their coffee. •

A sliding divider of Corten steel separates the café from the production facilities.

Stored in bags here, 30 different fine fair-trade Arabica's from all over the world are served by Elbgold.

Opposite Twelve custom-made coffee silos steal the show in the café.

At the back of the ground-floor level is the retail aspect of Ginette.

GINETTE BY RAËD ABILLAMA ARCHITECTS

A multifunctional Beirut venue where eating and shopping meet.

Photos Joe Kesrouani

Where Beirut, Lebanon
Opening December 2010
Client Ginette
Designer Raëd Abillama Architects → p.58
Floor space 301 m²
Capacity 26 seats (inside), 36 seats (outside)

Café and concept store Ginette lies in the heart of Gemmayzeh, a neighbourhood of Beirut with a range of bars and restaurants. Designed by Raëd Abillama Architects as an elegant multifunctional space, the interior architecture of this café has been kept to a subtle minimum.

The design team's aim was to merge all different components of the space into a natural flow, from the café, terrace and retail area on the ground floor to the gallery and USM furniture showroom on the first floor. Details are functional with clean lines, emphasized by the choice of materials: from the slabs of marble used for the café counter to the fair-faced concrete for the flooring and staircase, with its simple glass balustrade. Continuity has been maintained between the terrace and interior with the light wood tables and use of designer furniture, including Eames Plastic Side Chairs. The entrance of the café space is light, thanks to the white walls – painted or tiled – and the large oval window that dominates the façade. The window is constructed from an industrial-era system of small glass panels set in a steel framework and allows views from the terrace directly into the mezzanine-type first floor area, and vice versa. On entering the building, customers will notice the initial double-height space, emphasized by the delicately folded white paper chandelier designed by an origami artist. Custom-made reflector-plate lamps illuminate the eatery space and directional spotlights above the mesh ceiling are used in the retail area towards the back of the ground floor. •

Opposite top From the terrace, the imposing glass-front façade gives customers a clear view inside.

Opposite bottom Concrete stairs direct customers down to the café and shop, or upstairs to the furniture showroom.

RAËD ABILLAMA ARCHITECTS

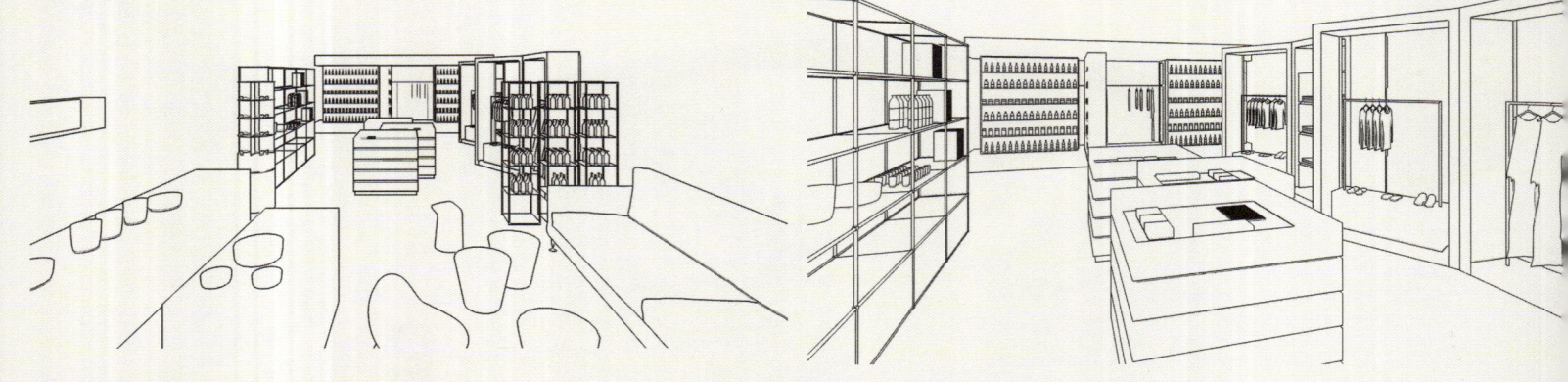

Drawing of the customers' perspectives as they move from the café into the shop at the rear of the lower level.

Renderings of the outside and inside dining areas.

First floor

Ground floor

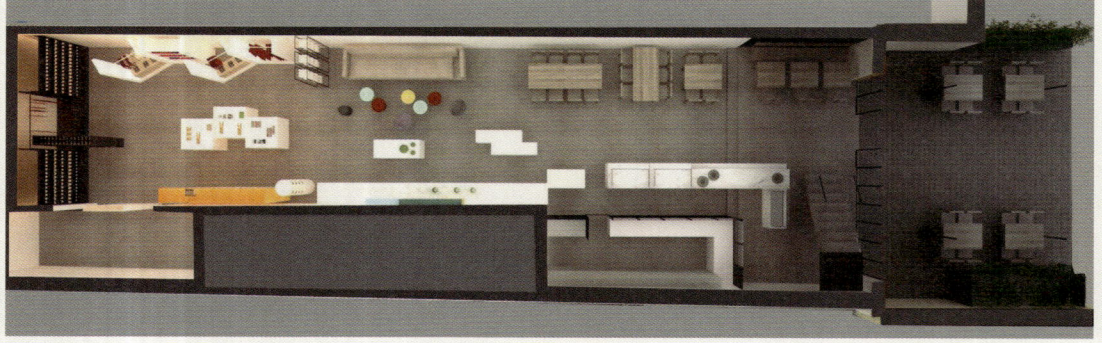

Hinged shelving detail

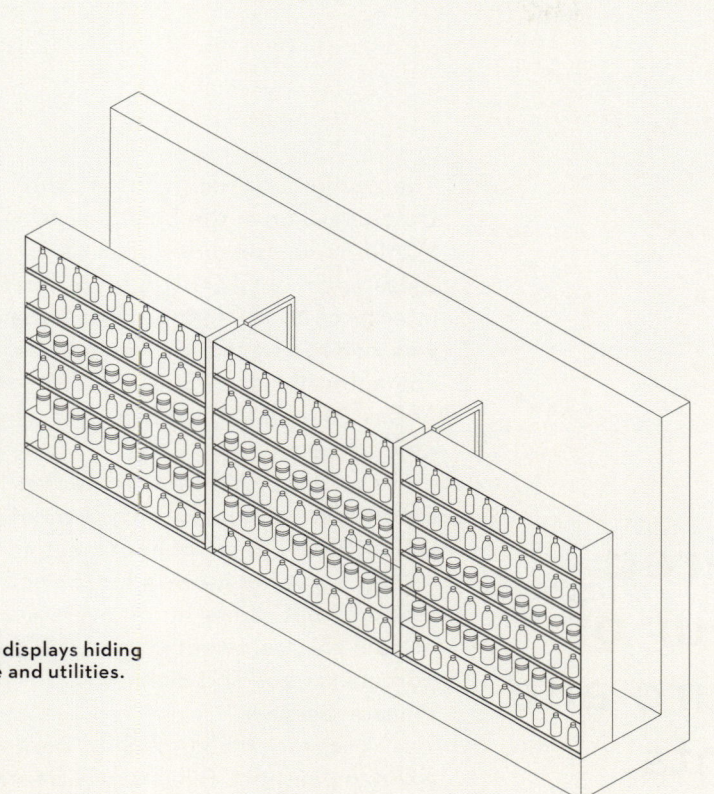

Closed displays hiding storage and utilities.

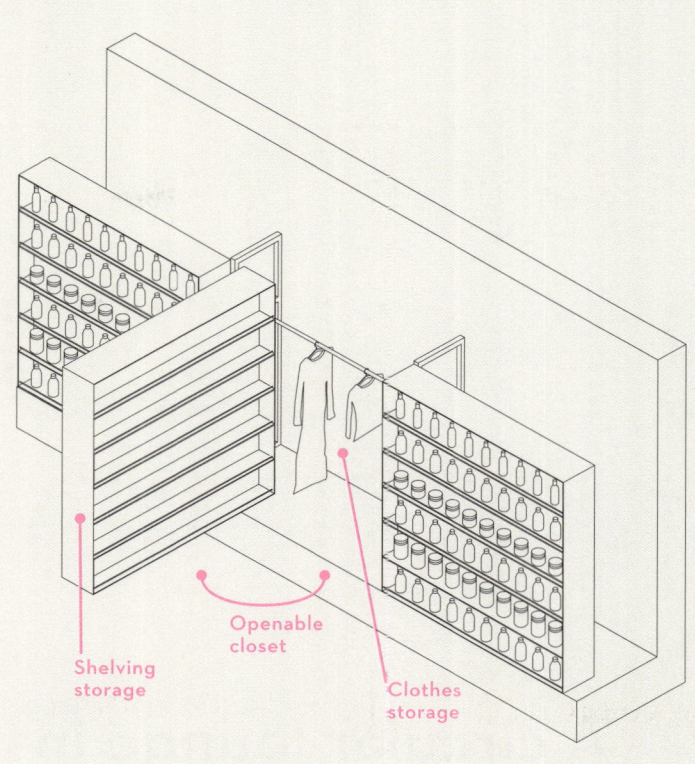

Open configuration.

Shelving storage
Openable closet
Clothes storage

First floor

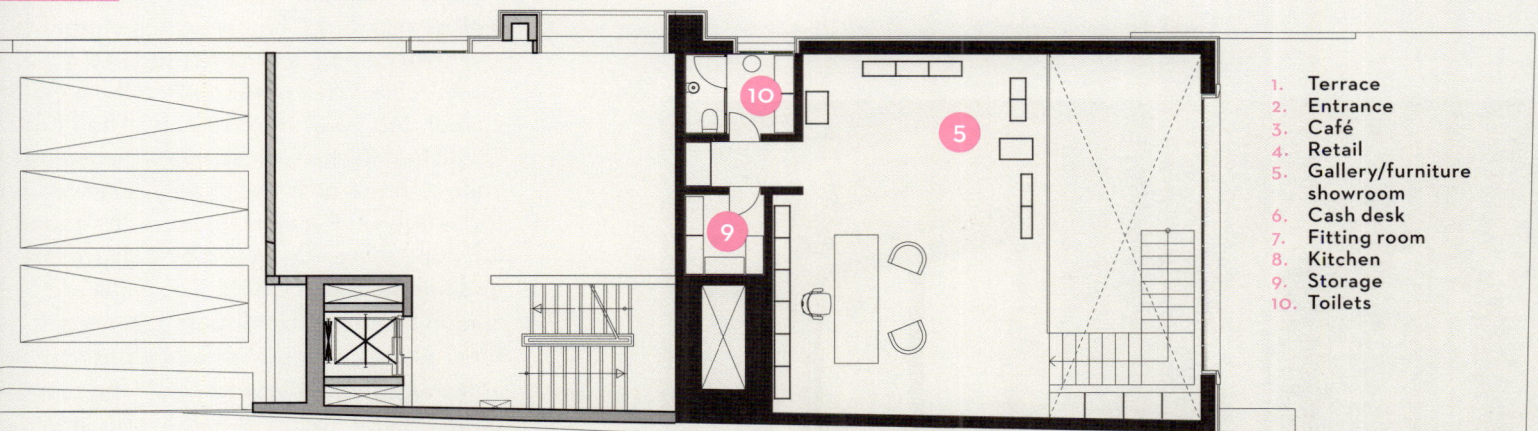

1. Terrace
2. Entrance
3. Café
4. Retail
5. Gallery/furniture showroom
6. Cash desk
7. Fitting room
8. Kitchen
9. Storage
10. Toilets

Ground floor

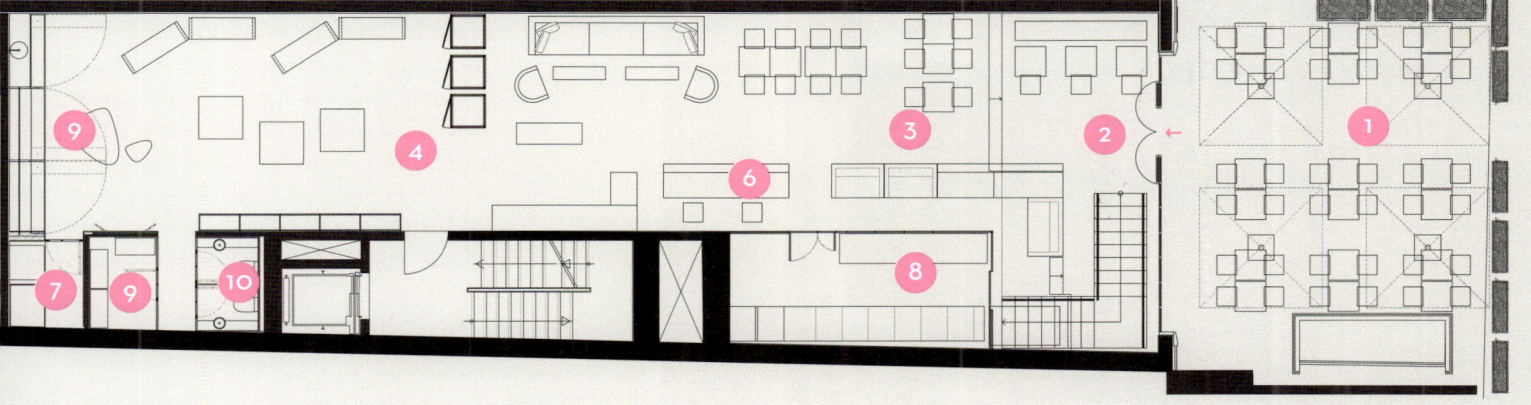

HAPPY VIP BY CLOUD-9 INTERIOR DESIGN

Where Shanghai, China
Opening May 2010
Client John Kormeling Architect
Designer CLOUD-9 interior design → p.58
Floor space 368 m²
Capacity 140 guests

A circular lounge inspired by the glitz and glamour of European royalty culture and Chinese iconic elements.

Photos Ingmar Swalue

The architect of Happy Street, the Dutch Pavilion at the Shanghai 2010 World Expo, asked designer Karin Rijlaarsdam of CLOUD-9 to design the interior of its VIP lounge. Rijlaarsdam was inspired by the festive and gregarious character of Happy Street and the shape of the VIP building itself, akin to a huge golden crown.

For Happy VIP she created an extravagant and joyful environment, almost an overdose of happiness and glitter. 'I was not looking for too serious a design, but rather for an overstatement of bold shapes, sweet colours, gold, porcelain, neon and diamonds,' Rijlaarsdam says.

A seasoned Shanghai resident with a Dutch passport, Rijlaarsdam creatively reinterprets elements freely from both worlds. For the design of the lounge she applied patterns and materials from Europe's fashion and royalty culture, as well as typically Chinese iconic elements.

The ceiling is ornamented like a gigantic baroque dress, with rich layers of suspended silver metal 'skirts'. The floor is finished in the Chinese imperial colour yellow, in the past exclusively reserved for the emperor. Every element in the round lofty space was designed by Rijlaarsdam and handmade in China. The walls are clad in specially developed porcelain tiles, a hand painted harlequin pattern and thousands of silver bows – the result of hours of meticulous handwork. The golden porcelain 'Happy VIP' tiles were inspired by the opulence of Shanghai's jet set and numerous VIP parties and VIP rooms in Chinese restaurants and clubs. The icing on the Happy VIP cake are the diamond-shaped lights, which Rijlaarsdam developed in China's porcelain city, Jingdezhen. Switched off, they seem to be solid sculptures; switched on, they turn into fragile glowing lanterns, enhancing the mesmerizing fairytale experience.

Every element in the round lofty space, like this huge golden bell light, was designed by Rijlaarsdam and made by hand in China.

The ceiling is adorned with layers of circular suspended metal mesh like a giant baroque dress.

A three-panel Chinese screen and hand-shaped pink lacquer columns adorn the lounge.

A close-up of the hand-carved golden porcelain 'Happy VIP' tiles.

Opposite Entrance area with an inviting organic security screen and door made of coloured glass to welcome the clients.

Where Utrecht, the Netherlands
Opening October 2011
Client Moos Mazid
Designer Workshop of Wonders → p.590
Floor space 200 m²
Capacity 80 guests

HI/LO BY WORKSHOP OF WONDERS

A smoking club with a split personality.

Photos Kasia Gatkowska

The 'sun' window lights up a 'heaven' filled with design furniture and lighting from Foscarini, Moroso and Hay.

The cubistic cloud-like forms of the reception desk and vending machine screen contrast harmoniously with the fluffy cloudscape of the wall art.

In the Netherlands, the sale of cannabis products is allowed in licensed 'coffeeshops', and Workshop of Wonders was commissioned to design one such smoking club in the city of Utrecht.

The brief asked for a contemporary high-end hospitality space in which customers can smoke in a context of security and comfort, using elements that make reference to an Arabic atmosphere inspired by the Moroccan roots of the owner. The interior concept was derived from the club's original name 'destination': as there are only two ultimate destinations – heaven and hell – Workshop of Wonders chose to recreate both.

For 'heaven', inspiration came from the idea of floating in a cloudscape: airy, light and high. This is depicted by fluffy clouds and a pinkish sunset wrapping around the white space. Shop Around was commissioned to create this wall art. Furthermore organic, curved shapes in the form of coloured glass elements are used at the entrance to control customer access. Custom-made cubistic cloudscapes create a sales counter and also screen off the vending machines. A circular yellow window has been incorporated into the back wall, fashioned as if it were the 'sun' through which light enters the space with radiating, dancing sun rays. A custom made circular couch together with the design lighting and furniture by Foscarini, Moroso and Hay add the final touch.

In contrast, when customers descend into 'hell', on the lower level, there is a much more mysterious atmosphere. This is a dark space, dimly lit and decorated with gold-chain curtains, large leather lounge couches, and Moroccan accessories. The space was inspired by the opium dens of the East, where one might stay for days on end under the influence.

This bipolar concept was given a new name Hi/Lo by Dietwee who are responsible for the graphic identity and branding of this high-end smoking club. Hi/Lo refers both to the heaven and hell concept and to the state a smoker can be in when either smoking weed or hash, being either high or stoned.

A secluded space on the lower level with large leather sofas is enveloped by a gold-chain curtain and illuminated with 'Cage' lights by Diesel.

THE LOWER LEVEL IS INSPIRED BY THE OPIUM DENS OF THE EAST

Once customers have descended into 'hell', they find themselves in a dark environment decorated with Moroccan tiles and accessories.

WORKSHOP OF WONDERS

The cloudscape/sunset wall art as created by Shop Around (→ p.588) and then translated into a wraparound wall covering for 'heaven'.

Dietwee - brand, design and communication (→ p.581) was responsible for the club's name, logo and visual identity.

A BIPOLAR CONCEPT OF 'HEAVEN AND HELL' IS AT THE ROOT OF THE CLUB'S INTERIOR DESIGN

Inspiration for the concept was taken from the *Cotton Candy Clouds* (2004, oil on linen, 75 x 100") painting by Will Cotton (left) and Brassaï's black-and-white self-portrait (right).
Courtesy of the Artist and Mary Boone Gallery

Basement

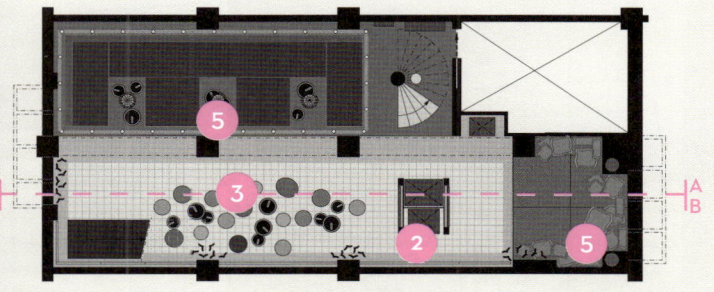

Ground floor

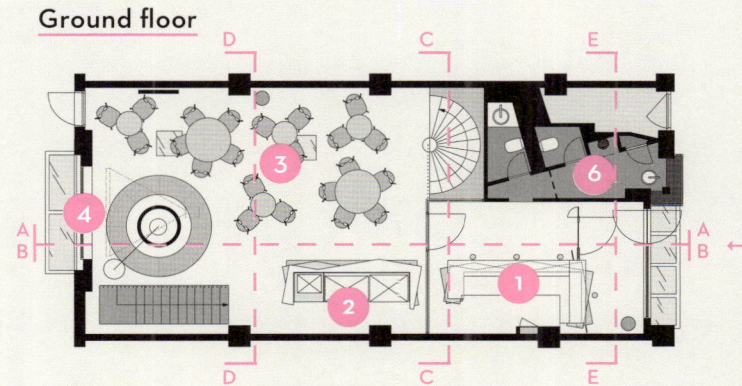

1. Sales counter
2. Vending machines
3. Seating area
4. Circular window
5. Lounge area
6. Toilets

Section AA

Section BB

Wall art

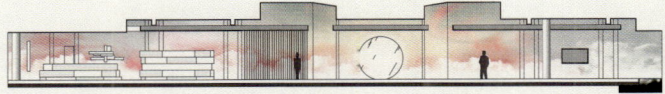

Design

Elevation

Section CC

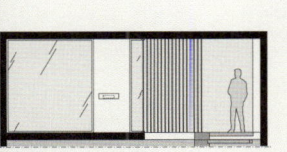

Section DD

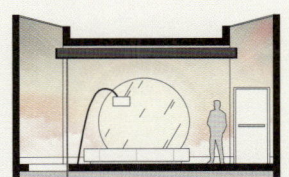

Section EE

HOUSE OF THE PURPLE

Opposite Retro design classics surround guests in the lounge, which has square wooden panels lining the walls.

HOUSE OF THE PURPLE BY ...,STAAT CREATIVE AGENCY

A members' club where everything is personally curated to resemble the home of a dear friend.

Photos Courtesy of ...,staat creative agency and Kasia Gatkowska

Where Seoul, South Korea
Opening April 2011
Client Hyundai Card
Designer ...,staat creative agency → p.578
Floor space 300 m²
Capacity 70 seats

In one corner, of the 'living room' a Drift bench by Amanda Levete can be seen.

...,STAAT CREATIVE AGENCY 293

Besides the interior design ...,staat creative agency was also responsible for the visual identity of the club as seen here at the entrance.

Guests can relax on the yellow sofa by Augusto Bozzi and enjoy the music that flows from an authentic vintage sound system.

THE VOYAGE BEGINS AT THE QUASI-THEATRICAL ENTRANCE

One of Asia's largest credit card companies, Hyundai Card, requested the development of a concept and design for a membership club for one of its premium credit cards, the Purple. ...,staat creative agency decided to focus on the two things money can't buy: friends and taste. The concept is based on the home of a dear friend who invites you in to relax and hang out amid his prized possessions. The idea was to change the whole perception of the Purple card member from card holder to friend with the message, 'my home is your home'. Together with the Hyundai Card project team and project coordinators Mr. Oh and Mr. Vlessing (Toal Impact Seoul) ...,staat creative agency started to work on this project.

The voyage into the House of the Purple begins at the quasi-theatrical entrance to this exclusive world, with plush velour curtains hanging from the ceiling, seemingly embracing the purple concierge desk before coming to rest on the glossy black wooden floor. The first impression guests get is of a club that immediately exudes elegance and exclusivity yet remains warm and welcoming. Continuing through into the living room, kitchen and reading room, the perfectly curated space – with its medley of inspired furniture and stunning works of art – has subdued lighting with a sophisticated nocturnal air. Relaxing and stimulating in equal measure, the venue allows guests to sit in an array of cosy room settings, depending on their mood. Here they can take the time to notice the plethora of curio items and assemblage of cool-looking conversation pieces surrounding them.

The kitchen area is a brighter and more open space, where daylight streams in through floor-to-ceiling white voile curtains. In this space, with its white ceiling and walls and marble serving counter, guests can gather around the large table or opt to eat in one of the more private spaces, or even retire to the terrace to enjoy the view of the organically sculpted vertical garden – a work of art in itself.

On the tiled wall behind the bar, the 48 arms of 24 small clocks spell out the time (Clock Clock by Humans Since 1982).

The restaurant area is as much for socializing as it is for dining.

THE PERFECTLY CURATED SPACE FEATURES A MEDLEY OF INSPIRED FURNITURE AND WORKS OF ART

The terrace is a veritable oasis in the heart of one of the world's busiest cities.

More secluded spaces are available just off the main kitchen area.

Opposite Members are greeted with a free drink and can sit down for a game of chess in the kitchen, just as they might at a friend's house.

A model of the complete membership club.

A last clean before the furniture pieces and works of art can be put at place.

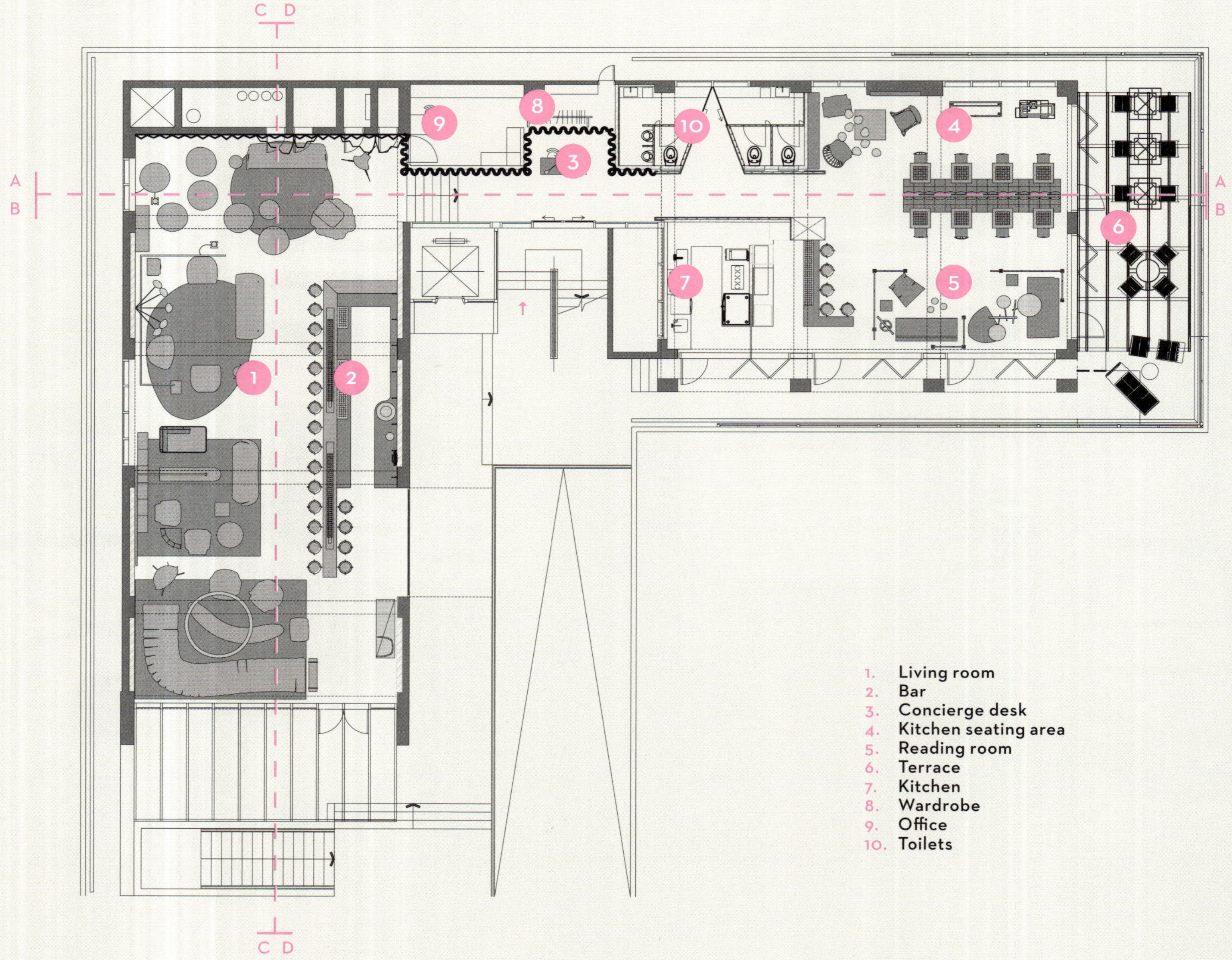

1. Living room
2. Bar
3. Concierge desk
4. Kitchen seating area
5. Reading room
6. Terrace
7. Kitchen
8. Wardrobe
9. Office
10. Toilets

THE CLUB EXUDES ELEGANCE AND EXCLUSIVITY, YET REMAINS WARM AND WELCOMING

Section AA

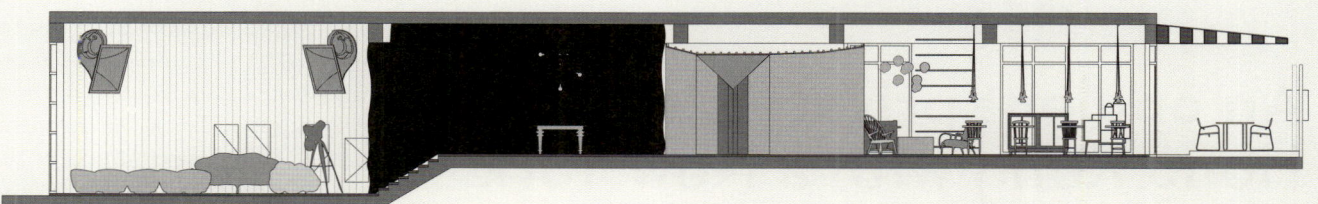

Section BB

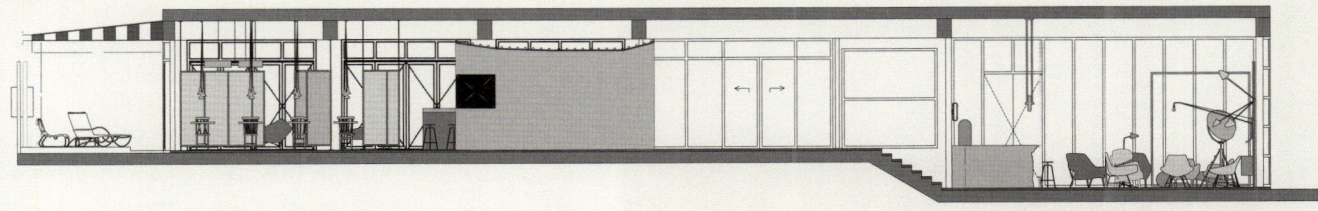

Section CC

Section DD

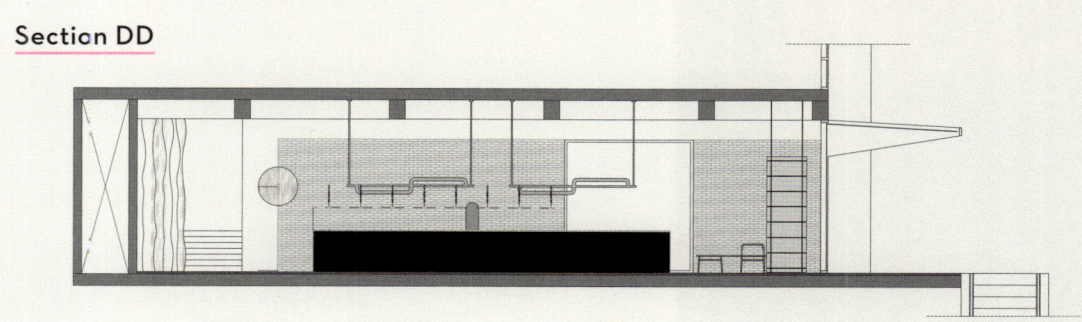

HYDE BY KINNEY CHAN & ASSOCIATES

An opulent private club in Hong Kong with a New York loft-type feel.

Photos Trio Photography

Opposite top Varied decorative lighting techniques are employed in the bar area.

Opposite bottom A dark, cosy space has been created for customers.

Hyde is a two-storey private members' bar, lounge and club situated in central Hong Kong. The client commissioned Kinney Chan & Associates to create an 'art clubbing experience'. The focus for the design team was to conjure up the desired atmosphere by the use of dynamic lighting and a sophisticated décor.

Styled with the use of natural materials, the completed space has been designed with a New York loft-type feel, with exposed brick, hardwood floors and leather sofas. Next to one of the bars and seating areas are three 2.4-m pool tables, each with designer lampshades looming above, adding to the luxurious atmosphere. Another central island bar – constructed of marble and illuminated around its bottom edge where it meets the marble-tiled floor – is also available for customers to congregate around. In this dark space, a different atmosphere is created, with spots of colour coming from the different illumination aspects, including the red strip lighting embedded in the textured felt walls and the industrial-style light installation over the bar itself. There is also a VIP room with extra privacy and three outdoor terraces where members and their guests can relax and enjoy the ambiance.

The restrooms also have an opulent edge, with a mixture of natural materials, velvet drapes and a quirky mix of modern-style parquet tiles laid on the floors as well as on the walls and ceiling, creating a curved sculptural walkway. ●

An art-like installation comprising red LED spotlights decorates the entrance area.

Where Hong Kong, Hong Kong
Opening September 2010
Client Hyde
Designer Kinney Chan & Associates → p.5
Floor space 1200 m²
Capacity 400 guests

KINNEY CHAN & ASSOCIATES

KISMET BY BLACKSHEEP

Where	Hyderabad, India
Opening	May 2011
Client	The Park Hotel
Designer	Blacksheep → p.579
Floor space	1068 m²
Capacity	250 guests

A fantastical and escapist club with nods to the past.

Photos Gareth Gardner

Craft traditions of the Hyderabad region have been woven into the concept, fused with highly contemporary aspects.

Hyderabad has always been a melting pot of different cultures and influences. Today, India's fifth-largest city is a cosmopolitan metropolis where traditional local crafts like jewellery making have been joined by new industries. The Park Hotel approached Blacksheep with the idea of creating a nightclub at the hotel that would reflect the energy, drive and optimism of this dynamic city.

Blacksheep's design transports guests into a fantastical and escapist environment where respectful nods to the past – the artistic traditions of the Hyderabad region – are seamlessly woven into an ultra-modern aesthetic – reflecting the city's high-tech present day. References to jewellery are particularly evident in an interior treatment layered with metallics, gem shades and iridescent materials. Guests enter the club via a spectacular tunnel, the walls of which are clad in faceted stainless steel panels, with inset lighting linked to the DJ's sound system.

The dance floor has four large booths, one at each corner, each lit by an illuminated bespoke chandelier made of traditional gilded ropes and beads. A massive central bar runs through both the VIP area and the main club. Smooth, sculptural and made of glistening Corian with inbuilt lighting, it provides a dramatic focal point for both areas. The distinctive hexagonal lighting units were inspired by iconic local Nizam jewellery designs. The VIP area boasts a dramatic feature: a void leading up from the club's ceiling to the bottom of the swimming pool above. The overall result is a nightclub that has not only established itself as Hyderabad's number one nocturnal destination but also rivals anything India has to offer. •

Opposite top If visitors look up through the ceiling void at the VIP area they can see the hotel pool above.

Opposite bottom The gilded ropes and beads in the jewel-lined booths were sourced from a local market.

BLACKSHEEP

KLUCHI BY ANTON GRECHKO, PETER KOSTELOV AND ALEXEY ROZENBERG

Where Moscow, Russia
Opening July 2011
Designers Anton Grechko → p.578, Peter Kostelov → p.587 and Alexey Rozenberg → p.578
Floor space 300 m²
Capacity 300 guests

Optical illusions in a modern Moscow nightclub with a historical context.

Photos Alexey Knyazev

Opposite Plinth-like tables are positioned in the bar area like pieces of a chess board.

The grey-hued chill-out area has leather-upholstered sofas for clubbers to lounge on.

Natural materials like wood, brick and ceramic tiles furnish the arched vaults where the toilets are located.

Regulars of the new Kluchi – a nightclub in central Moscow, first built in the 18th century – have seen it lovingly restored, with its original features emphasized and new modern shapes, approaches and materials implemented in the historical context of the interior. The full renovation was done by designers Anton Grechko, Peter Kostelov and Alexey Rozenberg.

The club is located in what used to be two separate buildings, with different ceiling heights due to different years of construction, and features two period fireplaces that became the very centre of the designers' motivation for the concept. In an effort to tie all the different architectural styles together, they opted for a modern interpretation of classical elements, incorporating unexpected surprises at every turn. An ultra-modern geometric bar counter, which serves as a white light box when illuminated from within, was positioned between the two historic fireplaces. In a separate room, traditional materials used for finishing contrast with the interpretation of how and where they are used: the bar ceiling is covered in parquet tiles in the same way as the floor, while the light fittings above the tall plinth-like wooden tables replicate their latter's shape. The mirror-image concept imbues a feeling of weightlessness and confusion due to the inverse space reflection. Similar principles have been applied in the concrete-clad chill-out area, with raw cubic slabs wrapping around every surface in the room and steel striations lining the interfaces between them. Curved cornice elements are positioned at different heights and angles, sometimes serving as a shelf running along one wall.

A final illusion is applied in the original arched brick vaults in the basement, where the lavishly decorated lavatories – with their hand-painted ceramic tiles – can be found. The cubicles are separated by what appears to be a wooden wall emitting bright light from gaps between its planks. In reality the wall is solid, and the source of the illusion is a built-in layer of LEDs. •

THE SPACE IS REPLETE WITH UNEXPECTED SURPRISES AND ILLUSIONS

An installation hangs in the stairwell below a chandelier made of black pipes of different diameters.

The intricately-carved white tiled fireplace is one of the original features, now set in a modern context.

ANTON GRECHKO, PETER KOSTELOV AND ALEXEY ROZENBERG

Opposite The custom-made white steel lanterns are completely open, mirroring the open sides of the white wooden surround on the terrace.

KUFRA LOUNGE BAR BY COLLIDANIEL-ARCHITETTO

An Italian hotel beach bar, inspired by the décor of Moroccan riads.

Photos Matteo Piazza

Three strips of intricate Corian detailing decorate the aqua-hued bar area.

Where Sabaudia, Italy
Opening June 2010
Client Oasi di Kufra Gestioni Alberghiere
Designer Collidanielarchitetto → p.580
Floor space 320 m²
Capacity 82 seats

COLLIDANIELARCHITETTO

Turquoise resin coats the wall surfaces and ceiling, applied by hand with various mixing and application techniques to obtain the desired textured effect.

Kufra Lounge Bar is located inside the Oasi di Kufra Hotel in Sabaudia, a coastal town south of Rome. It overlooks a beach with a view of Mount Circeo, important to local tradition as it features in Homer's *Odyssey*. The brief for the bar design called for a dual-spirited location, catering to beach leisure pastimes during the day and to a sophisticated nightlife once the sun goes down.

For the interior design of the beach bar, Daniela Colli and her team accentuated the architectural and functional space by using elegant decoration. White was used as the background colour, with vibrant hues of aqua blues picked out in the paintwork and tiles in the bar area, mirroring the ocean colours of the beachfront setting. Here, the décor incorporates intricate Corian detailing, of which the design is often found in the Moroccan riads, which produces a complex frieze. It becomes a three-dimensional element that marks the space, wrapping up and over the walls and ceiling.

The slender and geometrically pure counter is made of Corian. A glacier white solid has been chosen for the top, while the front sports a glacier ice illumination series. The white LED backlighting highlights the decoration that was produced by milling thick slabs. The result is a technologically refined three-dimensional lace.

In the seating area, the pre-existing wooden roof of the terrace has been modified only in its finishing and colour and is now equipped with a new lighting system that has the appearance of delicate lanterns shimmering overhead. They provide a dynamic effect and create a cosy atmosphere thanks to their mellow light and staggered heights. The interior of the lounge completely opens onto the terrace and the beach, offering magnificent views for guests, but also encouraging passers-by to walk in, even if they are not guests of the hotel.

COLLIDANIELARCHITETTO

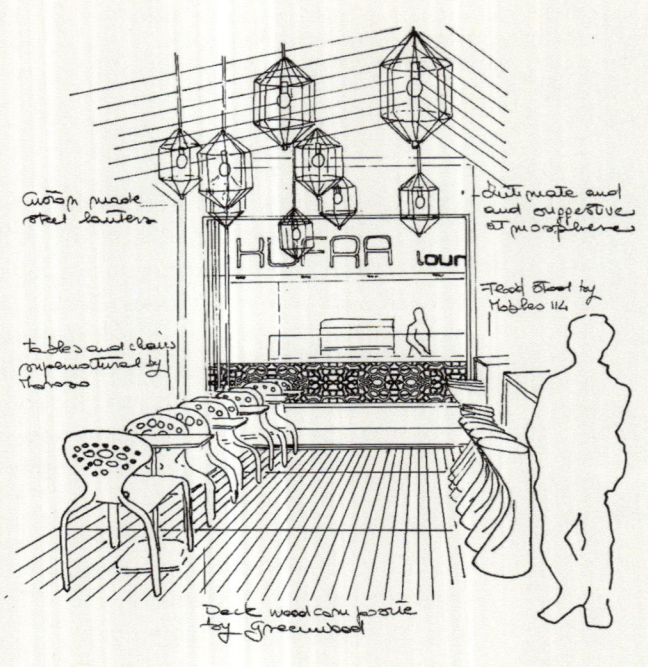

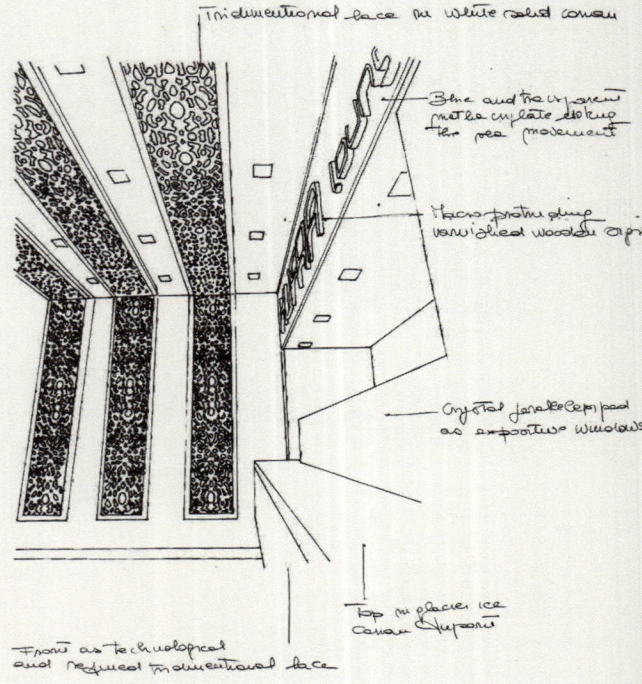

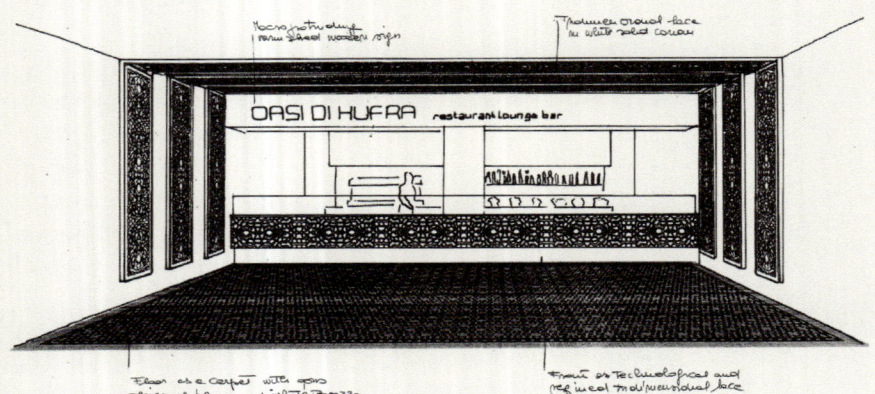

Initial sketches of the bar and seating area.

ELEGANT DECORATION ACCENTUATES THE ARCHITECTURAL AND FUNCTIONAL SPACE

Detailed sketch of the decorative panels.

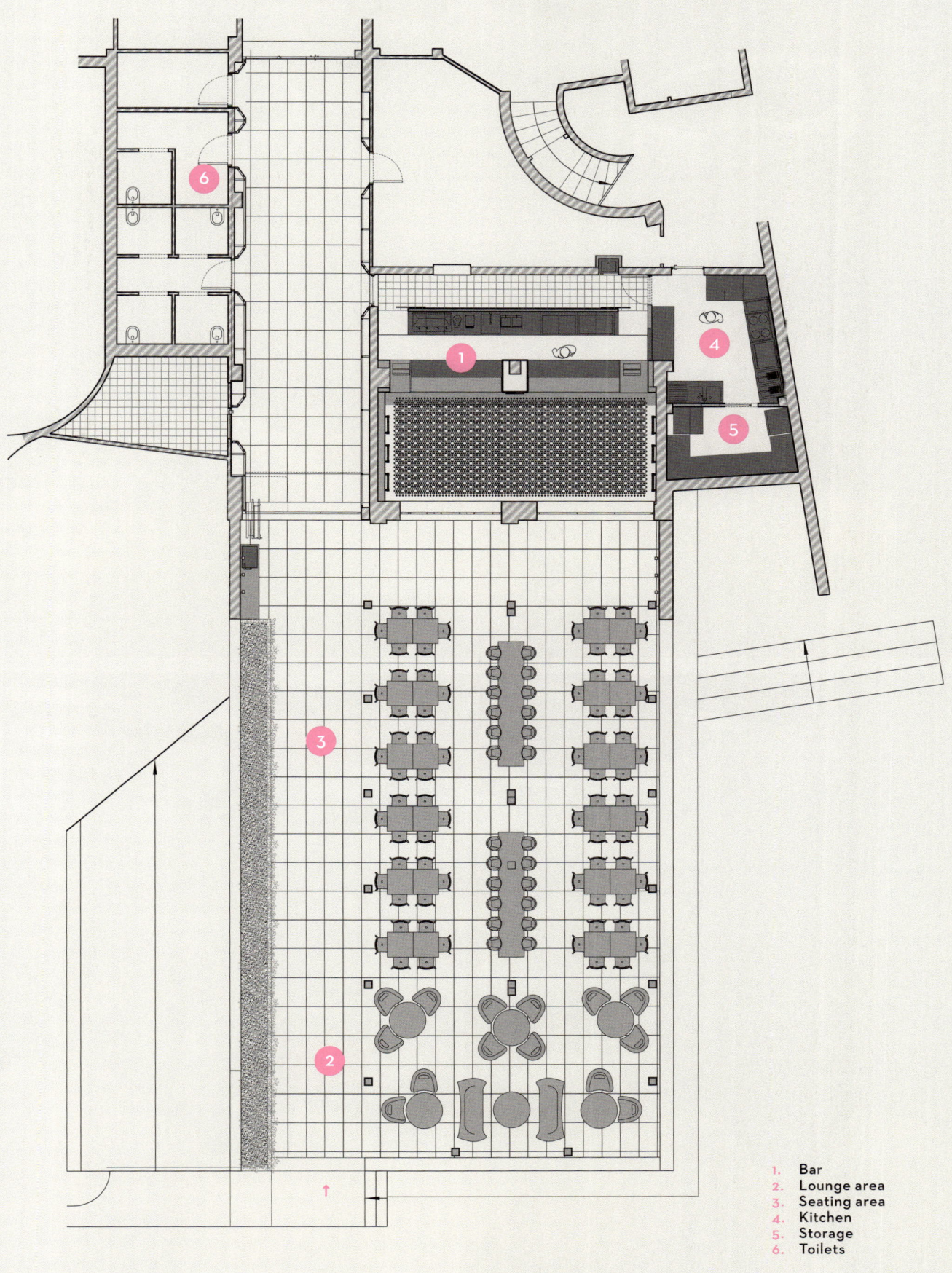

1. Bar
2. Lounge area
3. Seating area
4. Kitchen
5. Storage
6. Toilets

COLLIDANIELARCHITETTO

LA GAÎTÉ LYRIQUE

Opposite top and bottom Set against the magnificently historic décor is a modern cubist concept in which the light boxes also double as a bar counter (top).

Where Paris, France
Opening March 2011
Client City of Paris
Designer Manuelle Gautrand Architecture → p.585
Floor space 9500 m²
Capacity 1280 guests

LA GAÎTÉ LYRIQUE BY MANUELLE GAUTRAND ARCHITECTURE

A historic location in central Paris dedicated to the creative fields of digital art.

Photos Vincent Fillon, Jean Harixcalde and Philippe Ruault

From the grand, marble-clad entrance, visitors immediately see the mix of modern and historic aspects.

Programmatic and architectural challenges faced the design team while ensuring the best possible use of the space.

In 2001 a decision was made to renovate the historic Théâtre de la Gaîté lyrique, a Parisian theatre that dates back to 1862. The magnificent building was to be revealed in its new guise as a cultural centre dedicated to digital arts and contemporary music. The project, led by Manuelle Gautrand, aimed to create a venue open to all the different artistic fields related to digital art.

To enable all the architectural and programming needs to take shape, the design process began by focusing on the acoustic aspects. The result was a very effective sound-insulation system in relationship with the building's environment, made up of over 100 units more or less sharing the building's volume. The project is conceived according to the 'box within a box' principle, like Russian dolls, which gradually insulate the different spaces, down to the three most sound-oriented spaces at its core. Three successive layers of wrapping overlap to create increasingly powerful soundproofing as the visitor moves towards the centre of the building, where the three major presentation spaces are located, each of which can be adapted, in different proportions, to any kind of sound design, visual projection or staging.

In addition, there are the building's 'breathing spaces', which consist of more flexible aspects like the foyer, exhibition areas, the café, the resource centre, the video arcade and the spaces devoted to the artists. Throughout these aspects are small pieces of furniture grouped together in clusters to form seating areas, welcome stands, a few bars, and so forth. These are dotted around the public spaces like escorts and, dressed in translucent resin, they offer small luminous additions to the different spaces. Their dodecahedron shapes allow for many cluster formations. Set against the backdrop of the historic decor, they create an element of resonance with contemporary design. •

An interior was created that allows free circulation through the space.

LA GAÎTÉ LYRIQUE

Some rooms are padded to allow for acoustic and illuminative works of art.

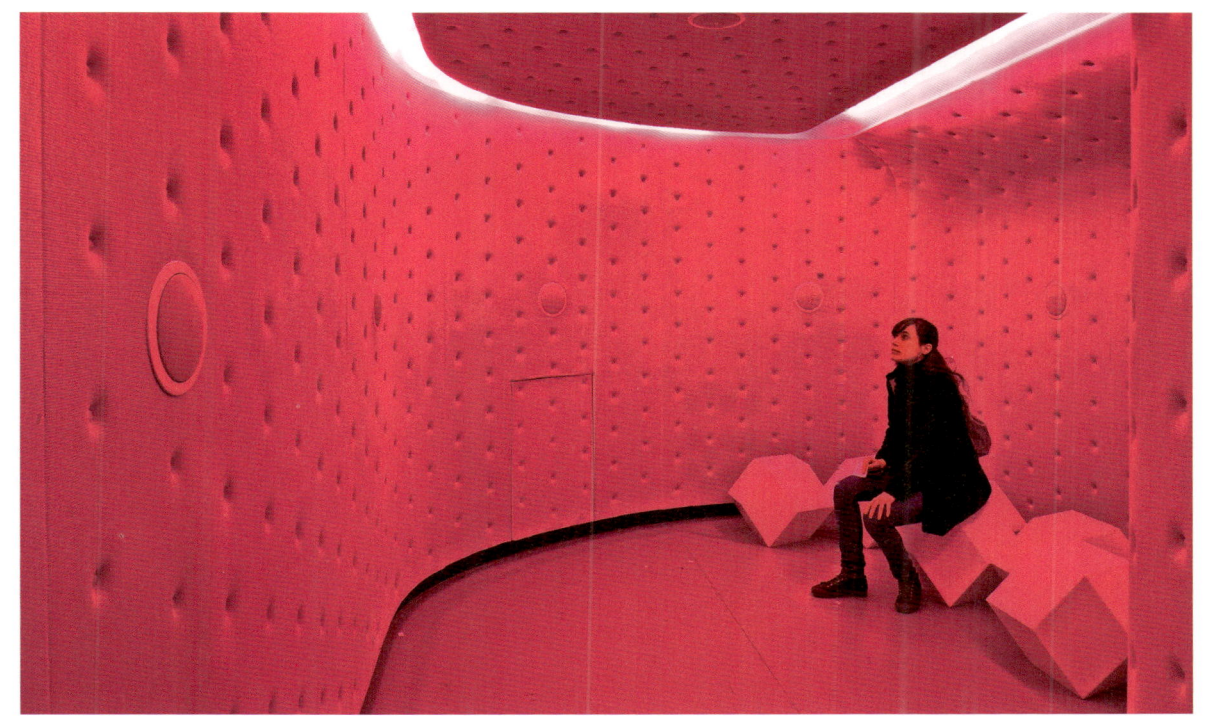

THERE IS INCREASINGLY POWERFUL SOUNDPROOFING TOWARDS THE CENTRE OF THE BUILDING

Soundproofed areas with visual projections await visitors at the centre of the building.

MANUELLE GAUTRAND ARCHITECTURE

There are 70 small, illuminated white boxes used in a modular format throughout the entire building.

THE PROJECT IS CONCEIVED ACCORDING TO THE 'BOX WITHIN A BOX' PRINCIPLE, LIKE RUSSIAN DOLLS

Many of the furniture elements used in the interior are fully movable, ensuring a great deal of flexibility in how the space can be used.

Visitors are welcome to relax in the futuristic sound and image modules.

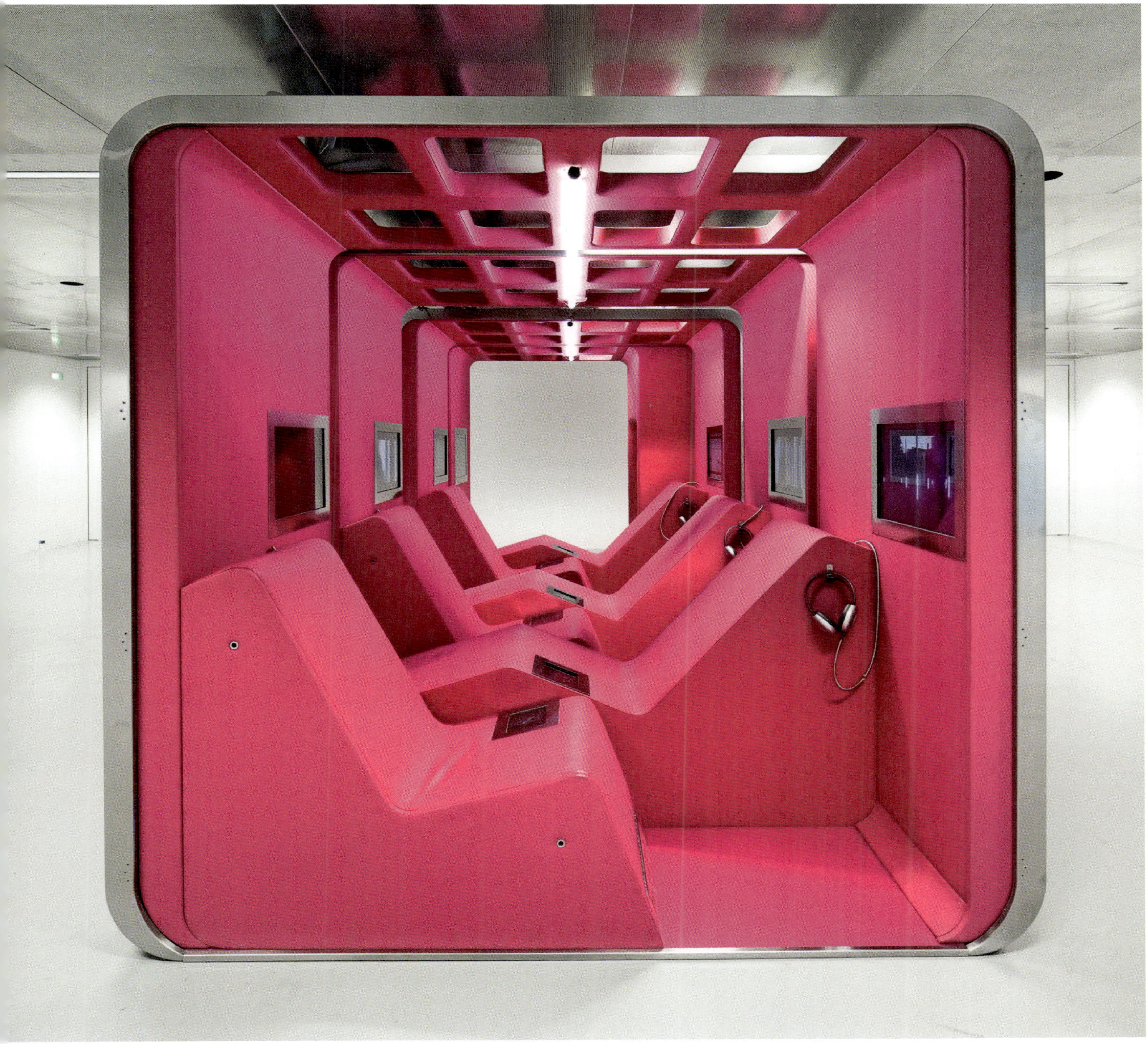

MANUELLE GAUTRAND ARCHITECTURE

Where **Brussels, Belgium**
Opening **October 2011**
Client **Le Fonograf**
Designer **Andrea Mantello Architetto** → p.578
Floor space **95 m²**
Capacity **42 seats**

LE FONOGRAF BY ANDREA MANTELLO ARCHITETTO

An ever-changing space with a cosmopolitan atmosphere.

Photos Laurent Brandajs

Opposite top The space can be easily adapted for exhibitions, workshops and live music.

Above and opposite bottom The sidewall system has both shelving and seating elements that can be used together or independently.

ANDREA MANTELLO ARCHITETTO

The metal strip is like a ribbon flowing from front to back, uniting the shelf system, the actual bar, the staircase and the DJ booth.

Le Fonograf was borne out of the initiative of three dynamic and night-loving young people – a Congolese DJ, a Belgian painter and an Italian sociologist – with high ambitions and a low budget. On this premise, the canteen and art café was inaugurated in October 2011 as a versatile bar in central Brussels. In answering the brief, which called for an ever-changing space that would reflect the city's cosmopolitan and neighbourly atmosphere, Andrea Mantello sought to integrate all these functions by using flexible seating and shelf fixtures.

A versatile wood and metal system has been fitted along the side walls, accommodating shelves and benches that can be effortlessly raised when the space is used as a large concert room with minimal seating facilities, or lowered for the regular café setup, with the long benches serving as seating. The top shelf at one side continues towards the back of the room, curving upward as a thick metal strip that embraces the bar and integrates into its counter. This same strip becomes the stairway's handrail leading up to the office space, twisting one last time against the wall, where it mutates once again, becoming a shelf next to the DJ booth.

A similar palette of materials is used on the façade, with overlapping panels of steel and wood used for the signage. Just as steel is used to link many components of the bar into one sculptural element, so the architect's guidance synergistically united the work of metalsmith Guillaume Thaveau, artist Enrico Gaido and designer Viviana d'Auria.

Detailed image of the metal strip.

AN INITATIVE OF THREE DYNAMIC AND NIGHT-LOVING YOUNG PEOPLE WITH HIGH AMBITIONS AND A LOW BUDGET

ANDREA MANTELLO ARCHITETTO

Sketch detailing the shelf/seat-combination of the side-wall system.

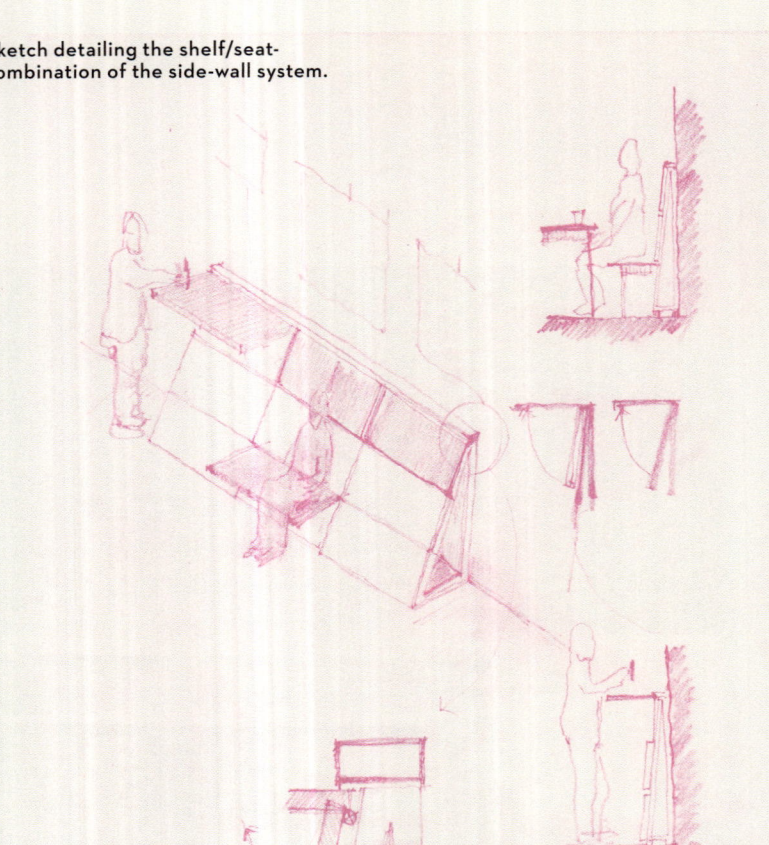

COMPONENTS OF THE BAR ARE LINKED INTO ONE STEEL SCULPTURAL ELEMENT

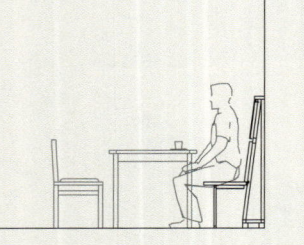

Layout option 1

Layout option 2

Layout option 3

Façade

324 LE FONOGRAF

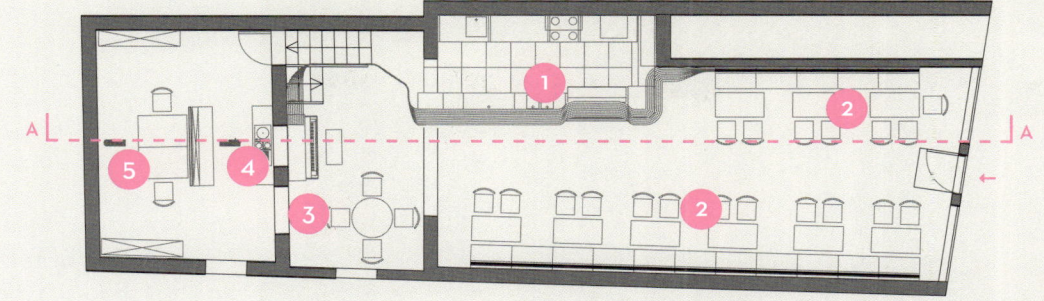

Layout option 1

1. Bar
2. Seating area
3. Stage area
4. DJ booth
5. Office
6. Wine cellar
7. Toilets

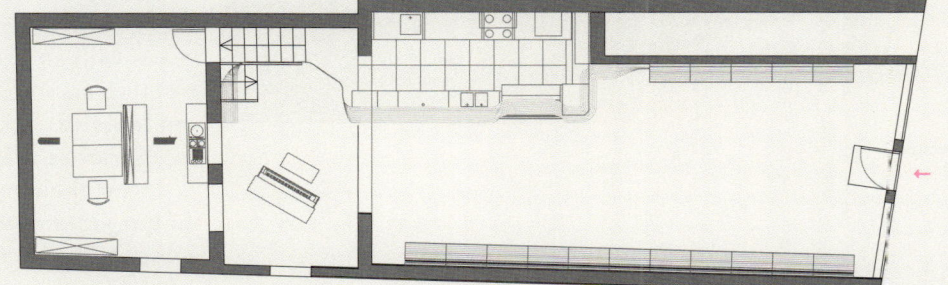

Layout option 2

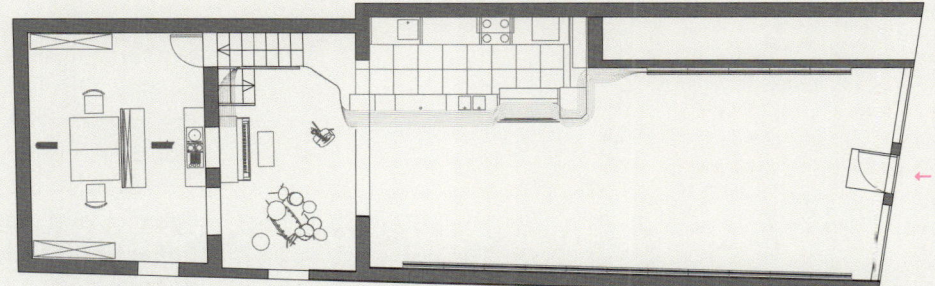

Layout option 3

Section AA

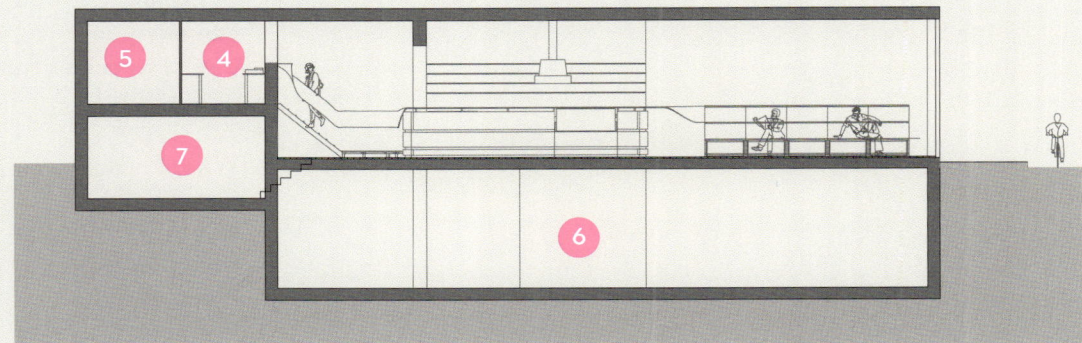

ANDREA MANTELLO ARCHITETTO

The main illumination in the restaurant comes from indirect light.

Opposite The natural spruce timber slats stand out against the original dark floor tiles and black-painted ceiling.

LOOKOUT CAFÉ BY DESIGN SPIRITS

A veritable forest of thin spruce boards.

Photos Toshihide Kajiwara

Near the top of the mountain in Niseko on Hokkaido sits a cosy café that serves as a retreat for skiers and mountain adventurers. The owners commissioned design spirits to renovate the original wooden structure, built 28 years previously. The idea was to produce a space with an exotic Japanese character, creating an ambiance where customers can feel the outside-world atmosphere in an interior space.

The challenge for the team was that the project needed to be completed within a 40-day time frame – before the impending winter. An added challenge included working on a construction site in such a remote location, inaccessible by car or ski lift in the off-season. This required materials that could be easily transported up the mountain by Caterpillar and then be assembled quickly. This led to the idea of covering the interior with approximately 2500 wooden louvers made of local spruce.

Built on a concrete base with wooden columns and diagonal braces for support, the existing building was enhanced by decorating the interior with slats of light-coloured timber. The layout of the café includes one long room; peering into the space, guests get the feeling that they are looking down a Japanese alleyway, with lattice-work ceilings of differing heights producing interesting dimensions. Small booths are thus created, like individual houses, with low tables positioned beside the windows through which customers can enjoy the view – whence the secluded eatery gets its name.

Where Niseko, Japan
Opening November 2010
Client YTL Hotels
Designer design spirits → p.581
Floor space 172 m²
Capacity 80 seats

MELTINO BAR & LOUNGE

MELTINO BAR & LOUNGE BY LOFF

Where Braga, Portugal
Opening December 2010
Client Meltino Espaços
Designer LOFF → p.585
Floor space 182 m²
Capacity 91 seats

An eye-catching bar made with coffee in mind.

Photos Fernando Guerra

View of the bar and lounge seen from the outside.

Opposite top A geometric, spherical layout is given to each of the side-by-side structures.

Opposite bottom Illumination comes from indirect light from diachronic and halogen lamps.

The double-wall design reinforces the perforated elements and lends solidity to the structures.

THE VENUE IS BASED ON GEOMETRIZED COFFEE BEANS

LOFF, a Portuguese lighting design and architecture practice, was asked to design a charismatic and unique bar in a shopping centre for the coffee brand Meltino. The idea was to build a bar inside the mall, transparent but still maintaining a sense of privacy for every visitor. How to be inside and have the feeling of being outside was a guiding concept throughout.

The venue, based on geometrized coffee beans, is divided into three areas: two volumes and a terrace, which is elevated above the mall floor. The terrace is an open space that integrates with the mall and the two volumes are enclosed by perforated walls. The two volumes are identical but have different uses and furniture. The first volume, the lounge area, houses a relaxation area where gourmet coffee is served. In the second volume, the bar area, the public can order express coffee.

Coffee beans were drawn on many scales – used as a mould to perforate the walls – and then a matrix was created: three panels which were then inverted, for a total of six distinct panels. The designers wanted to emphasize the bean perforations, so the walls and ceilings were duplicated. The central part of the ceiling is raised to give the space a more dynamic feeling. The structure is built of pine wood, which is light and easy to assemble. The walls, ceilings and balconies are clad in white-painted MDF. The white and brown colours were chosen because of their association with coffee. The furniture was designed with detailed attention to aesthetics and comfort. The tables are covered with a unique and new material derived from a coffee by-product.

The perforated walls play with the natural light and shadows dance in the space, making this bar hard to forget for anyone who enters the mall.

The outer shell of each volume resembles the basic shape of a geometricized coffee bean.

Initial sketch of the geometric structure moving from a singular volume concept to two side-by-side volumes.

Elevations

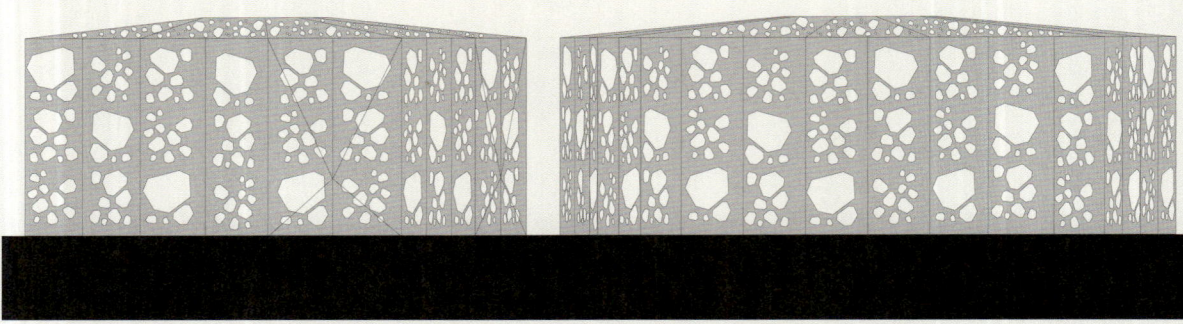

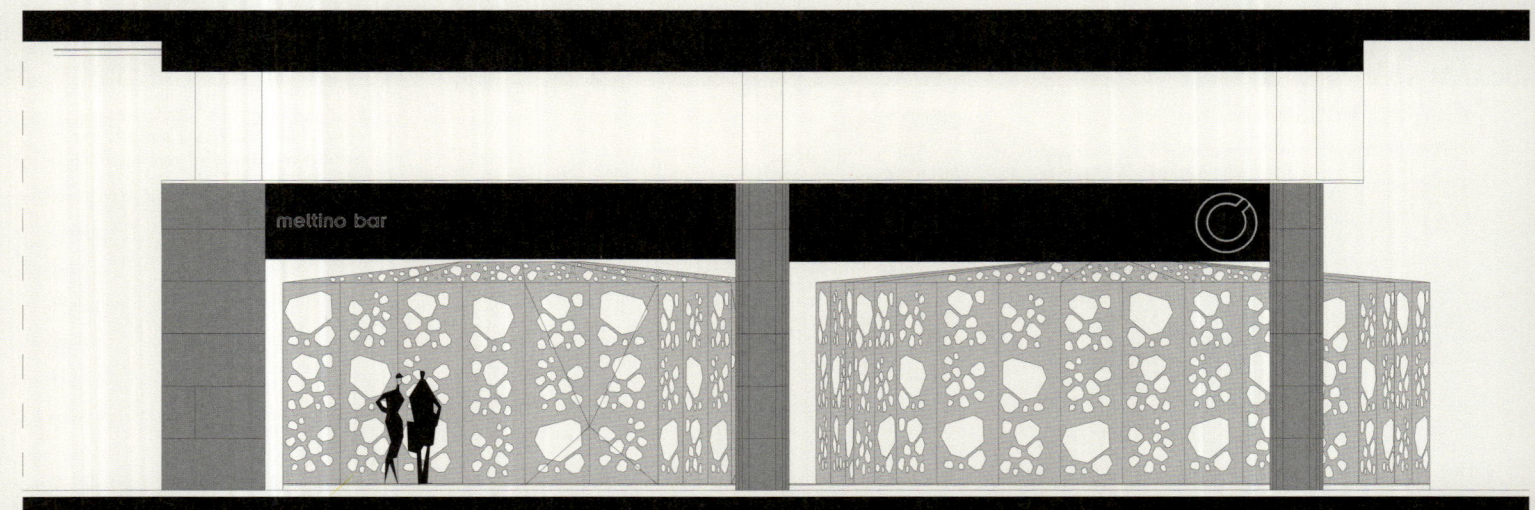

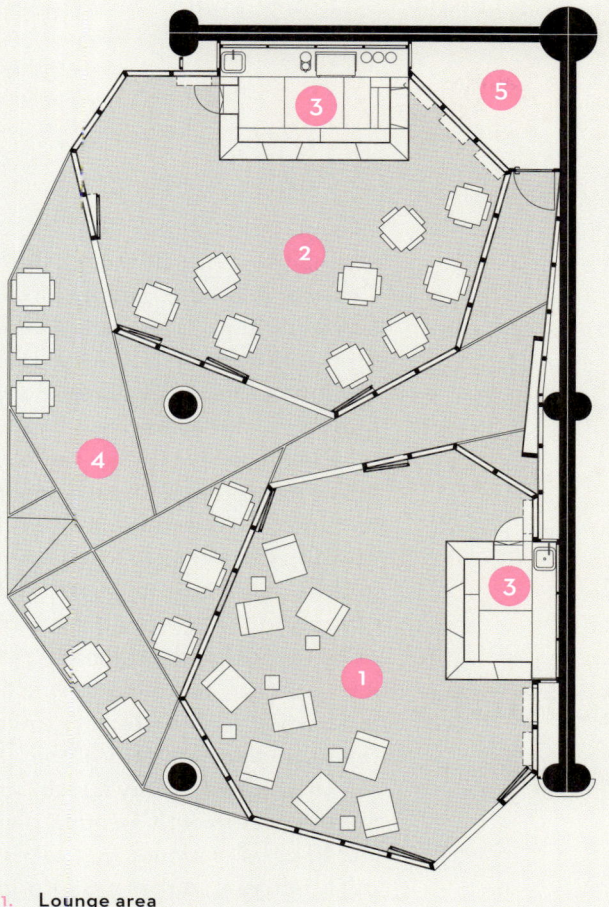

1. Lounge area
2. Bar area
3. Bar
4. Terrace
5. Storage

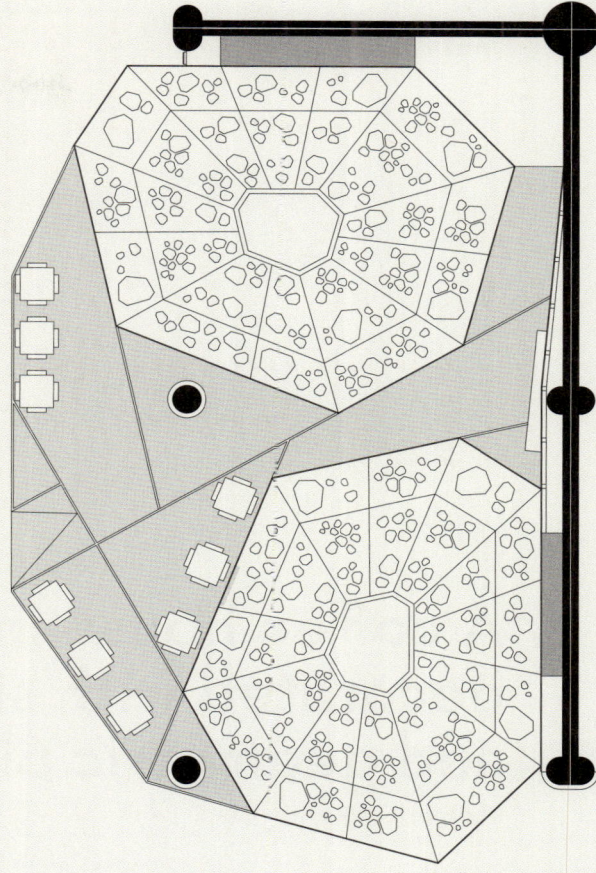

Pattern of the ceiling seen from above.

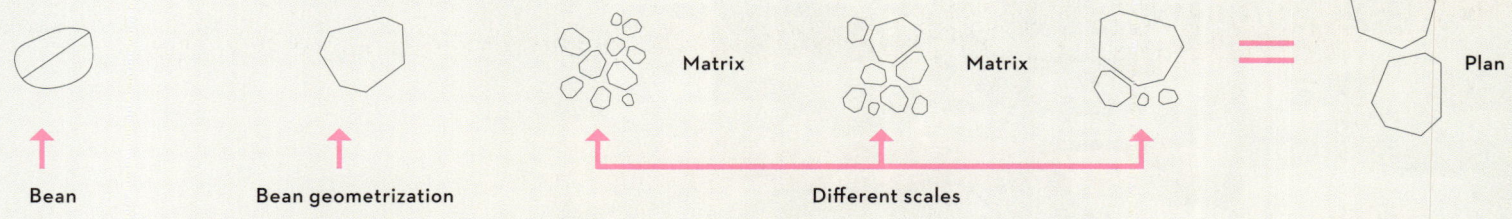

Bean

Bean geometrization

Matrix

Matrix

Different scales

Plan

Development of the geometrized coffee bean shape.

LOFF

MOCHA MOJO BY MANCINI ENTERPRISES

A coffee house in India decorated with strong colours and geometric planes.

Photos courtesy of mancini enterprises

Mocha Mojo is a meeting place in Chennai geared towards coffee and conversation. The client's design brief asked for an interior inspired by the 1970s, which is what mancini enterprises delivered.

The concept is inspired by this era, which mastered distinctive wallpaper, with strong colours and geometric shapes, as well as a nod to the early modernists' approach towards interiors. Only in the 1960s and 1970s were the old qualities of 'opulence' and 'ornament' re-infused into interiors, resulting in spaces of great intensity. It is this intensity the design team sough to embody within this project.

In the two-storey space, surfaces are decorated with wooden planks, laid in parallel planes and playing with perspectives, so that the interior seems to extend into the distance – enhanced in addition by the use of strong colours on the floor and the ceiling. Painted in a myriad of blues, reds and khaki greens, the elongated boxes are layered on the walls to create a full-height 3D effect, creating a scene not unlike that of a childhood Lego world. This visually satisfying quality adds a fun and familiar aspect to the space, which also has a cosy ambiance that draws customers in to nestle in the niches and relax on the cushions and spherical design classic chairs. •

Opposite The colourful timber-clad coffee house has a cosy quality.

Conduits are boxed in on the ceiling, reflecting the box-like booths below that run the length of the space.

Where Chennai, India
Opening January 2010
Clients Impresario Entertainment & Hospitality and Oneworld Impex
Designer mancini enterprises → p.585
Floor space 350 m²
Capacity 110 guests

MANCINI ENTERPRISES

Opposite and right The mobile wooden booths are reminiscent of the transport crates in an art warehouse.

MS CAFÉ BY WUNDERTEAM

A modern café resembling an art warehouse.

Photos Olo Rutkowski, Jakub Stepien and Ula Tarasiewicz

Where Łódź, Poland
Opening March 2009
Client Muzeum Sztuki
Designer Wunderteam → p.590
Floor space 315 m²
Capacity 54 seats

The booths offer more private seating arrangements for the guests.

IN ORDER TO EMPHASIZE THE HISTORIC BEAUTY OF THE PALACE, THE DESIGNERS USED SIMPLE MATERIALS

The original ceilings of the 19th-century palace contrast with the contemporary interior.

The cloakroom and the museum pass office are linked by a shared counter. Clothing is stored in slide closets with glass fronts.

In order to modernize the ground floor of the Museum of Art in Łódź and adapt it to its new function, design duo Magdalena Koziej and Paulina Stępień of Wunderteam were asked to create the interior design of the bookshop and café. The client requested they pay respect both to the avant-garde tradition and to the building's historic function.

After entering the gateway passage, the visitor is directed by means of clear signs towards the exhibition or the MS Café and bookshop. Opposite the exhibition entrance there is an information and ticket desk, designed with a strong note of red, providing a powerful counterpoint to the rest of the interior. The greatest challenge was the area of the building where the designers situated the MS Café and bookshop. This area includes a glassed-in box with a bookshop opening into the café, two rooms housing the café, as well as a cloakroom and toilets. The cafeteria is also open outside the museum's exhibition hours, hence the need for a separate entrance to this part of the building.

In order to emphasize the historic beauty of the palace interiors, the designers used simple materials like plywood, metal and glass. The result is a contrasting interior juxtaposing the 19th-century interior with contemporary design. The design duo was also looking for direct references to the museum as a building and came up with an interior that resembles an art warehouse. They designed mobile furniture, reminiscent of transport crates used to carry works of art, including lounge sofas and stools. Moveable booths with two benches flanking a table offer guests more intimate seating.

The café features a crystalline bar. The designers wanted to build a structure that resembled a fragment of some mysterious sculpture – a form growing right out of the floor and walls. At the same time, the bar was supposed to be comfortable and visually attractive. They managed to build a crystalline structure out of plywood and lit-up Plexiglas, simultaneously respecting the principles of ergonomics. The result is a perfect match for the bar stools designed by Konstantin Grcic. •

The bar is made of wooden triangular planes with back-lit Plexiglas panels.

THE MOBILE FURNITURE IS REMINISCENT OF TRANSPORT CRATES USED TO CARRY WORKS OF ART

The different pieces of custom-made furniture can be combined to create different lounge seating islands.

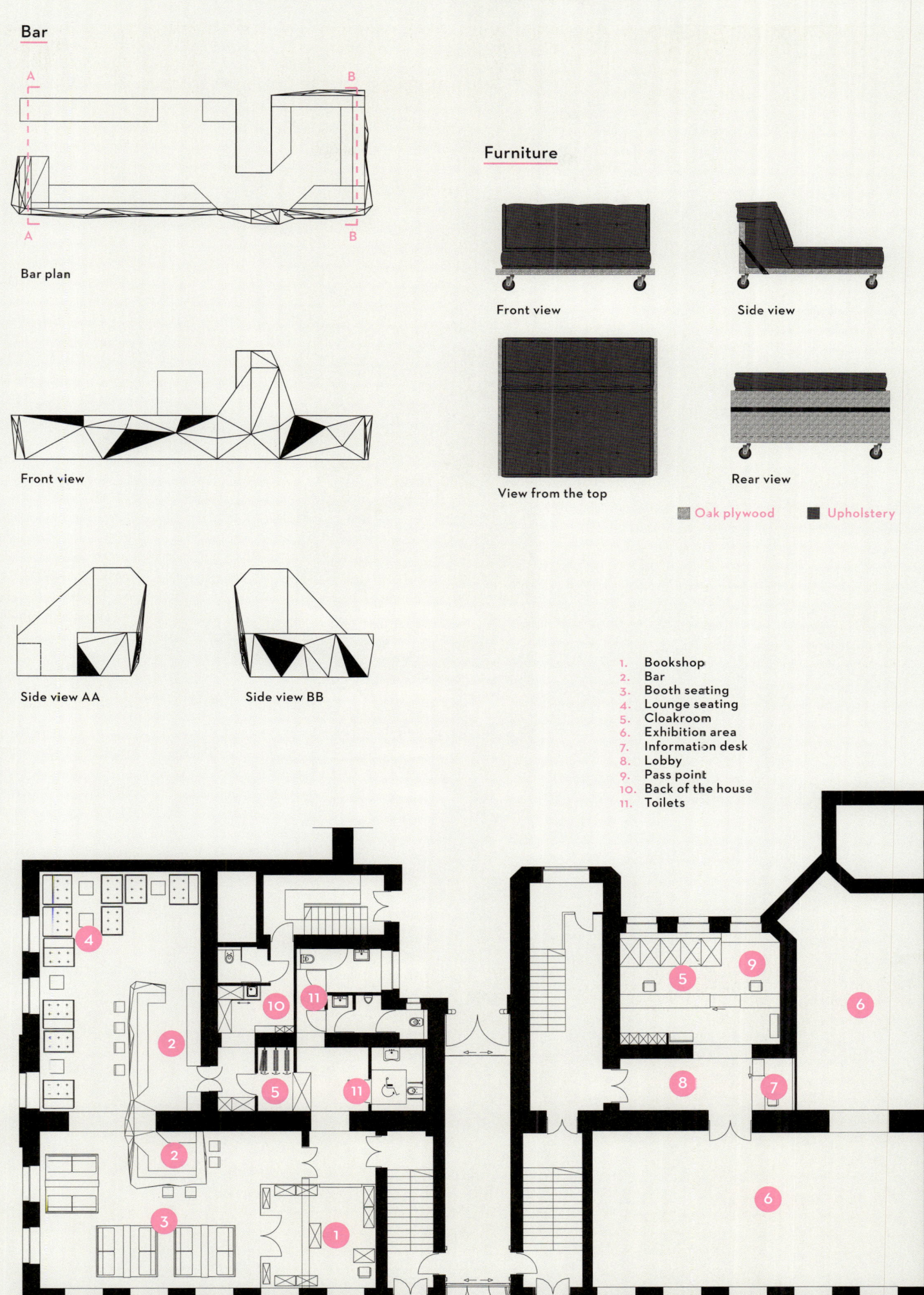

Opposite The 'curtains' that softly drape the walls of the foyer are not actually made of fabric but are sculpted waves of Corian.

Illumination is an important aspect in the space, adding to the luxurious atmosphere.

OZONE BY WONDERWALL

An opulent bar in Hong Kong is a multilayered, mesmerizing experience.

Photos Nacása & Partners

Where Hong Kong, Hong Kong
Opening May 2011
Client Sun Hung Kai Properties
Designer Wonderwall → p.590
Floor space 755 m²
Capacity 250 guests

Wonderwall's aim was to design an incredibly extraordinary space for the world's highest bar.

WONDERWALL 343

Left and opposite The faceted bar counter is assembled to look like it's made out of a single block of white marble.

Next spread Instead of trees, Katayama's Eden features a forest of quirky, curving columns, finished in high-gloss white.

THE SIGNATURE PATTERN FEATURED IN THE FOYER CONTINUES THROUGHOUT THE INTERIOR

In May 2011 the 118-storey Ritz-Carlton Hong Kong opened its doors, becoming the tallest hotel building in the world. Capping the tower is Ozone, the highest bar in the universe – and probably the closest to heaven a person can get. Even the breathtaking skyline of Hong Kong is far below. Here you are 500 m above ground and surrounded by the extraordinary.

The shelves behind the bar are made of solid ebony.

Japanese designer Masamichi Katayama, founder of Wonderwall, was thrilled to be asked to design this space in Kowloon. To prevent it from being overwhelmed by the energy of the city, the design called for luxury at its most extreme. Katayama intentionally abandoned the Ritz-Carlton's style of Asian Art Deco and came up with a concept he calls 'Edenic Experiment', in which he envisioned a world of naturally inspired idealized forms filled with a sense of wonder.

Moving at a speed of 9 m per second, guests arrive on the 102nd floor in 55 seconds, where they step into the Ritz-Carlton's reception lounge. Awaiting them in one corner are two narrow lifts clad in black leather and mirrors, poised to carry them the remaining 16 storeys to Ozone. When the doors open on the 118th floor guests arrive in the foyer, where floor-to-ceiling Corian 'curtains' line both side walls, contrasting with the high-impact, geometrically patterned marble floor and fragmented-glass motif of the ceiling.

The signature pattern featured in the foyer continues throughout the interior, repeated on walls and ceilings and in different materials to produce interesting layers of texture. Behind the main bar, the pattern is translated into a stainless steel, wooden shelf for wines and spirits. This shelving unit extends to the ceiling, where the pattern becomes part of the lighting scheme. Stools and couches shine in the dark like irregularly shaped diamonds, and giant spiralling sculptures double as structural columns. The result is a seamless landscape of visual elements forming an imaginary world.

Lighting plays a key role in all of Katayama's designs. In Ozone, he combined natural and artificial lighting and used mirrors and other reflective materials to capture the movements of people, to enlarge a space and to exert a strong influence on the desired ambiance. In the sumptuous dining room, a dazzling plethora of spherical pendants hang from the ceiling, while lighting in the lounge area bathes guests in subtly changing colours. Illumination throughout the various areas enhances the glamorous crowd and extends the beauty of the city below. •

WONDERWALL

Computer modelling produced the series of sinuous columns.

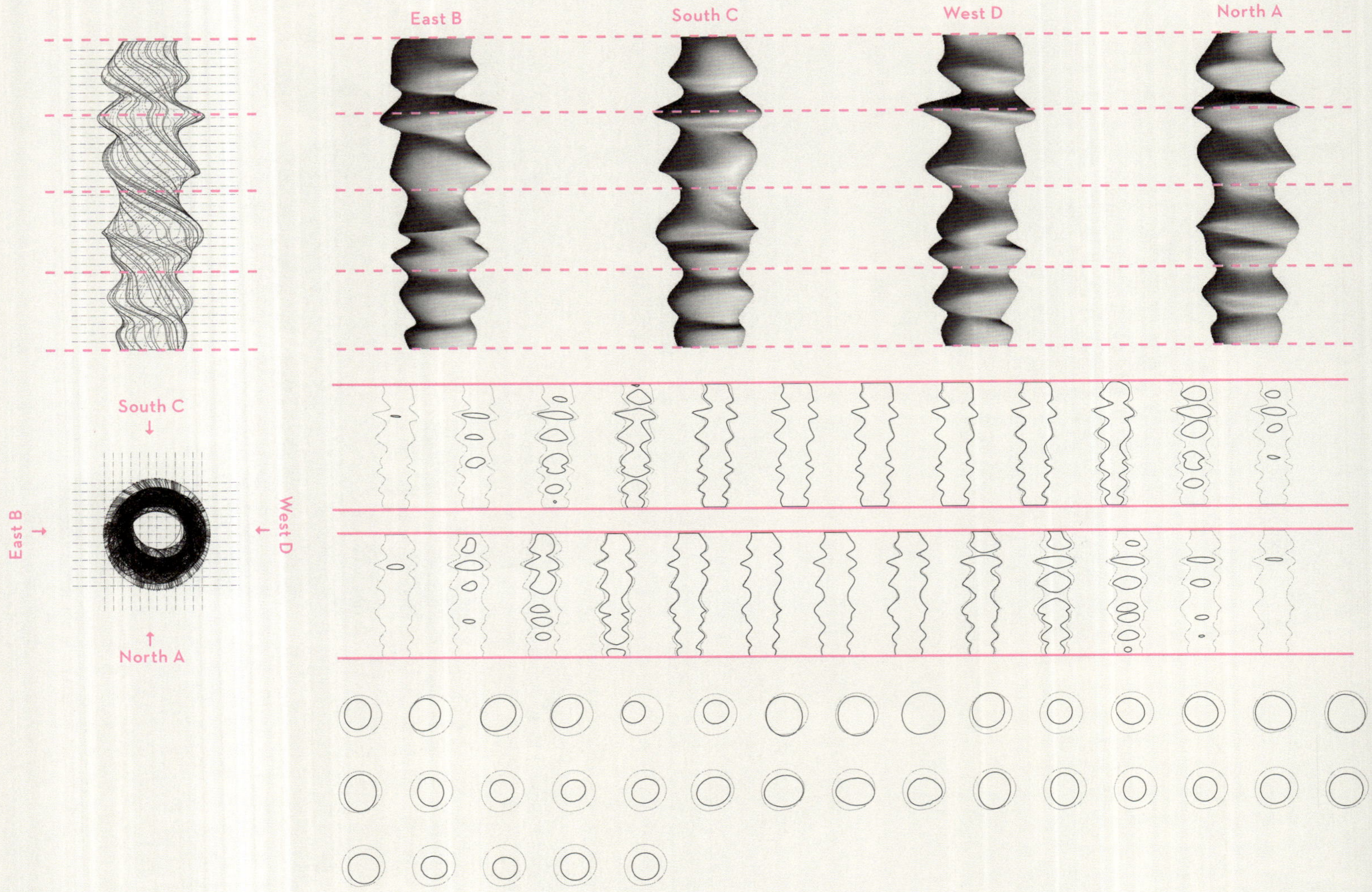

East B
South C
West D
North A
South C
East B
West D
North A

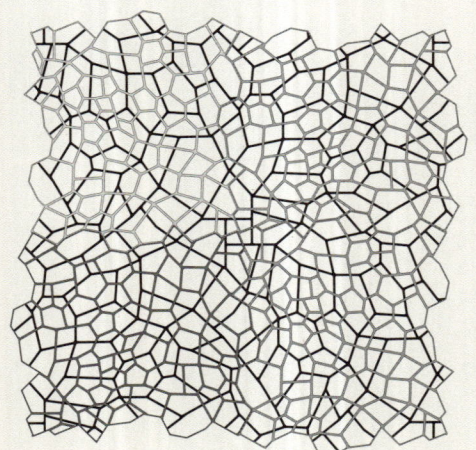

Layered over each other, the Voronoi screens add texture and complexity to the ceiling.

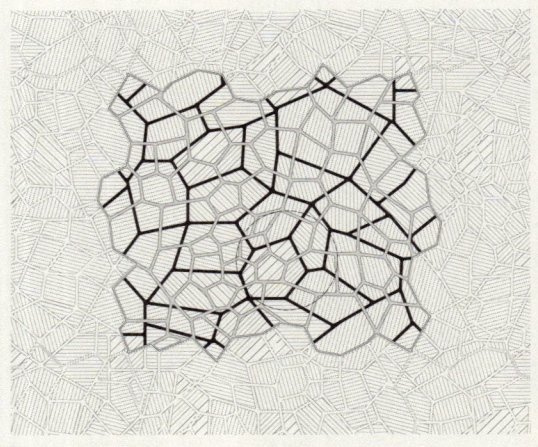

Voronoi diagrams provided the geometric blueprint for much of the design.

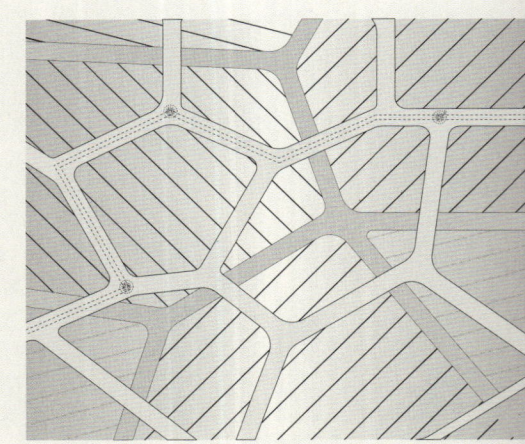

Diagram showing the contrasting layers of the Voronoi ceiling screens.

GUESTS ARRIVE ON THE 102ND FLOOR IN 55 SECONDS

1. Entrance hallway
2. Bar
3. Lounge area
4. Corner seating area with 270-degree views
5. Private dining room
6. Sushi bar
7. Dining area
8. Outdoor lounge area
9. Stone Garden
10. Toilets
11. Lifts

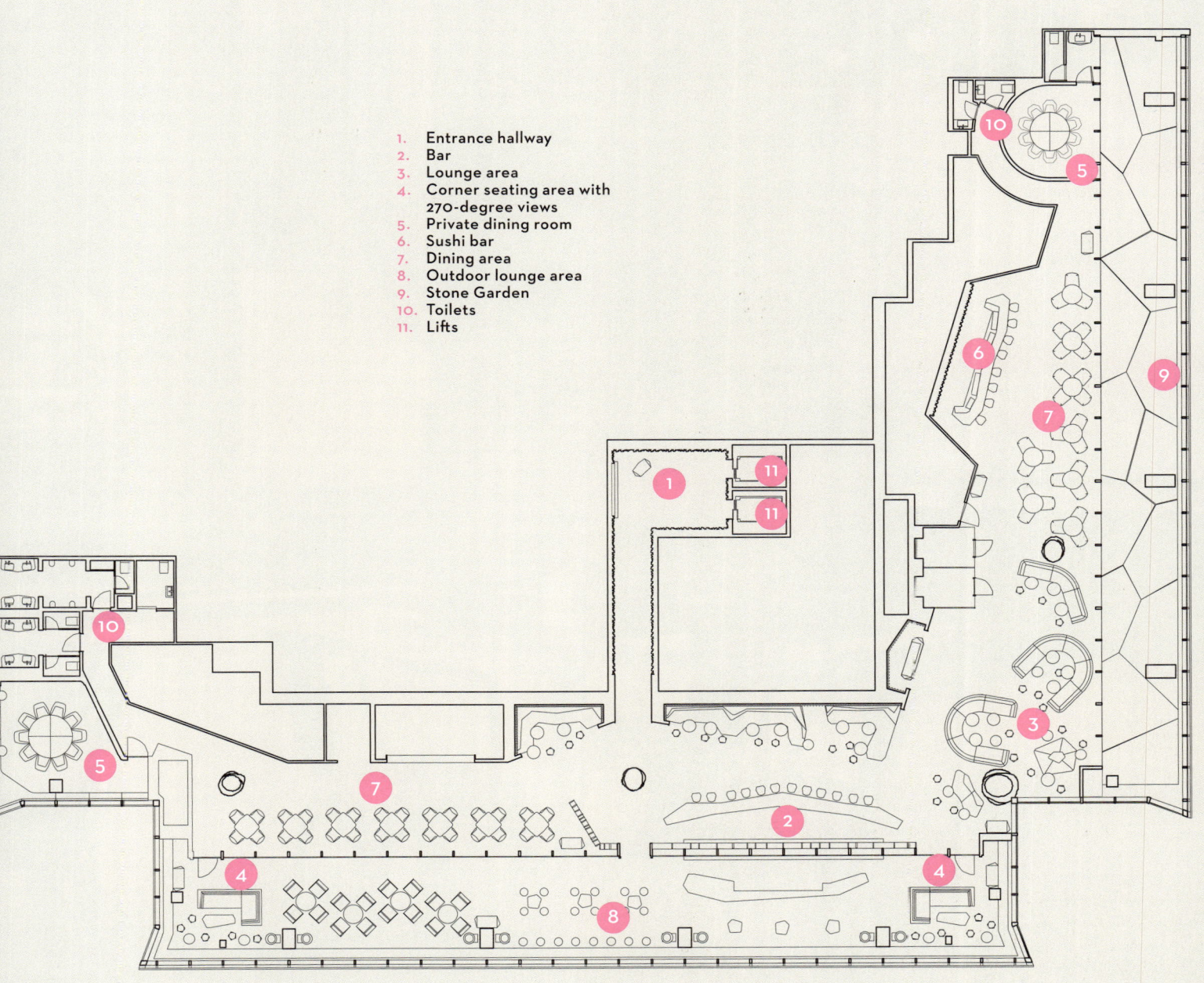

WONDERWALL

PLAZA BY AROMA

Where Zurich, Switzerland
Opening November 2010
Client Plaza Kosmos
Designer Aroma → p.579
Floor space 900 m²
Capacity 800 guests

A nightclub in Zurich's first silent-movie theatre with timeless flair.

Photos Mischa Scherrer

The stage at the main room has the exact same place and dimension of the former cinema screen.

Opposite Around the dance floor are candlelit tables and shiny metal Tolix chairs.

AROMA

The extravagant and larger-than-life bird imagery was painted by local artist Onur Dinc using UV-photosensitive colours, which really come alive when illuminated by a certain incidence of light.

LARGE PAINTINGS OF VIBRANTLY PLUMED BIRD DRAWINGS ADORN THE WALLS

A striped décor in a cosy corner has neon strip lights radiating outwards overhead.

The building that housed Zurich's first silent-movie theatre in the 1920s has recently been renovated, injecting the city's nightlife with a touch of glamour, the likes of which may not have been seen since the days Greta Garbo or Rudolph Valentino graced its movie screens. The modern-day requirements of the space called for it to be multifunctional, with a timeless flair adapted to all kinds of visitors and events. Aroma was commissioned to oversee the project's concept, design and total transformation into the Plaza club, with its various bars, lounges and dance floors on two levels.

The concept encapsulates a sumptuous atmosphere right from the start, with illuminated signage details that appear to hark back to the building's original 1920s' features. The interior near the entrance features a rich décor of dark walls and velvet curtains, giving guests the impression of entering the Plaza club through the back door, which forms a contrast to the vivid rooms that follow. In the basement area there is a unique sense of space that preserves the essence of the former cinema. An extra-large LED frame surrounding the stage – where the screen would have once been positioned – gives the room a contemporary twist. Striking features that adorn the walls throughout are the large paintings of vibrantly plumed bird paintings by artist Onur Dinc, inspired by 19th-century animal illustrations. These not only create a colourful atmosphere but also give the club a vivid identity, used in branding materials and on its website. Other specialists who collaborated with Aroma on this project include Zmik, who designed the first floor space, and Designersclub, responsible for the graphic design of the rebranding process.

AROMA

PONCELET CHEESE BAR

Opposite A tapestry of foliage is woven into the vertical garden that sits behind the diners.

PONCELET CHEESE BAR BY GABRIEL CORCHERO STUDIO

A gastronomic haven for cheese lovers.

Text Sarah Martín Pearson
Photos Pasquale Caprile

The menu offers customers a selection of more than 140 different kinds of cheese.

Where Madrid, Spain
Opening July 2011
Client Poncelet
Designer Gabriel Corchero Studio → p.583
Floor space 700 m²
Capacity 100 seats

GABRIEL CORCHERO STUDIO   355

The interior has white textured surfaces mixed with blond oak wooden floors, with splashes of subtle colour coming from the upholstered seating arrangements.

Guests can savour cheese and wine while sitting around the curved Corian counter.

A 30-M² VERTICAL GARDEN SERVES AS AN OXYGENATING LUNG

Poncelet Cheese Bar is a Madrid concept restaurant whose *raison d'être* revolves around this dairy delicacy. Gabriel Corchero Studio conceived the interior of this gastrobar with a clear emphasis on nature to evoke the original cheese-making setting.

The studio not only used sustainable materials and finishes, it also brought some of the outdoors in by growing a 30-m² vertical garden that serves as an oxygenating lung while also providing acoustic comfort. Near this foliage-covered wall is a multicoloured, kaleidoscopic mural designed by Corchero himself. Other features evocative of nature include a wall covered in plastered branches and mushroom-shaped light fittings that seem to pop out the ceiling. But the main focus of the restaurant is the diamond-shaped cheese case that occupies a central position in the dining area. This custom-designed glass display case is framed in oil-treated, vaporized cedar and its function is to ensure ideal humidity and temperature conditions for maturing and preserving cheese.

The restaurant layout is intended to provide customers with a relaxed gastronomic experience in an atmosphere inspired by the home. A variety of seating areas allows diners to enjoy a sense of intimacy whether gathering around a communal oak table, sitting on cosy armchairs around lower tables, or heading for the cushy, upholstered bench with its own individual lighting overhead. Others can choose the library upstairs for a further insight into the world of cheese found in literature or theme-specific books, to be enjoyed on restful, colourful armchairs. And finally there is a space for those who prefer to observe the cheese connoisseurs from one of the undulated, white Corian surfaced bars, in front of the case or by the entrance, while watching the masters cut their favourite piece and serve it in sushi chef fashion.

PROJECT

Opposite A type of amphitheatre with overhead canopy has been created for the seating booths around the dance floor.

PROJECT BY RAW DESIGN

Project keeps you entertained into the early hours.

Photo Richard Southhall

Varied, ambient lighting elements are an important aspect of the design concept.

Where Norwich, United Kingdom
Opening February 2011
Client Luminar Leisure
Designer Raw design → p.587
Floor space 3770 m²
Capacity 1630 guests

RAW DESIGN 359

The chill bar is playfully lit-up by the lime-green Spacewalker pendant lamps by Constantin Wortmann.

Light projections and graphics on the walls create visual interest in the seating areas.

Project is a nightclub with two main rooms, live stages and a karaoke suite. The client's brief specified that the spaces in the venue needed to interconnect but also stand alone as separate entities. Matt Rawlinson of Raw Design began with an empty shell and created a journey through the evolving spaces.

The stairwells and corridors have been kept deliberately stark, except for the designer light fittings. Inside the main room, positioned at the heart of the club, all industrial ductwork has been left exposed, with the walls wrapped in graphics of fashion imagery juxtaposed on an ethereal landscape of urban wastelands. This aspect can be changed periodically to create new identities for the space. Dynamic lighting enhances the nightclub's atmosphere with large colour-changing Oblivion pendant lights positioned around the edge of the main dance floor, along with illuminated cubes used as tall tables. A colonnade of white aluminium truss structures with polypropylene cellular roof and walls encloses the seating booths, thus creating a type of amphitheatre. Radiating from this central space is the chill bar, with reflective black stretch PVC ceilings, green vinyl seating and Spacewalker light fittings, the VIP area positioned behind cellular semi-transparent glass, and the karaoke suite – defined by pink studded rubber flooring, retro cellular ceiling tiles and Japanese-style wall decorations. The second room is characterized by a floating timber installation ceiling which extends to envelop the bar and seating areas at either side as well. Large LED floodlights swathe the room in sweeping shards of luminosity, casting shadows onto the concrete dance floor and the walls, decorated with graffiti-style art work to create a raw aesthetic.

A FLOATING TIMBER INSTALLATION CEILING ENVELOPS THE SPACE

Tree-like trusses grow up and over the bar area in the second room.

Pot shelves rise from the floors around the edge of the dance floor, breaking up the space.

RAW DESIGN

Sketches outlining the initial concepts for specific rooms in the club.

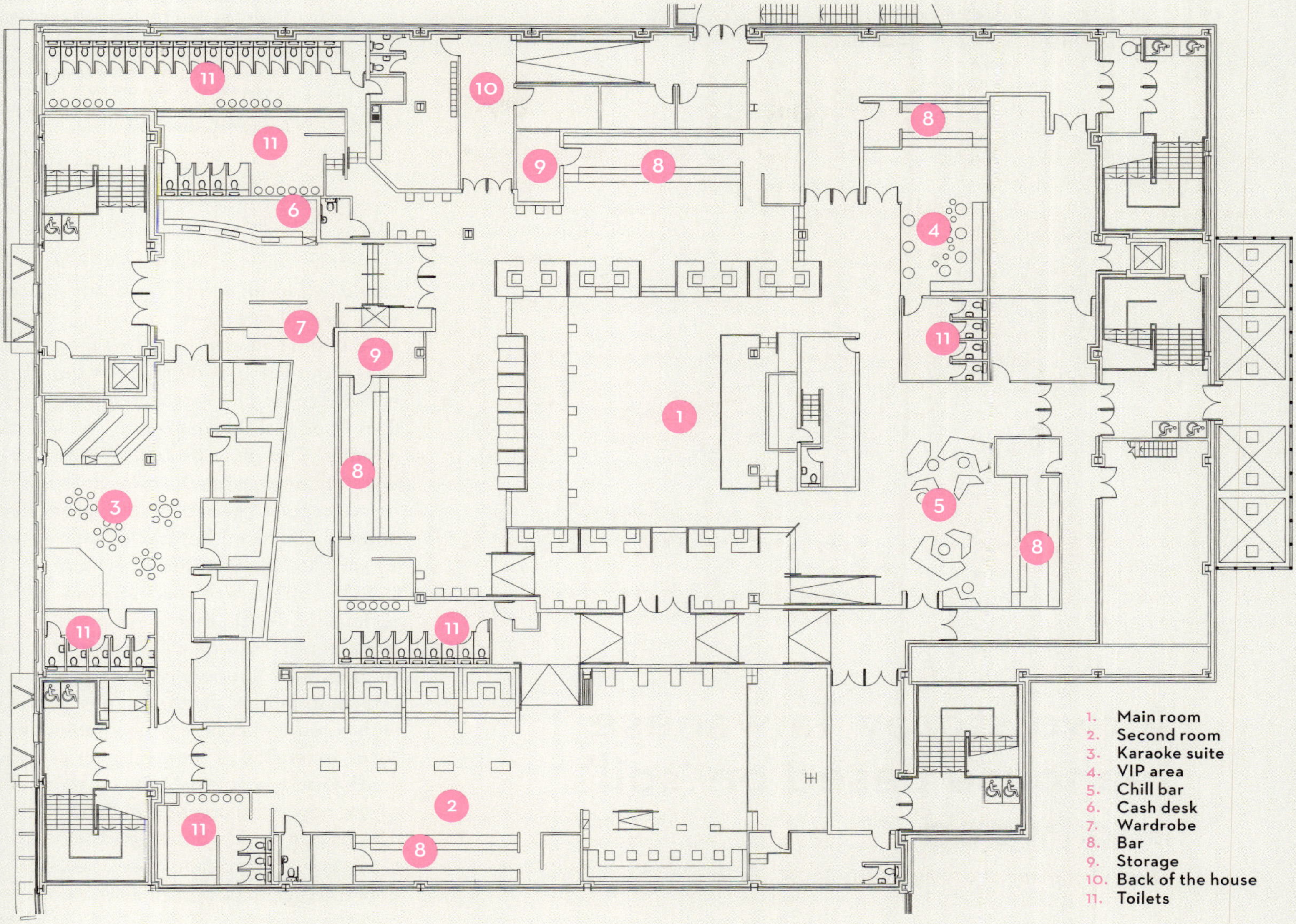

1. Main room
2. Second room
3. Karaoke suite
4. VIP area
5. Chill bar
6. Cash desk
7. Wardrobe
8. Bar
9. Storage
10. Back of the house
11. Toilets

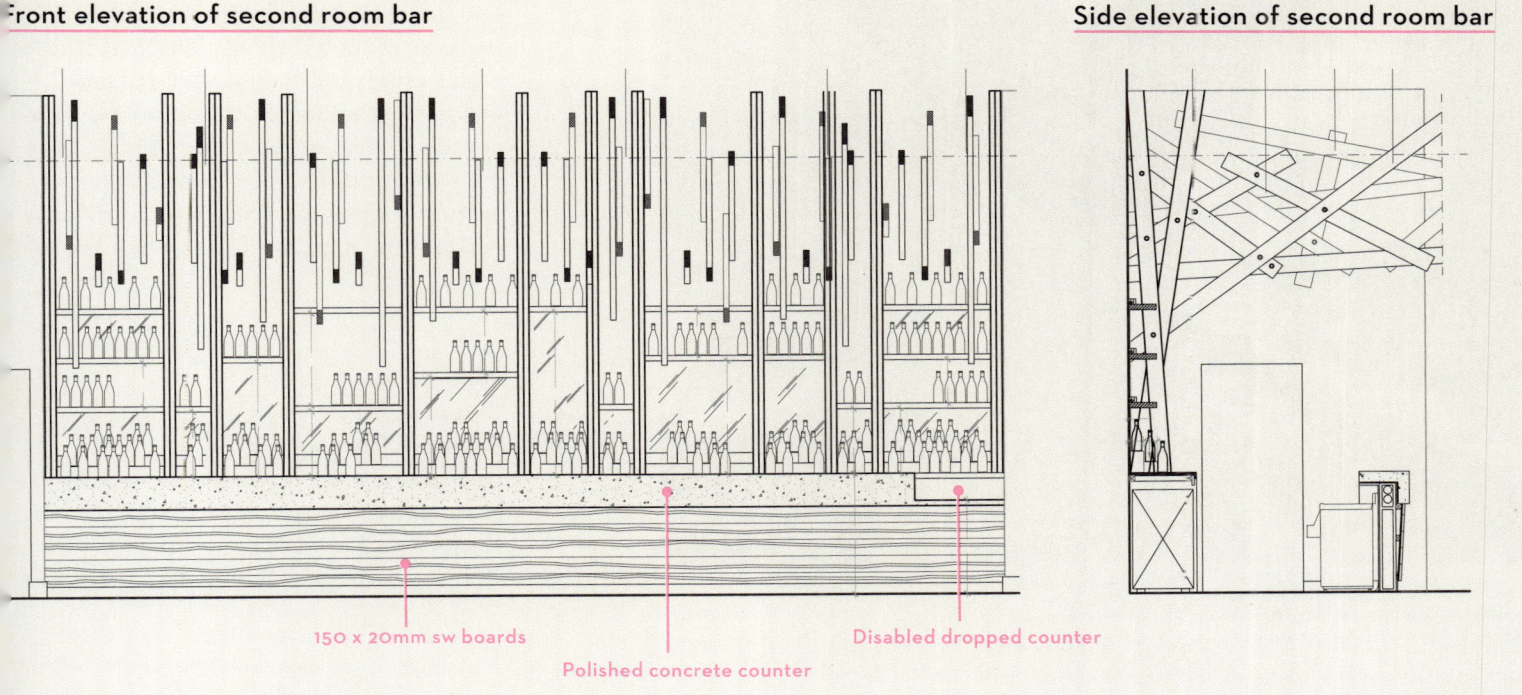

Front elevation of second room bar

Side elevation of second room bar

150 x 20mm sw boards

Polished concrete counter

Disabled dropped counter

RAW DESIGN

SMITH&HSU TEAHOUSE BY CARSTEN JÖRGENSEN

A two-storey Taiwanese teahouse based on 'soil' and 'wood'.

Photos courtesy of smith&hsu

Opposite top Designer furnishings include Y Chairs by Hans J. Wegner on the ground floor, Eames Plastic Side Chairs on the first floor and pendant lights by C. Jörgensen.

Opposite bottom On the upper level, the books that line the walls come from the customers themselves and from a few generous donors.

Contemporary tea brand smith&hsu is based in Taiwan and offers premium loose teas, as well as accessories and gourmet food to accompany the refreshing beverage. The brand has a number of teahouses, and its location on Nan Jing East Road in Taipei is its fifth and latest addition. Designed by Danish designer Carsten Jörgensen, the two-storey tea house seats 48 guests on the upper floor and ten guests in the spacious lower level, which also incorporates a tea shop.

The space is refreshingly raw, with an interior design that is minimalistic and uncluttered. Materials have been chosen to reflect the subtlety of fine tea and to appeal to guests' aesthetic sensibilities, with wood and concrete predominating. As an extension of the design of previous smith&hsu tea houses, the key elements of the new store are 'soil' and 'wood'. The colour palette has an earthy feel of stone colours and pale greys. Screed concrete surfaces on the floors, walls and ceilings wrap around the space, which is decorated with wooden furnishings to add a sense of organic warmth.

Custom-designed wooden tables, counters and shelves feature a simple cubic shape that is repeated over the two floors. Boxes of different dimensions make attractive display elements, stacked high to form full-height wall units as well as suspended from the ceiling over central islands in the shop. Upstairs, the piles of wooden cubes form a shelving system lined with books, which customers can leaf through as they sip their tea.

Where Taipei, Taiwan
Opening May 2011
Client smith&hsu
Designer Carsten Jörgensen → p.580
Floor space 172 m²
Capacity 58 seats

The tea house is a place where people can gather to chat and enjoy tea, as well as pick up smith&hsu products.

CARSTEN JÖRGENSEN

STARHILL TEA SALON BY DESIGN SPIRITS

A contemporary and classic tea salon with an Oriental twist.

Photos Toshihide Kajiwara

Where Kuala Lumpur, Malaysia
Opening October 2011
Client Autodome
Designer design spirits → p.581
Floor space 515 m²
Capacity 98 seats

Starhill Tea Salon is located on the ground floor of the Starhill Gallery Shopping Mall in Kuala Lumpur, surrounded by shops for international luxury brands like Louis Vuitton, Christian Dior, Bottega Veneta and Gucci. Malaysia, once colonized by the British, now has hardly any venues that serve authentic tea. Therefore the client asked designer Yuhkichi Kawai of design spirits to create a classic and authentic tea salon.

As the designer felt it was crucial to create a profit-making venue, he didn't want the concept to just be classical. He therefore came up with a combination of classic and contemporary design with an added sparkle of Oriental style. The tea salon is owned by a Malaysian company, so Kawai decided to use Oriental style tea tins throughout the design. Huge columns made of large and small tins, each in its own *ton-sur-ton* colour scheme, create a colourful pattern – from green to blue, purple, pink, orange and all the way to yellow – throughout the space.

The salon's organic shape with a natural flowing and curving look is echoed in the curvy furniture and the patterns used on the ceiling and carpets. The open space is separated from the shops by illuminated cabinets on the floor and borders hanging from the ceiling.

The designer faced a shortage of tea tins for display purposes because of budget constraints. He met this challenge by creating graphics of tea tins and using prints inside the side cabinets – the perfect lighting ensures that the prints cannot be distinguished from real tins.

Clusters of gold powder-coated tea cans are affixed to the ceiling over the bar.

Opposite top The curvaceous illuminated perimeter is made of clear 5-mm-thick acrylic and overlaid with a laser-cut gold-coloured sticker and lenticular sheet.

Opposite bottom Colourful columns turn product presentation into an architectural form.

DESIGN SPIRITS

Natural wood frames the skylights and the vertical windowpanes.

A challenge for the design team was to strike a balance between the enclosed air-conditioned, the shaded and the open spaces.

TANJONG BEACH CLUB BY TAKENOUCHI WEBB

A tropical venue in a classic yacht club style.

Photos Jeremy San

Opposite The interior décor is light and airy thanks to the glazed front wall and the double-height ceiling.

Opposite bottom The beach bar effortlessly combines both indoor and outdoor spaces.

For Tanjong Beach Club in Singapore, the client's brief was for a venue that seamlessly brought together all the elements of a private club with an indoor restaurant, outdoor bar and a large infinity pool. The venue needed to be flexible and cater to activities ranging from all-day dining to beach parties. Takenouchi Webb created a concept for the club that mirrored its location, with a tropical style and a marine colour palette.

Inspired by classic yacht clubs, mid-20th-century modernism and aspects of the local architecture, the design combines the warmth of natural materials with the lush landscaping of the site. Linking the outside and inside was a major priority, with striking views facilitated for customers dining in the restaurant, which is a single space 6-m high, with an additional mezzanine dining level. The ceiling is punctured by a series of circular skylights and clad in natural timber planks, which also line the walls in diamond-shaped patterns interlaid with gold-coloured strips.

A slatted-timber screen runs across the length of the front glass façade, providing a shimmering array of shadows from the surrounding palm trees. The aqua-blue shades of the upholstery in the restaurant are also repeated in the custom-made tiles that line the counter of the outdoor bar, as well as in the large pendant lampshades that hang above it. With a faceted marble front, the bar is bounded by a perforated concrete block wall and is located close to the pool, which has lounge seating at one end and a covered cabana pavilion at the other. •

Where Singapore, Singapore
Opening June 2010
Client The Lo & Behold Group
Designer Takenouchi Webb → p.589
Floor space 1515 m²
Capacity 130 seats (inside), 210 seats (outside)

TAKENOUCHI WEBB

The flawless stainless steel bar counter provides an eye-catching reflection of the blue wire chandelier.

Opposite Strong steel cables hold the tables rigidly in place.

UNPLUGGED BAR BY C4ID INTERIEUR-ARCHITECTEN

A transformable bar to get really social.

Photos Roos Aldershoff

Where Amsterdam, the Netherlands
Opening November 2011
Client WTC Amsterdam
Designer C4ID interieurarchitecten → p.5
Floor space 215 m²
Capacity 60 seats

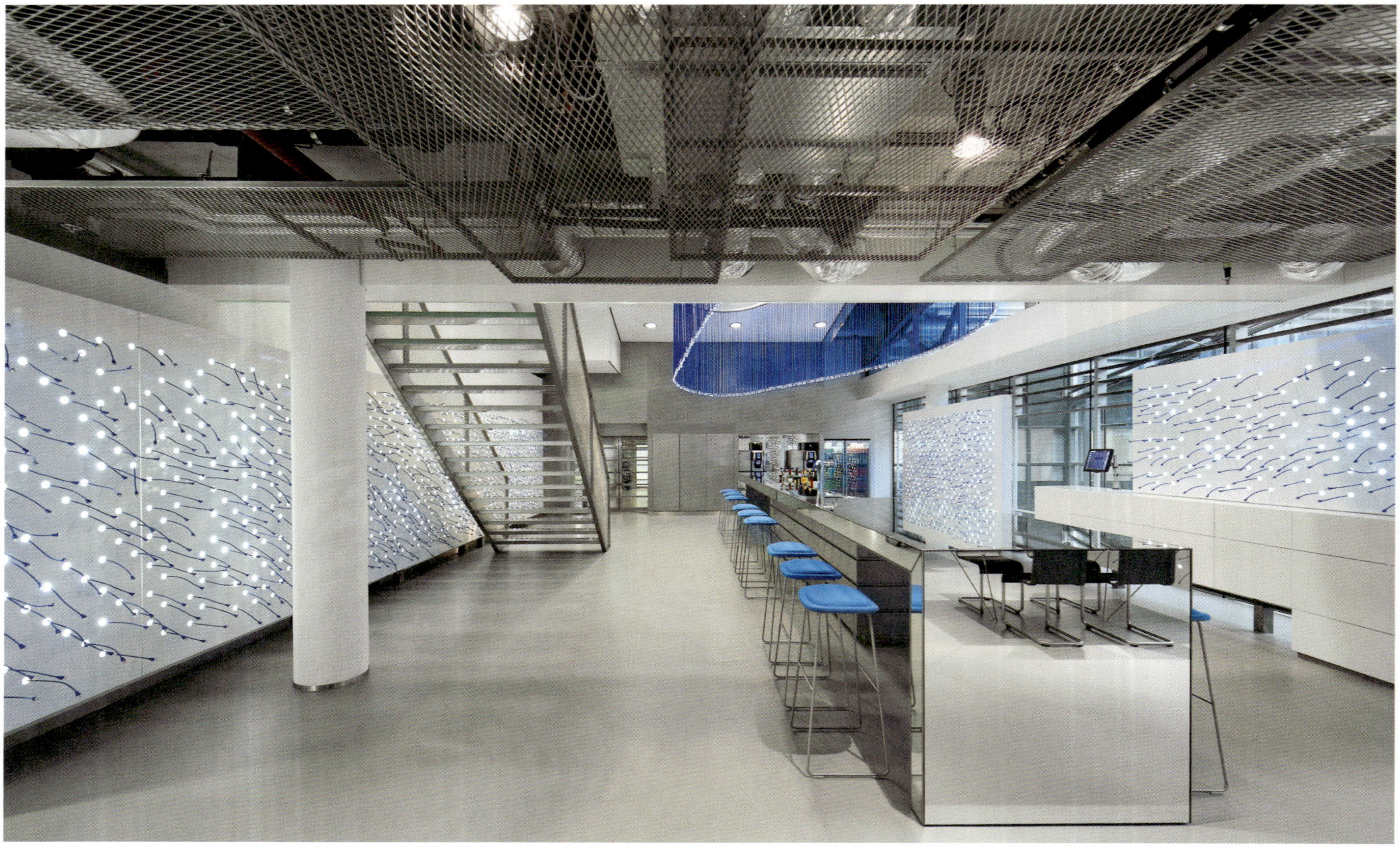

The tall Hi Pad stools were designed by Jasper Morrison for Cappellini.

THE TABLES CAN BE LIFTED TO CEILING LEVEL WHERE THEY BECOME PART OF THE MASHED STEEL PANELLING

The glossy HPL white walls are perforated with back-lit holes through which an array of blue cut data wires poke.

Picture a business, located in the middle of the Amsterdam World Trade Centre, that has no clients. The only people who enter this multifunctional bar space are employees. Young and talented people, casually dressed, with a heavy workload since they operate in a worldwide financial web. They need to break out, relax, eat, drink, watch a match and party together. It was C4ID's task to fulfil the client's wishes, who asked for an ambiguous space: it had to be industrial and forceful, yet it had to be sociable and nightlife-like when in use.

Transforming an office environment into a convincing bar area made the designers realize they had to go beyond the borders of 'corporate identity'. To give the bar personality, C4ID analysed the daily routine of its users. The match they found is that everyone involved is permanently busy in a digital world. So to create a real change, the team decided to design an Unplugged Bar, where only human contact remains. They exploited this concept by stripping typical data elements of their function and reducing them to decorative elements. The side walls are decorated with thousands of blue data wires, with only three red wires actually connected to the network. The huge chandelier above the bar is also made of data wires, attractively reflected in the mirrored panelled bar.

Another wish of the client was to be able to get rid of the tables and chairs to organize a business update with all the employees together. This is where the floating tables came in. Using electric motors and steel cables, the designers were able to create tables that can be stable as a rock without having legs. The anchoring effort of the cables and the electric motors in combination with the right triangular shapes do their job surprisingly well. Once released from their floor connectors, the tables can be lifted to ceiling level, where they become part of the mashed steel panelling. During the day the Unplugged Bar looks fresh and clean, in the evening hours it transforms into a vibrating and fashionable space, where unplugged people connect to each other easily. •

At the flick of a switch, electric motors reposition the tables, making the space multifunctional.

When the steel platform tables are in their lowered positions, employees can relax on Vitra .05 chairs.

YOUDO STONE CAFÉ BY LITTLE

Where Kanagawa, Japan
Opening February 2011
Client Youdo
Designer Little → p.585
Floor space 186 m²
Capacity 25 seats

A café with a simple, sleek design and sparkles of glamour.

Photos Kenta Hasegawa

The concept for the space is based on ancient mysticism and the food is motivated by ancient medicine, with Studio Cultivate providing customers with a seasonal organic and herbal menu.

Opposite Customers enter a simple space with concrete flooring, a solid iron cash desk, and brown painted walls.

Upstairs, oak floorboards direct customers to the first-floor terrace where fresh herbs grow.

THE CONCEPT UNITES MODERN LIFESTYLE AND ANCIENT LEGEND

The top floor with the boutique.

Youdo Stone Café is in Kamakura, an ancient city in Japan, in the Kanagawa Prefecture to the south of Tokyo. Saori Miwa of design office Little was responsible for overseeing the renovation of the three-storey building in which the café is located.

The café serves up healthy organic food and is spread over two floors, with the top floor housing a boutique for gems and quartzes. The idea behind the space is that customers can have a coffee and a bite to eat while waiting for their bespoke jewellery order to be completed. The concept behind the design comes from a legend of the local area, where a formidable dragon was said to have lived. The client had a specific request for the designer linked to this legend, in that the third storey of the building could be designed as a dwelling for the white dragon, with the lower levels providing the nourishment – in the form of the gems, quartzes, plants and vegetables produced here. In the design, Saori Miwa united aspects of both modern lifestyle and the spirit world of ancient times.

A simple and sleek design was implemented for the interior, which includes oak flooring and white walls. Touches of glamour are also incorporated with the use of tiny crystals in the decoration. The client deals in many kinds of gems and quartzes, which are believed to confer good luck and are often used as talismans. For this project, small gemstones were therefore used – adorning the wall surfaces and hanging from lampshades – to enhance the space in which customers can relax. On the ground floor a glass-fronted niche is embedded into the side wall to display larger gemstones and jewellery samples.

Opposite top Crystals are hanging from the lampshades and cover the complete wall with its sunken cabinet.

Opposite bottom All the tables, cabinets, chairs, stools and sofas, upholstered in plain-weave fabric, were custom designed.

LITTLE

Where Shanghai, China
Opening December 2010
Client David Laris
Designer Dariel Studio → p.581
Floor space 125 m²
Capacity 30 guests

The U-shaped bar counter is a central focus for customers.

YUCCA BY DARIEL STUDIO

The spirit of Salvador Dali is conjured up in a Shanghai lounge bar.

Photos Derryck Menere

Perched on the third floor of a grand, traditionally-styled building in the former Shanghai French Concession, Yucca is a swanky Mexican lounge bar. The mansion is the headquarters of Yucca's creator, Australian-Greek chef David Laris, and it also houses three of his other restaurants

The word 'Mexican' in connection with restaurants and bars tends to conjure up a host of tired old clichés and stereotypes of cacti and sombreros, which Thomas Dariel of Dariel Studio was determined to avoid. Instead, they paid homage to the rich visual cultures of Latin America and opted for a quirky yet chic-and-sleek interior design featuring a mismatch of styles and shocking colours. With exuberant style, walls are splashed in vivid blocks of blue and pink and the floor is a study in Op Art with a mosaic of custom-made blue-and-white tiles in geometric formations laid out at haphazard angles. A photograph of blue-hued women festooned with Moorish designs extends from the entrance up the double-height wall to the top floor lounge, which is connected by a cerise spiral staircase leading up to the lounge area for private parties.

In the main lounge, the theatrical space is dominated by the glass-topped marble bar, which at one end features a glass shelf extending from the counter, positioned at a lower level for the convenience of guests sitting in the luxurious armchairs that surround it. In a secluded room to the back of the lounge is the VIP area, with walls decorated in vivid red and black stripes. In every corner of the bar, decorative elements have been carefully selected to instil a spirit of exuberance while still creating a warm, cosy and harmonious atmosphere. ●

One wall has a larger-than-life photo divided into parallel-positioned frames.

Opposite Solid blocks of vibrant colour are juxtaposed with navy blue-and-white patterned floor tiles.

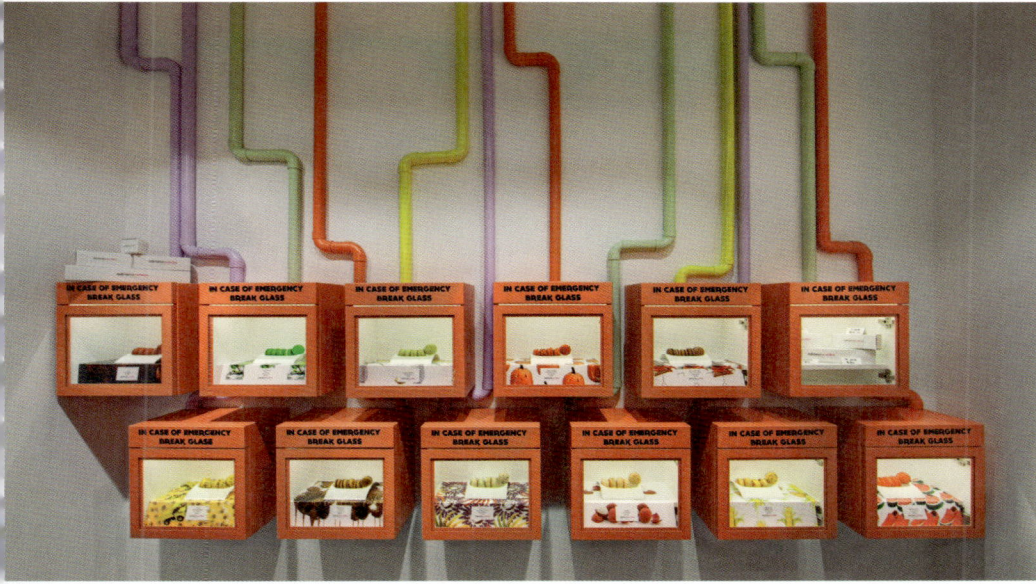

Luchetti Krelle custom-designed a lot of the furnishings in the eatery, including the imaginative display boxes.

Opposite From the street, customers can gaze in childlike wonder at the colourful feast inside Zumbo's 'house of fun'.

Where Sydney, Australia
Opening October 2011
Client Adriano Zumbo Patissier
Designer Luchetti Krelle → p.585
Floor space 182 m²
Capacity 16 seats

ZUMBO BY LUCHETTI KRELLE

A colourful dessert bar with a fun, factory feel.

Photos Murray Fredericks

The Willy Wonka design concept was borne out of the Wonka tattoo on Adriano Zumbo's arm.

CUSTOMERS SEATED AROUND A MOVING VISUAL FEAST: THE SUSHI BAR-STYLE DESSERT TRAIN

The kitchen wall is clad in black-and-white tiles laid in a pattern which is reminiscent of a measuring jug.

Adriano Zumbo's new 'dessert bar', located in an inner-city suburb of Sydney, offers a daily array of delectable delights; Luchetti Krelle was commissioned to create an equally delicious design for the interior.

The team drew inspiration from the fact that the client is often referred to as 'the Willy Wonka of Australian patisserie', aiming to instil a fun, factory feel in the small space. From the street, the glass façade helps to entice customers into the kinetic fun world of Zumbo. With a view into the kitchen from both the retail and dining areas, the concept creatively incorporates references to a moving assembly line, with customers seated around a moving visual feast: the sushi bar-style dessert train.

A fresh pastel palette adds splashes of colour to the white space, from the furniture and fittings to the custom-made wallpaper on the back wall, decorated with macaroons. Childhood memories are evoked with display stands and cages designed like the various components of the Mouse Trap board game. Customers will spot these aspects throughout the space, including the bathtub filled with cakes, the 'in case of emergency, break glass' display cases on the walls and the storefront display of telescopic stands on top of which some sweet treats have been trapped. •

The bespoke macaroon wallpaper – inspired by the designer's memories of lickable wall coverings from his childhood – is lit up by Ism Objects' spherical halogen lamps.

25HOURS BY ALFREDO HÄBERLI

Where Zurich, Switzerland
Opening October 2012
Client 25hours Hotel Company
Designer Alfredo Häberli → p.578
Floor space 8000 m²
Capacity 126 rooms

The starting point for a city-wide treasure hunt.

Photos courtesy of 25hours

All rooms have bespoke desk units decked out with a flat-screen TV and high-tech docking station.

Opposite The guest rooms are a comfortable and colourful retreat, packed full of custom-designed upholstery, furniture and fittings.

The décor questions familiar ideals and elicits a smile with some of the cutesy touches, in particular the contemporary illustrations on the walls.

Quirky styles and curved edges await guests in the bathrooms.

The stories and hints about the city of Zurich can be discovered on the shelves.

The character of Zurich West, a thriving and trendsetting district of the city, is influenced by a mixture of former industrial buildings. A cultural quarter, with art galleries, small theatres, bars and clubs, it is also now the new home of 25hours hotel Zurich West, designed by Alfredo Häberli. As with the concept all 25hours hotels, the brief called for a design that was inspired by its location and Häberli set out to combine his usual witty product with new, exciting ideas.

The pointedly organized, timeless interior of the first 25hours hotel in Switzerland greets its guests in the generously sized lobby, decorated with elegant fabrics and a nod and a wink to a paint jar, instilling a lively atmosphere. With the working title of 'the smile of my hometown', the hotel is brimming with artistic and graphic interventions that lead the guests on a tour of the design team's favourite spots. Adding value to the different elements throughout the hotel, Häberli's vibrant designs make a statement in the lobby, the central bar area and right through to the meeting rooms and up to the top-floor sauna suite, with its décor of placid natural materials and breathtaking views across the city.

The 126 guest rooms and suites are adorned with custom-designed multifunctional furniture in a range of silver, gold and platinum categories. Striking shapes and colours are a key feature in the rooms, from the swirling designs of the mirrors to brightly patterned hand-tufted carpets. The revelation of the personal travel tips from the designer himself is the best-kept secret: sightseeing recommendations have been written on the walls in the rooms, even behind curtains and on surfaces around the building at seemingly random intervals, surprising guests and leading them on a city-wide treasure hunt.

THE HOTEL IS BRIMMING WITH ARTISTIC AND GRAPHIC INTERVENTIONS

ALFREDO HÄBERLI

White painted timber planks are incorporated into the lobby décor.

Opposite Just like a circus troupe, hotel guests are always on the move.

25HOURS BY DREIMETA

A hotel that plays with the dreams and sensations of the circus world.

Photos courtesy of 25hours and Steve Herud

Found circus memorabilia is set alongside bespoke leather-upholstered furniture.

Where Vienna, Austria
Opening March 2011
Client 25hours Hotel Company
Designer Dreimeta → p.582
Floor space 1050 m²
Capacity 34 rooms

The individual floor plans and selected design elements make every guest room unique.

BEARDED LADIES, JUGGLING CLOWNS AND STRONG-CALVED HORSES SCURRY ABOUT THE WALLPAPER

The bathroom is lit up like a theatrical dressing room.

Opposite The guest rooms have circus-related furniture elements and artwork on the walls.

The 25hours hotel Vienna is one of the 25hours Hotel Company's latest venues. The basic principle of the 25hours hotels is that each hotel is entirely unique and tells a different story. The client asked design studio Dreimeta to design this Austrian hotel.

Vienna has always stood for sensationalism and show, for seeing and being seen. In 1808, the first fixed circus opened at the Vienna Prater. The circus at that time was a mixture of human zoo, freak show and vaudeville. The hotel concept is drawn from the traditions of the circus institution as a symbol of spectacle. Found pieces from that era were put together and re-treated without hiding their age. Instead of conspicuously vintage pieces, Dreimeta chose memorabilia with history. Custom-designed tables, sofas and armchairs fit perfectly into the eclectic style.

An eye-catching design element in the guest rooms is the wallpaper with exclusive illustrations by Berlin artist Olaf Hajek. Matching the colour concepts of the rooms, he depicts circus scenes, blurring fantasy and reality, space and time. Bearded ladies, juggling clowns and strong-calved horses scurry about the wallpaper. Other than the illustrations, the suites are quite reserved, but no less playful in their use of the circus motif: lighting in the bathrooms alludes to dressing rooms, fixtures create the idea of a circus wagon and accessories refer to the lively leitmotif.

Besides the 34 rooms Dreimeta also designed the public areas with its relaxing lounge Dachboden (which simply means attic or loft). Improvisation is a circus device: everything is temporary. The designers also wanted to establish an improvised atmosphere, but one that is cosy and does not appear unfinished. The floor in the public areas is minimally finished instead of covered with the usual materials. Room dividers, reminiscent of big cat cages, divide the loft area into atmospheric zones, but keep the rooms open, transparent and flexible.

The relaxing lounge with bar is overlooking the rooftops of Vienna – giving a little preview of what is to follow in the second stage: in the winter of 2012/2013 25hours will include another 185 rooms, a spa, conference rooms, as well as several dining areas.

Opposite Vintage suitcases are used as television cabinets.

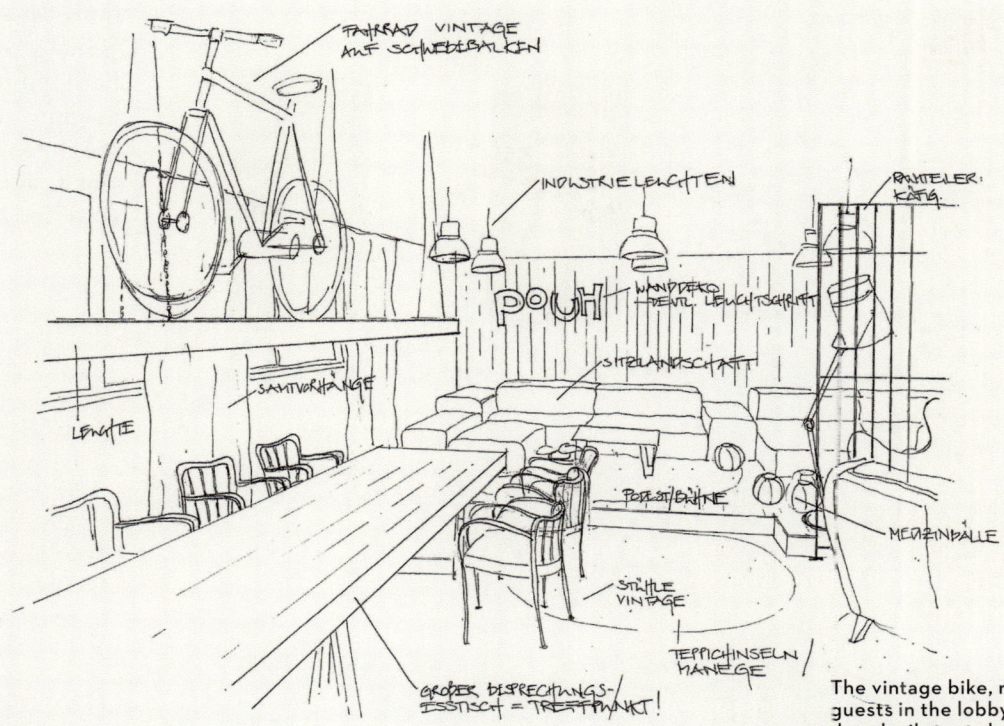

The vintage bike, riding high above guests in the lobby, brings to mind daredevil stunts by tightrope walkers.

Lobby

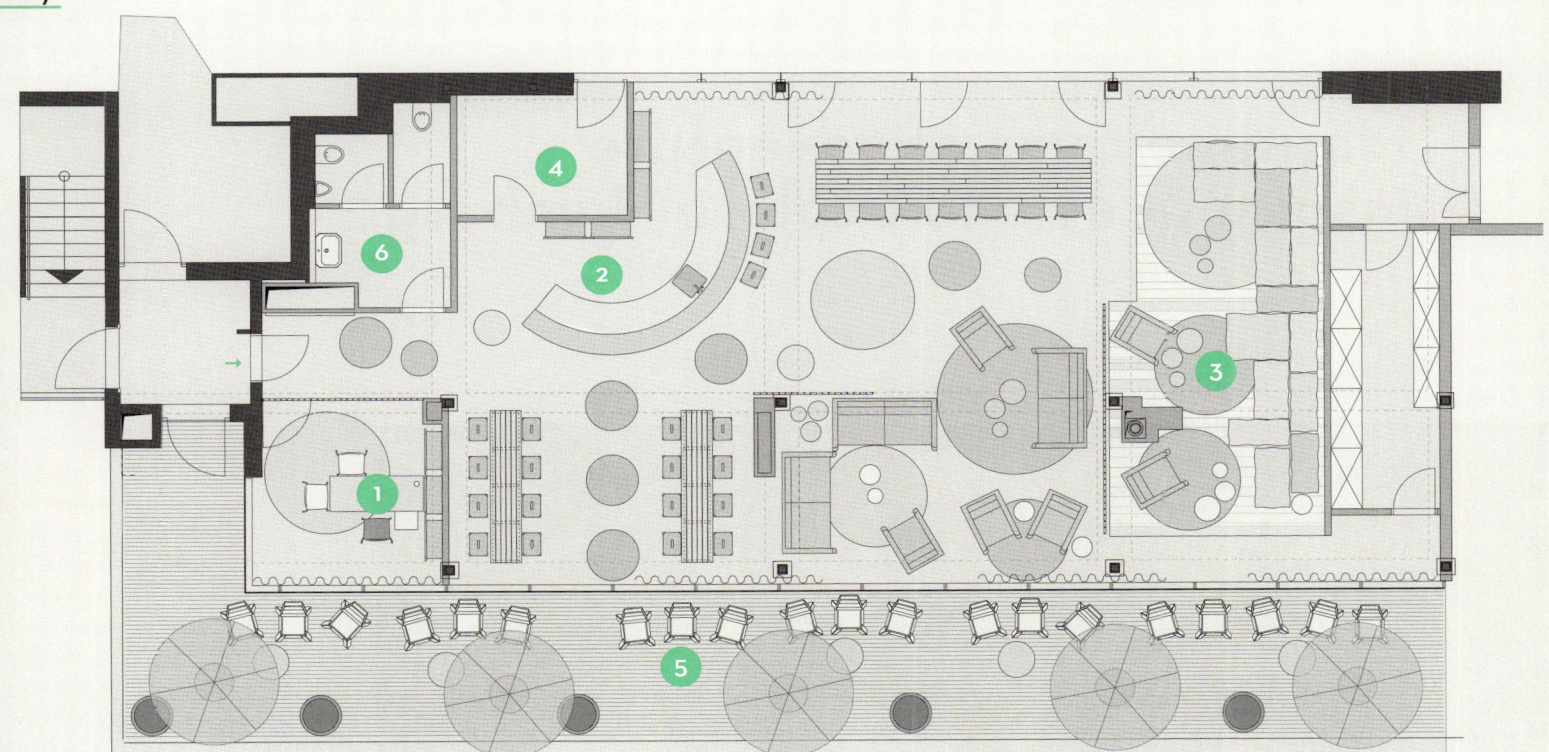

1. Reception
2. Bar
3. Lounge seating
4. Kitchen
5. Terrace
6. Toilets

Guest room

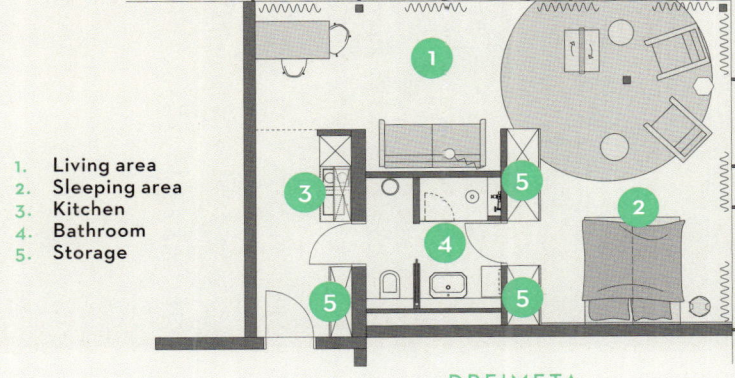

1. Living area
2. Sleeping area
3. Kitchen
4. Bathroom
5. Storage

The Dreimeta team designed sofas and wing-backed armchairs to fit comfortably in the eccentric interior.

DREIMETA

25HOURS BY STEPHEN WILLIAMS ASSOCIATES

Where **Hamburg, Germany**
Opening **July 2011**
Client **25hours Hotel Company**
Designer **Stephen Williams Associates** → p.589
Floor space **7500 m²**
Capacity **170 rooms**

Maritime tales of adventure inspire guests to explore Hamburg.

Huge signs on the floor, as seen here at the reception desk, provide clear routing throughout the hotel.

Opposite Hapag-Lloyd, a Hamburg shipping company, donated the shipping container that forms one of the conference rooms.

STEPHEN WILLIAMS ASSOCIATES

The first floor Club Room and opposite Vinyl Room feature vintage furniture.

Through the void of the first floor guests can look down at the hotel lounge.

The washbasins in the public toilets refer to the tubes inside ships.

The window storage – which runs along one of the ground floor walls – features niches for intimate dining.

A new district is emerging in Hamburg, where old port warehouses are being replaced by offices, hotels and shops, creating a lively city quarter that is a microcosm of modern life. The district is HafenCity, where people can come together, mingle, confer and celebrate, and there is now a new 'hang-out' in the neighbourhood. The 25hours hotel HafenCity was designed by Stephen Williams Associates as a welcoming 'living room', filled with signs and symbols that refer to the history of the district. A multidisciplinary team (including Fabian Tank, Konnie Kotte and Markus Stoll) worked collaboratively with the client, inspired by sailors and the city's seafaring past.

The interior is packed with elements and materials reminiscent of the shipbuilding industry, spun together with some seamen's yarns. The tales of 25 mariners are adapted into semi-fictional stories – of dangerous passages, romantic encounters, wild storms and painful farewells – that became one of the guiding themes of the design concept. The hotel offers a classical typology of spaces but comes up with some surprising interpretations, from the business centre called the 'Radio Room' decked out with salt-bleached driftwood, to the rooftop sauna built within a rusty container with panoramic views over the industrial harbour.

The hub of the hotel is on the ground floor, with its open lobby, restaurant, bar and shop presenting a comfortable and relaxed version of harbour living. The décor has an elegant industrial aesthetic: warehouse shelves, rough wooden boxes, stacks of oriental carpets and an eclectic range of maritime finds that are not only decorative but also multifunctional, open to being reconfigured at a whim; the floor markings provide an order to many different layout options available.

The bedrooms are cabin-style suites, with cosy built-in bunks and a 'travel trunk' that opens up to provide visitors with all that they require for their stay: information, desk space and even a log book. Intended to inspire the guests to explore the city, the log books are illustrated with the seamen's stories, which are also brought to life in the drawings on the bedroom walls.

STEPHEN WILLIAMS ASSOCIATES

Each room has a 'travel trunk' that serves as a desk and small storage space, and also includes the minibar.

Opposite The bunk beds resemble sleeping berths on ships.

GUESTS CAN RETREAT TO THEIR CABIN-STYLE SUITES

The bathroom also features nautical elements.

The guest rooms' bespoke wallpaper is illustrated with adaptations of classic seafarer tattoo art.

STEPHEN WILLIAMS ASSOCIATES

Initial sketch of the window storage and restaurant area.

Section AA

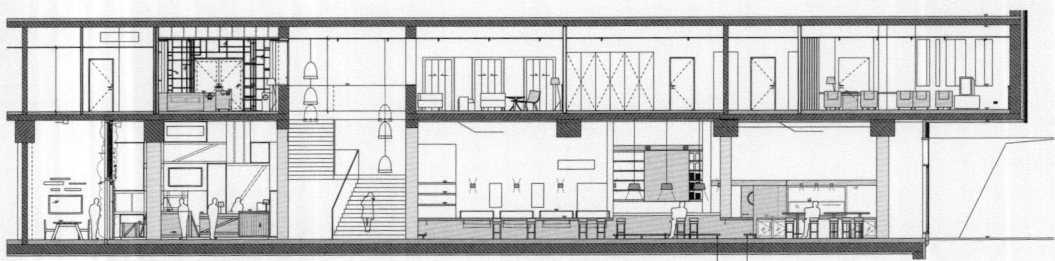

Section BB

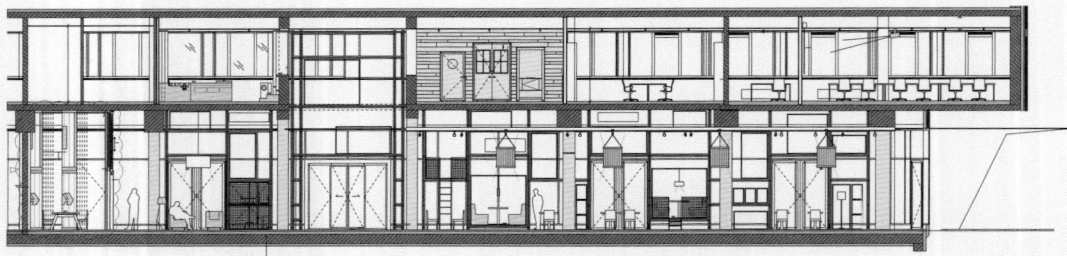

Elevations

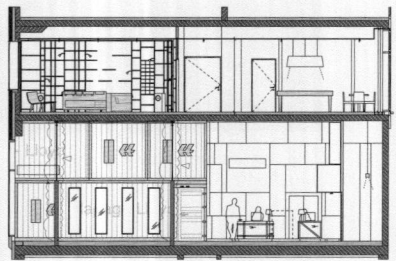
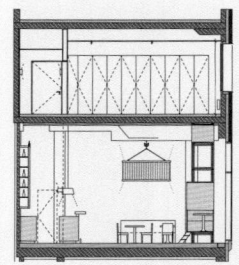
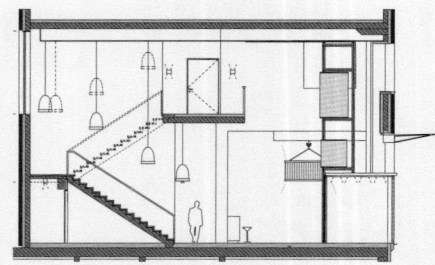

First floor

1. Radio room
2. Vinyl room
3. Conference room
4. Club room
5. Guest rooms
6. Lifts

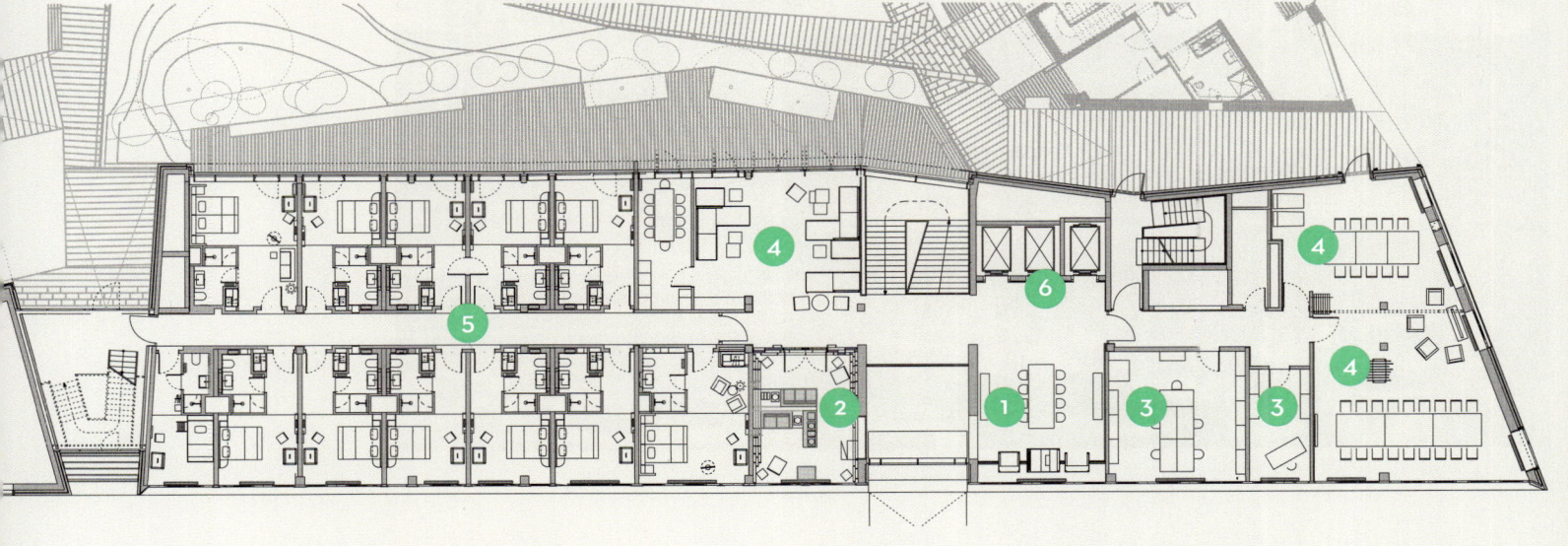

Ground floor

1. Reception
2. Lounge
3. Bar
4. Restaurant
5. Conference room
6. Kitchen
7. Lifts
8. Back of the house

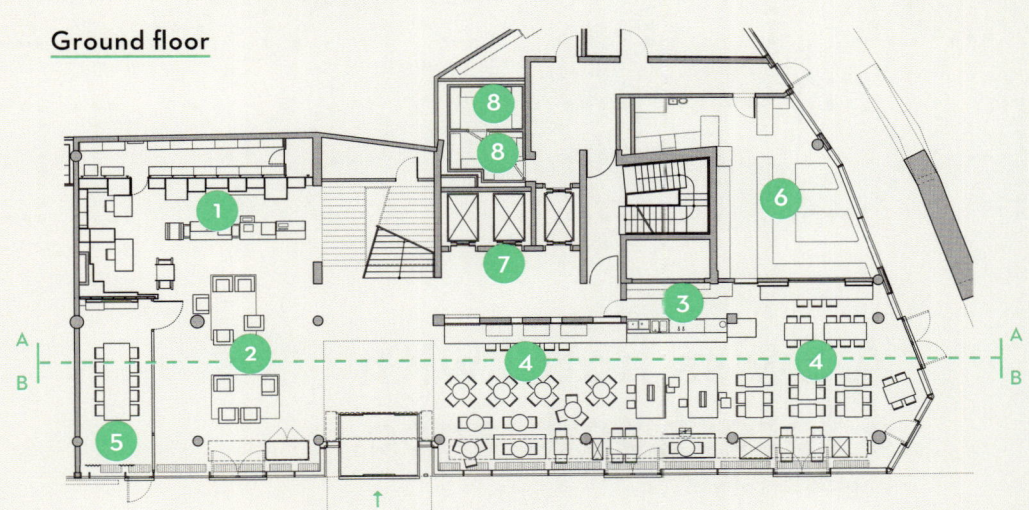

THE CONCEPT IS INSPIRED BY THE CITY'S SEAFARING PAST

STEPHEN WILLIAMS ASSOCIATES

The mirrored exterior reflects the park foliage that surrounds the hotel.

Opposite top Architectural elements, such as the angled mirrored columns, are incorporated into the interior décor.

Opposite bottom Tall tables in the bar were designed by IDA 14 to neatly slot together or stand alone as required.

CITY GARDEN HOTEL BY IDA 14

A Swiss hotel with a forest ambiance.

Photos Urs Wyss

Where Zug, Switzerland
Opening January 2010
Client Parkhotel
Designer IDA 14 → p.584
Floor space 4368 m²
Capacity 82 rooms

Velvety upholstery and deep-pile rugs in a burnt orange hue give an autumnal forest feel to the lobby.

THE DESIGN TEAM CONCENTRATED ON WARM MATERIALS

The architecture firm EM2N has succeeded in engaging the City Garden Hotel in Zug in a dialogue with the nearby park thanks to spectacular architecture. The three-dimensional façade covered in chromium steel panels and the rhythm of the corridors lend the hotel a unique character. The mirrored finish of the staggered façade, a theme continued in the interior, draws in the park's natural elements and combines with the modernity of the interior space. The design and execution of the interior was done by interior architecture office IDA 14.

Inside, the design team concentrated on warm materials such as wood but also on rough elements like concrete. In the ground-floor restaurant, mirror finishes were used on columns scattered throughout the room to connect the interior with the exterior. Together with design company The Chair, IDA 14 developed special lounge sofas and wooden tables in various sizes.

The ambiance of the rooms and suites is characterized by simple elegance. A luxurious, airy atmosphere was achieved in the rooms by reducing the amount of furniture and using high-quality materials. In each room, the eye is immediately drawn to large decorative textile bedhead panels. They are unique design pieces from the Glinka Güell textile collection created by Jakob Schlaepfer, whose colours subtly blend in with the room's prevailing ambiance. For the bathrooms, the designers choose a semi-open plan with glass or mirrored surfaces and slick white washbasins. The dark oak parquet contrasts with upholstery materials in yellow and green tones or the delicate purple curtains.

A kaleidoscopic rhythm is imbued in the hotel's monochromatic corridors.

Bespoke furniture designed by IDA 14 is also to be found in the guest rooms, including the luggage rack at the end of the bed.

Colours from the magnificent floral headboard are picked out and used in the furnishings or surfaces in the rooms.

COSMO HOTEL

COSMO HOTEL BY DUKA DESIGN AND SEHW ARCHITEKTUR

Where Berlin, Germany
Opening January 2010
Client Europe Hotels International
Designers duka design → p.582
and SEHW Architektur → p.588
Floor space 5600 m²
Capacity 84 rooms

A play with tactility in a Berlin hotel.

Photos Studio 9 für Ardex, Andreas Süß and Kathi Weber

Opposite top The interior is a mix of materials, from the roughly-finished metallic bronze walls to the richly upholstered sofas.

Opposite bottom The lush velvety fabrics on the dining chairs echo the metallic materiality of the hotel's décor.

The central block on the ground floor consists of the reception desk, positioned at one corner, and the bar at the other.

Large fabric-covered headboards are a feature in all the rooms.

The silvery tones of the feature wall match with the metallic silver blinds, and the golden fabrics with the rich grain of the woodwork.

Animal print wallpaper is used to make a statement.

Mix 2 cl of vodka, 1 cl of Cointreau, 1 cl of lime juice, 2 cl of cranberry juice and crushed ice in a cocktail glass and you have a Cosmo. The recipe for the new Cosmo Hotel in Berlin Mitte, however, is completely different. Its premise is more a reaction to a monofunctional and overtly saturated real-estate market. An office building built only a few years ago and abandoned shortly after completion due to a lack of tenants became the shell into which the design hotel was poured.

The exterior, in natural stone, is a reference to the critical reconstruction of Berlin, practically hiding the entrance, creating an introverted feel. Inside, SEHW Architektur opened up the ground floor, creating a bright lobby zoned by a dominant golden core consisting of service spaces. The lobby is cloaked in a light flowing curtain, blurring the threshold between inside and outside. The plan for the upper floors appropriates the existing office building grid and then emancipates itself in its design. The existing service core at the interior of the building was partially opened up to accommodate special functions, including a cigar lounge, spa and sauna. Walls, ceilings and floors are coloured dark brown. Orientation is provided by specially designed pictograms, which are back-lit and lend atmosphere to the hallways.

The dark interior of the hallways contrasts with the effect upon entering the rooms, where a pleasant flow of light and a wide view of the city welcome the guest. Duka design opted for a restrained attitude with a whiff of glamour in all 84 rooms. The elaborate choice of colours draws attention to the meticulous composition of materials. The designer duo clearly took great pleasure in playing with tactility by using hard and soft, smooth and rough, matt and shiny surfaces next to one another. Furthermore, the intelligent zoning creates crucial visual axes. For the furniture, duka design combined three functions in one simple element by creating a bench that turns into a sideboard and finally a wardrobe. The sophisticated atmospheric lighting concept and subtle design references to opulent grand hotels of the past show that the Cosmo is the Berlin of today, without being retro. ●

DARK HALLWAYS CONTRAST WITH THE LIGHT AND OPEN CHARACTER OF THE ROOMS

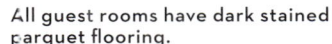

All guest rooms have dark stained parquet flooring.

EMPIRE HOTEL BY AS DESIGN SERVICE

An aristocratic style for an 'emperor's' deluxe suite.

Photos Sum Sing

Whereas most of the furnishings have a cubic shape, curves can be seen in the designer sanitary ware.

Opposite top Although the rooms are devoid of bright colours, texture and intrigue are created by the use of tactile materials on every surface.

Opposite bottom Monochromatic relaxation awaits guests in the guest room spa.

Where Hong Kong, Hong Kong
Opening May 2010
Client Empire Hotels
Designer AS Design Service → p.579
Floor space 95 m²
Capacity 1 room

The concept uses exquisite textural layering as a visual language to realize a deluxe design hotel.

Thanks to the crisp white illumination, the luxuriously dark décor has a sense of lightness.

Darkened mirroring emphasizes the elegantly sleek interior.

THE DESIGN TEAM USED THE TERM 'BLACK ELEGANCE' AS A STARTING POINT

Simple slabs of a marble-like material light up the room number.

AS Design Service was asked to redesign the 95-m² deluxe suite for the Empire Hotel in Hong Kong. They used the term 'Black Elegance' as their starting point.

The design team – Four Lau and Sam Sum – used black as the sole colour. The design is a break from the traditional hotel room and was inspired by the constant demand of consumers for new innovations. The room symbolizes the aristocratic style and poise of the 'Empire', where guests can indulge in the extravaganza 'in the dark'. The suite is furnished with sophisticated materials; every single wall is decorated with materials of different textures, creating a metropolitan atmosphere that creates not only visual but also tactile sensations. The design team integrated seven elements, including wooden surfaces made with special techniques – like Bamboo wallpaper, velvet wallpaper, crystalline marble floor tiles, fabric, glass, steel, and basket-weave floor mats.

The suite is completed with different kind of luxury features, such as big flat-screen televisions and an integrated surround sound system. The luxurious bathroom features a tailor-made waterbed along with a rainforest shower and a massage bed. All to ensure that guests feel like emperors themselves.

Opposite The ambiguity of the stepladder overhead allows the visitor to dream up their own story of the original forester's house.

FORSTHAUS AM EISWOOG BY NAUMANN. ARCHITEKTUR

A forest fairytale hotel that preserves its orginal soul.

Photos Zooey Braun

The hotel is situated in a forest to the southwest of Frankfurt.

Where Ramsen, Germany
Opening September 2010
Client Landgasthof Forelle
Designer naumann.architektur → p.586
Floor space 288 m²
Capacity 9 rooms

The moss green flooring in the entrance area was manufactured by Carpet Object.

Nothing in the house is without meaning and historical context, although what this might be is up to the guests' imagination.

ONLY UPON CLOSER INSPECTION DOES ONE NOTICE THE CHANGES

Forsthaus Am Eiswoog is a rural hotel in Southwest Germany. Located in a building that had been a forest ranger's house for ages, it was successfully transformed into a hotel by German agency naumann. architektur. While the soul of the building was preserved and its original dimensions maintained, alterations and additions were made to meet the requirements of a modern hotel. Each of its original eight rooms has its own feel and ambiance, and the ninth room is located in the former wash house.

At first glance, the house's transformation is not apparent. Although newly painted, the building's colours are as they've always been. Only upon closer inspection does one notice the changes: 'Es War Einmal' (once upon a time) is written on an Umbra grey metal sheet and folded around the corner of the house. Other metal sheets show phrases like 'Auf Der Lauer' (on the lookout) and 'Die Erde Still Geküsst' (the ground kissed silently).

Guests enter the Forsthaus through the dark entrance, with its dark painted walls and ceiling and flooring made to look like fallen leaves and moss. Spots accent the room doors, with written quotes below the room numbers. Each room has its own story and character. The unmodified staircase stands like an accessible, functional sculpture or historical relic.

The choice of material for the rooms was inspired by the surroundings; Douglas Fir plywood, concrete blocks and solid oak timbers – simple but strong materials. Except for chairs and lighting, the architects designed all the furniture themselves – the furniture is directly related to the building and is an organic component of it. Narrow, untreated tree trunks above an armoire are prime examples of this. When viewed along with the large wooden posts surrounding the four-poster bed, they serve as 'visual aids' that enhance the sensation of sleeping in the forest among the trees.

An intriguing forest of tree trunks is slotted into the space above the natural wood wardrobe, seating and shelving unit.

The simple stencils on the walls accentuate the story of the previous inhabitants of the house, as well as the wildlife of the surrounding countryside.

NAUMANN.ARCHITEKTUR

Façade

North

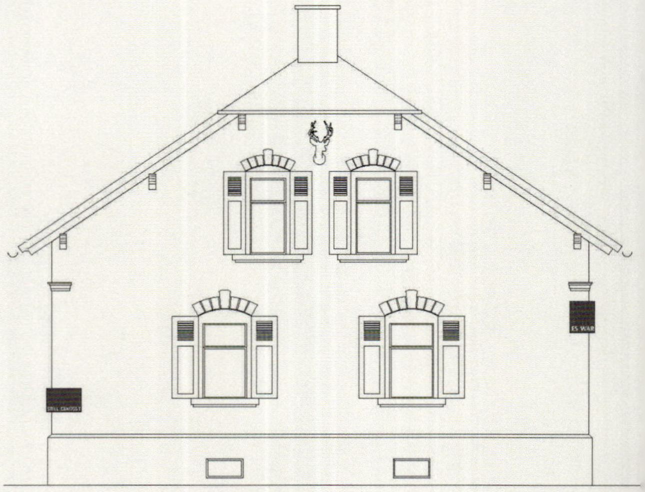

East

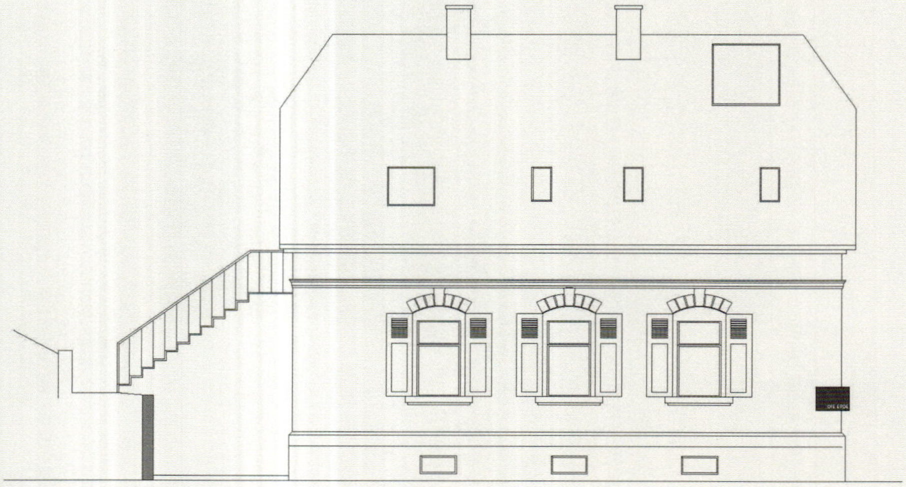

South

West

Site plan

1. Hotel
2. Room 9
3. Vegetable garden
4. Barn
5. Garage
6. Slaughterhouse

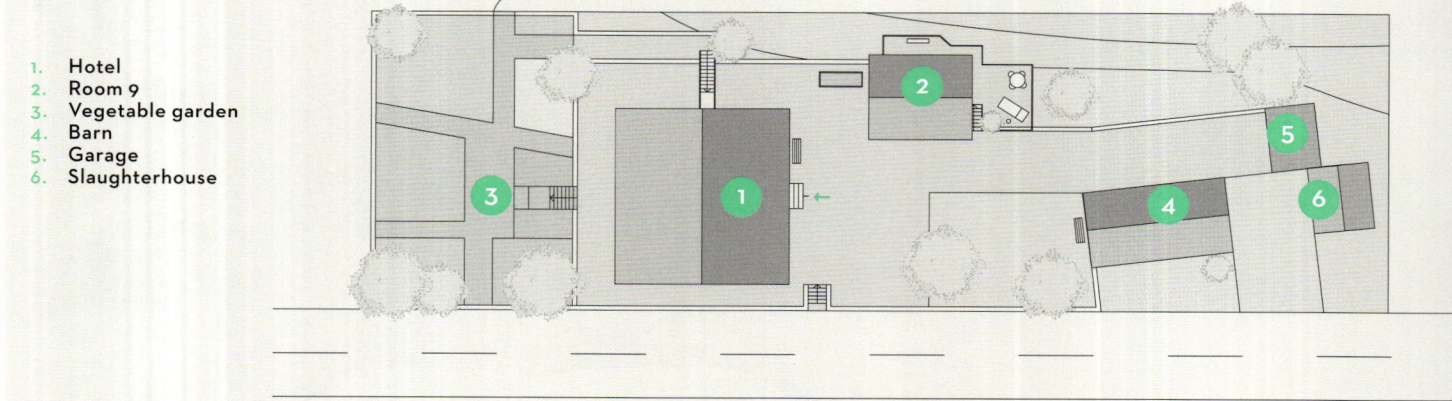

THE CHOICE OF
MATERIAL FOR
THE ROOMS WAS
INSPIRED BY THE
SURROUNDINGS

Section AA

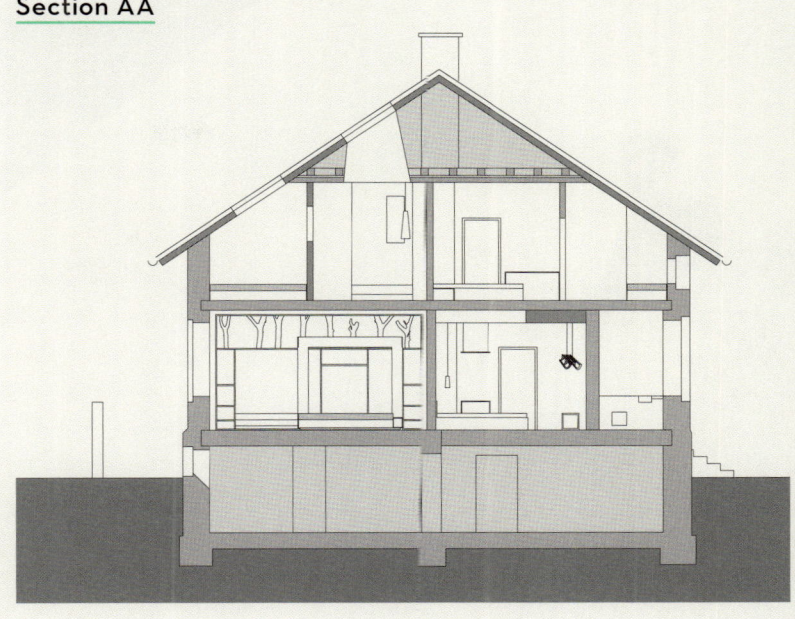

Ground floor

First floor

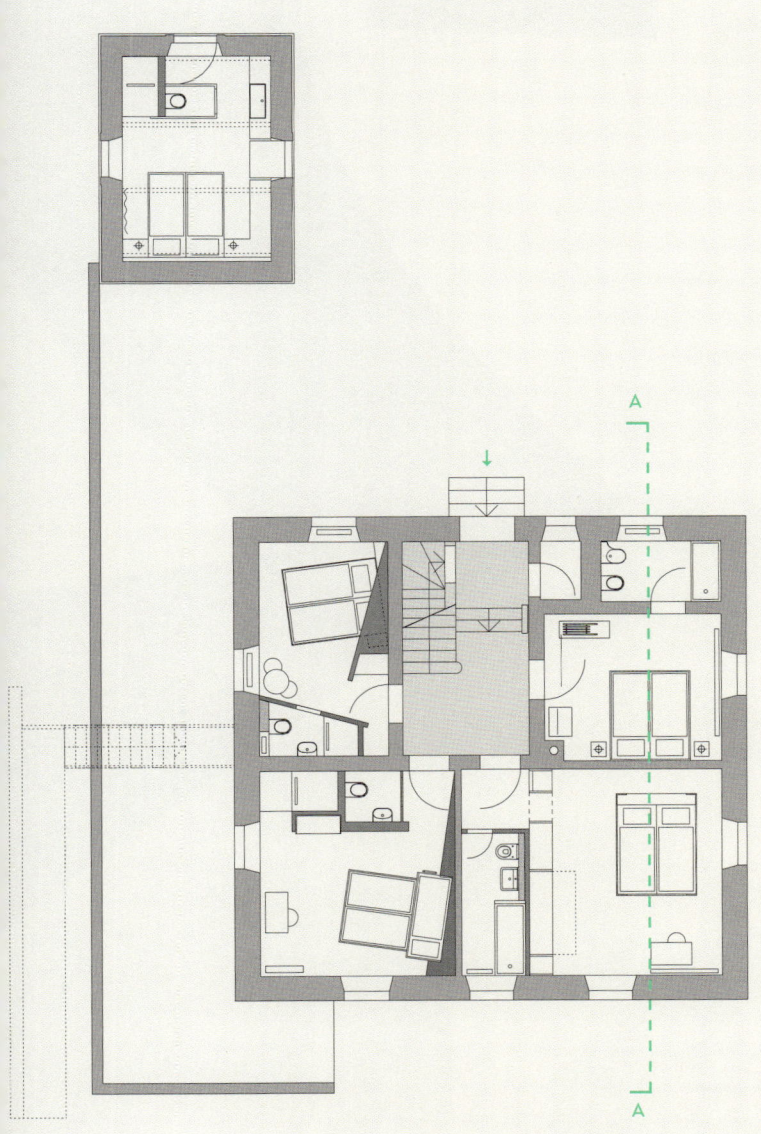

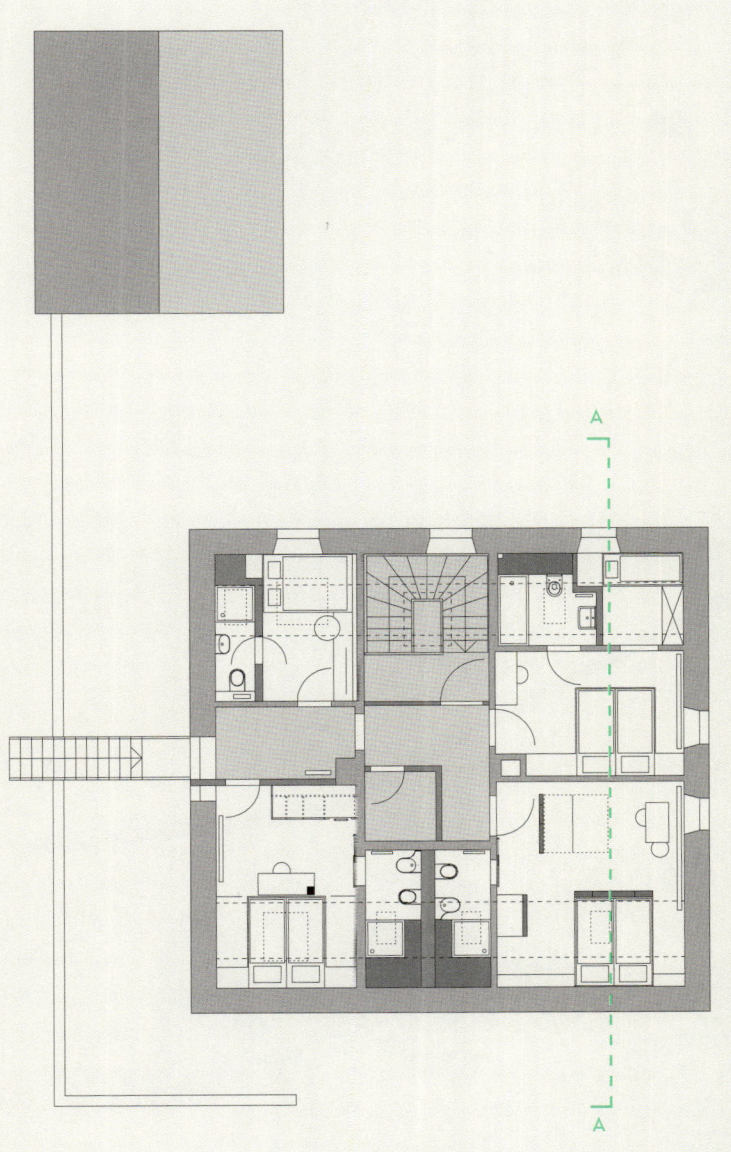

NAUMANN.ARCHITEKTUR

The bar area has a black and yellow colour scheme.

GOLI+BOSI BY STUDIO UP

Naked and barefoot in Split.

Photos Robert Leš

A yellow glow emanates from all the windows in the building.

Opposite Bold, black numbering stands out against the bright yellow of the stairwell.

Where Split, Croatia
Opening September 2010
Client Safir
Designer Studio UP → p.589
Floor space 1360 m²
Capacity 138 guests

STUDIO UP 425

The historic Savo building, located in the centre of Split, can be found within the walls of the Roman palace built in the fourth century by Roman emperor Diocletian. The exterior of the building is grand and looks like a 1920s-era department store, which is pretty much what it was until Studio UP undertook some guerrilla design, transforming the entire space into a design hostel in just 100 days. The original escalators, customer lift and staircase were left unchanged, with what used to be the shopping areas being partitioned by a system of walls that contain all the necessary components for a hostel – beds, lavatories and showers.

The spacious ground floor level offers a reception, bar area and restaurant, leading off which are the escalators that dominate the core of the building. Blocks of colour create a solid and vibrant décor in the interior, with the bar area being dominated by black surfaces – for the counter, walls and ceiling – while epoxy resin in a brilliant yellow colour is spread across the floor. This sulphurous yellow is also used for the circulation areas and stairs. From outside, this colour glows from the windows, establishing the identity of the hostel and evoking memories of the city's sulphurous hot springs that originally drew the emperor to this site.

The design team shoehorned 29 rooms into the four-storey building, all cloaked in white, ranging from singles to a dormitory sleeping eight in wall capsules, and angular duplexes that occupy the attic floor. The concept is not a million miles away from a Japanese capsule hotel, with a raw and basic aesthetic instilled in the space, which also links to the hostel's name: 'goli' and 'bosi' literally translates to 'naked and barefoot'. •

Opposite The white dormitory 'pods', which incorporate eight beds and one wash basin, have a cubist design.

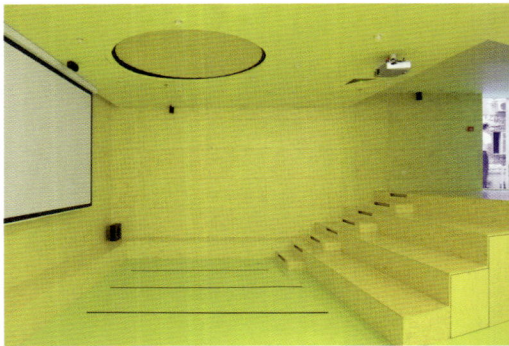

An all-yellow surround is seen in one of the communal areas.

The hostel makes use of every bit of available space, with upper bunks accessed by step ladders.

BLOCKS OF COLOUR CREATE A SOLID AND VIBRANT DÉCOR

Some rooms have built-in entertainment systems.

Opposite The sleeping areas have an all-white décor, with informative graphics printed on the yellow floor.

First floor

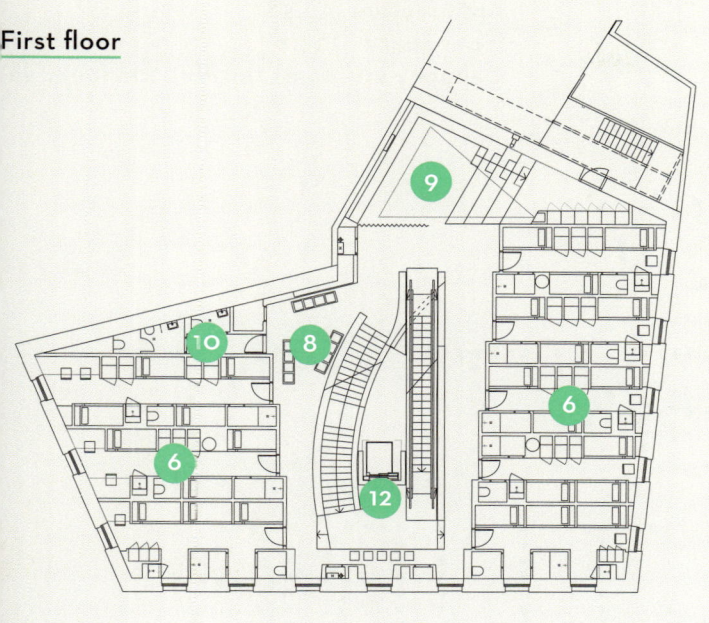

Third floor

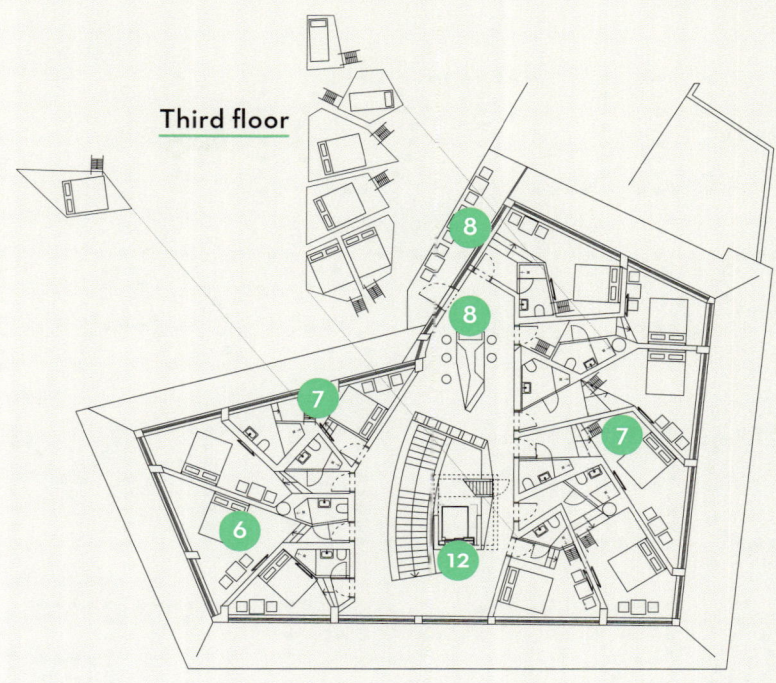

Ground floor

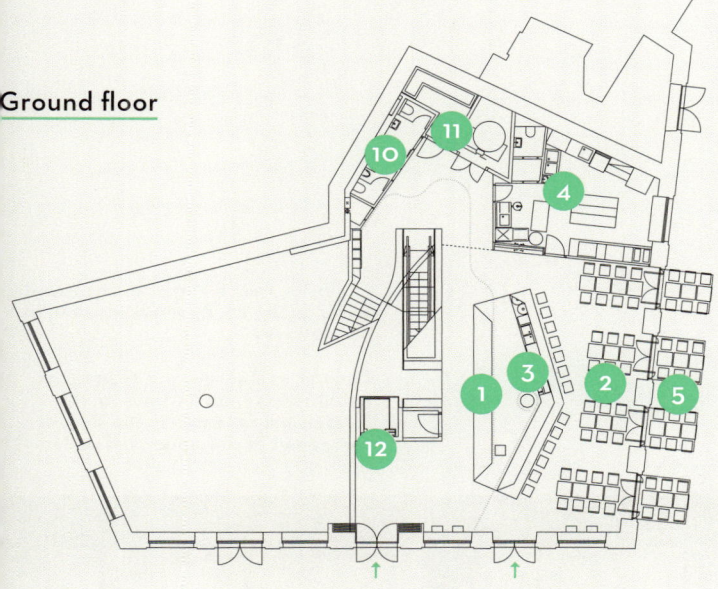

Second floor

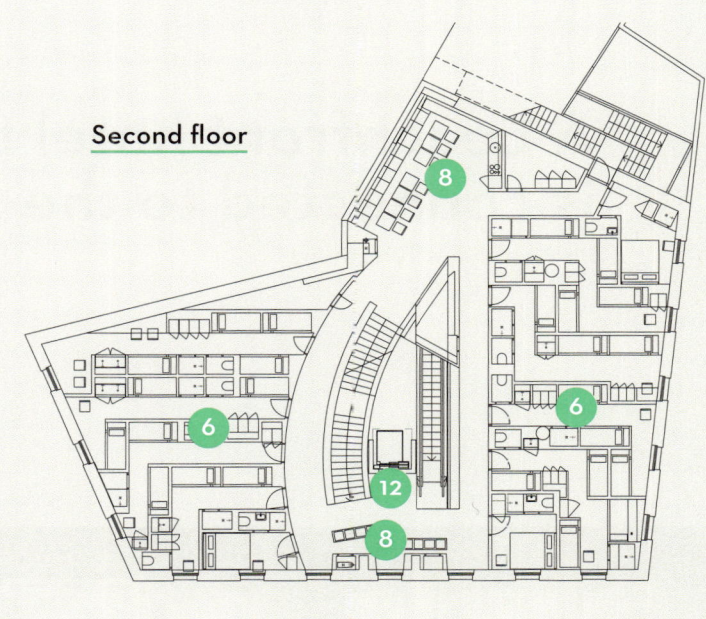

Façade

1. Reception
2. Restaurant
3. Bar
4. Kitchen
5. Terrace
6. Regular room
7. Duplex room
8. Lounge area
9. Theatre
10. Toilets
11. Back of the house
12. Lifts

STUDIO UP

HILTON PATTAYA BY DEPARTMENT OF ARCHITECTURE

Where Chonburi, Thailand
Opening November 2010
Client Central Pattana Public
Designer Department of Architecture → p.581
Floor space 3100 m²
Capacity 205 seats (inside), 106 (outside)

A beachfront hotel that is connected to the sea.

Photos Wison Tungthunya

Opposite The ceiling of the captivating lobby on the 17th floor was inspired by ocean waves.

Organic oval shapes are seen in the pebble lamps and daybeds on the terrace and repeated in the alcoves carved out of the wood-clad wall in the bar.

Linking passageways gave the designers opportunities to implant site-specific installations integral to the overall interior concept.

The interiors of several common areas at the luxurious Hilton Pattaya in Thailand were designed by Bangkok-based Department of Architecture, inspired by the sea just outside this impressive building. The design team was responsible for the lobby, the bar, the two restaurants and connecting spaces within the building.

Waves were the inspiration for the wavy ceiling installation, made from natural fabrics, found in the main lobby. Its dynamic wave lines lead arriving visitors towards the seafront beyond. At night the ceiling installation becomes a main feature of the space, as strip lighting accentuates the fabric's linear pattern and the ceiling volume becomes a gently glowing source of light, lending the overall space a pleasant ambiance. At the end of the lobby the bar area is arranged linearly along the building's edge, parallel to the sea and open to the ocean view. At the back of the bar area is a wooden wall with alcoves where the day beds are partially tucked into the wall. In front of the indoor bar is a terrace with a large reflecting pond, catching the reflection of both the sky and the droplet day beds and lamps scattered around.

In the Edge restaurant, visual elements in the space are reminiscent of an underwater landscape – sea fans and translucent, luminous ocean creatures. The interior surfaces are almost transformed from their original materiality into thin Gorgon-like membranes wrapping the space. Clusters of glowing organically shaped lamps suspended at random heights in varying sizes and colours are scattered throughout the space.

In the Flare restaurant, the design team explored the mediation of the demarcation of space between pockets of private dining areas. A translucent volume of sheer fabric occupies the intermediate space, resulting in an elegant, mystifying atmosphere, simultaneously engaging and disengaging different spaces.

Various connecting spaces throughout the hotel have been designed to make maximum use of their potential – as spaces to connect, to introduce and to invite people to start their little journey to their destination.

VISUAL ELEMENTS IN THE SPACE ARE REMINISCENT OF AN UNDERWATER LANDSCAPE

Opposite The design team used oversized chairs and soft furnishings juxtaposed against the wooden textured surrounds of the Edge restaurant.

Journeying along one corridor, guests glimpse shards of light coming through the walls and ceiling.

Opposite Rich colours, textures and sheens abound in the Flare restaurant.

AT NIGHT THE WHOLE CEILING VOLUME BECOMES A GENTLY GLOWING SOURCE OF LIGHT

Some of the connecting spaces have the simplest of surface treatments, ensuring a tranquil atmosphere.

The white bar stools on the pool terrace were designed by Christophe Pillet for Emu.

HOLIDAY INN BY ROOMS

From Soviet era to comfortable design.

Photos Courtesy of Rooms

Opposite top The Solar Walk chandelier was custom-designed by Rooms and takes pride of place in the lobby.

Opposite bottom The square shape of the concrete columns is reflected in the furniture design, from the chairs to the pendant lights of the bar.

The green-hued hotel tower can be seen from afar thanks to the strips of illumination that run up the entire length of the brick-clad end walls.

Where Tbilisi, Georgia
Opening December 2010
Client Adjara Group
Designer Rooms → p.588
Floor space 15,730 m²
Capacity 126 rooms

ROOMS

Michelin-star chef Thomas Muller offers up a menu of modern cuisine in the hotel's restaurant.

The high ceiling in the restaurant is emphasized by the eye-catching black pendant lights with their draped electrical wires.

Hand-printed designer wallpaper is seen in the guest rooms, including the trompe l'oeil bookcase wallpaper by UK artist Deborah Bowness.

The magnificent 21-storey glass building housing the Holiday Inn used to be the symbol of the city during the Soviet era. Following its transformation, first changing the façade in 2008 and now the interior, Holiday Inn Tbilisi now accommodates guests in 126 rooms. Design company Rooms did the redesign, and the brief from the client was to create a design hotel, different from any that already exist in its hotel chain. The concept was to create a comfortable, stylish and high-quality hotel using premium materials and furniture.

Guests are welcomed in a double-height lobby, with an atrium affording a view up to the first floor, where the bar and lounge are located. Big, grey concrete columns are scattered throughout this ground-floor area, all bearing big numbers, to serve as meeting points. These columns are also a feature of the ground-floor restaurant, where the grey colour is also used for the upholstered benches and the walls. Rooms used a custom-designed wallpaper with an old Persian carpet motif; the same motif is used on the floors of the bar and lounge.

BIG, GREY CONCRETE COLUMNS ARE SCATTERED THROUGHOUT THE GROUND-FLOOR AREA

In every guest room the spacious feel is enhanced by high ceilings and floor-to-ceiling windows. Each room features a seating area and a desk, and the designers used only white and grey tones, complimented with wooden materials, to create a comfortable atmosphere.

Rooms is also responsible for the design of the pool garden, where Eu/phoria chairs by Paola Navone for Eumenes, Vondom's Pillow seats, Emu's bar stools and the Heracleum lamp by Bertjan Pot for Moooi were used. It's a genuine oasis in Georgia's hot summers. •

Dark grey, textured tiles line the floor and walls in the bathrooms.

ROOMS

HOTEL ACTA MIMIC BY EQUIP

Where **Barcelona, Spain**
Opening **July 2010**
Client **Inversions Riera Sant Miquel**
Designer **Equip** → p.582
Floor space **4744 m²**
Capacity **92 rooms**

A bold palette pinpoints an eclectic Barcelona hotel.

Photos **Adrià Goula**

Opposite The mural-clad rear façade overlooks an organically-shaped opening that offers a glimpse into the hotel's lower level.

The exterior façade has a mural by local artist Héctor Francesch.

HOTEL ACTA MIMIC

Behind glass doors at street level is the hotel's yellow mosaic-tiled reception desk.

A look back at history revealed that a stately theatre once stood in the midst of the maze of streets known as the Raval in Barcelona. Since 2011 the Hotel Acta Mimic has called the building home, following its transformation by architecture practice Equip.

The designers decided to preserve the historic façade, more for the sake of sentimentality than for any aesthetic considerations. Guests approaching the hotel catch sight of a gigantic polyester screen featuring a mural by local artist Héctor Francesch. The main entrance is linked directly to a patio, where another of Francesch's works covers the hotel's rear façade. The playful graphic façades give way to a splendidly retro static lobby with exposed concrete, bold colours and 1970s-style furnishings. A spiral staircase on one side of the lobby area lends access to a lower-level lounge, and on the other side guests find a small reception area.

Compared with the colourful public spaces, the rooms in the hotel are more minimal and decidedly functional. By pushing the shower towards the window and framing it with glass, the designers have achieved a light, airy feeling seldom found in tightly packed, budget hotel rooms. For the rest, guests find simple beds wrapped in white cotton sheets in their rooms, offering a place to relax while watching TV on a large flat-screen high on the wall.

The hotel, albeit a place of rest for the tourist, seeks to remain ultra urban, its interior peppered with a dose of the exterior, with objects and combinations in the public areas and views of the street from the rooms. Hence the building is akin to a door onto the street and, in turn, onto the hidden, private and heterogeneous parts of a historic district. ●

From the reception area, guests can look down into the communal seating area in the basement.

The interior is a conglomeration of curved lines, with glass-lined stairwells that offer clear sight-lines across the entire basement level.

THE COLOURFUL PUBLIC SPACES ARE IN CONTRAST WITH THE MORE MINIMAL GUEST ROOMS

In contrast to the public spaces in the building, the guest rooms have an almost entirely white décor.

EQUIP

Model of the hotel plot showing the front and back elevations.

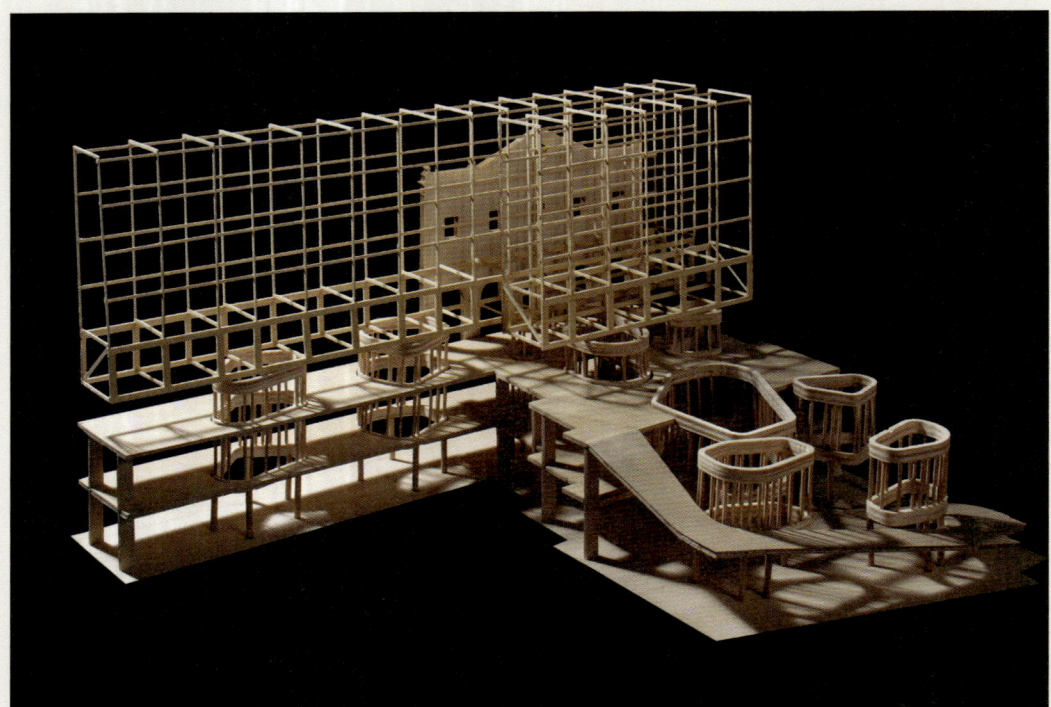

Construction photos of the main stairwell being installed.

444 HOTEL ACTA MIMIC

Upper floor

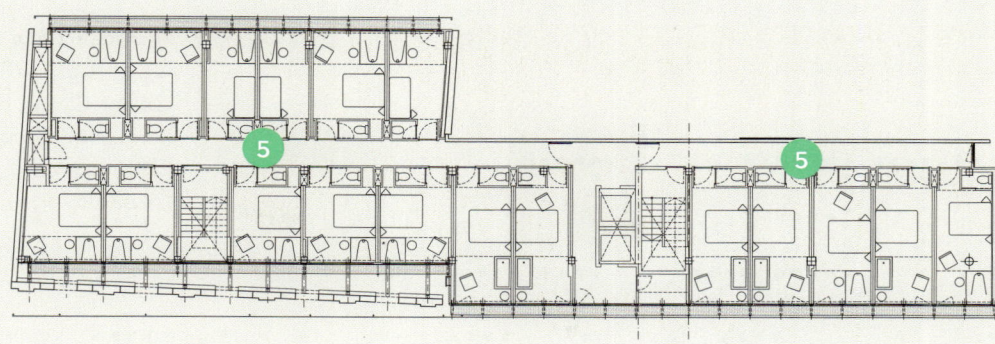

Ground floor

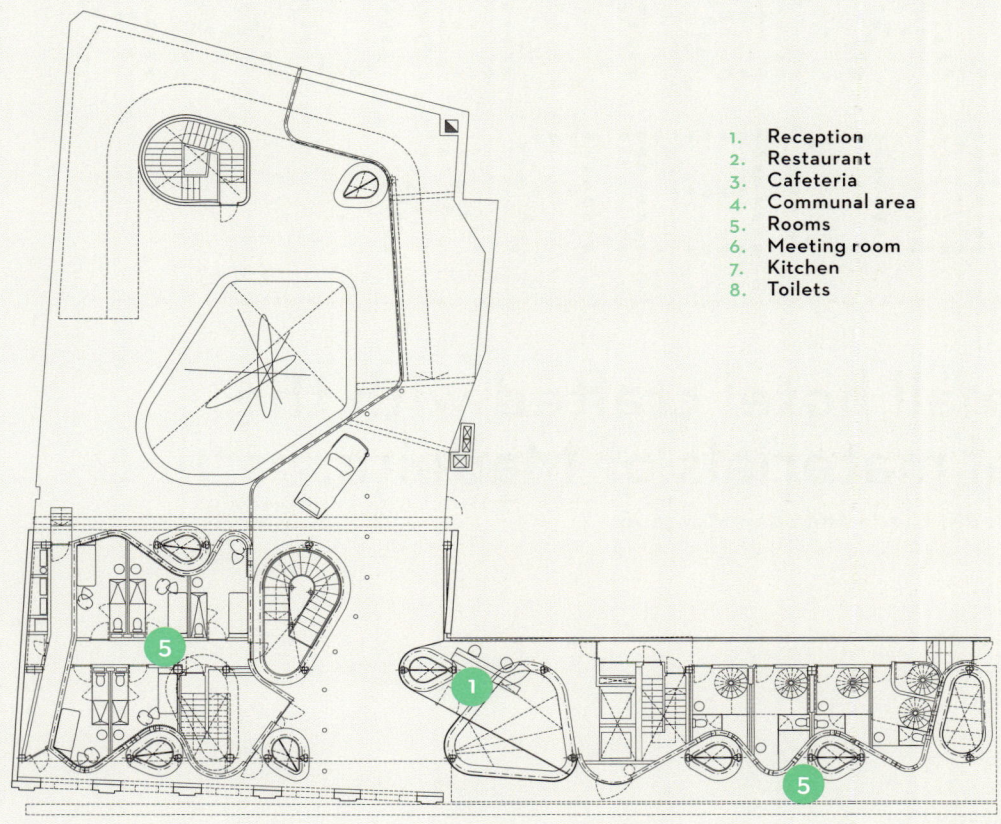

1. Reception
2. Restaurant
3. Cafeteria
4. Communal area
5. Rooms
6. Meeting room
7. Kitchen
8. Toilets

Basement

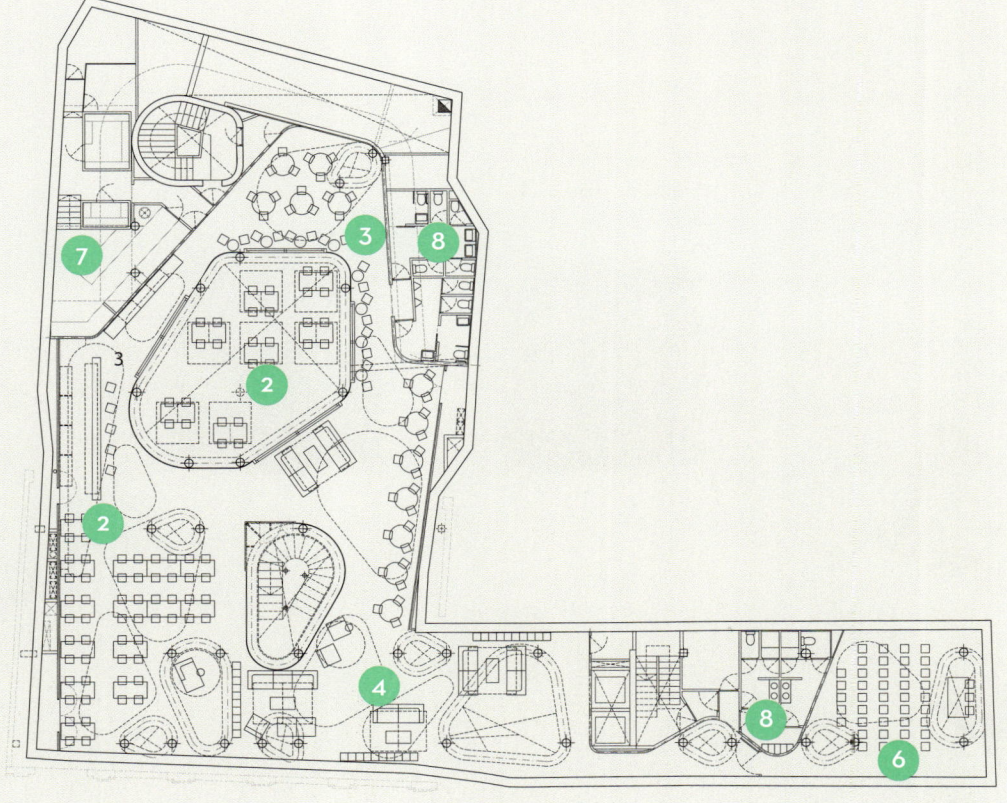

HOTEL DA VILA BY DUARTE CALDEIRA

Where Ponta do Sol, Portugal
Opening April 2010
Client Costa de Baixo Turismo
Designer Duarte Caldeira → p.582
Floor space 955 m²
Capacity 15 rooms

A small hotel crafted with the local materials of Madeira.

Photos Pedro Clode and Joao Morgado

Opposite The custom-designed furniture is made of natural wood, and tree branches seemingly emerge through the wall to support the desk.

Except for the wooden elements, the guest rooms have an all-white décor.

Hotel da Vila is a small hotel, located in Ponta do Sol, a village on the southwest coast of the island of Madeira. It stands on the sunny seafront of the village, with magnificent views of the Atlantic Ocean. The architectural practice Duarte Caldeira was asked to design the interior of the hotel.

Given the very tight budget, the design was kept simple and raw, using inexpensive materials. Taking inspiration from the rural culture and its ingenuity, the design team used local materials, like wood and stones from the surrounding mountains, for bespoke objects and furniture. Objects like the floor and table lamps, the plastic and wheat-straw bed pillows or the naked ceiling lamps of the restaurant, reveal an unexpected and humorous wit. The building's interior is completely clad in black and white, including the furniture in the guests' rooms, which is mostly white. The table and floor lamps were custom-made from natural wood, and even the white TV matches the room colour.

Upon crossing the 'cartoon-like' hotel front door, guests are welcomed by a glass desk with two wooden stools. On the left hand side a door invites them to have a drink at the bar/restaurant, in an area that contrasts starkly with the hotel's white interior. It features a wood-covered ceiling and wall with two windows facing the blue-tiled kitchen. The other wall is an irregular pleated surface that opens to an outside terrace where coffee or meals can be enjoyed in the shade of old palm trees. In this restaurant, locals and tourists mingle and relax, drinking and listening to music during the island's warm evenings.

A room of two halves: natural wood grain versus raw black surfaces.

Guests can relax on the seafront terrace with its modern storm lanterns.

33 *quarto trinta e três*

Both letters and numbers appear on the guest room doors.

INSPIRED BY THE RURAL CULTURE AND ITS INGENUITY, THE DESIGN TEAM USED LOCAL MATERIALS

DUARTE CALDEIRA

The hotel's interior is bright and bold, with a fringe chandelier dominating the double-height lobby.

Opposite top Echoing the sand and sea that surrounds the hotel, a rich gold and turquoise colour palette has been incorporated into the décor.

Opposite bottom Missoni carpets and fabrics feature throughout.

HOTEL MISSONI BY GRAVEN IMAGES

True to its location, Hotel Missoni Kuwait has a colour palette of gold, turquoise and beige.

Photos Gerry O'Leary

Where Kuwait City, Kuwait
Opening March 2011
Clients Al-Tijaria CRC, Missoni and The Rezidor Hotel Group
Designer Graven Images → p.583
Floor space 17,000 m²
Capacity 169 rooms

GRAVEN IMAGES

Vibrant colour-blocking complements the checked and striped fabrics in the guest rooms.

THE INTERIOR SPACES ARE AS ATMOSPHERIC AND EXOTIC AS FASHION SHOOT LOCATIONS

Bathrooms are stocked with Missoni products, including fragrances, linens and towels.

HOTEL MISSONI

Each of the three types of suite has a distinct colour palette, with the Missoni suite being decked out in pastel blues and honey hues.

Under the creative direction of Rosita Missoni, Graven Images has delivered the interior for Rezidor's second Hotel Missoni, a 169-room property – located in Kuwait City – bursting with the bold patterns and vibrant colour palette for which the Italian fashion house is known. As Graven Images' design director William Nolan explains, 'The brief was essentially about integration, both in a design sense and as a cooperative working process.'

It was essential for Graven Images to understand the Missoni brand, in terms of both design and life values, and to make these tangible within a hotel context. It is intrinsic for the hotel brand to be a reflection of the Missoni personality. By acknowledging these cornerstones and aspirations, the designers worked to help create spaces that are as atmospheric and exotic as fashion shoot locations, while embracing the social interaction that a successful hotel environment thrives on.

As the superstructure of the complex and the hotel shell had already been formed, the public areas and guest room schedule had to plug into an existing footprint. The irregular building plan and spatial dynamic of the circular forms gave rise to some great opportunities to explore visual connections between the public spaces and to play with spatial volumes, natural light and perspective, to help animate the public spaces and guest experience.

The design team was required to examine how the hotel would be used by guests. For example, the sale and consumption of alcohol is prohibited in Kuwait, hence the absence of a bar. Instead, the hotel has gained larger social spaces like the Luna restaurant on the 18th floor. Thanks to the region's warmer climate, leisure facilities have also been extended with an outdoor pool tiled in the signature Missoni stripe.

Interiors are a reflection of Missoni's bold personality combined with references to the Arabian Gulf and bespoke features. The double-height lobby is flanked by two oversized mosaic urns decorated in the colour scheme of the property. The lobby has neutral stone wall and floor claddings as a base, overlaid with highlight features in colour and material: purple fringe chandeliers with 8-m drops, walls in purples and orange, gold metalwork and a mosaic-clad water feature in purples and blues. The 106 guest rooms and 63 suites, all of which have views of the Persian Gulf, continue the palette of gold, turquoise and beige seen throughout the property and are accented with bold, emphatic patterning. All guest rooms feature white oak floorboards, furniture by Knoll and Artifort, and coordinating upholstery, wall coverings and rugs from the Missoni Home collection. Bathrooms are clad in mosaic in shades of green, blue or yellow to respond to the respective room scheme and showcase Italian sanitary ware.

The Missoni brand is iconic and instantly recognizable, and Graven Images stayed true to the company's ethos.

GRAVEN IMAGES

MANDARIN ORIENTAL HOTEL BY PATRICIA URQUIOLA

A richly-textured visual concept awaits guests at a former bank in Barcelona.

Photos George Apostolidis and Vargas Urquiola

Opposite On entering the hotel, visitors walk through the soaring atrium, which slices up through all eight floors of the building.

Where Barcelona, Spain
Opening November 2009
Client Reig Capital Group
Designer Patricia Urquiola → p.587
Floor space 17,000 m²
Capacity 98 rooms

Bronze frameworks and textured wall coverings are a feature of the interior.

The hotel has an exclusive spa with a 12-m swimming pool, as well as a rooftop dipping pool.

Bank vaults are incorporated as a sleek decorative element on walls and ceiling.

THE HOTEL BAR TAKES ITS DESIGN CUES FROM THE BUILDING'S FORMER FUNCTION: A BANK

In the very heart of Barcelona an elegant 20th-century building, formerly the head office of Banco Hispano-Americano, has revamped its interior thanks to the touch of designer and architect Patricia Urquiola. The Mandarin Oriental Hotel is a surprising space on different levels: an ascending access ramp crosses an impressive atrium that exposes the hotel's full height of eight floors and leads to the hotel lobby, where metal grids afford a glimpse of the hall below.

At the core of the public area, located on the lower floor, guests can find the Blanc restaurant and lounge, where light filters in from the atrium through large skylights. Large, rectangular, metallic grids suspended over the restaurant tables articulate the space and allow for greater privacy. The Banker's Bar and Moments restaurant are situated on the mezzanine level on either side of Blanc. Banker's Bar features steel safety deposit box fronts from the bank that formerly occupied the premises, now used to adorn the ceiling and walls.

The hotel's 98 rooms sparkle in shades of cream and white, with avant-garde furniture well-matched to oriental details. Light oak floors and large bespoke beige rugs add warmth, while the bathrooms are adorned with mosaics by Mutina and Bisazza that were conceived as magical boxes of coloured glass.

The spatial layout and furniture design, the ceiling decorations and the beautiful hand-woven carpets were all carefully chosen by Urquiola, making this hotel a perfect getaway in Barcelona.

The carpeted, ascending walkway from the entrance and through the atrium ends at the mirrored-ceilinged lobby.

Next spread A geometric 'veil', in the form of a white metallic framework, wraps around the lounge area.

PATRICIA URQUIOLA

THE HOTEL ROOMS SPARKLE IN SHADES OF CREAM AND WHITE

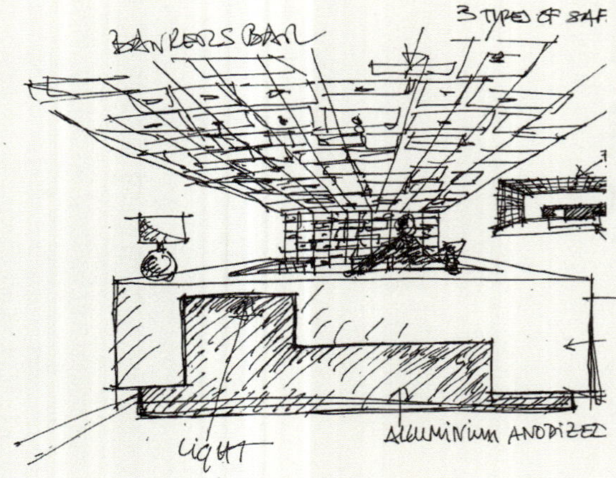

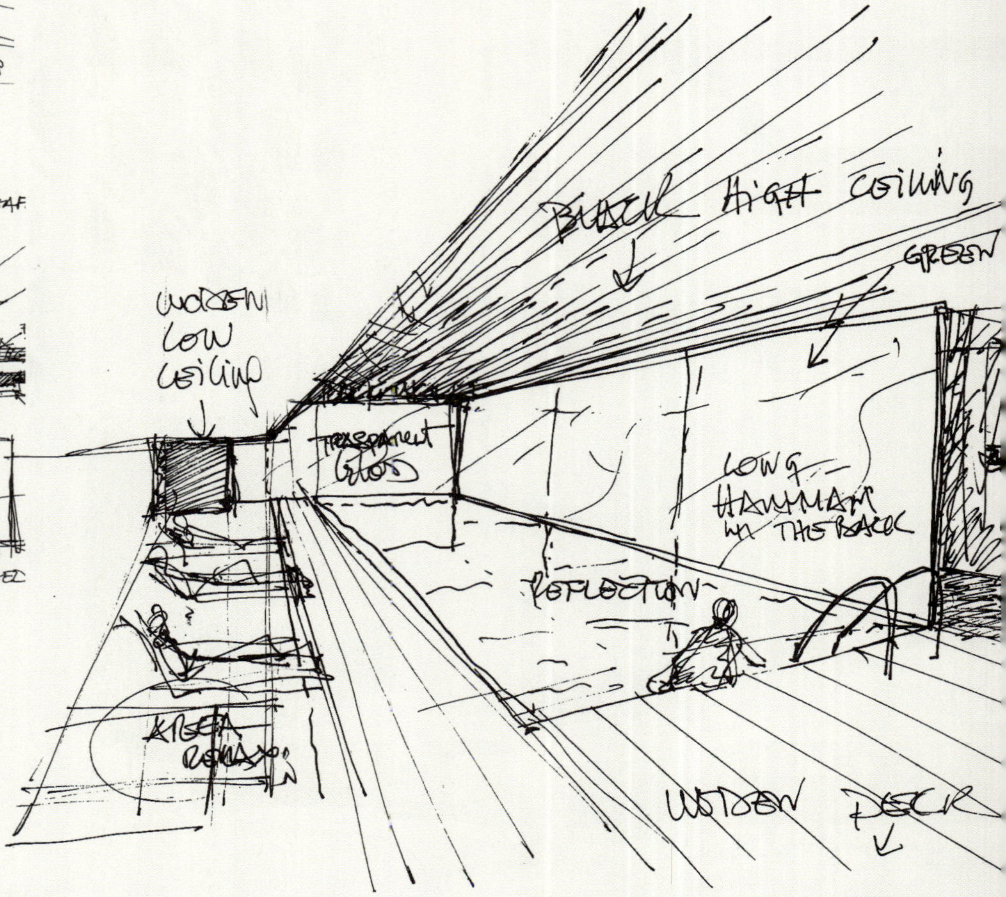

Initial sketches of Moments restaurant, Banker's Bar and the spa.

Section AA

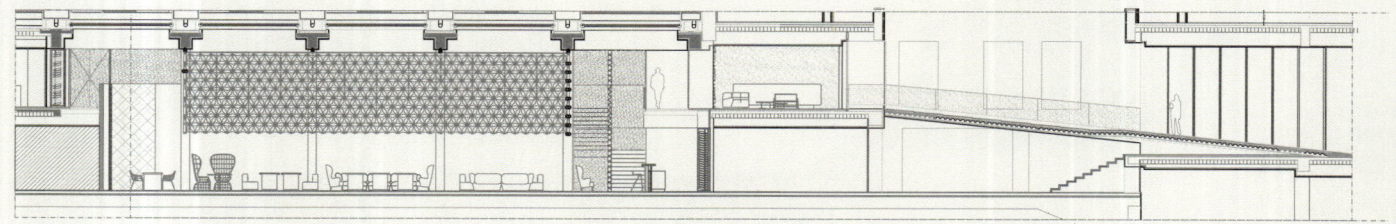

Section BB

Ground floor

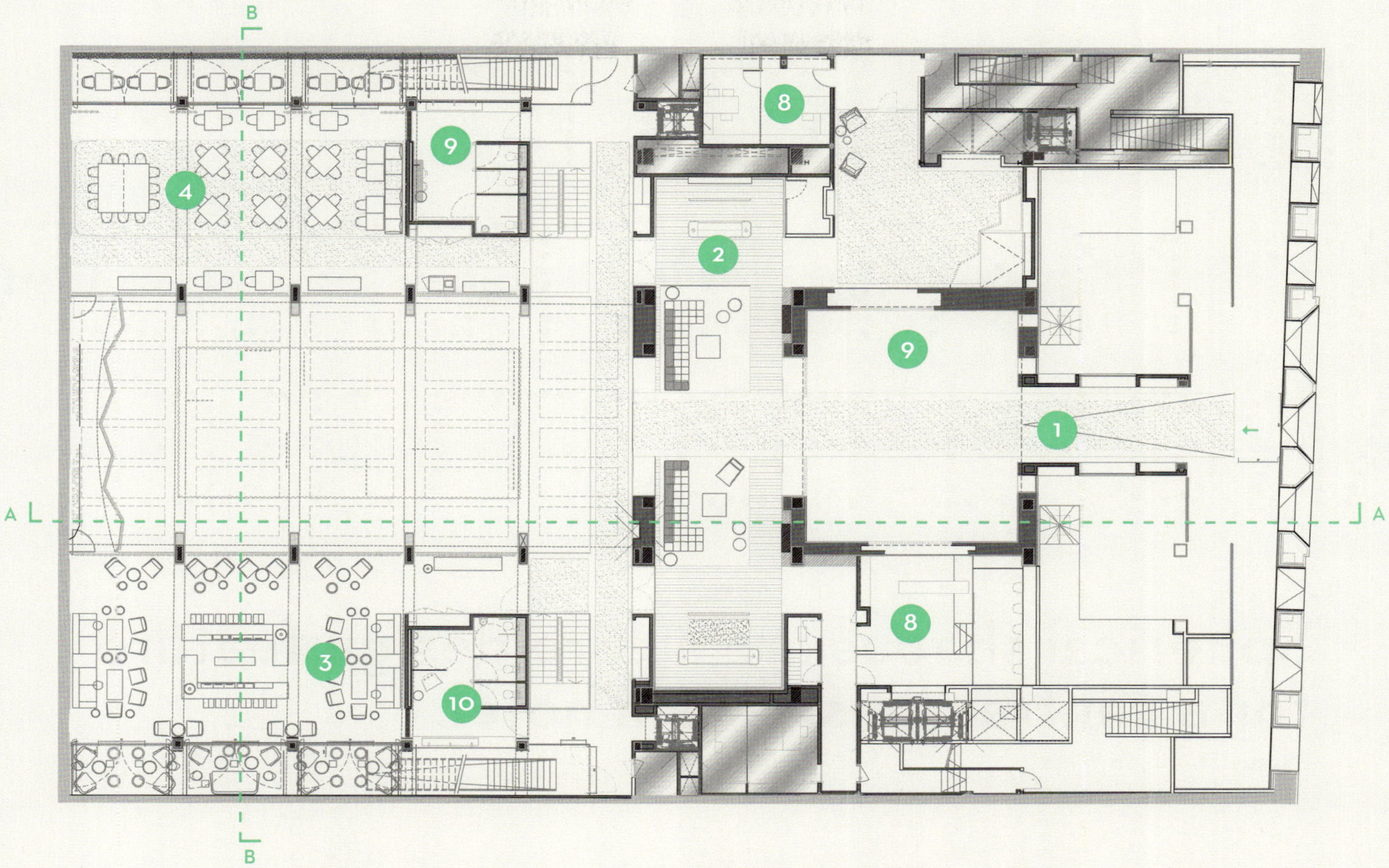

Basement

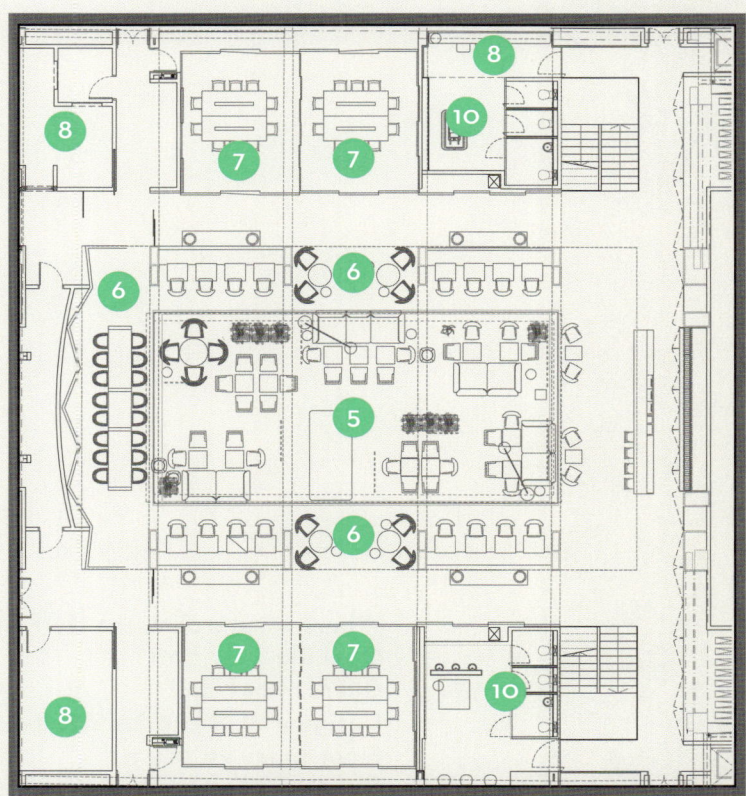

1. Access ramp
2. Lobby
3. Banker's Bar
4. Moments restaurant
5. Blanc lounge area
6. Blanc restaurant area
7. Meeting room
8. Back of the house
9. Atrium
10. Toilets

MINT HOTEL BY M+R INTERIOR ARCHITECTURE

Opposite Padded panelling is a feature in the interior décor, with blocks of vibrant red and lime green interspersed with striped fabric.

Spherical shapes are a core design feature for a central Amsterdam hotel.

Photos Studio de Winter

Smoked oak parquet has been laid in the lounge and restaurant.

Where Amsterdam, the Netherlands
Opening June 2011
Client Mint Hotel
Designer M+R interior architecture → p.5
Floor space 29,700 m²
Capacity 553 rooms

The shape of the spherical, mirrored structures in the lobby was inspired by stacked whisky barrels.

With its 553 rooms, the Mint Hotel Amsterdam (now called DoubleTree by Hilton) is one of the largest hotels in the Netherlands. The hotel is situated next to Central Station on the Oosterdokseiland. According to architect Hans Maréchal of M+R interior architecture, who designed the interior, the building is rather 'sharp and forbidding', so he opted for soft and round shapes. M+R took inspiration for the design from the hotel chain's Scottish roots.

M+R translated those Scottish origins, among other things, into an idiom of forms based on stacked whisky barrels. This reference is made clear by the sculpture in the City Café on the ground floor, which consists of a number of stacked round elements with a mirrored front. Several circles contain video screens, turning the sculpture into a multifunctional wall. The ambiance of stacked wooden whisky barrels not only occurs in the round shapes but also in the special wooden cladding of the bars. The same wooden finish has been added to the floors. The City Café, actually a restaurant, is a large, long space, divided only by transparent curtains in order to create more intimate spaces. The dominant colour in the restaurant is grey. Behind the restaurant is the East Dock Lounge; a large round window between the two venues keeps them light and open. The colours in the lounge are mainly red, as featured in the wall coverings and upholstery, which were chosen to fit the Scottish theme. Designed with ambient lighting and a comfortable mix of low and high-level seating, the lounge has been dubbed the new 'living room of Amsterdam'. •

THE DESIGNERS TRANSLATED THE HOTEL'S SCOTTISH ROOTS

Illumination from the spherical lampshade casts shadows on the dining area.

Opposite M+R's concept for the interior is based on high quality and a business-like atmosphere.

Opposite The restaurant's terrace, on the first floor, affords diners with the best seat in the house from which to take in the view.

One of Damien Hirst's spot paintings stands out against the dark walls of the first floor restaurant.

MIURA BY LABOR13

The Czech Miura Hotel is like a spaceship that has landed on Earth.

Photos Zdenek Ernest, Tomas Soucek, Ondřej Straka and Martin Vomastek

The geometric shape of the building is complemented by David Černý's 'Cubeople' sculptures, one of which sits on the roof.

Where Celadna, Czech Republic
Opening July 2011
Client Miura Hotel
Designer LABOR13 → p.584
Floor space 4774 m²
Capacity 44 rooms

LABOR13   467

The elongated and sloping architecture of the building is echoed in the sloping concrete ramp that takes customers up to the first floor.

EXCEPTIONAL 'CUBEOPLE' SCULPTURES SIT IN PLACES YOU LEAST EXPECT

Located on a flat plain surrounded by the foothills of the Beskydy Mountains in the Czech Republic, the Miura hotel opened its doors to the public in the summer of 2011. The team behind the whole concept is LABOR13, an architecture studio from Prague.

The Miura Hotel is not just a building: it is a sophisticated blend of architecture, design and art, with a clear concept and expression. The building looks like a spaceship from another world that has brought a family of five sculptured 'Cubeople' to Earth. Rather than create a barrier in the landscape, the hotel's dynamic spaceship shape is designed to preserve views through the site by raising the structure on piles, leaving the landscape relatively untouched. The main material used is concrete, combined with rusting Corten steel sheets and purple glass on the outside. Inside, the concrete alternates with wood, stainless steel sheets, glass and Corian.

The building is divided into three parts, one of which seemingly levitates above the ground. The hotel rooms are located in the two side wings of the hotel and all face south towards the golf course, which is part of the hotel. Some have balconies and an incredible view of the surrounding mountains. In the geometric centre of the building is the functional centre of the hotel, with the main entrance, lobby and restaurant. These spaces are smoothly connected by a concrete ramp. The restaurant is located on the second floor and glass walls offer panoramic views on the surrounding hills. Two conference rooms and the hotel's pride and joy – the Miura spa – are found in the basement. The colour scheme throughout the hotel is minimalistic, with shades of grey, black and white with some splashes of fuchsia.

The entire hotel is literally riddled with art. As you walk through or past the hotel you come across art in places you perhaps would not even expect it, like Czech sculptor David Černý's exceptional 'Cubeople' sculptures sitting on the roof or leaning against the outside wall. •

The guest rooms have muted grey tones, accented by a flash of fuchsia in the bathrooms.

Vast windowpanes give guests a forest view.

The shower is designed as a concrete-clad wet room with the sink positioned outside, in the bedroom.

Sketches of different views of the elevated end of the hotel.

THE DYNAMIC SPACESHIP SHAPE OF THE HOTEL IS DESIGNED NOT TO CREATE A BARRIER IN THE LANDSCAPE

The building has an irregular and elongated volume.

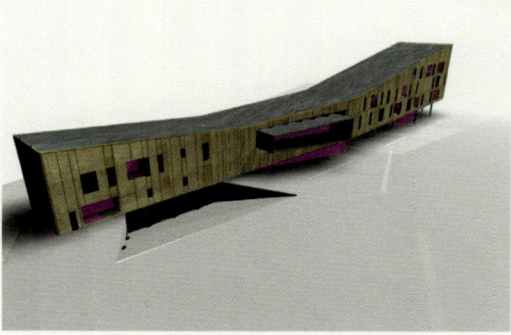
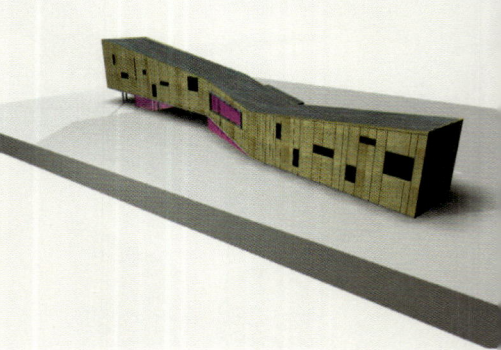

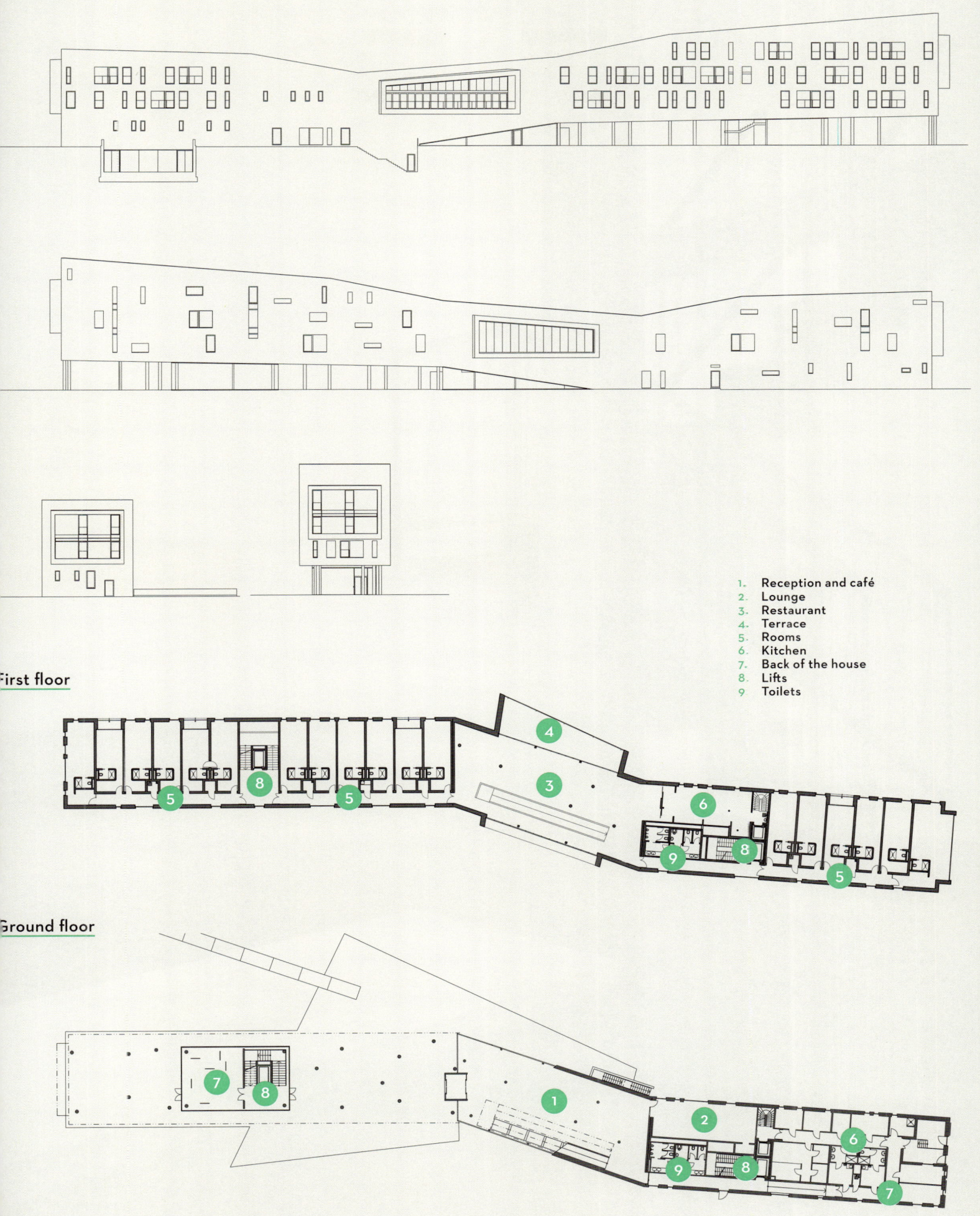

Opposite The graphic elements in the hotel are phrases of the famous novel *Three Golden Keys* by Petr Sys.

MOODS BY VRTIŠKA·ŽÁK

Literature graphically permeates the interior of a Czech boutique hotel.

Photos Filip Slapal

Passers-by can see the colour scheme of the hotel, which is located in a former bank building.

Where Prague, Czech Republic
Opening June 2010
Client Santanex Investment
Designer Vrtiška·Žák → p.590
Floor space 1800 m²
Capacity 51 rooms

The reception area contains a moss wall and a custom-made sofa wrapped around a central chromed column.

A colourful new destination was established in the Czech metropolis of Prague in the summer of 2010 with the opening of a new design boutique hotel. Seen from the street, the signage and the room windows of Moods exude a multicoloured vibrancy. The design duo Vrtiška•Žák was commissioned to undertake a complete renovation of the building, situated close to the Old Town in the medieval heart of the city. Linking the space to its locality, the design incorporates a quirky aspect with extracts from a Prague-based book – a magical tale of journeying to landmarks in the city – appearing on the walls of the hotel, in the lobby, lounge and even in the guest bedrooms.

Hotel Moods has a unique, contemporary and light atmosphere. The concept is based on the use of organic and natural materials, such as wood, bamboo and moss, contrasted with concrete, glass and metal. Guests are immediately greeted in the reception area by a variegated moss wall, opposite which is another creative surface of cut-bamboo sticks. These line the wall behind the reception desk, and guests can also see back-lit bamboo in the bar area. Other concrete, grey-coloured and wallpapered walls form an ideal backdrop for vibrant designer seating.

Textures, patterns, colours and graphics are delightfully combined in the 51-room hotel, which features its fair share of atypical pieces of furniture, bespoke fittings, lighting and design accessories. The overall concept focuses on the details, with numerous graphic accents permeating the interior. These can be seen throughout the building, but particularly in the bedrooms. In this soothing grey setting, albeit with clashing contemporary colours of blue and pink emanating from the headboards, guests can lie down to sleep with a literary extract painted on the wall above them, as if in a white cloud or dream-bubble.

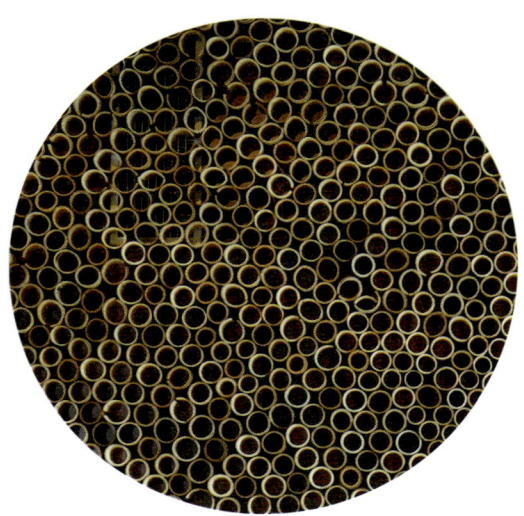

Behind the bar is a wall made of cut bamboo sticks.

Each floor has a designated hue, from bright pink to sunshine yellow to vivid turquoise.

A MAGICAL TALE OF JOURNEYING TO LANDMARKS IN THE CITY LINKS THE SPACE TO ITS LOCALITY

The headboards of the beds in each guest room are made of turquoise cushions. Guests can choose and change the lighting behind them.

Initial sketch of the reception area.

Above and right Photo and sketch of the stairwell interior.

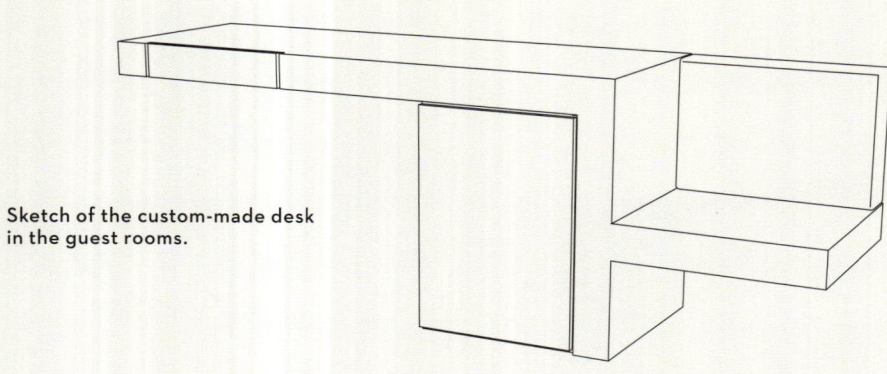
Sketch of the custom-made desk in the guest rooms.

Façade

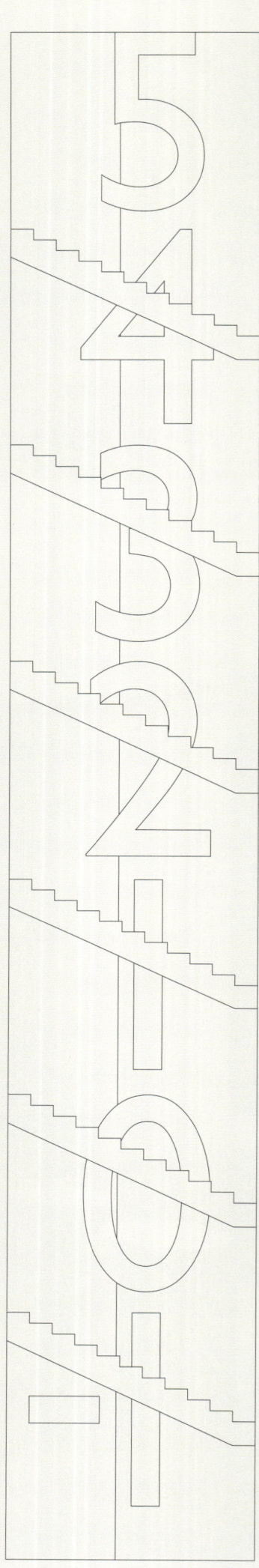

GUESTS ARE INVITED TO ENTER A SPACE THAT EXUDES A MULTICOLOURED VIBRANCY

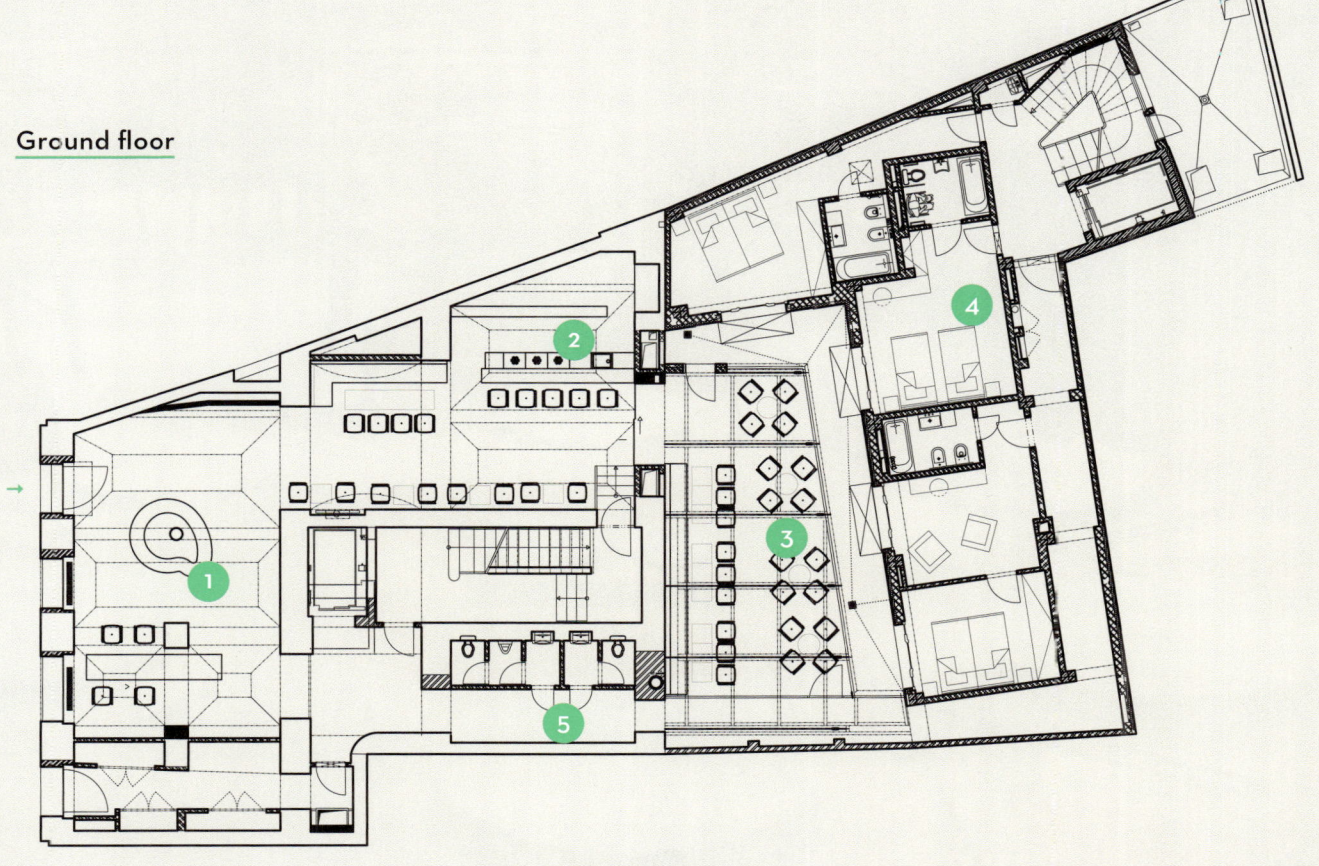

Upper floor

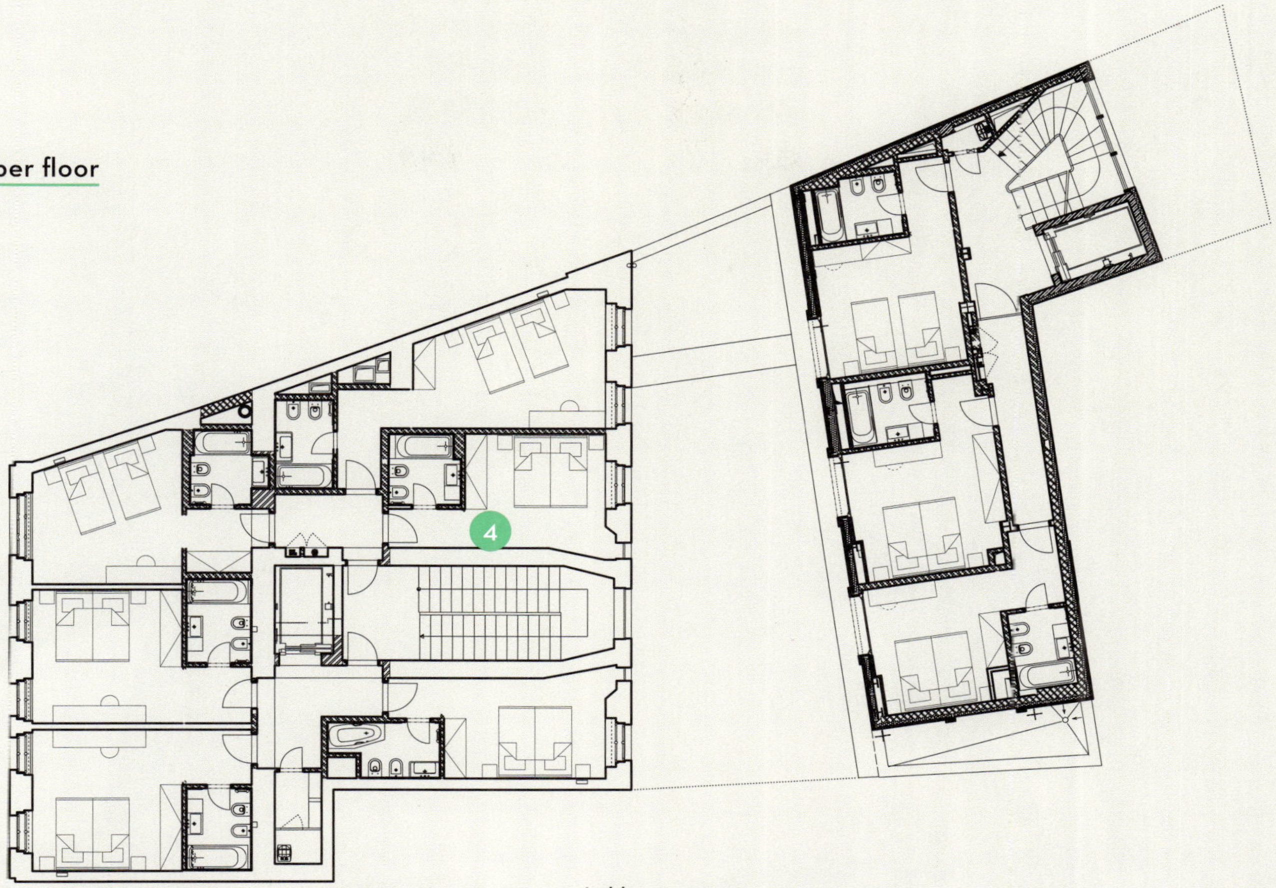

Ground floor

1. Lobby
2. Bar
3. Restaurant
4. Rooms
5. Back of the house
6. Lifts
7. Toilets

Modern furniture in the reception area sits alongside the original 1940s marble staircase.

NEW HOTEL BY ESTUDIO CAMPANA

Historic Athenian elements, contemporary art and urban Brazilian inspiration.

Photos courtesy of Yes! Hotels

Where Athens, Greece
Opening July 2011
Client Yes! Hotels
Designer Estudio Campana → p.582
Floor space 3674 m²
Capacity 79 rooms

Opposite The imposing golden lampshade is made of shiny sheets of metal hammered together into a bell shape.

ESTUDIO CAMPANA

The jagged-edged mirror doubles as a wall divider between the bathroom and bedroom.

New Hotel in central Athens is part of the Yes! Hotels group, whose philosophy is 'young, enthusiastic and seductive'. Owner Dakis Joannou, an avid collector of modern art, lured sibling designers Fernando and Humberto Campana away from their native Brazil when he commissioned them to redesign the hotel. The brief called for a blend of the old with the new, creating a contrast between historical Athenian elements and astounding contemporary touches.

This was the design duo's first architectural refurbishment project and, given their love of restoring, recycling and sharing, the brothers decided to work with 20 young architects from the local university on the project. Using insights into the local culture gained through the students, the designers worked three traditional Greek themes into the hotel's décor. The themes – old Athens, folklore and superstitions – are portrayed in the rooms with historic postcards, fictional characters and an 'evil eye' guarding against bad omens. New interpretations and hybrid approaches to the pre-existing spaces gave new lustre to items of furniture and objects found in this old modernist building, originally the Olympic Palace Hotel, dating back to 1958.

Striking interiors greet guests at every turn, with quirky bespoke furniture and handmade fixtures throughout. The team worked around some of the original features, including the 1940s black marble staircase with its solid wood balustrade. The art installation that covers the ground floor reception area and restaurant – with its tree-like structures climbing around the supporting columns – is made of reclaimed wood as a tribute to the hotel's history. In keeping with the hotel's new name, the designs and works of art in the interior encapsulate a new vision for surfaces and a new way of handling materials. Wood features highly on many surfaces within the interior, even in the Peruvian carpet lining the upper corridor walls and room doors, which was made of processed bark from the Moraceae plant family.

All the guest rooms showcase striking solid brass washbasins in the shape of fragmented rocks. This fragmented shape, inspired by the jagged contours around Brazil's favelas, is also used in the shapes and layout of various other items within the rooms, including the large wall mirrors, the wooden panels on the console tables and even in the arrangements of the historic postcard collages on the wall above.

'Karagiozis' is a mysterious character from Greek folklore, often depicted as a shadow figure or puppet.

In the rooms with an 'evil eye' theme, a wave of handmade glass eyes on one wall watches over guests as they sleep.

The console tables have a hinged mirror incorporated into them.

THE INTERIOR WAS DESIGNED USING INSIGHTS INTO LOCAL CULTURE

Opposite the headboard padded in grey velvet is a vibrant pink wall adorned with golden folklore characters.

ESTUDIO CAMPANA

Elevations

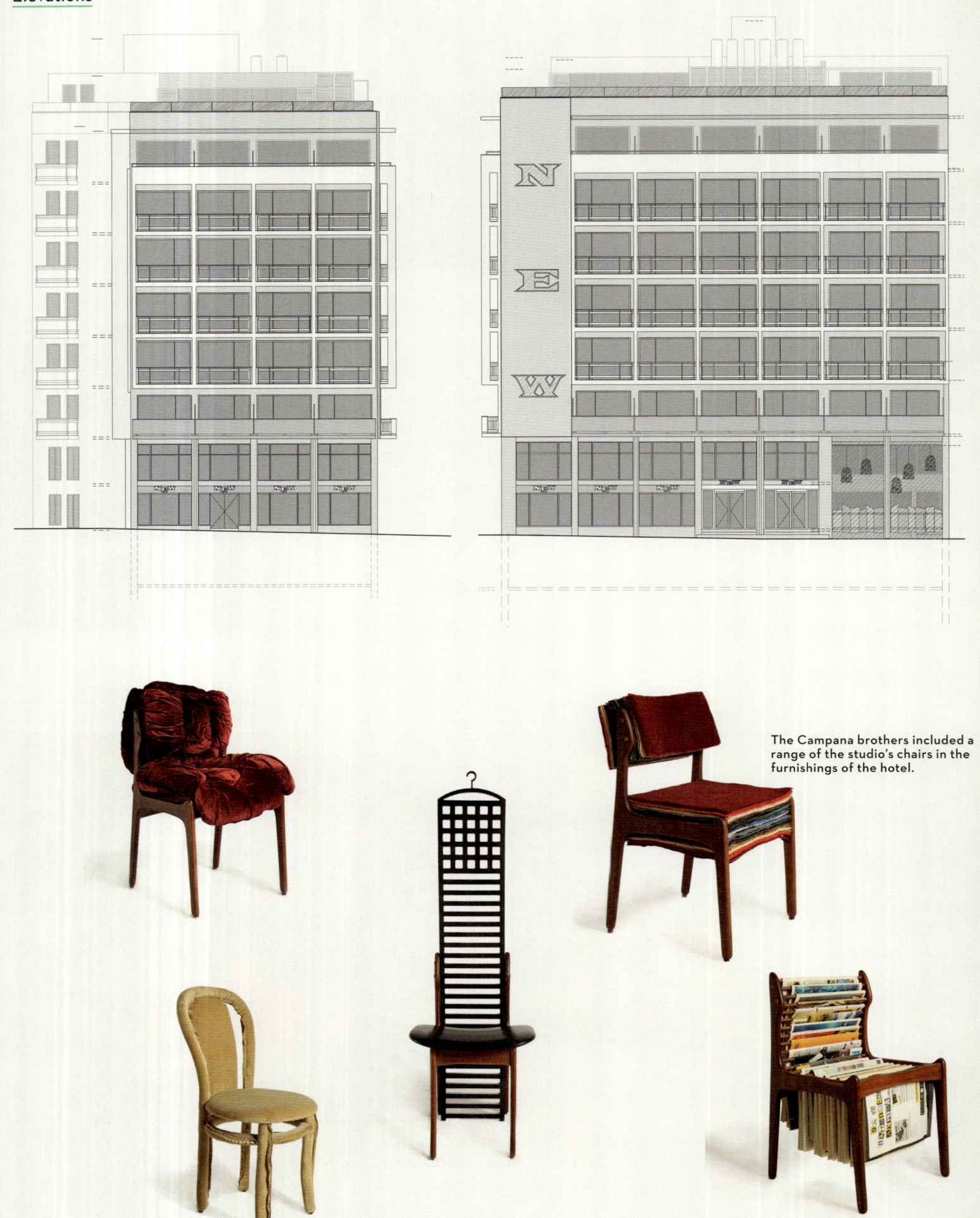

The Campana brothers included a range of the studio's chairs in the furnishings of the hotel.

Upper floor

Ground floor

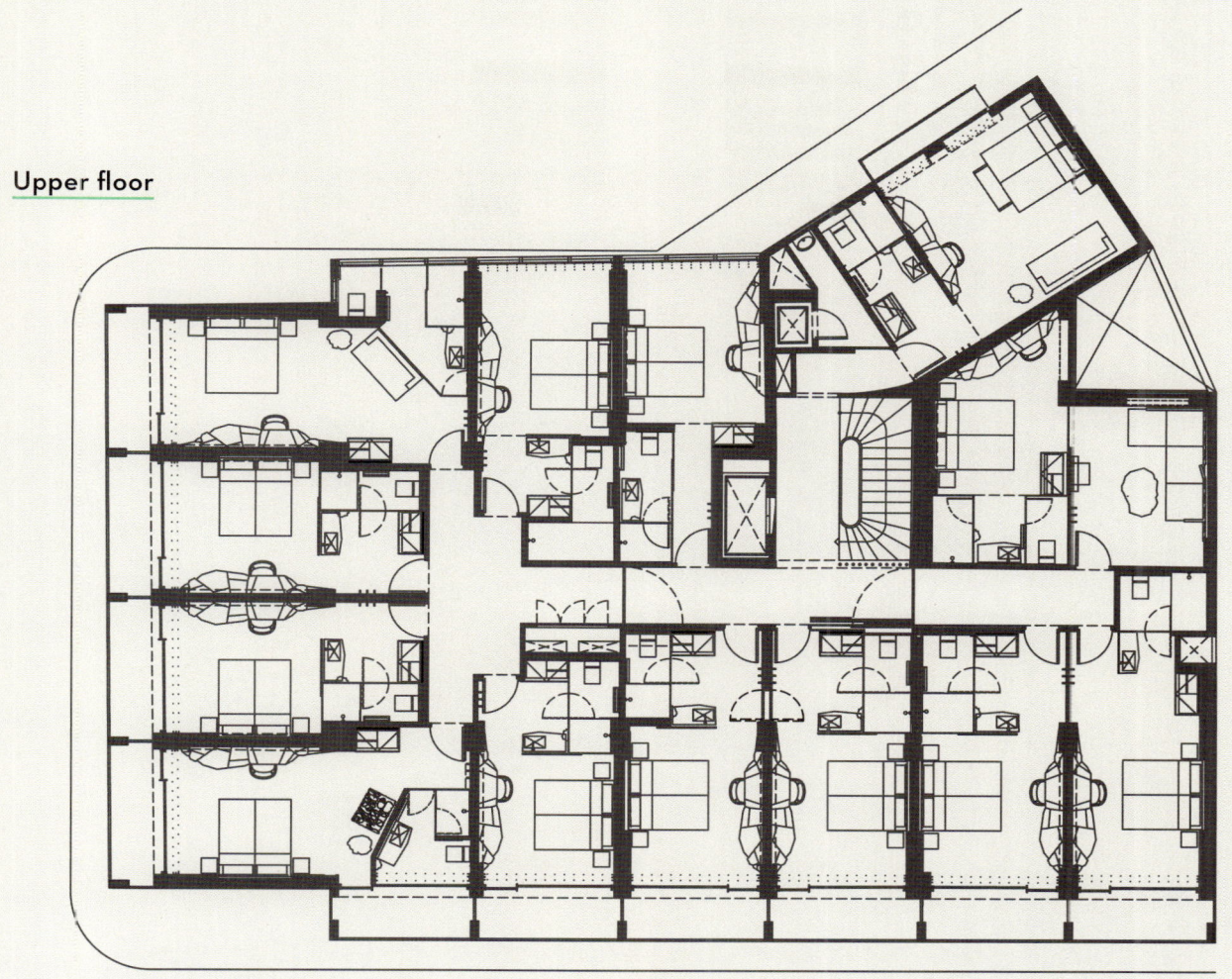

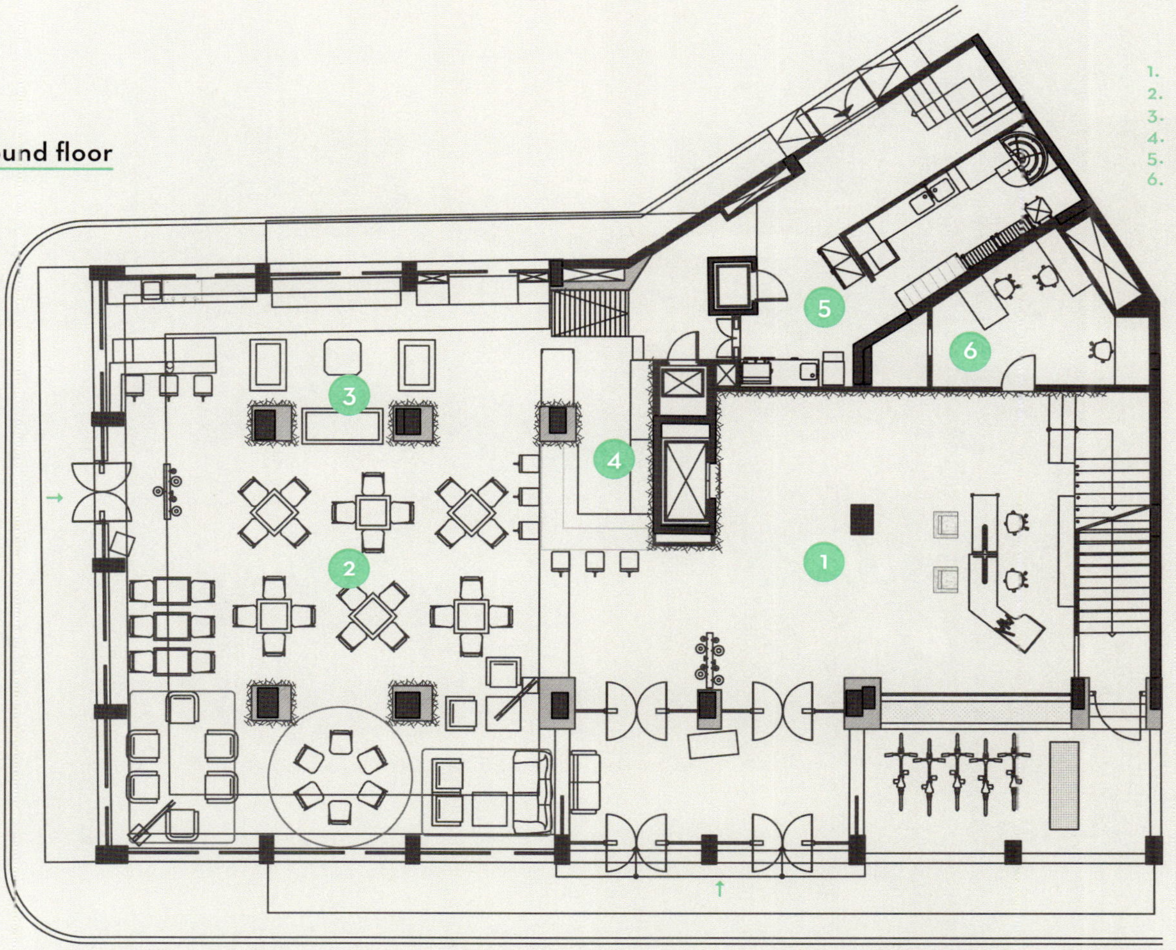

1
2
3
4
5
6
1. Reception area
2. Restaurant
3. Bar
4. Brasserie
5. Kitchen
6. Office

The custom fibreglass sculptures – including the reception desk seen here – were constructed by Hecker.

NHOW BY KARIM RASHID

A techno-organic landscape of data-driven art and spaces.

Photos Lukas Roth and courtesy of NH Hotels

the guests seated around the circular ar counter look up, they will notice a iant golden head seemingly spinning n its axis.

Opposite High-gloss pink features ighly in the interior décor.

Where Berlin, Germany
Opening January 2011
Client NH Hotels
Designer Karim Rashid → p.584
Floor space 29,000 m²
Capacity 304 rooms

NH Hotels asked Karim Rashid to create the interior design for the new nhow hotel in Berlin. They wanted a hotel that celebrates the *zeitgeist* of modern Berlin. Set on the Spree River, the old line between East and West Berlin, Rashid's objective was to create an original esoteric place (like Berlin itself) yet still pragmatic and in tune with the NH standards. He wanted nhow to connect to the rest of the world by creating a techno-organic landscape of data-driven art and spaces, bridging the digital age of information and the physical and spiritual needs of visitors.

Guests are greeted by the dramatic reception desk: a sensuous sculpture made of high-gloss fibreglass with inset lighting. Similar sculptures in the restaurant and bar serve as both art and object; for instance the central sculpture in the dining room is used to serve meals during the day. Sheer custom curtains with a digipop pattern act as art work, colouring the scenic view of the Spree River. Printed ceramic floor tiles provide dimension and texture, the pattern represents the transference of digital data that exist around us.

The East Tower rooms feature a sunrise/sunset colour scheme of warm golds and invigorating pinks. The West Tower technolux rooms have cooler colour schemes of grey, blue and pink. Modern digital needs are accommodated, as guests can play their own tunes from a complimentary iPod dock and connect their laptop to the television in the guestrooms. The lighting can be personalized to create different pre-set moods: work, play and relax. In premium rooms, a curved wall divider separates the bedroom from living area. An inset television rotates within the wall for viewing from multiple vantage points in the room.

Rashid tried to address all the needs intrinsic to living in a simpler, less cluttered, more sensual environment. He always questions whether the physical world is as experiential, seductive, connective, inspiring, personalizable and customizable as the digital world. This is what he tried to achieve with the nhow hotel by making a space that coexists with the data-driven, digital world.

A four-storey block with a mirrored underside hangs 25 m above the ground.

The organic sculptures are functional in the daytime, but in the evening their sole purpose is as art objects.

The swivelling aspect in the wall has a dual purpose: the flat-screen TV has a mirror on the reverse side.

SCULPTURES SERVE AS BOTH ART AND OBJECT

Techno-organic shapes are evident in the guest rooms, from the patterns on the floor and wall coverings to the voluptuous contours of the wall divider.

KARIM RASHID

Ground floor

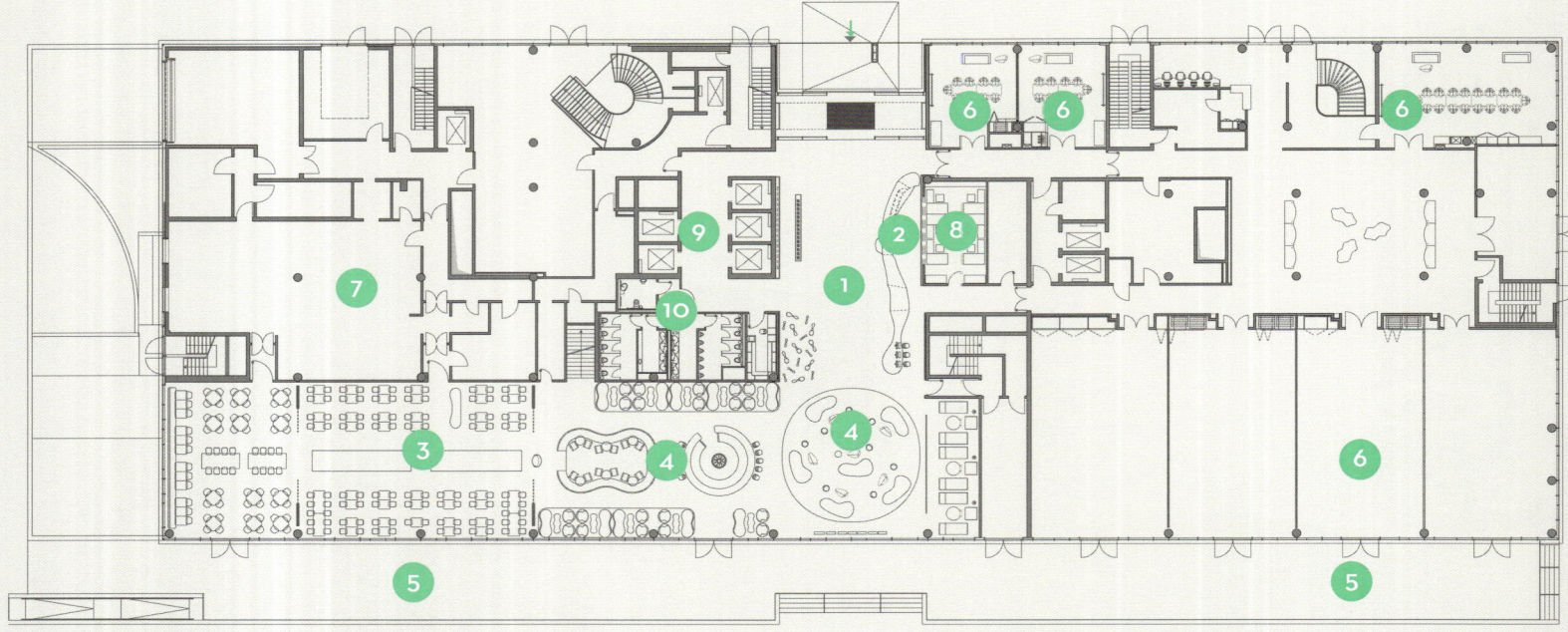

1. Lobby
2. Reception desk
3. Restaurant
4. Bar and lounge
5. Terrace
6. Meeting room
7. Kitchen
8. Back of the house
9. Lifts
10. Toilets

The design concept, showing the customer's perspective on entering the hotel, walking through the lobby towards the bar (clockwise from top left).

Suite

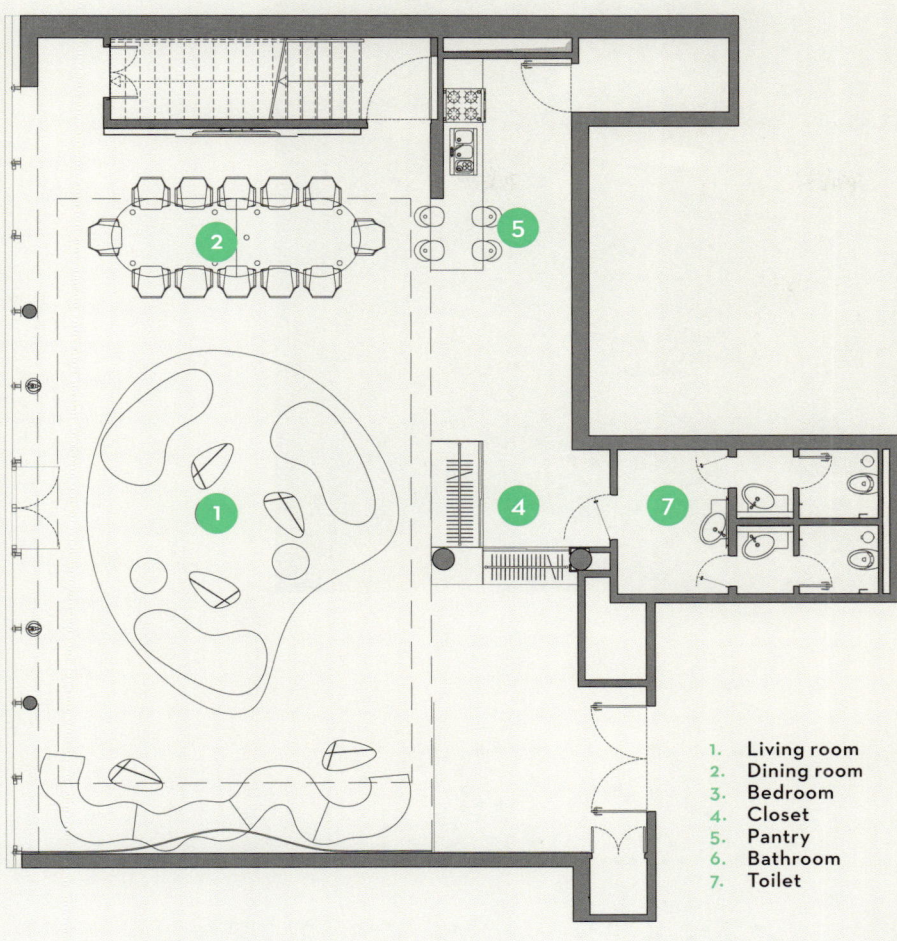
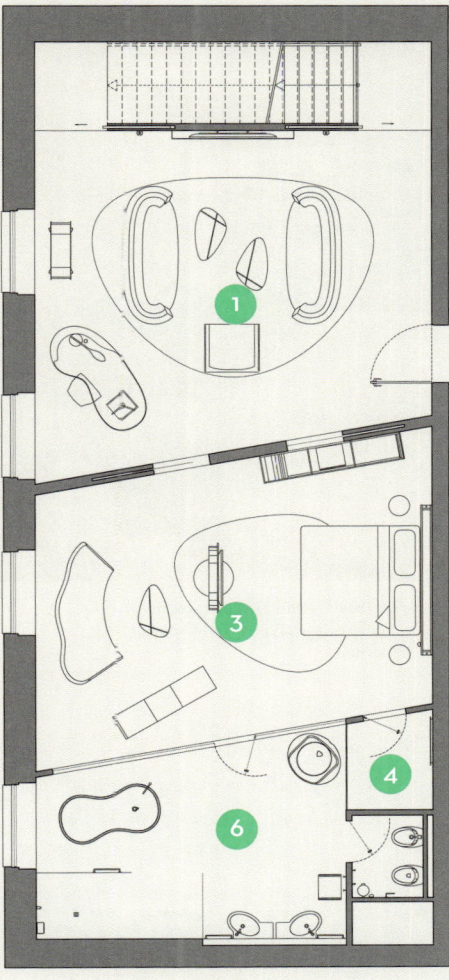

1. Living room
2. Dining room
3. Bedroom
4. Closet
5. Pantry
6. Bathroom
7. Toilet

Guest room

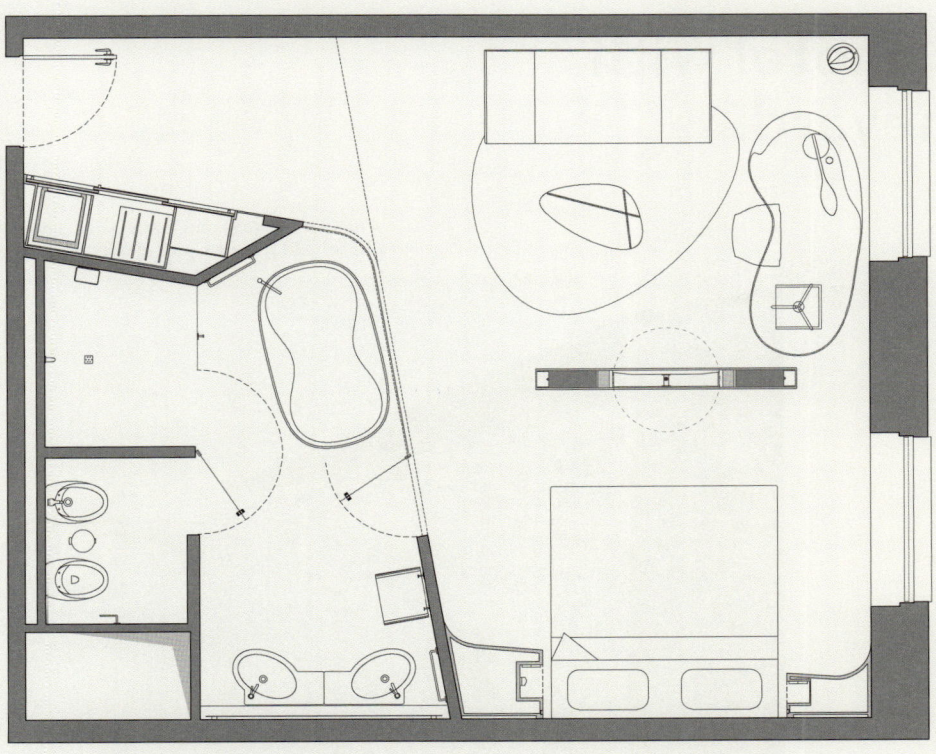

KARIM RASHID

Throughout this Italian retreat, natural materials perfectly match with Opera 02's philosophy.

Opposite Contemporary furnishings deck out the communal areas.

OPERA 02 BY COSTA GROUP

A harmonious hotel with views of a vineyard.

Photos Moreno Carbone

What once was an ancient stable is now a hotel and spa with an outdoor pool.

Where Levizzano di Castelvetro, Italy
Opening May 2010
Client Cà Montanari
Designer Costa Group → p.581
Floor space 530 m²
Capacity 8 rooms

COSTA GROUP

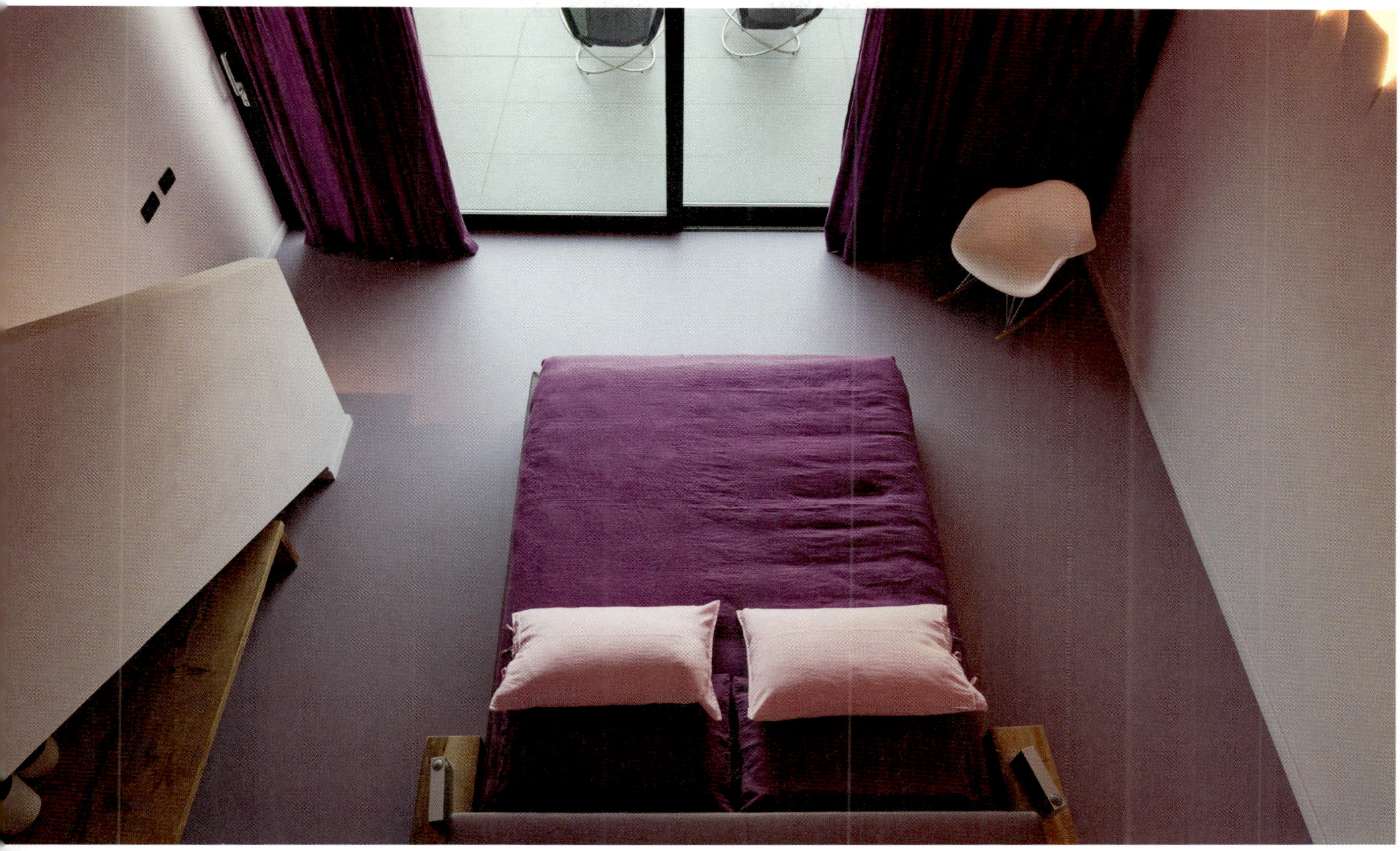

Guest rooms are furnished simply and classically.

Opposite Marble counters, stone tiles and exposed roof beams ensure the farmhouse feel of the location.

THE STRUCTURE HAS SIMPLE, ESSENTIAL LINES ENRICHED BY NATURAL MATERIALS

Each terrace is secluded on either side so there are no distractions from the magnificent vista ahead.

In the Emilia region, in a village called Levizzano di Castelvetro, the Montanari family has implemented its own idea of territory with the creation of Cà Montanari farm, covering an area of 45 hectares. Opera 02 is the name of this project aimed at promoting agricultural activity and preservation of traditions. The location is a perfect example of Emilian culture, carefully combining food, wine, balsamic vinegar, organic products, a swimming pool, a spa and eight comfortable rooms.

The design of the restaurant, reception and rooms was entrusted to the Costa Group, which carried out the project in a functional way, creating a harmonious and elegant location. The structure has simple, essential lines enriched by wooden details and natural materials. The designers enriched the lobby and restaurant with pieces of wooden furniture, a white marble bar counter, comfortable warm-coloured sofas covered in jute and Iroko wood on the walls. Some designer furniture pieces were added as a counterpoint to the natural materials, but also to amplify each other.

The eight rooms of the inn are dedicated to the main products of the surrounding countryside, with names like plum, wine and honey. Each room is hued in the colour of its given name, used in simple details like curtains and bed linen. The design of the rooms is kept simple in order to keep the focus on the spectacular views over the vineyard.

Opposite The dining area has a crisp interior furnished with designer chairs by Eames and NaughtOne.

PURO HOTEL BY BLACKSHEEP

Where **Wroclaw, Poland**
Opening **May 2011**
Client **Genfer Hotels**
Designer **Blacksheep** → p.579
Floor space **4200 m²**
Capacity **102 rooms**

A Polish urban hotel with innovative technology.

Photos Gareth Gardner

The colourful illuminated façade fits in with the hotel's urban oasis concept.

The lobby is for lounging, with its interactive media wall and contemporary furniture by Ligne Roset.

BLACKSHEEP 495

Oak wood panelling is featured throughout the hotel interior.

The leaf motif appears above the bed and on the door to the glass-walled bathroom.

PURO HOTEL

tuated near the historic centre of Wroclaw, Puro is the first in an innovative new chain of hotels that are 'budget-intelligent' without compromising on comfort and quality. Blacksheep's brief was to create an urban oasis where technology enhances the hotel experience without dominating it.

Puro's owners, Genfer Hotels, envisaged the ground floor as a busy and sociable open space where guests are encouraged to mingle. With its self-check-in desk, luxurious Ligne Roset seating, iPads on custom-made stands, vending machines with drinks and snacks and an espresso machine, the Puro lobby is perfect for those who want to eat, drink or socialize. The bar area has a relaxed but energetic feel, with soothing grey tones enlivened by greens and yellows. Richly stained oak walls add warmth to the scheme of the ground floor area, while the bespoke carpet features a motif inspired by the leaves of the Bartek, an ancient Polish oak. This leaf motif is subtly echoed on the walls of the 102 bedrooms. The rooms are compact, but space is optimized with a range of clever solutions. All come equipped with a laptop safe and integrated desk/wardrobe unit. The beds are large and comfortable and each bathroom consists of a glass unit with a curtain for privacy. Finally, a touch-screen 'tablet' lets guests control every electronic item in the 'intelligent' rooms.

Puro is a ground-breaking concept in an emerging market, introducing technology in innovative but above all user-friendly ways. •

SPACE IS OPTIMIZED BY BESPOKE FURNITURE

The wood-clad wardrobe and desk form one integrated unit.

BLACKSHEEP

Where Poznań, Poland
Opening February 2011
Designer mode:lina → p.586
Floor space 100 m²
Capacity 6 guests

QUOTEL BY MODE:LINA

An apartment-style hotel on a budget.

Photos Marcin Ratajczak

opposite All three guest rooms have small yet functional work spaces.

Custom-made furniture, constructed from plywood and metal strips, are placed in the centre of the room as a prominent feature.

Are you hungry?

The cheeky phrases on the walls tie in with the room's function.

The custom concrete flooring in the kitchen is highly polished.

Leading off from the living is a small terrace.

USING BUDGET FURNISHINGS THE APARTMENT IS GIVEN A TAILORED ATMOSPHERE

A splash of colour awaits guests in the green mosaic-tiled shower.

An apartment-style hotel popped up in 2011 in Poznań, Poland, offering guests a no-frills lodging destination. Polish mode:lina architects Jerzy Wozniak and Paweł Garus created the 100-m² space specifically for visitors to the Poznań International Fair. The client asked the architects to create an apartment that would stand out from other similar apartments for fair visitors.

Designed on a budget, the apartment had to convey a sense of comfort for its guests, and what seemed to be a problem in the beginning ended up being an opportunity. Using budget furnishings from IKEA, plus plywood and recycled pieces, the apartment is given a unique, tailored atmosphere.

In the main bedroom the designers created a custom-made furniture element, made of one piece of plywood, which encompasses a bed, bookshelf, nightstand and wardrobe. To continue the project's originality, Wozniak and Garus wrote funny phrases on each wall of every room. These phrases are a cheeky form of art, in line with the tight budget. Most of the interior has been kept white – only the brownish hue of the wooden furniture and some splashes of red and green add life to the design.

The goal of the architects was to make low-budget materials look like custom-made designs and give the impression of being high-end.

The central structure in the master bedroom is modern and multifunctional.

THE CONCEPT USED LOW-BUDGET MATERIALS FOR CUSTOM-MADE DESIGNS

A good laugh and a long sleep are the best cures in the doctor's book

The bespoke bed is a much-admired feature in the space.

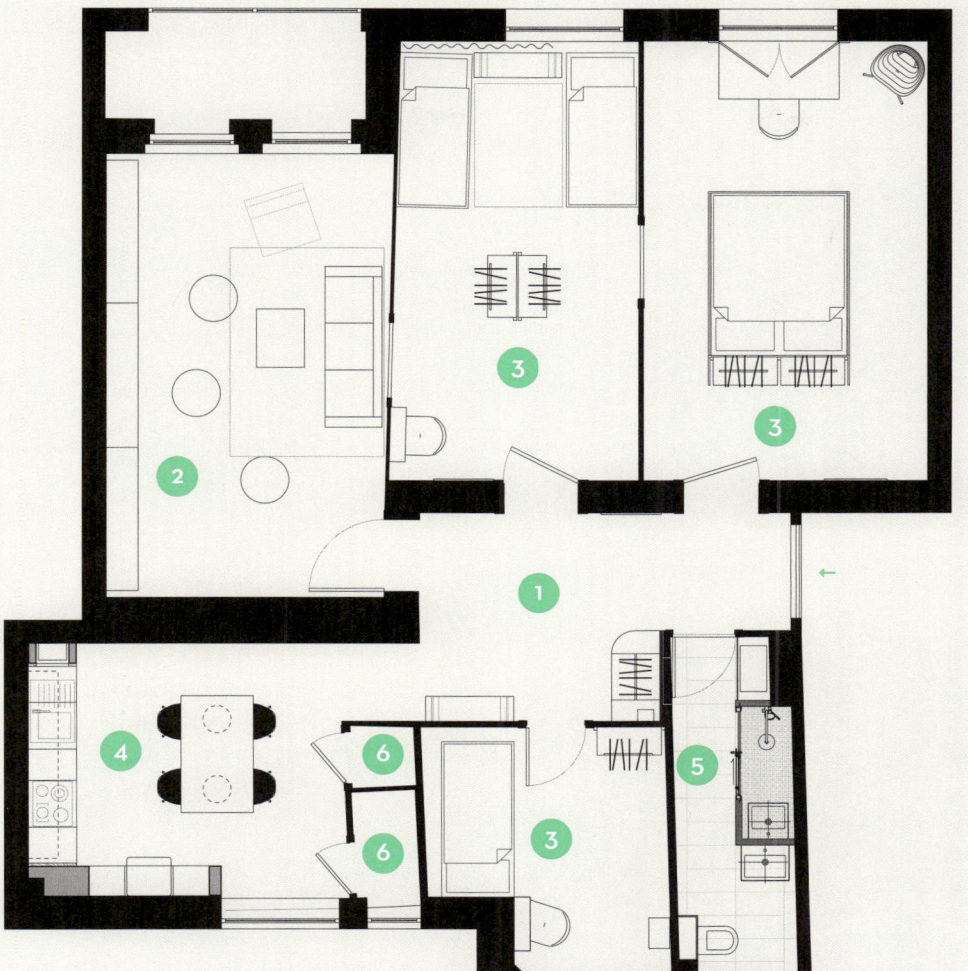

1. Hall
2. Living room
3. Bedroom
4. Kitchen
5. Bathroom
6. Storage

...enderings of each of the spaces.

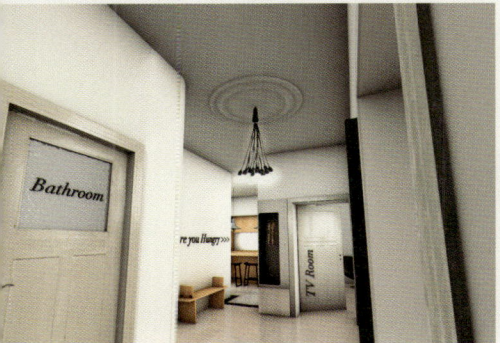  

Opposite Ziru sofas are situated in the double-height lobby.

SANA BY FRANCESC RIFÉ STUDIO

A Berlin hotel with a Barcelona philosophy.

Photos Fernando Alda

An expanded metal mesh covers the lobby walls and reception desk, creating textured surfaces with a natural green hue.

Where Berlin, Germany
Opening December 2010
Client Wolte
Designer Francesc Rifé Studio → p.582
Floor space 15,710 m²
Capacity 166 rooms, 42 apartments

A combination of wood, smoky mirrors and brilliantly lacquered MDF has been used in the suite corridor.

Opposite top and bottom The bathroom mirror, affixed to the laminated smoky glass wall, is the only spherical shape in the guest room.

A NEUTRAL DÉCOR IS THE ESSENCE OF THE INTERIOR

Mirrored walls and illuminated vertical surfaces decorate the customer bathrooms.

The latest SANA hotel, designed by Francesc Rifé Studio, is situated in the centre of Berlin. With its black granite façade, the hotel occupies its location in a neutral way in this continuously changing avant-garde capital. The design of the façade and the round corners maintain a clear dialogue with the inside of the building, aiming for an integrating philosophy, the essence of the Barcelona-based design studio.

The layout of the granite façade tiles has its origin in the windows, which strategically rest against green-coloured retro-illuminated modules, showing the silhouetted building. Both the lobby and the restaurants on the ground floor are demarcated by transparent glass, offering views of the public areas of the hotel. Only the main entrance's revolving door is made of green laminated glass, similar to the illumination found in the façade, with reference to the inside cladding of the lobby as well as to the rest of the public areas.

The green-coloured texture of the double-height lobby is achieved with expanded metal mesh cadmium finishes. Curved lines fuse together the letters 'ber', for Berlin, and 'bar', for Barcelona. The walls sinuously lead customers to the two restaurants, the lounge bar and the pub. Upholstered sofas are found along the main lounge of the lobby and the front desk is designed as a prolongation of one of the meshes, totally integrated in the main structure.

Through the dark atmosphere of the corridors guests are led to the rooms, which are strongly illuminated, both artificially and by natural sunlight, thanks to huge windows. Guest rooms have been designed using two different finishes: bright lacquer and oak. Two elements define the rooms: the bathroom, with a laminated smoky glass partition with an integrated round mirror, which allows visibility to the rest of the room depending on the light used inside; and a straight module containing a wardrobe, a mini-bar, a television and a desk that runs along the room, in front of the bathroom and the bed area. All of these modules, of which the finishes vary, have been designed according to the same idea as the façade and the lobby. ●

FRANCESC RIFÉ STUDIO

Ground floor

1. Reception
2. Lobby
3. Restaurant
4. Lounge bar
5. Pub
6. Conference room
7. Kitchen
8. Terrace
9. Toilets

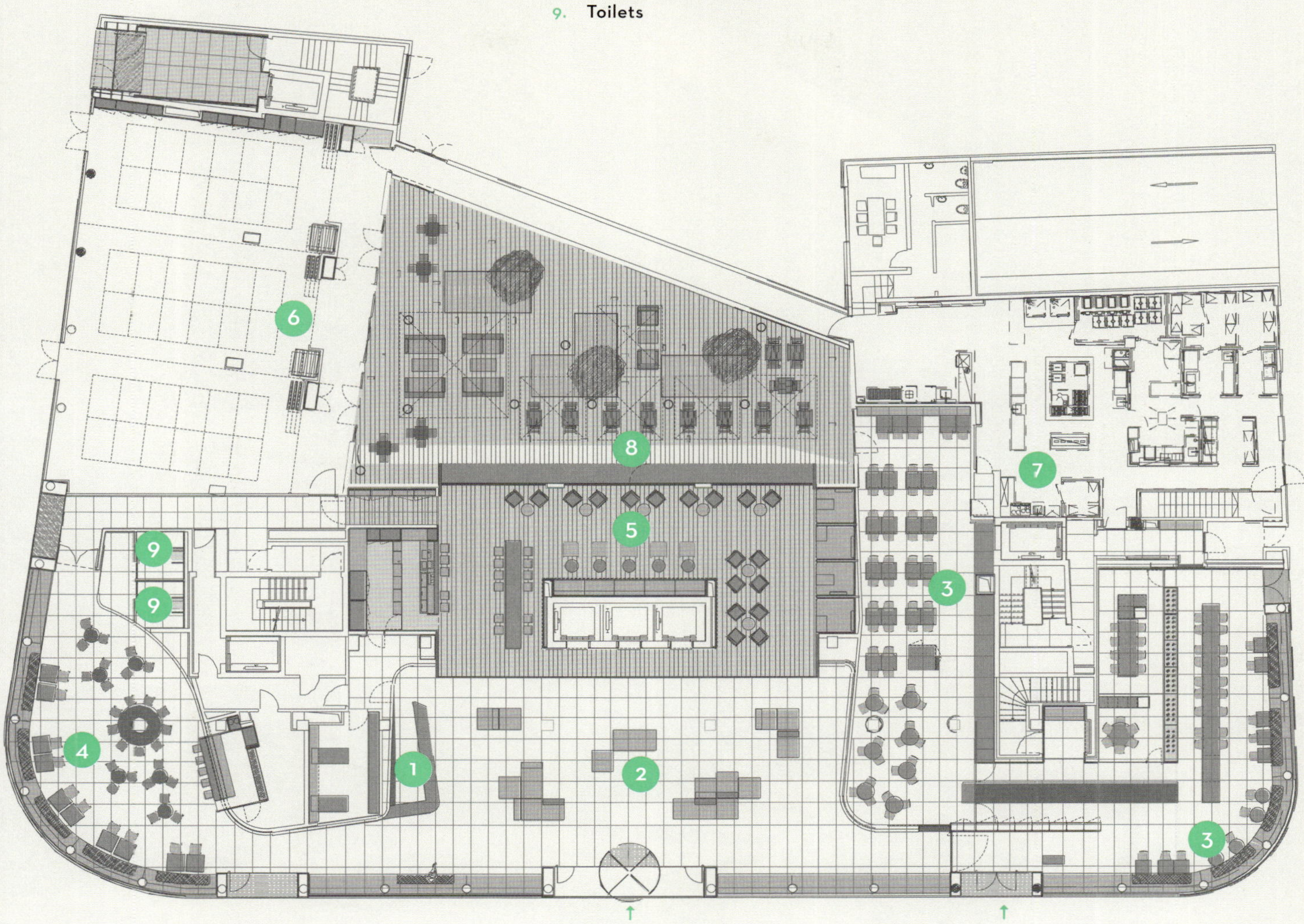

Guest room

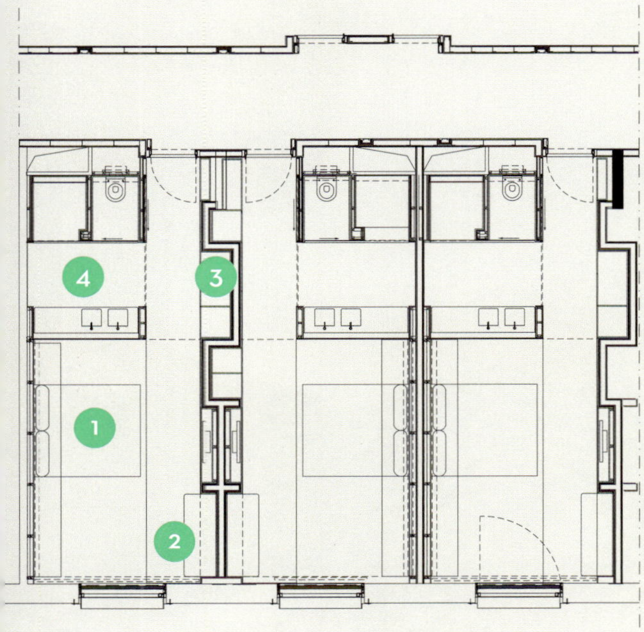

1. Bed
2. Desk
3. Closet
4. Bathroom

TWO DIFFERENT ELEMENTS DEFINE THE GUEST ROOMS

Opposite The sinuously curved lobby walls effortlessly guide customers in the right direction.

FRANCESC RIFÉ STUDIO

Opposite Koncept incorporated bulb lighting elements into the copper railings that run between the seats.

Where **Stockholm, Sweden**
Opening **October 2011**
Client **Scandic**
Designer **Koncept Stockholm** → p.584
Floor space **15,093 m²**
Capacity **391 rooms**

SCANDIC GRAND CENTRAL BY KONCEPT STOCKHOLM

An urban theatre where you can stay overnight.

Photos **Patrik Lindell**

Specially-designed concrete floor tiles with a floral print are laid across the entire bar and restaurant area.

KONCEPT STOCKHOLM

Wall panels are incorporated into all guest rooms in five different colour schemes.

In every guest room there is at least one photo by Mattias Edwall of a local personality, and one quote from a musical song.

Aqua blue 'Cage' lights by Diesel make a statement over the brass-topped tables.

NEW FURNITURE IS COMBINED WITH ACCESSORIES FOUND AT AUCTIONS

Graphic lettering on the corridor walls spells out song lyrics.

Since October 2011, hotel guests, music lovers, restaurant visitors and conference participants are welcome at the new Scandic Grand Central in Stockholm. Architects at Koncept Stockholm designed this new hotel in a magnificent, grand Vienna-style city palace from 1885. Scandic's brief asked for a hotel that could help them attract a new younger target audience without alienating its existing clientele.

With the vibrant urban and cultural life of theatres and jazz clubs in the neighbourhood, the hotel becomes part of the street scenery. The interior design is a great love affair between the old building and the street life of Stockholm, as the materials used in the late 19th-century collide with the rougher street materials, the combination lending the hotel a unique and vibrant atmosphere as well as a sense of unpretentiousness.

Behind the amazing huge windows the restaurant and bar Teaterbrasseriet and the bar Acoustic are clearly visible from the street. With a focus on food, drinks and events such as acoustic live shows, the idea for the hotel is to be open for everyone. The hotel expresses plenty of character and personality and has the quality of an instant classic – it's modern, creative and has a classical twist. The design also includes references to the world of entertainment and makes guests feel they are in the spotlight. The public areas are destinations in themselves and create the heart of the hotel, where guests and locals mingle and meet. New design furniture is combined with accessories found at auctions and original building details. Specially designed carpeting with patterns taken from the city's manhole covers lines the hotel corridors, and portraits of famous Stockholm personalities decorate the walls.

Upon entering the rooms you become aware of their non-generic design and creative vibe, which is contemporary but not cold or minimalistic, personal with a feeling of warmth and comfort. It's like stepping into the room of a well-travelled global nomad who has left traces from his travels around the globe. Rooms are designed to suit both business and leisure travellers and exude a genuine sense of comfort and care, seldom to be found in big-city hotels.

KONCEPT STOCKHOLM

Opposite Calligraphy-style graphics greet guests in the reception area, the corridors, the lifts and the guest rooms.

Where Singapore, Singapore
Opening May 2010
Client Harry's Hospitality
Designer Ministry of Design → p.586
Floor space 1950 m²
Capacity 22 rooms

THE CLUB BY MINISTRY OF DESIGN

A luxurious boutique hotel that is related to the past with a modern twist.

Photos CI&A Photography

LED lights behind the metal patterned wall can be changed at the bartender's whim, from blue to pink to yellow, to suit his mood and his drinks.

The designers aimed for a colonial chic aesthetic with a tongue-in-cheek slant that would put a smile on the customers' faces.

CALLIGRAPHY-STYLE WORKS OF ART ADORN THE HOTEL'S WALLS

The designers incorporated a black circular dial at the door that guests ca turn to leave messages for hotel staff.

The bathrooms are the only place in th hotel where the chequerboard design climbs the walls.

THE CLUB

Each guest room is unique. All of the rooms have custom-made furniture, from the headboards to floor-to-ceiling decorative frames at the foot of the bed.

The Club, housed in a stately 1900s' heritage building, is a 22-room luxury boutique hotel on Ann Siang Road, one of Singapore's most fashionable districts. Designed by Ministry of Design (MOD), the establishment brings the area's rich heritage to life with a stylish blend of contemporary minimalism and antique, Oriental highlights.

In conceptualizing The Club's branding, MOD orchestrated a unified design vision for all related collateral, signage and spatial environments. The monochrome hotel features undulating folds of fabric hanging from the ceiling as well as black illustrations.

The design team drew its inspiration from two sources. The first is Singapore's colonial past: the designers pay tribute to Sir Stamford Raffles, British statesman and founder of Singapore, by placing a larger-than-life statue of him with his head in the clouds (where would Singapore be if he didn't dream of its future?). Re-created traditional terrazzo flooring and antique pendant lamps also tell the story of the building's legacy and the area's heritage. The second inspiration was drawn from the area's popularity as a remittance centre for Chinese immigrants at the turn of the 20th century, from which hard-earned money and wistful letters were sent back to the homeland. Guests are escorted from the lobby to their rooms by a flock of messenger birds bearing directions, resonating with a playful theme of friendly 'messengers', which refers to the Chinese immigrants. The theme recurs in calligraphy-style works of art that adorn the bedroom walls, featuring animals like humming birds, squirrels, frogs, carp, mice – inspired by MOD and individually hand-painted by local artist Wyn-Lyn Tan. Besides the wall graphics each room also sports a bold design feature, such as a bed framed by a pair of grand columns adorned with traditional Chinese carvings. The striking bathrooms are, like the entire hotel, all in black and white.

Guests have the option of checking in at the ground-level lobby or in the panoramic rooftop Sky Bar. Two other food and beverage areas were designed by Jane Yeo: the lobby lounge and ground-floor tapas bar.

THE MET HOTEL BY ZEGE ARCHITECTS

Where Thessaloniki, Greece
Opening March 2010
Client Chandris Hotels & Resorts
Designer Zege Architects → p.590
Floor space 15,000 m²
Capacity 212 rooms

An urban landmark for art lovers.

Photos Vangelis Paterakis

Guests can spot works of art throughout the hotel, including the Flying Car UFO by Austrian artist Erwin Wurm.

Opposite top Sivec white marble tiles create a high-gloss walkway underfoo[t]

Opposite bottom A touch of golden glamour is given to the wall behind the bar in this angled, monochromatic interior.

ZEGE ARCHITECTS

THE MET HOTEL

Opposite top Oak, walnut linings, black marble and glass are all used in the lobby décor.

Opposite bottom A muted grey colour palette is interspersed by splashes of rich purple.

The bedrooms are cosy havens for the guests.

THE SEA AND THE DOCKS LEND THE BUILDING ITS SPECIAL FORM

The Met Hotel is a five-star hotel designed entirely by Zege Architects for the Chandris Group and located in the port of Thessaloniki, Greece's second-largest city. The hotel has become a new urban landmark, attracting people to an industrial area that in the past was hardly ever visited by the public at large. It is contributing to the redevelopment of the port, setting an example of how to breathe new life into such environments.

The building is in a dialogue with its context: the sea and the docks lend it its special form. The wavy surfaces of its façades – made of black and white marble – challenge the standard hotel typology, and the zigzag lines of the bar, the reception desk and the restaurant create a sense of movement that prevails over the straightness of the enveloping spaces. Big windows and transparent bathroom walls in the rooms make the view of the port an integral part of the design and the visitors' experience.

The hotel's interior has a kind of futuristic atmosphere, with a darkly muted palette of greys and blacks, which turns cosy and warm with its contrasts of white and other pops of colour. In the corridors leading to the bedrooms, guests experience volume and warmth through the structural wood panel forms. Inside the bedrooms there is the presence of wood, lacquer and glass. These finishes are combined with smooth fabrics to create a luxurious but approachable space.

With the use of large surfaces of wood, marble and glass, the designers created an environment of clean aesthetics and discrete contrasts that allows visitors to quickly decipher the logic of the space and its uses. But as they move through the hotel, surprises await them: comfortable lounges, cosy fireplaces, quiet reading corners and exits to the inner courtyard, with its distinct clean lines and Mediterranean plants. Gold-leaf wallpaper behind the bar, wooden walls in the restaurant and a deep black reception desk make these areas recognizable and add to the visitors' sense of direction. Works of art by artists such as Bill Viola and Erwin Wurm from the private collection of the Chandris family enhance the gallery-like atmosphere of The Met Hotel and make it a major attraction for art lovers. ●

Guests can reflect on the neighbourhood's industrial past as they take a dip in the infinity-edge pool.

ZEGE ARCHITECTS

Opposite A relaxing vibe is imbued in the spa area.

Contemporary furnishing and glass dividing walls are essential aspects of all the guest rooms.

WORKS BY INTERNATIONAL ARTISTS MAKE THE HOTEL A MAJOR ATTRACTION FOR ART LOVERS

524 THE MIRROR

Opposite While relaxing in the lounge, guests are accompanied by the hotel's sculpted angels, created by artist Christoph Mertens.

THE MIRROR BY GCA ARQUITECTES ASSOCIATS

A hotel with a touch of heaven.

Photos Jordi Miralles

The patio, located at the centre of the building, contains the vertical communication formed by the stairs and glass lifts.

Where Barcelona, Spain
Opening January 2011
Client Hotel Mirror
Designer GCA arquitectes associats → p.583
Floor space 3300 m²
Capacity 63 rooms

ENDLESS REFLECTIONS OF THE ALL-WHITE INTERIOR ABOUND FROM A UNIVERSE OF MIRRORS

From the streets people can have a look into the bar area of the hotel.

The reception desk and bar flow into each other because of their similar design.

The hotel restaurant is run by renowned Spanish chef Paco Pérez.

GCA arquitectes was asked to refurbish an old office building into a four-star hotel. The team was led by designer Josep Riu. The Mirror Barcelona became an avant-garde showpiece, both in its architecture and interior design. The design of the interior fuses the use of white with endless reflections from a universe of mirrors to create this boutique hotel's unique character.

The open-plan ground floor is dominated by a grand counter, which links the reception desk to the bar. Leading on from there is the central patio, which serves as the hotel lounge. An enormous tapestry of mirrors, two panoramic lifts and several white sculptured angels – the guardians of the hotel – adorn this area. Behind the patio, the serene and neutral ambiance of the restaurant – with its white tables and chairs and fresh white linen, accented with mirrors and stainless steel details – is in keeping with the use of white and mirrors throughout the hotel. The hotel rooms are interspersed to make optimal use of the building's 12-m width and obtain four rooms along each façade, eight per floor. Again the use of mirrors creates a sense of space, and the different shades of white help to create a feeling of calm and relaxation. A huge headboard, which spans the wall behind each bed but also the ceiling above, is made of white leather and incorporates subtle lighting. In each guest room, the bathroom is atomized: the toilet, washbasin and shower or bathtub are positioned autonomously at various points in the room. The shower or bathtub and the toilet are white glass boxes built into the walls.

The personality of the rooms is extended to the hotel's common areas, creating a unified whole.

Behind the mirrored wall in each room is a separate unit for the shower, toilet and washbasin.

A SERENE AND NEUTRAL AMBIANCE IS INFUSED INTO THE HOTEL'S DÉCOR

The use of white in different shades and tones creates a neutral atmosphere.

THE MIRROR

Elevation

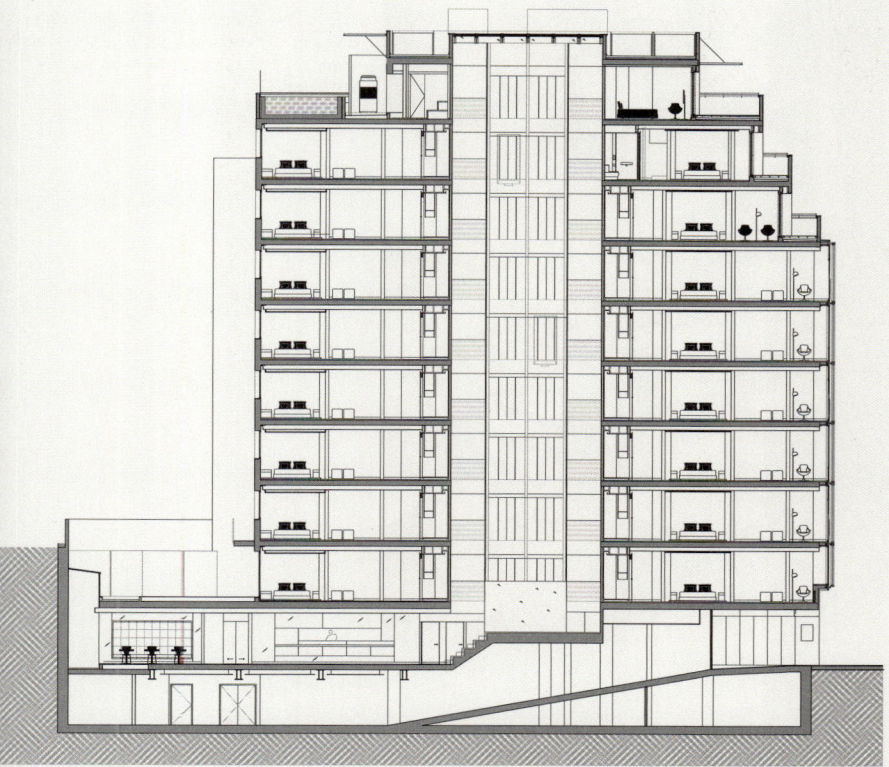

1. Lobby
2. Bar
3. Lounge
4. Restaurant
5. Kitchen
6. Lifts
7. Back of the house
8. Rooms
9. Patio

Mezzanine

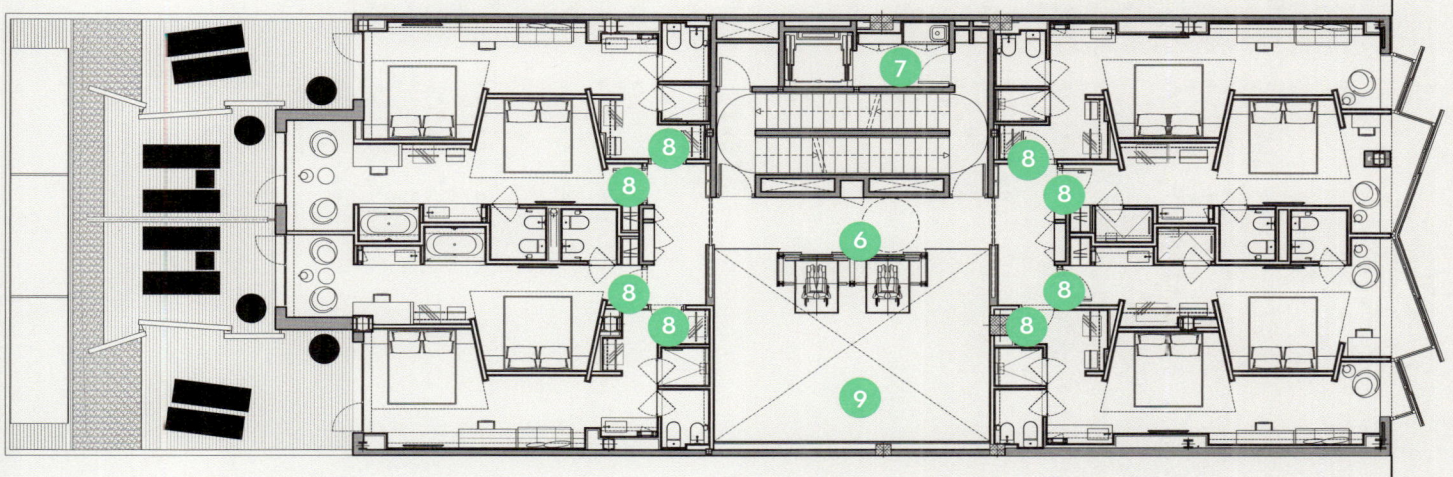

Ground floor

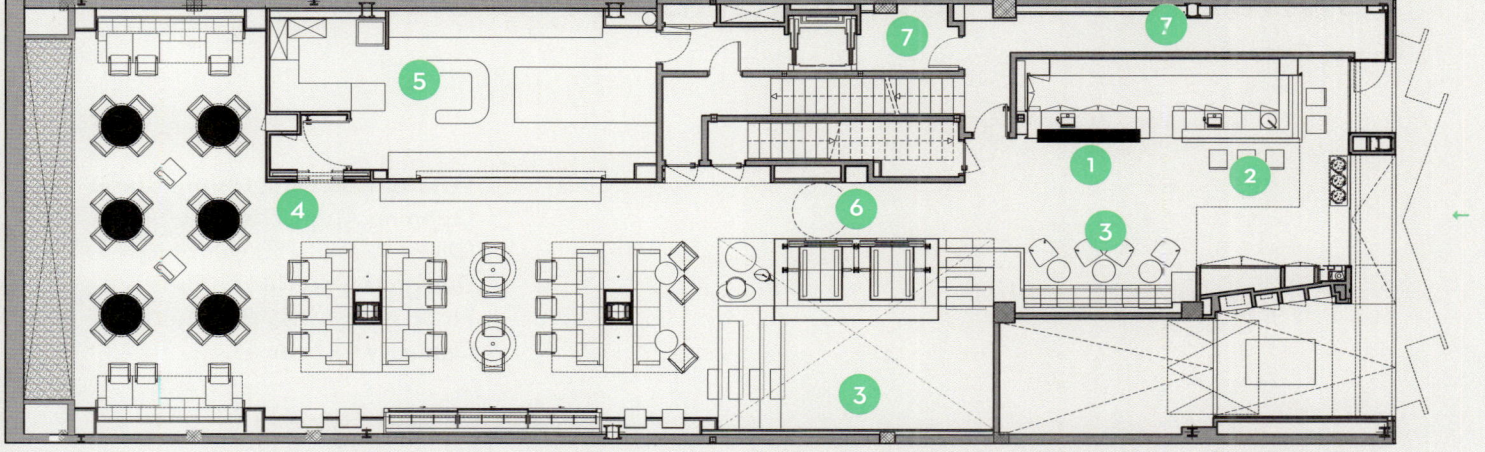

GCA ARQUITECTES ASSOCIATS

The ground floor level is sunken below street level.

Opposite The double height in the bar area affords space for an extensive wine rack that reaches high up the end wall.

THE NOLITAN BY GRZYWINSKI +PONS

A boutique hotel with a strong connection to the neighbourhood.

Photos Floto+Warner

Where New York, United States
Opening August 2011
Client Veracity Development
Designer Grzywinski+Pons → p.583
Floor space 2235 m²
Capacity 55 rooms

Corner guest rooms have windows with panels of both clear and frosted glass.

GRZYWINSKI+PONS PARTICULARLY WANTED TO FOSTER A CONNECTION WITH THE NEIGHBOURHOOD

The Nolitan Hotel is a 55-room boutique property in downtown Manhattan that also features a restaurant and a roof deck. The building, interiors, restaurant and rooftop were designed by Grzywinski+Pons.

The Nolitan is located on the corner of Elizabeth and Kenmare Streets. Kenmare is a wide thoroughfare with a comparatively larger scale than the neighbourhood – Nolita – it bisects. It was the design team's intention that the hotel act as architectural and programmatic connective tissue joining the northern and southern parts of the district. The lot itself is a rather constrained trapezoid, but it offers a lot of façade and exposure.

Grzywinski+Pons particularly wanted to foster a connection with the neighbourhood at the street level, so the façade on the ground floor is made entirely of glass. The designers also sank the ground-floor restaurant and lounge 60 cm below street level and left portions of both the restaurant and reception at double height. The idea was to abstract the view of the street with this lower perspective from the dining room, and a ceramic frit was also added to the glass here. In the lobby the double-height point-supported glass provides a more direct, unfettered connection to the street.

Some guests can enjoy the street life from private balconies; other guests have floor-to-ceiling windows in their rooms that provide an unobstructed view of the neighbourhood and the skyline. The use of channel glass in the rooms opens up the space to the streetscape below without compromising privacy.

The material palette for the entire project was chosen to be elemental rather than a surface treatment; the intention is that – with use and age – the materials will develop a patina or richness rather than become shabby. The exterior is comprised largely of terraced terracotta shingles, exposed concrete, glass and wood. Grzywinski+Pons carried the same materials through to the interiors. They used European oak floors, exposed concrete, ceramic tiles, leather, felt, blackened steel – all real, elemental finishes that share the characteristics of warmth, texture and authenticity. •

The hotel gets its name from the Nolita neighbourhood it borders.

A simple and sleek décor sees surface treatments of paint, timber and exposed concrete.

The bathing areas are positioned in a corner of the guest rooms.

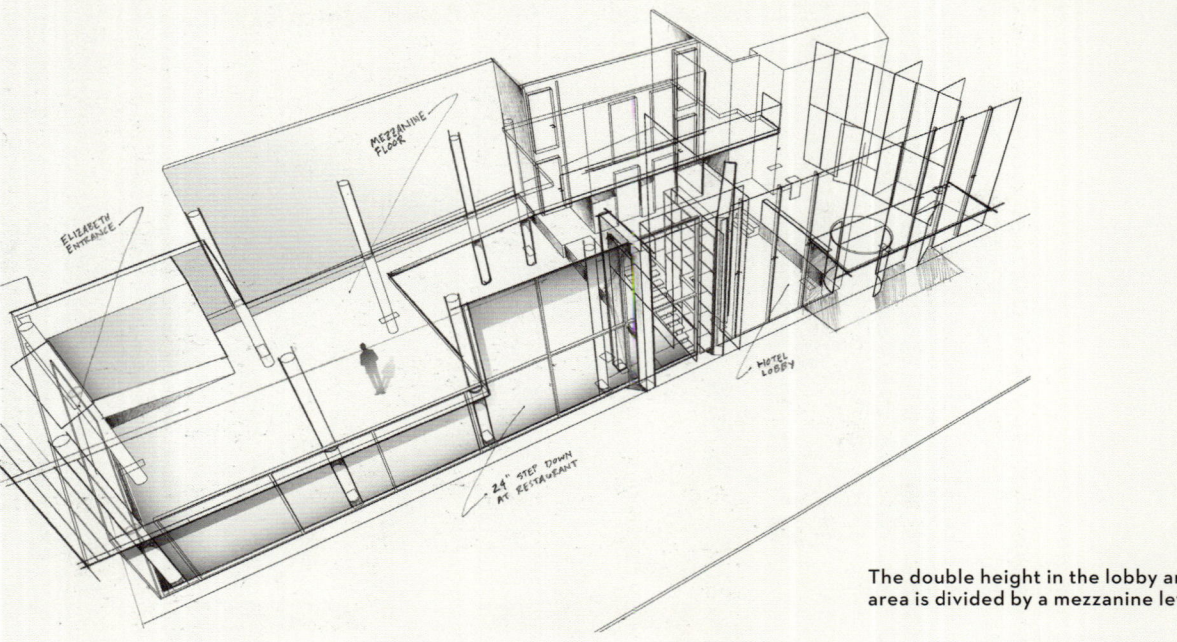

The double height in the lobby and bar area is divided by a mezzanine level.

TO ABSTRACT THE VIEW OF PASSING TRAFFIC, THE DESIGNERS SANK THE GROUND FLOOR 60 CM BELOW STREET LEVEL

Sidewalk dining is imagined in a rendering of the hotel.

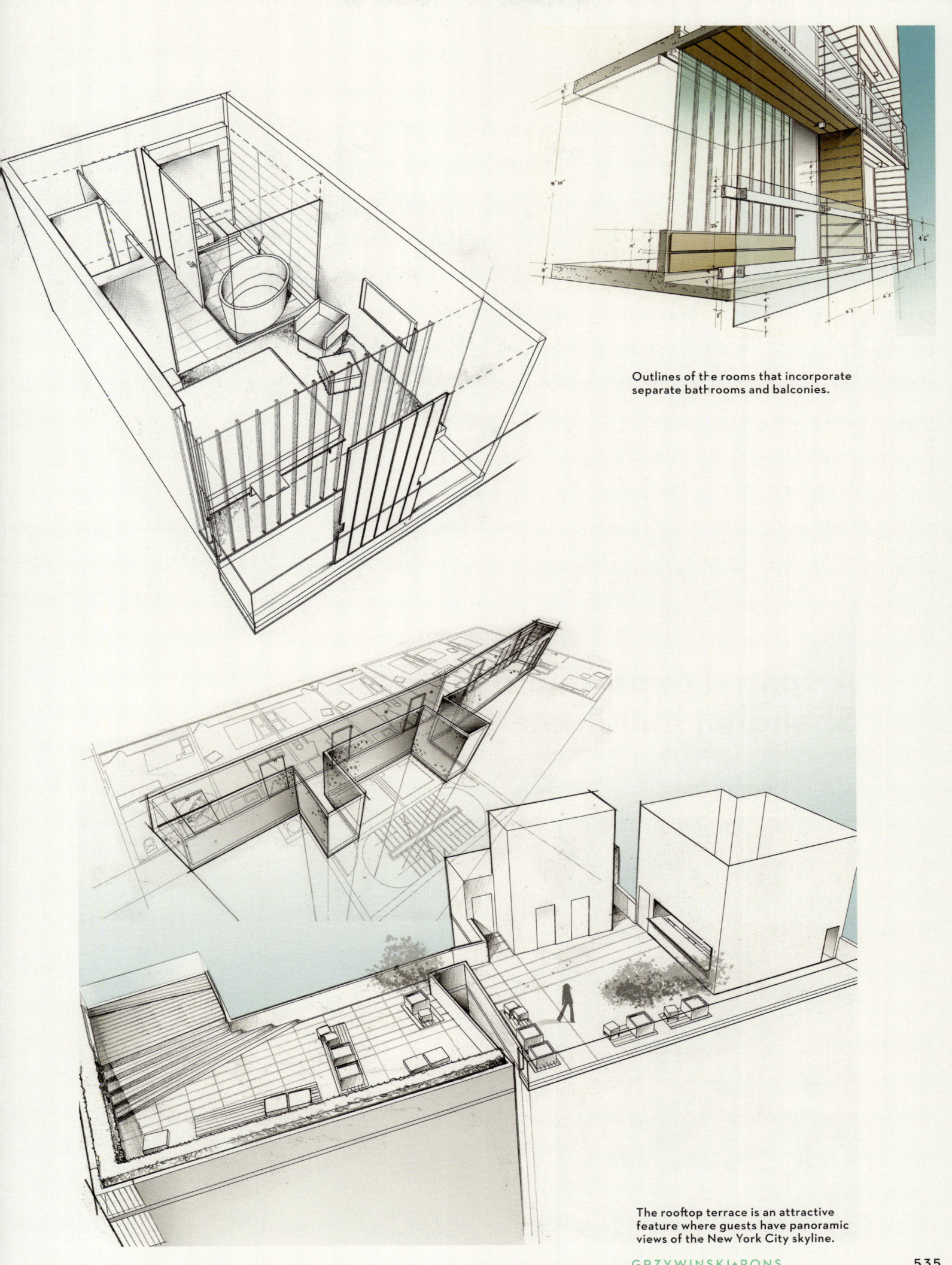

Outlines of the rooms that incorporate separate bathrooms and balconies.

The rooftop terrace is an attractive feature where guests have panoramic views of the New York City skyline.

Opposite One guest room has a view into the lobby through the large vertic window above the reception desk.

THE WATERHOUSE AT SOUTH BUND BY NERI&HU DESIGN AND RESEARCH OFFICE

A spatial experience in an old Shanghai building.

Photos Derryck Menere and Tuomas Uusheimo

The top level of the building, with its rust-coloured steel surround, now houses a roof deck bar.

Where Shanghai, China
Opening May 2010
Client Cameron Holdings
Designer Neri&Hu Design and Research Office → p.586
Floor space 2800 m²
Capacity 19 rooms

Concrete and metal-clad columns separate three vast windows on either side of the restaurant.

THE CONCEPT RESTS ON A CLEAR CONTRAST BETWEEN OLD AND NEW

An industrial-style entrance, both very simple and rather imposing, is set in the original façade.

Located at the South Bund District of Shanghai, the Waterhouse is a four-storey, 19-room boutique hotel built in an existing three-storey Japanese army headquarters building from the 1930s. The boutique hotel fronts the Huangpu River and looks across to the gleaming Pudong skyline. The architectural and interior concept behind Neri&Hu Design and Research Office's (NHDRO) renovation rests on a clear contrast between old and new.

While the original concrete building has been restored, the designers made a new extension on the roof of Corten steel, reflecting the industrial nature of the ships passing on the river, providing an analogous contextual link to both history and local culture.

NHDRO was also responsible for the design of the hotel's interior, which is expressed through a blurring and inversion of the interior and exterior, as well as of the public and private realms, creating a disorienting yet refreshing spatial experience for the hotel guest who longs for an unique five-star hospitality experience. The public spaces allow one to peek into private rooms while the private spaces invite one to look out at the public arenas, such as the large vertical room window above the reception desk and the corridor windows overlooking the dining room. These visual connections of unexpected spaces not only create an element of surprise, but also confront hotel guests with Shanghai's urban condition, in which visual corridors and adjacencies in narrow *nong-tangs* (alleyways) define the city's unique spatial flavour.

The geometrical shapes of the dark, reclaimed wood shutters open into the courtyard, accentuating the space.

The guest rooms have exposed brick, concrete and white painted walls, as well as a vast window affording magnificent views across Shanghai.

Darkened glass lines the bathrooms and showers.

THE WATERHOUSE AT SOUTH BUND

Second floor

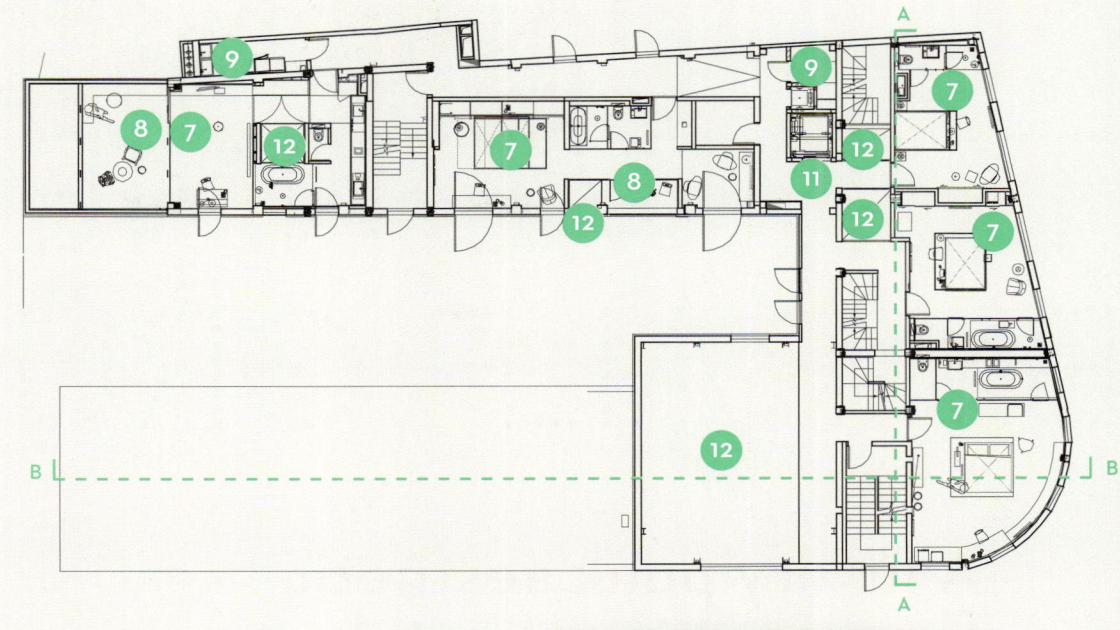

1. Lobby
2. Lounge
3. Restaurant
4. Private dining room
5. Courtyard
6. Kitchen
7. Rooms
8. Terrace
9. Back of the house
10. Toilets
11. Lifts
12. Void

Ground floor

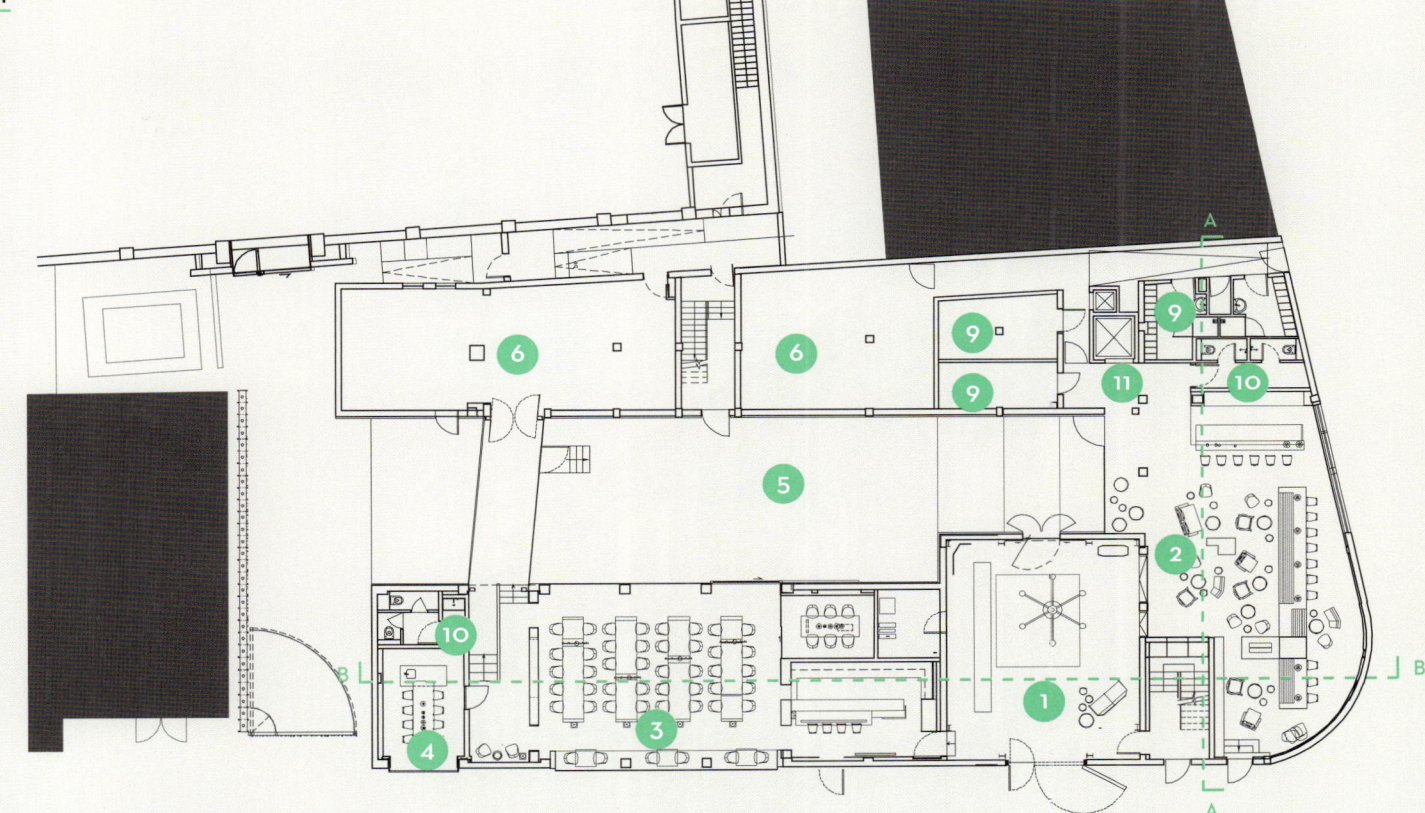

Section AA

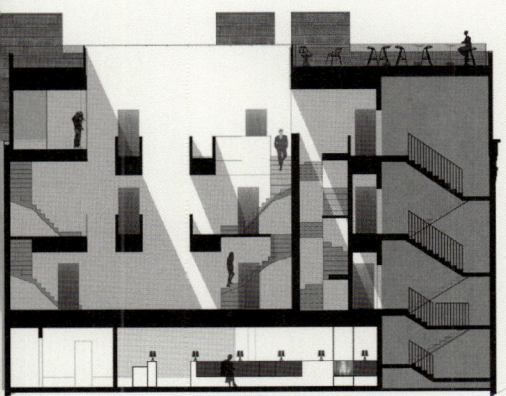

Section BB

Opposite A colourfully creative doorway greets guests at the entrance

THE WEINMEISTER BY RALF GRÜNDER

A luxury punk aesthetic for a creative clientele.

Photos Courtesy of Lux 11

The building has a flat, matt-golden metal, avant-garde front that resembles a cage.

Where Berlin, Germany
Opening July 2010
Client chambers group
Designer Ralf Gründer → p.587
Floor space 4500 m²
Capacity 84 rooms

Specially crafted lamps are integrated into the bar and the low lounge tables.

THE INTERIOR AIMS TO CAPTURE THE ESSENCE OF MODERN COOL

Aside from the colourful graffiti art, a natural palette of browns and beiges runs through the hotel's entire interior décor.

THE WEINMEISTER

The monumental beds are like ships waiting to set sail into the night.

Storage facilities are incorporated at the back of the vast headboard.

Mitte is a district of central Berlin that is a hotspot for art, culture, fashion, shopping and clubbing. It is here that the Weinmeister Berlin-Mitte is located, a hotel project by Ralf Gründer with a luxury punk aesthetic. The concept was to create a destination where guests feel part of the true Berlin and that captures the essence of modern cool.

The hotel exudes style and elegance, produced with both restraint and opulence along with a healthy dose of creativity and urban style – from the graffiti art on the walls to oversize angular furniture. Guests enter the striking foyer past a mural by local graffiti artists and continue onto the Schwarz Bar where the walls and surfaces are clad in the richest of natural textures: the counter has varnished strips of wood, the walls are a patchwork of beige-hued padded materials, and the structural columns are dressed in deluxe grey felt, stitched together like a threaded corset. Also on the ground floor is the Club Lounge, with its gigantic couches and chairs that appear to envelop guests as they sit back and unwind. The furniture is all handcrafted with a theatrical aesthetic and creates moments of Alice in Wonderland whimsy.

In each guest room, the undisputed show-stopper is the huge bed positioned as a wing-backed installation that takes centre stage. Large mattresses measuring 2 x 2 m and oversized cloth-covered frames have nearly floor-to-ceiling headboards that doubles-up as a built-in amenities closets. The stark and minimal décor is complemented by muted colours and materials both organic and luxurious, including bathroom shelves made of slabs of natural oak and handcrafted lamps.

opposite The circular shape above the beds in the yellow apartment is repeated in the bathroom, which has a luxurious round tub.

TOWN @ HOUSE STREET BY SIMONE MICHELI

A home away from home in an apartment-style Milan hotel.

Photos Juergen Eheim

Where Milan, Italy
Opening April 2010
Client Alessandro Rosso
Designer Simone Micheli → p.588
Floor space 130 m²
Capacity 4 rooms

The 'yellow' suite is the only apartment within the Town @ House Street urban concept that primarily uses metal tubular elements in the furniture.

SIMONE MICHELI

A project born in Milan but intended for the leading metropolises of the world. A commercial space on the first floor of Via Goldoni 33 has been transformed into a four-suite hotel, an idea conceived by Alessandro Rosso and implemented by architect Simone Micheli. A new contemporary hospitality concept is brought forth by the desire to retrain degraded or abandoned metropolitan spaces. The basic hotel stereotypes are totally refuted: the reception, lobby, stairs, lifts and corridors have been omitted.

Every suite looks straight onto the city street, each having an independent access directly from its glazed door facing the street, electronically controlled by an alphanumeric keyboard on which the reservation code obtained from the hotel's website can be entered.

Entering the suite is done without any additional filters, crossing the threshold of a former commercial space. The room becomes the city and vice versa – home away from home. The macro-photographs on the walls by Maurzio Marcato depict breathtaking views of the city, encompassing squares, streets and revealing monuments. The iconic views of the city serve to identify and name the four suites as 'the street', giving each one a different flavour.

The four suites, approximately 35 m² each, emerge as real mini-apartments complete with every comfort, all equipped with a bed, wardrobe, bathroom and kitchen. Each suite is different, not only in its main colours and its digital printed images but also in the design solutions applied to each furniture component.

The first suite greets guests with a long blazing green tongue. Coming up from the floor, the tongue flowingly bends and grows along the entire wall, turning into desk, the small kitchen, and the bed. The second suite is characterized by the colo orange and almost entirely resolved into a single plastic gesture. An impressive headboard bends and leans forward at 90 degrees, housing a LCD monitor. In the third suite each element – bed, desk, table – is divided into two parts. The mai parts, like the table top, are made of soli white surfaces, wrapped by yellow tubul steel – which serves as table and bed leg for instance. The fourth suite, open on both ends, houses a desk with fluid and s lines, integrated with the kitchen furnitu that occupies a whole glass window, and lightened by the red colour that underli all the finishes.

EVERY SUITE IS DIFFERENT, NOT ONLY IN THE MAIN COLOURS BUT ALSO IN DESIGN SOLUTIONS

The bed's support is made out of a C-bent structure that stretches out to become the bedside tables.

This is a pilot project for the concept, which is to redevelop redundant urban retail spaces across the world.

The vibrant colours of the glossy furnishings contrast with the monochromatic digital prints that cover all the walls.

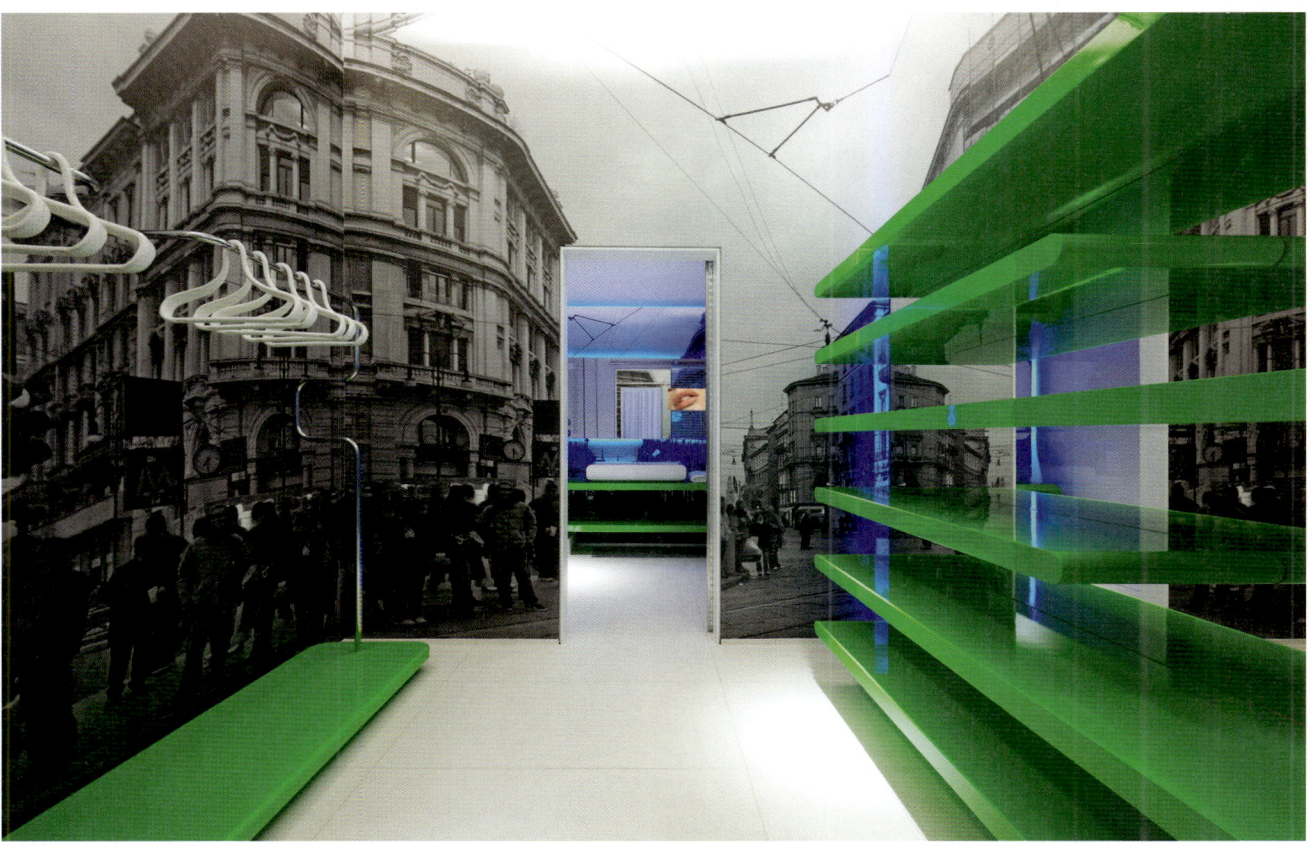

Behind what appears to be a mirrored wardrobe is actually a built-in kitchen, complete with sink, fridge and microwave.

PHOTOGRAPHS ON THE WALLS DEPICT BREATHTAKING VIEWS OF THE CITY

All rooms have blue-tinged recessed lighting supplied by Targetti Poulsen.

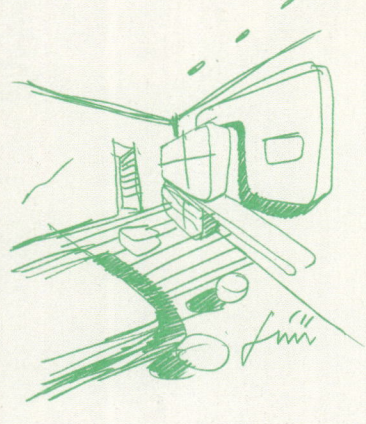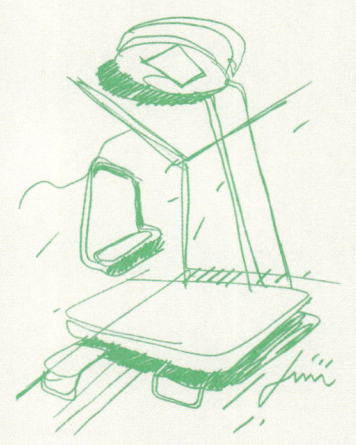

Sketches showing the various options for the integrated, bespoke bedroom furniture.

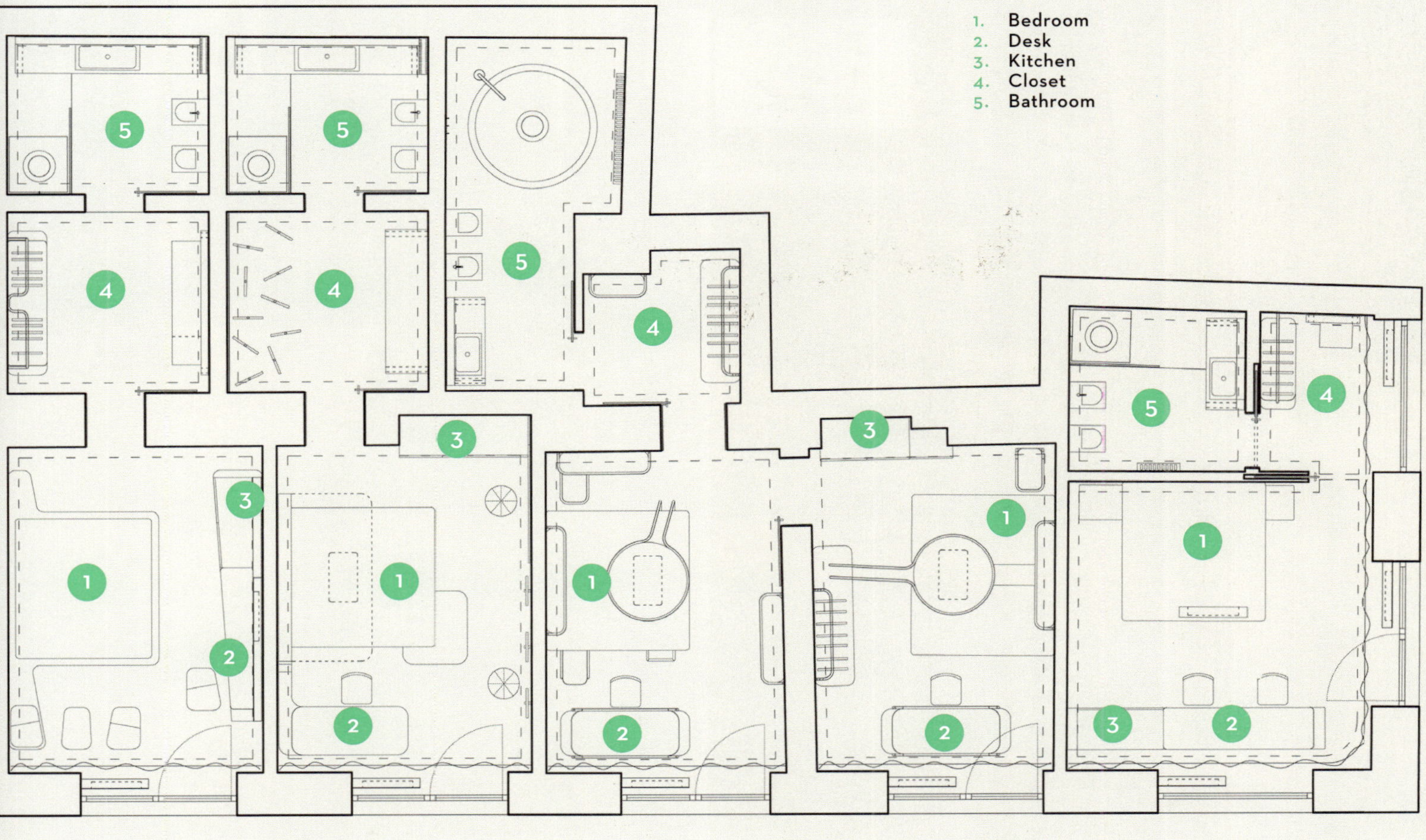

1. Bedroom
2. Desk
3. Kitchen
4. Closet
5. Bathroom

SIMONE MICHELI

Architectural angles emphasized by coloured lighting define the reception area.

TULIP CITY BY SPACE ARCHITECTS & DESIGNERS

An Istanbul hotel that has a utopian atmosphere.

Photos Mirhan Bilir

Where Istanbul, Turkey
Opening July 2010
Client Marsan Marmara Holding
Designer Space Architects & Designers → p.589
Floor space 1957 m²
Capacity 64 rooms

Opposite The mirrored ceiling creates impressive reflections of the metallic gold lamps.

ÇETINKAYA SET THE TONE OF TULIP CITY AS 'HETEROTOPIA'

From the rooftop, guests can enjoy magnificent views across Istanbul.

Top and left An opulent and somewhat futuristic atmosphere is incorporated within the décor.

This modern take on the Turkish bath can be illuminated in different colours.

A digitally printed trompe l'oeil wall-hanging features in the guest rooms as a contemporary headboard.

Having completed numerous boutique hotel projects, Kaan Çetinkaya – founder of Space Architects & Designers – was asked by Marsan Holding to design the interior of the Tulip City hotel in Istanbul. The interior design of the hotel creates a timeless atmosphere in which divergent themes combine to produce a feeling of fullness and excitement.

Çetinkaya set the tone of Tulip City as 'Heterotopia'. Starting in the 1950s, modern forms could be created thanks to new materials that could be produced in specific and creative shapes. The possibilities of creating new architectural products created a new attitude towards architecture; ideas about the future and about design became utopian in this new architectural era. Every movie about the future made at the time represented a utopian world that would follow the modern era: sterile places and planets shaped by metal. The interior of Tulip City is based on this concept.

Guests enter the lobby of the hotel and are welcomed by a crystallized, sculpted reception desk covered in metal plates. The sculptural form of the reception desk extends into the elevator section towards the reading area. Mirrors cover the ceiling to achieve a utopian atmosphere.

While aiming to satisfy the growing needs of travellers in a rapidly globalizing world, the hotel remembers to embed the local characteristics and cultural heritage of Istanbul within its enjoyable and dynamic environment. The basement *hamam* (Turkish bath) couldn't be left out, as it is an essential component of traditional Turkish culture. Meanwhile, the 64 home-like rooms are equipped with all modern conveniences. In the rooftop Up Lounge bar, crystalline forms steal the show again. The kitchen area is hidden from view by a structure covered in wooden panels, and guests can enjoy stunning views of modern and traditional Istanbul from the upholstered couch with zigzag back. ●

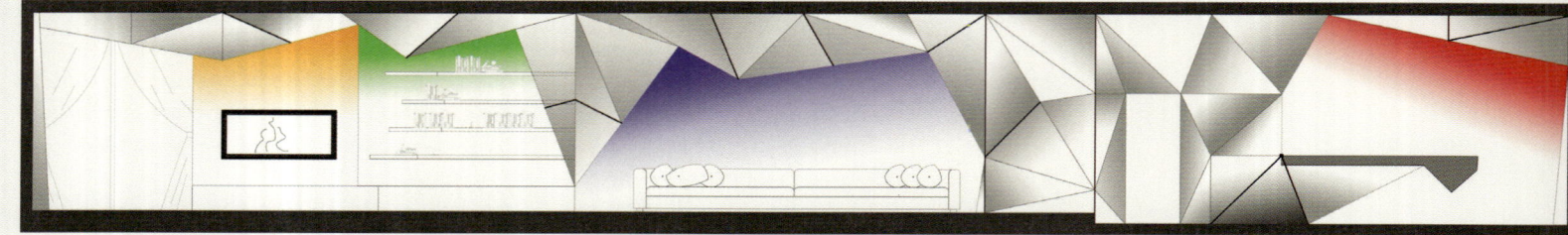

Metallic triangular shapes and atmospheric lighting creates a geometric landscape on the interior walls.

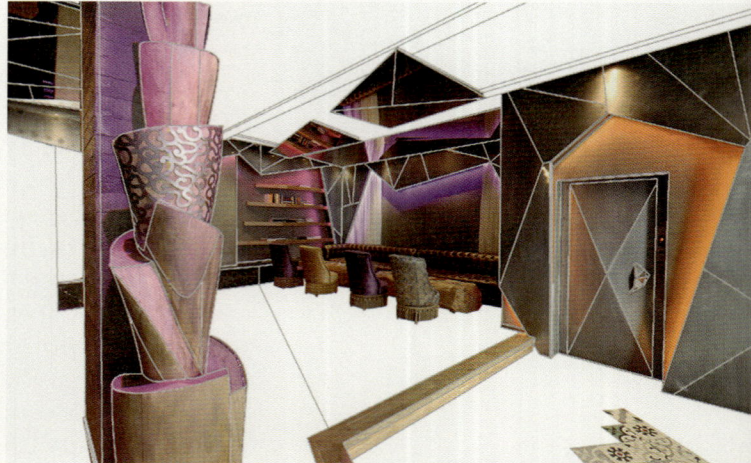

All furniture and fittings in the space were custom-designed by Space Architect & Designers.

CRYSTALLIZED, SCULPTED SURFACES CREATE AN ARCHITECTURAL AESTHETIC IN THE LOBBY

Up Lounge

1. Bar
2. Seating area
3. Kitchen
4. Toilets
5. Lifts

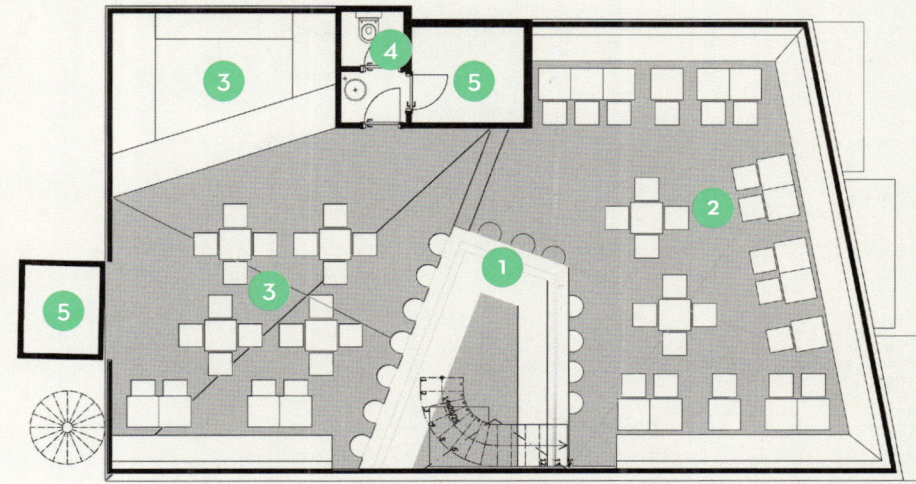

First floor

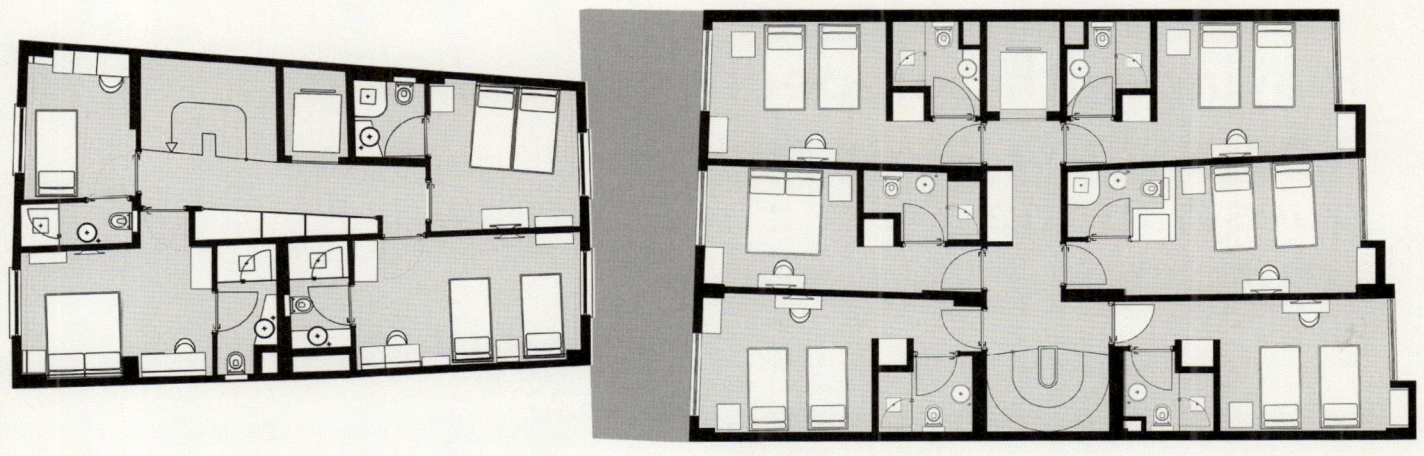

Ground floor

1. Reception
2. Lounge
3. Library
4. Business area
5. Breakfast room
6. Toilets
7. Lifts

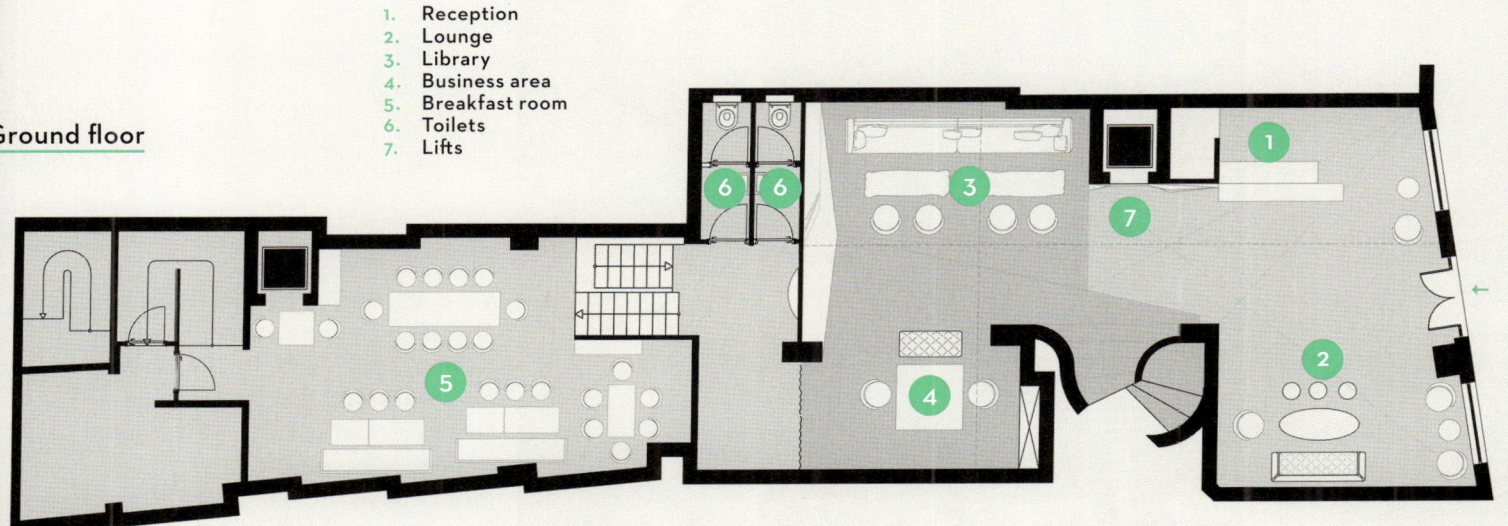

SPACE ARCHITECTS & DESIGNERS

W LONDON BY CONCRETE ARCHITECTURAL ASSOCIATES

Playing with perspectives, a plush interior awaits guests in the West End.

Photos Ewout Huibers for Concrete

Opposite A striking framework of vertical blinds is positioned behind the Chesterfield couch.

Maurice Brill Lighting Design was responsible for all the lighting solutions featured in the hotel, including the illuminated 'W' that greets guests at the entrance.

Where London, United Kingdom
Opening February 2011
Clients McAleer & Rushe Group and Starwood Hotels & Resorts
Designer Concrete Architectural Associates → p.581
Floor space 8100 m²
Capacity 192 rooms

On the shelves of the cabinet that climbs one wall is a display of plates designed by byviv and Marcel van der Vugt.

Opposite An impressive lighting installation, which draws customers' eyes upwards, makes the most of the vast height in the W Lounge.

THERE'S A SURPRISING SHIFT IN PERSPECTIVE WITHIN THE SPACE

The screening room has recessed lighting with angled, illuminated lines streaking across all surfaces of the space.

W London is a five-star hotel on Leicester Square, in the heart of London's West End. The client commissioned Concrete Architectural Associates to create an interior that was all about being part of London's business-club and party culture. The design concept invites guests to experience the dual personality of a true Londoner by mixing private and social, work and play, formal and party, reserved and outrageous, day and night.

On walking into the hotel, glitz and glamour abound, with guests immediately dazzled by reflections of a sparkling sculpture in the entranceway. Supported by black glass walls and dynamic spotlights that point towards the cloud of 280 disco balls, guests are guided up to the first-floor welcome area, past the W Store and into the W Lounge. Here, a broad and bright passage with an impressive height features a plush customer seating area. Sofas, cushions and stools are upholstered in traditional textiles and patterns, giving the space a modern look, positioned next to a high white book case. A contemporary twist sees the dark parquet tiles of the floor extend up the end walls and across the ceiling. With the vast lighting installation above made up of constituent parts that mirror the shape of the seating below, there is a surprising shift of perspective within the space.

Mirroring effects also feature in the rich décor of the lounge bar, with lighting reflected onto the gold-leaf ceiling and in the highly polished tiles around the edge of the room. A luxurious, 37-m-long Chesterfield couch sets a winding landscape as it curves around everything, including the end-grain oak flooring, following its path. Next door in the Wyld bar, a late-night atmosphere is instilled with its spicy red and black leather furnishings and a grand disco ball 3 m in diameter.

Amid the hotel's silver and gold mirrored and frosted glass walls, guests can treat themselves to pampering sessions in the spa or gym or indulge themselves in the ultimate dressing rooms within their own rooms. The bedroom interiors are a soft antidote to the highly polished surfaces, walls and natural tiled floors of the dressing room areas. There is also a play on perspectives, with mirrors positioned so that reflections cleverly expand the space; quilted, padded panels on the walls enhance this effect. •

CONCRETE ARCHITECTURAL ASSOCIATES

The trio of welcome pods are made of polished stainless steel and Corian Bisque, with recessed purple LED lighting around the bottom.

GUEST ARE GREETED BY GLITZ AND GLAMOUR

The bespoke cocktail tables have glass tops and red LED up-lights.

Mirrored reflections appear to expand the space.

A dark-stained oak walk-in wardrobe has drawers with front panels upholstered in champagne-coloured artificial leather.

CONCRETE ARCHITECTURAL ASSOCIATES

Lighting is also an important aspect in the guest rooms, with strip lighting above and beneath the beds.

A central bath and vanity unit is positioned on the crème Mosa floor tiles.

GUEST ROOMS ARE SOFTENED WITH QUILTED MATERIALS AND PADDED PANELS

Sixth floor

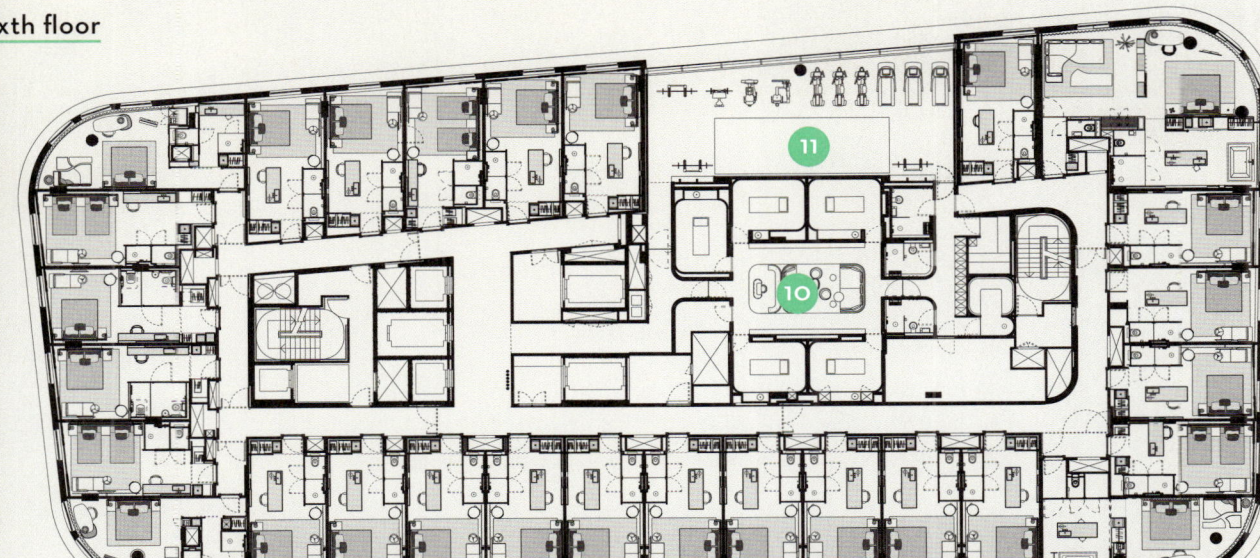

1. Reception area
2. W shop
3. W lounge
4. W lounge bar
5. Wyld bar
6. Screening room
7. Kitchen
8. Guest rooms
9. Meeting rooms
10. Spa
11. Gym

Second floor

First floor

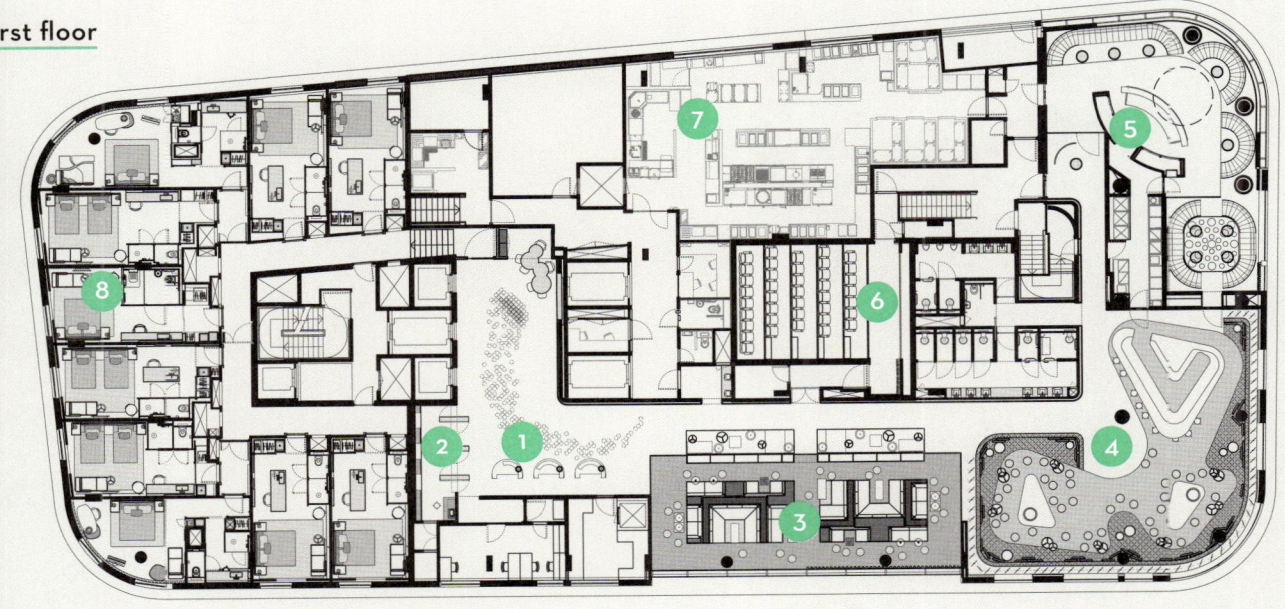

W RETREAT & SPA BALI

Opposite At this private spa facility in the extreme WOW suite couples lie under an imposing circular skylight.

W RETREAT & SPA BALI BY AB CONCEPT

A resort with a surprising and ultra-modern twist on Balinese design.

Photos Chester Ong

The large daybeds on the terraced W lounge are open to the coastal breeze.

Where Seminyak, Indonesia
Opening April 2011
Client W Hotels
Designer AB Concept → p.578
Floor space 31,000 m²
Capacity 158 suites and retreats, 79 villas

AB CONCEPT

The bathrooms of the three-bedroom villas have slatted ceilings that let in sunbeams.

ARCHITECTURAL MOTIFS REINTERPRET TRADITIONAL BALINESE ART

Much of the furniture is made of natural materials, including local timber and volcanic stone.

The villas all have a private pool and outdoor living area.

Light weathered oak has been used for surfaces, while bedside tables in thick sheets of float glass confirm the strong contemporary impression.

The bathrooms are vast, symmetrical landscapes of terrazzo with stepped architectural profiles.

next spread In tribute to the island's Hindu traditions, the W lounge ceiling features an intricate henna design.

Located along Bali's über-chic Seminyak strip, W Retreat & Spa Bali, designed by Hong Kong-based studio AB Concept, offers a surprising, ultra-modern twist on Balinese design. Fusing festive colours, distinctive architectural shapes and traditional elements, AB Concept has created a luxury retreat of uncompromising quality.

Comprising 158 suites and retreats and 79 one-, two- or three-bedroom private villas, the resort covers 31,000 m² over four floors. AB Concept designed the interiors of this beachfront resort, including the stunning terraced lobby and W Lounge. Oversized day beds and billowing curtains exude a relaxed vibe, while the quirky contours and palette of hot pinks and purples hint at the designers' adventurous spirit. While dispensing with the teak-and-terrazzo formula so popular in many of Bali's resorts, the design team remains respectful of the island's rich cultural heritage. Architectural motifs reinterpret traditional Balinese art while the open-plan lobby provides natural ventilation for much of the year, blurring the boundaries between indoors and outdoors. Lampshades woven from synthetic rattan resemble pagoda roofs while terrazzo tiling, cut to resemble leaf veins, shimmers with inlaid seashells.

Inspired by the colours of Bali's sunsets and seascapes, the scheme pulls in the coastal landscape at every opportunity. From the violet-hued lustre of the lobby, to the aquatic greens of the guest retreats, AB Concept has seamlessly integrated natural elements into the design. Bed throws are hand-stitched with a leaf pattern, skylights carved above the bath welcome the sunlight, and the library features furniture made of tropical timber and pillars of local volcanic stone. Adding a new level of luxury, the 79 self-contained villas offer a sense of relaxed outdoor living and boast a private pool allowing guests to soak up the elements, open to the sky.

YOTEL BY ROCKWELL GROUP AND SOFTROOM

Where **New York, United States**
Opening **June 2011**
Client **Yotel**
Designers **Rockwell Group** → p.588
and **Softroom** → p.588
Floor space **21,368 m²**
Capacity **669 rooms**

A semi-futuristic space in a 21st-century city.

Photos Nikolas Koenig

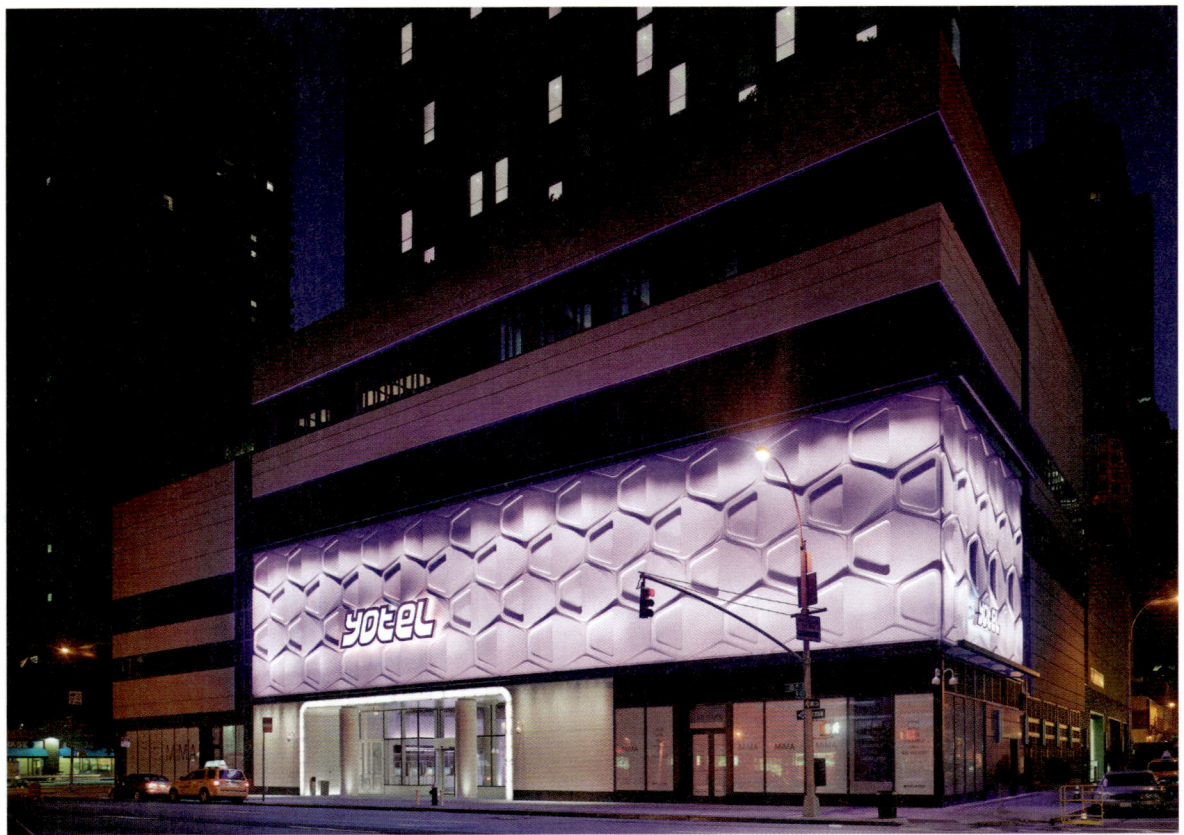

The signature lozenge shape of the Yotel brand has been incorporated in the illuminated purple façade.

Guests are welcomed by Yobot, a mechanical white robot that makes the experience of 'checking your bags in' quite the futuristic spectacle.

Trinity modular seating from sixinch and Air stools by Héctor Serrano for Gandia Blasco furnish the terrace.

The colourful 10-m-chain curtain in the lobby was designed by Japanese artist Shinpei Naito and manufactured by KriskaDecor.

Opened in June 2011, YOTEL New York features over 669 stylish cabins. This is the brand's first property outside its current international airport locations and was designed jointly by Rockwell Group and Softroom. Besides the standard Premium Cabins, YOTEL New York has 19 First Class Cabins and three VIP Cabin Suites. The large footprint also allows 1700 m² of public space, including a lounge and bar, restaurant, gym, studio space for events and a 370-m² outdoor terrace.

Centred on a concept of 'affordable luxury', the overall vision of the design was to create technologically sophisticated and vibrant spaces. YOTEL is focused on delivering the optimum guest experience, balanced with affordability and practicality. At the same time, it was paramount that the hotel communicate a sense of fun, warmth and welcome to its guests.

The presence of the hotel is communicated at street level: a dramatic custom-designed white concrete cladding system in the form of giant low-relief tiles covers the façade over three storeys, and a curvaceous, white, sculpted, lozenge-shaped canopy embraces the point of entrance. In the entrance lobby, the design of the check-in and luggage storage functions has been given a radical twist. Check-in desks have been eliminated, replaced with a row of self-check-in kiosks. The star attraction of the lobby is the automated luggage storage: a service normally hidden away has been made highly visible and transformed into an ambassador for the hotel experience. Guests wishing to deposit their bags are able to entrust their belongings to the power and security of Yobot – a giant white robot arm. Bags placed onto a loading tray housed within an elegantly designed enclosure are whisked away by Yobot. This fascinating mechanical spectacle is theatrically lit and revealed through a huge window facing onto the lobby and also visible from the street outside.

Each cabin features a comfortable bed, a large, fully glazed bathroom area, a 'technowall' guests can use to customize the lighting and audio, and enough storage for all their belongings. The VIP Cabin Suites also boast fireplaces, a convertible pool table, a round rotating bed with unparalleled views of the Manhattan skyline, and a wrap-around terrace with a Jacuzzi.

The overall palette of YOTEL is clean and simple, in line with the values of the brand. Pure whites are used across a variety of textures, from the pre-cast concrete of the façade to the sheer curtains dividing the sleeping and bathroom areas of the cabins. Some warmth is added by the use of bamboo and oak timber, while signature purple is used primarily in upholstery and is echoed in accent lighting in both the public spaces and cabins.

the guest rooms, the bedroom
and bathroom can be separated by
sheer curtains.

the VIP suite, the Aramith 'Fusion'
table intriguingly transforms from a
dining table to a pool table.

ROCKWELL GROUP AND SOFTROOM

360id studio
3 Alexandrou Soutsou Street
10671 Athens
Greece
+30 210 361 7348
info@360id.gr
360id.gr

p.138

Alexandros Tsikordanos is a Greek interior designer who founded his Athens-based design company, 360id studio in 2005. The studio has a wide-ranging portfolio of private residence, offices and commercial spaces. 360id studio approaches each project in a collaborative spirit with the client to create harmonic, familiar spaces with symbolic meanings. Bespoke objects and furniture are designed to fulfil the client's needs. The studio also collaborates with creative consultants to deliver high-quality detail and construction.

…,staat creative agency
De Ruyterkade 143
1011 AC Amsterdam
the Netherlands
+31 20 572 1388
contact@staatamsterdam.nl
staatamsterdam.nl

p.292

The international creative agency …,staat is based in Amsterdam, where it has been operating since 2000. The team, led by creative director Jochem Leegstra and partners Julia Kortekaas, Michiel Steyn and Martijn Tamboer, passionately develops projects in the realms of design, branding, architecture, advertising and everything in between.

A00 Architecture
135 Guang Yuan Lu, 2nd Floor
200030 Shanghai
China
+86 21 5465 3616
ss@azerozero.com
azerozero.com

p.100, 162

A00 Architecture is a Shanghai-based practice led by Montreal-born architects Sacha Silva and Raefer Wallis. Founded in 2004, A00 quickly developed a niche creating highly personalized modern residences in Shanghai's historic district, feature restaurants and the conversion reuse of many industrial warehouses, including the award-winning URBN hotel. This reputation for innovative and iconic projects has led them to develop a diverse portfolio spanning interiors and architecture from China to Sri Lanka. A00 is internationally recognized for pioneering solutions that combine ecological, social and economic sustainability.

AB Concept
1801 Leighton Centre
77 Leighton Road
Causeway Bay, Hong Kong
Hong Kong
+852 2525 2428
info@abconcept.net
abconcept.net

p.566

Since its formation in 1999, AB Concept has developed a vision and reputation that spans continents and cultural themes. With a team of design masterminds with an eye for the unique, Hong Kong-based AB Concept focuses on high-end hospitality projects around the world. Directors Terence Ngan and Ed Ng have a gift for balancing stimulation with a sense of deep tranquillity, and through it they aim to anchor each project to a client on a physical and emotional level.

Alexey Rozenberg
Prospekt Mira 118/104
129164 Moscow
Russia
+7 916 610 4229
ar4229@gmail.com

p.304

Alexey Rozenberg was born in 1957 in Tomsk, Russia. After graduating from Almaty Architecture and Construction Institute, he undertook a teaching position at the same institute. In 1998, he received his master's degree in architecture at the Research Institute of Educational Buildings in Moscow where he now works as a professor. Rozenberg also undertakes projects for his own architectural practice with a portfolio that includes multiple residential houses, and also residential and commercial interiors.

Alfredo Häberli
Seefeldstrasse 301a
8008 Zurich
Switzerland
+41 44 380 3230
studio@alfredo-haeberli.com
alfredo-haeberli.com

p.388

Argentinian-born and Swiss-based designer Alfredo Häberli established his own studio in Zurich in 1991. He manages to unite tradition with innovation, joy and energy in his product designs and marries bold Argentinian colours to Swiss simplicity. His portfolio also includes interior architecture for hotels, shops and trade fair stands.

Andrea Lupacchini Architetto
Via Degli Scipioni 252
00192 Rome
Italy
+39 069 784 3563
info@lupacchini.it
lupacchini.it

p.254, 260

Andrea Lupacchini graduated from the Sapienza University in Rome with an honours degree in architecture. He works as a freelance designer and architect, creating interiors within the hospitality, corporate and public sectors. His portfolio also includes landscape and graphic design projects, as well as exhibition spaces. In addition, he is a teacher at the School of Architecture and Design in the University of Camerino.

Andrea Mantello Architetto
Rue de Venise 29a
1050 Brussels
Belgium
+32 475 357 372
mail@andreamantello.com
andreamantello.com

p.320

Trained at the Politecnico in Turin, Andrea Mantello is an architect and designer. He set up his own firm in 2004 in Turin and extended its practice to Brussels 2 years later. His portfolio features exhibition spaces, retail design and the conception of single objects, such as chairs and lamps. His curiosity for the synergistic intermingling of architecture, art, design, space and light has also led to his collaboration with lighting design offices across Europe. Since 2010 Mantello is co-founder of thesignLab and AV[z].

Anton Grechko
aagrechko@gmail.com

p.304

Anton Grechko, who was born in Moscow in 1979, graduated from the San Francisco Academy of Art in 2002 with a degree in new media. He has worked as an art director in several network agency's like BBDO and Rapp Collins, as well as a concept artist for several production studios and art director for numerous photo shoots and advertising campaigns. Currently, Grechko cooperates on interior design projects and undertakes book illustration commissions.

Aroma
Binzmühlestrasse 170
8050 Zurich
Switzerland
+41 44 208 2222
mail@aroma.ch
aroma.ch

p.350

Lukas Meier founded Aroma in 1995 in Zurich. This 3D communication agency offers a wide range of services, focusing on interior design and event architecture. Aroma employs over 20 specialists in design, communications and construction, all united under one roof. The team's strengths lie in creation and design, giving brands, products and companies unique spatial identities, whether temporary or long-term.

AS Design Service
Room B1, 7th Floor, Yeung Yiu Chung Ind's Building
19 Cheung Shun Street
Lai Chi Kok, Hong Kong
Hong Kong
+852 2191 6433
info@as-hk.com
as-hk.com

p.204, 414

With a vast imagination, great market sense and determination to work together and achieve success with clients, AS Design has grown into a thriving design firm in Hong Kong. The team of AS Design provide professional and comprehensive design services to international brand labels in Hong Kong, the mainland of China and the South Pacific region. The strength of the design agency lies in image renovation for brands, as well as interior design of retail, hospitality, commercial and residential spaces.

Barzileye Concept & Design
Molenstraat 15
2315 BH Den Haag
the Netherlands
+31 70 361 1711
info@barzileye.com
barzileye.com

p.072

Interior designer Angelika Kok is the owner and founder of Barzileye Concept & Design, which she established in 2007. Her approach to finding the true identity of a project entails intensive and extensive research, delving deep into its cultural, geographical, historical and literary origins. By collaborating with highly trained experts and utilizing state-of-the-art technology, she weaves the past into the future for projects in the realms of interior design, leisure projects (hotels, cruise ships), private houses and exhibition and event design.

Bates Smart
1 Nicholson Street
Melbourne VIC 3000
Australia
+61 3 8664 6200
enquiries@batessmart.com
batessmart.com

p.114

With offices in Sydney and Melbourne, Bates Smart is a leading Australian practice offering full services in architecture, as well as interior and urban design. Bates Smart works with diverse clients across a range of sectors from commercial, multilevel residential and health care projects to hospitality venues. The practice is committed to research-based design focused on delivering excellence and innovation as well as exceeding client expectations.

Beers|Brickworks
Molenbochtstraat 35
5003 DG Tilburg
the Netherlands
+31 6 1059 9027
nicole@beers-brickworks.nl
beers-brickworks.nl

p.090, 268, 276

In 2008, Nicole van Beers (Beers) and Kariene van Steenoven (Brickworks) joined forces to found Beers|Brickworks. The design firm specializes in venues for drinking, eating, sleeping and partying. What characterizes the designs of Beers|Brickworks is a constant search for contrasts and the ideal balance between order and chaos.

BEHF Architects
Kaiserstrasse 41
1070 Vienna
Austria
+43 1 5241 7500
behf@behf.at
behf.at

p.124

Armin Ebner, Susi Hasenauer and Stephan Ferenczy established their own architecture company BEHF Architects in 1995. Today, the Vienna-based company consists of about 100 architects with competencies and experience ranging from project planning to implementation to completion, and its network extends far beyond Austria's borders. An understanding of architecture as communication for companies and institutions is at the heart of BEHF. The firm's projects are characterized by a reduction to a few but clearly and consistently applied architectural elements, not bombastic but focusing on the essentials of the task.

BK Architecture
39 Ehad Haam Street
65205 Tel Aviv
Israel
+972 3560 9914
bk@bkarch.co.il
bkarc.com

p.086

BK Architecture was established in Tel Aviv in 1999. At the time, the studio's co-founders, Alon Baranowitz and Irene Kronenberg, had been carving out their own careers in urban and interior design, and their combined experience meant they could apply design solutions to projects of varying scales, from the micro to the macro. BK projects are narratives that instil the design process with a multidisciplinary approach. The studio's portfolio includes residential buildings, private villas and civic centres as well as the interior design of restaurants, offices, hotels, bars and shops.

Blacksheep
13-19 Vine Hill
London EC1R 5DW
United Kingdom
+44 20 7713 7413
contact@blacksheep.uk.com
blacksheep.uk.com

p.060, 302, 494

Formed in 2002 by Tim Mutton and Jo Sampson, Blacksheep has a global reputation for creating exceptional hospitality environments. From its London studio, Blacksheep creates aspirational lifestyle spaces, delivering slick, branded concepts that exemplify timeless style and contemporary glamour. The studio boasts specialist teams who understand the importance of an all-encompassing, holistic hospitality design service, including local market analysis, brand positioning and integrated graphics and branding.

blazysgérard
2030 Pie IX Suite 108
Montreal QC H1V 2C8
Canada
+1 514 303 0711
info@blazysgerard.com
blazysgerard.com

p.108

Founded in 2003 in Montreal, studio blazysgérard was established by Alexandre Blazys and Benoit Gérard when they decided to join their talents and knowledge to create an office of design and architecture working primarily on prestigious interior projects. Reflection and knowledge are key players in the studio's approach, with a dynamic team offering flawless execution and impeccable service to its commercial and residential clients.

Brinkworth
4–6 Ellsworth Street
London E2 0AX
United Kingdom
+44 207 613 5341
info@brinkworth.co.uk
brinkworth.co.uk

p.178

Brinkworth is a design-led company working in architecture, interiors and furniture design as well as creative brand strategy and graphics. Formed in 1991 by founder Adam Brinkworth, one of its three directors along with Kevin Brennan and David Hurren, the company is based in London and has active projects around the world.

brownbag lab.
1-14-25 Kyomachibori,
Nishiku
550-0003 Osaka
Japan
+81 6 6449 1711
info@brownbag.jp
brownbag.jp

p.026

Designer Shingo Abe established his own design office in Osaka, Japan in 2002. brownbag lab. offers total design solutions for interiors. The studio's portfolio includes interior design projects, mostly in the eating and drinking category.

C4ID interieurarchitecten
's Gravelandseweg 38
1211 BT Hilversum
the Netherlands
+31 35 785 2128
info@c4id.nl
c4id.nl

p.370

C4ID interieurarchitecten – Concepts for Interior Design – was founded by Casper Schwarz in 2006. This Dutch design studio focuses on business environments for both commercial and government clients. The C4ID designers raise the needs and wishes of a client to a higher or more specific level by creating an open way of communication and cooperation. In this way, each project becomes a well-balanced group achievement. The studio's major clients are legal, consultancy and financial companies.

C+L Studio
Via Maggio 7
50125 Florence
Italy
+39 055 265 7672
info@cipiuelle.net
cipiuelle.net

p.046

Camilla Lapucci and Lapo Bianchi Luci founded their own architecture and design office, C+L Studio, in 2002. The company explores different areas, ranging from architecture to interior design, from graphic design to art direction. The studio's projects cover both the public and private sectors and vary from hotels and restaurants to luxury boutiques and private villas and apartments.

Carmody Groarke
21 Denmark Street
London WC2H 8NA
United Kingdom
+44 207 836 2333
studio@carmodygroarke.com
carmodygroarke.com

p.158

Carmody Groarke is a London-based architecture studio established by Kevin Carmody and Andrew Groarke in 2006. A strong emphasis is given to a critical design process within the studio, after a thorough investigation of each project's unique situation. Undertaking projects of highly varied typologies, the studio's international portfolio includes public buildings and spaces, exhibition design, residential spaces and offices.

Carsten Jörgensen
Seestrasse 95
6047 Kastanienbaum
Switzerland
+41 41 362 2075
admin@joergensen.ch
joergensen.ch

p.364

Carsten Jörgensen is a painter and graphic designer by education, and a product designer by experience. After working for 25 years as creative director for Danish coffee-maker manufacturer Bodum, he now divides his interests and activities among product design, design consultancy, lecturing and writing on art, design and architecture.

Clemens Bachmann Architekten
Balanstrasse 73
81541 Munich
Germany
+49 89 2300 0700
info@cbarchitekten.com
cbarchitekten.com

p.146

Clemens Bachmann Architekten is a multidisciplinary office involved in architecture and design. It was established by architect Clemens Bachmann in Munich, Germany in 2004. The practice has completed a number of large- and small-scale projects and its portfolio includes projects ranging from interior design to large-scale planning and architecture.

CLOUD-9 interior design
1326 Huai Hai Zhong Road,
516
200031 Shanghai
China
+86 134 8212 4129
karin@cloud-9.nl
cloud-9.nl

p.284

CLOUD-9 interior design, based in Shanghai since 2005, was founded by Karin An Rijlaarsdam in the Netherlands in 2000. CLOUD-9 has produced designs for restaurants and hotels in China and elsewhere, sustainable showrooms for furniture brand Haworth, and develops its own interior products and handmade porcelain lights, collaborating with local craftsmen to explore new ways of using local materials and techniques. In 2012, CLOUD-9 will open a second studio in Rio de Janeiro, Brazil.

COLLIDANIEL-ARCHITETTO
Via Sannio 61
00183 Rome
Italy
+39 069 761 0447
info@collidaniela.com
collidaniela.com

p.308

Architect Daniela Colli founded her own studio in Rome in 2009. Her distinctive trademark is rooted in a capacity to combine a contemporary vision with knowledge of the historical and cultural roots of interior design, producing results that blend the past with the future. Her work ranges in scale from furniture to architecture and urban design, with a focus on craftsmanship, detailing and precision. The practice includes a young, dynamic team that works on residential projects and commercial spaces such as shops, showrooms, salons, spas, offices, cafés, restaurants and hotels.

Concrete Architectural Associates
Oudezijds Achterburgwal 78a
1012 DR Amsterdam
the Netherlands
+31 20 520 0200
info@concreteamsterdam.nl
concreteamsterdam.nl

p.152, 558

Concrete Architectural Associates is based in Amsterdam, the Netherlands. It is a design studio that focuses on developing holistic concepts for businesses and institutions. Visual marketers, interior designers, product designers and architects work on various projects in multidisciplinary teams with a focus on the hospitality and retail sectors.
Photo Ewout Huibers for Concrete

Corvin Cristian
3 Pictor Stahi Street,
Apt 7, Sect. 1
010187 Bucharest
Romania
+40 744 537 079
corvin@corvincristian.com
corvincristian.com

p.228

The Bucharest-based designer Corvin Cristian is a trained architect and has worked for the last ten years as an art director for movie sets, including many major builds, from period films to contemporary fiction. He is also responsible for interior design projects ranging from bars, restaurants and clubs to trade fair stands and retail spaces and offices, as well as the scenography for brand launches and other corporate events.

Costa Group
Via ValGraveglia Zai
19020 Riccò del Golfo (SP)
Italy
+39 0187 769 309
info@costagroup.net
costagroup.net

p.046, 490

Costa Group is an Italian company specializing in food entertainment. Established by brothers Franco and Sandro Costa in the 1980s, the company has seen steady growth over the years and now has 100 employees at its headquarters. The group focuses on architectural projects, as well as the design and realization of interiors. Its mission is to have 360-degree interaction with clients at every stage of the process and, in order to achieve this, the group works with architects, designers and communication experts.

d-raw
23b Goodge Place
London W1T 4SN
United Kingdom
+44 207 636 0016
info@d-raw.com
d-raw.com

p.018, 208

London-based architecture and interior design collective d-raw has a diverse portfolio of bespoke design that covers every creative niche. Experts in branded environments, retail design and renovation, the team has a passion for unusual commissions and an uncompromising understanding of the dialogue necessary to create great design. With its creative home remaining in the heart of London and a satellite team of specialist creative talent stretching across the globe, the company performs on both the local and international level.

Dariel Studio
3rd Floor, Building 1, Lane 12
1384 Wan Hang Du Road
200042 Shanghai
China
+86 21 6191 0102
contact@darielstudio.com
darielstudio.com

p.378

Dariel Studio is a Shanghai-based creative agency founded by Thomas Dariel in 2012, borne out of Dariel's previous company Lime388. Originally educated as a designer in Paris, Dariel moved to Shanghai in 2006 and specializes in interior design for luxury private homes (villas, lofts and apartments), creative offices and high-end hospitality projects (hotels, clubs, bars and restaurants). The agency aims to be an open platform for creativity, bringing together international designers, architects, scientists, universities, artists and other participants from the creative industry.

Department of Architecture
18th Floor, Smoothlife Tower
44 North Sathorn Road,
Bang Rak
10500 Bangkok
Thailand
+66 2 633 9936
dept.of.arch@gmail.com
departmentof
architecture.co.th

p.430

Bangkok-based Department of Architecture was founded by Amata Luphaiboon and Twitee Vajrabhaya Teparkum in 2004. The firm specializes in architecture, interior design, landscape design and other related design disciplines in a broad range of programmatic requirements and scales. It focuses on developing ideas in architecture, carries out research on social, cultural and physical contexts, and explores the use of alternative materials.

Designliga
Hans-Preissinger-Strasse 8,
Halle A
81379 Munich
Germany
+49 89 6242 1940
hello@designliga.com
designliga.com

p.264

Designliga is a company specializing in visual communication and interior design. Founded in Munich in 2001 by product designer Saša Stanojcic and communication designer Andreas Döhring, the firm has grown into a strong team of experienced designers, consultants and interior designers. Stanojcic now is Designliga's Creative Director while Döhring is the Creative Director Art. Christina Koepf is Head of Interior Design and Philipp Heitsch is Chief Operating Officer. The firm's clients include companies such as Adidas, Cartier, Marc O'Polo and Sony BMG.

design spirits
2-18-2-2002 Ohara, Setagaya
156-0041 Tokyo
Japan
+81 3 3324 9901
info@design-spirits.com
design-spirits.com

p.326, 366

Yuhkichi Kawai is a Tokyo-based designer who graduated in space design in 1997. After working for other firms, he established his own studio, design spirits, in 2003. Fulfilling his lifelong passion for design, Kawai concentrates on creating interior spaces for cafés, restaurants and hotels. In 2011, he also began lecturing at his alma mater, the Kuwasawa Design Institute in Tokyo.

Dietwee
Kruisdwarsstraat 2
3581 GL Utrecht
the Netherlands
+31 30 234 3555
gerard@dietwee.nl
dietwee.nl

p.286

Dietwee is a branding, design and communication agency with track-records and awards in all categories. With a team of 30 they develop, revitalize and bring brands to life with a straightforward in your face attitude and mentality. Above all: Dietwee is very much Dietwee.

Dreimeta
Ernst-Reuter-Platz 10
86150 Augsburg
Germany
+49 82 1455 7950
info@dreimeta.com
dreimeta.com

p.392

Dreimeta's goal is to create interiors with identity and character. Founded in 2003 by Armin Fischer, this team of creative minds works on both international projects and local or regional tasks. The emphasis is on hotel, restaurant and shop design. Dreimeta works interdisciplinarily and is complemented by a network of architects and interior designers, restaurateurs and designers, marketing experts and psychologists. The goal is always to strengthen the identity and philosophy of the customer by way of daring interpretations.

Duarte Caldeira
Rua da Mouraria 9, 4º c
9000-047 Funchal
Portugal
+351 291 225 334
info@duartecaldeira.com
duartecaldeira.com

p.446

Founded by Portuguese architect Duarte Caldeira in 2001, the studio focuses on architectural design on every scale. Its portfolio includes public buildings, hotels, commercial and residential developments, as well as interior design and furniture. Its concept-based approach aims to create buildings, objects and spaces that engage their users and respond to their ambitions, cultures and contexts. The practice is fuelled by talented and experienced architects who develop projects from the initial sketches to on-site supervision. Every project involves a multidisciplinary team, sometimes with external consultants, who focus their knowledge, expertise and imagination into a fresh and innovative approach to design.

duka design
Tumblingerstrasse 28
80337 Munich
Germany
+49 89 8898 8848
info@duka-design.de
duka-design.de

p.410

Located in Munich, duka design is an interior design firm that was founded by Dagmar Duchow and Anja Kalusche in 2007. The studio's main focus is on hospitality projects situated in Europe. The team believes the main key to running a successful hotel is the combination of good and functional design, regardless of the size or category of the accommodation.

Elenberg Fraser
160 Queen Street, Level 3
Melbourne VIC 3000
Australia
+61 3 9600 2260
mail@e-f.com.au
e-f.com.au

p.190

Elenberg Fraser is an architecture firm based in Melbourne that was established by founding directors Zahava Elenberg and Callum Fraser in 1998. Combining the creativity of a design studio with the outcome-orientation of a commercial firm, the team works on the premise that high design value and commercial success follow on from one another. The studio's mission is to carry out ambitious building projects of multiple scales and programmes, with a commitment to innovation, design and sustainability.

Equip
C. Pellaires 30-38 G1
08019 Barcelona
Spain
+34 93 303 4660
equip@equip.com.es
equip.com.es

p. 440

Equip is a multidisciplinary architecture practice based in Barcelona founded as ADD+ in 1990 but operating under its current name since 2006. To the team of architects and industrial designers led by Xavier Claramunt, the development process is just as important as the end product. In a desire to offer constant innovation, the practice just launched a new approach to projects: 'Responses'. This initiative combines the disciplines of architecture, interior design, industrial design and jewellery, areas in which the team has been active since 1990. Besides opening its own office in China in 2005, Equip also works together with Ferran Adrià, Hospes Hoteles, BMW, Chic&Basic and Cosmic.
Photo Jaume de Laiguana

Esrawe Studio
Alejandro Dumas #16
Col. Polanco
11560 Mexico City
Mexico
+52 55 5553 9611
infoshowroom@esrawe
esrawe.com

p.180

Esrawe Studio, the workshop founded by industrial designer Héctor Esrawe, focuses on developing concepts for furniture, product and interior design. The company is composed of an experienced group of designers and architects who, through a method based on listening, analysis and exploration, develop creative and pioneering ideas that allow its customers access to harmonious and unique life experiences.

Estudio Campana
São Paulo
Brazil
+55 11 3825 3408
press@campanas.com.br
campanas.com.br

p.478

Brothers Fernando and Humberto Campana have worked together in Brazil in the field of design since 1983. Their focus has been to transform something plain into something decadent and opulent. By experimenting with high- and low-tech materials and using artisanal techniques, the Campana brothers are able to define a new aesthetic based on experimentation and advanced technologies in product design and interior design.

FFD
2324 North Miami Avenue
Miami, FL, 33127
United States
+1 305 576 7556
info@ffdmiami.com
ffdmiami.com

p.168

François Frossard founded his design firm FFD in Miami in 1998. He is an industrial designer who has developed a signature grand style infused with 'high bold drama' that can be seen in the chic interiors he has created for hospitality venues around the world. He confronts each project with a careful meditation on style, function and originality: a marriage of art and business with a profound understanding of his clientele.

Francesc Rifé Studio
Escoles Pies 25
08017 Barcelona
Spain
+34 93 414 1288
f@rife-design.com
rife-design.com

p.504

With a double degree in interior and industrial design, Francesc Rifé's professional career began as an undergraduate with independent commissions for various design and architecture studios, while at the same time undertaking his own projects. After several years of training, he established his own studio in 1994. Based in Barcelona with a team of more than ten designers and architects, the studio specializes in commercial and private projects that encompass spatial order and geometric proportion with a portfolio covering interior and industrial landscapes.

Gabriel Corchero Studio
San Ildefonso 25
28012 Madrid
Spain
+34 91 506 0661
info@gabrielcorchero.org
gabrielcorchero.org

354

Gabriel Corchero Studio is a multidisciplinary studio based in Madrid, devoted to graphic design, product design, interior design, packaging design, web design and art direction. Its ideas evolve into exclusive projects: as it firmly believes in the singularity of each piece, it uses only spotless materials and gives impeccable finishes to customize each of its works. Gabriel Corchero Studio gathers a qualified team of professionals who can also collaborate, when needed, with third parties that complement the team's skills in projects involving architecture photography, video production and social media. Cutting-edge, craftsmanship and versatility define their work.

GCA arquitectes associats
Valencia 289
08009 Barcelona
Spain
+34 93 476 1800
info@gcaarq.com
gcaarq.com

p.042, 524

Josep Juanpere and Antonio Puig founded GCA arquitectes associats in Barcelona in 1986; associates Josep Riu, Jesús Hernando, Jordi Castañé, Lluís Escarmís and Francisco de Paz joined the team later. The studio, currently boasting a team of more than 50 professionals, opened a second office in Shanghai in 2010. The architectural team – a multidisciplinary group of professionals – brings interior designers, engineers, graphic designers, landscape architects and photographers on board for each specific project. GCA plans and develops commissions in architecture, urbanism and interior design for the public and private sectors.

Giorgio Gullotta Architekten
Rathausstrasse 12
20095 Hamburg
Germany
+49 40 3251 390
office@giorgiogullotta.com
giorgiogullotta.com

p.024, 278

Giorgio Gullotta Architekten, founded in 2006, specializes in architecture and interior design. The studio's work ranges from small private family homes and refurbishments of historic buildings to large-scale hotel projects, for clients in Germany and abroad. The designs are often playful and generous but also precise and clear-cut.

Girbau Mateu
Carrer Perú 118, Local A
08018 Barcelona
Spain
+34 65 411 2991
girbaumateu@girbaumateu.com
girbaumateu.com

188

Architects Neus Mateu and Quim Girbau founded their Barcelona-based studio in 2001. The studio consists of architects and interior designers dedicated to creating comfortable atmospheres and corporate image design. Mateu and Girbau combine their work in the design studio with teaching at the School of Architecture of Barcelona.

Glenn Sestig Architects
Fortlaan 1
9000 Ghent
Belgium
+32 9 240 1190
contact@glennsestigarchitects.com
glennsestigarchitects.com

p.140, 246

Glenn Sestig studied architecture at the Henry Van de Velde Institute in Antwerp and went on to found his own architecture firm in 1999. The focus of the firm is on chic, contemporary projects. He aims to facilitate the evolution of cities into better places by applying his signature cosmopolitan and luxurious style to shops, bars, nightclubs, residential buildings, renovations, temporary projects and product design.

GM Architects
Verdun Centre (Concorde Building), 10th Floor
113-5204 Beirut
Lebanon
+961 1 346 770
arch@gm-architects.com
gm-architects.com

p.030

GM Architects was established by Galal Mahmoud in Beirut in 1996. Now with offices in Beirut and Abu Dhabi, GM Architects has a multidisciplinary and holistic approach to architecture. The firm is driven by its founder's deep belief in the power of good design and architecture to positively affect the well-being of society. This is reflected in the meticulous attention to detail shown throughout the interior and exterior designs in its wide-ranging portfolio, which covers the hospitality, commercial and residential sectors.

Graven Images
175 Albion Street
Glasgow G1 1RU
United Kingdom
+44 141 552 6626
info@graven.co.uk
graven.co.uk

450

Glasgow based design studio Graven images is respected for its approach to, and delivery of, diverse and consistently successful projects for a global clientele. Led by founding director Ross Hunter, Graven Images has been providing leading-edge design consultancy services, including interior environments and branding and communications design, for the corporate, public and hotel and leisure sectors for over 25 years. A highly experienced team of 25 individuals, including architects, interior designers, graphic designers, 3D artists and exhibition designers.

Grzywinski+Pons
594 Broadway, Suite 1214
New York, NY, 10012
United States
+1 64 6536 2716
matt@gp-arch.com
gp-arch.com

p.530

Grzywinski+Pons is a New York-based practice, founded in 2002, led by principals Matthew Grzywinski and Amador Pons. The company has developed a diverse body of built work including retail, commercial, hospitality and residential commissions. The practice is committed to design excellence predicated on quality, beauty, innovation and a rigorous approach to detail. With each commission, Grzywinski+Pons endeavours to serve the programmatic and functional essence of the project through the application of concept-driven design.

Honest Entertainment
117 Great Western Studios
65 Alfred Road
London W2 5EU
United Kingdom
+44 20 3214 3310
info@honestentertainment.co.uk
honestentertainment.co.uk

p.270

Honest Entertainment was founded in 2007, bringing together Tanya Clark's and Heston Harper's combined 20 years of experience in film, theatre, food and set design. The Honest team designs, creates and stages events for companies and individuals around the world. The dedicated and passionate team members pride themselves on nurturing and challenging all aspects of event production.

IDA 14
Im Viadukt...7
Viaduktstrasse 73
8005 Zurich
Switzerland
+41 44 463 12 33
atelier@ida14.ch
ida14.ch

p.406

Zurich is home to IDA 14, an architecture firm founded by Karsten Schmidt-Hoensdorf in 1993. The emphasis of the design practice is on interior architecture and, more specifically, on restaurants and hotels. IDA 14 also designs and advises on art and culture projects, refurbishes private houses and apartments and offers its own design furniture collection (IDA collection). The firm follows the philosophy that the requirements of use and the interior design/design details have to come together in a harmonious and highly functional whole.

Imagine Native
Room 305, Tesbusy Centre
28 Queen's Road East
Wanchai, Hong Kong
Hong Kong
+852 2529 9917
info@imagine-native.com
imagine-native.com

p.078

Imagine Native is a Hong Kong based architecture and interior design firm founded by Edmond Tse, C. Lai and F. Fung in 2009. With extensive experience in various types of projects, Imagine Native believes that innovative ideas and new design forms are developed through critical analysis of project parameters, such as site, marketing strategy and other specific design criteria. To maximize the design potential, the firm also aims for a cross-descipline approach, ensuring that clients and specialists work together to find the most appropriate design solution.

Ippolito Fleitz Group
Augustenstrasse 87
70197 Stuttgart
Germany
+49 711 993 392 330
info@ifgroup.org
ifgroup.org

p.080, 198

Ippolito Fleitz Group is a multidisciplinary, internationally operating design studio based in Stuttgart. The studio is made up of identity architects and aims to develop products, architecture and communication projects that are part of a whole and yet distinctive in their own right. The team conceives and constructs buildings, interiors and landscapes along with the development of products and communication measures.

Joey Ho Design
Unit 1601-1602, 16th Floor,
Car Po Commercial Building
18-20 Lyndhurst Terrace
Hong Kong
Hong Kong
+852 2850 8732
enjoy@joeyhodesign.com
joeyhodesign.com

p.224

Joey Ho Design was established in 2002 with a young and energetic team of talented individuals, all with their own skills, styles and disciplines, the studio creates dynamic and engaging commercial and residential spaces. Driven by the pursuit of quality, the team is always concerned about the physical context of works and sensitive to the community, as well as mindful of the well-being of users.

Karim Rashid
357 West 17th Street
New York, NY, 10011
United States
+1 212 929 8657
office@karimrashid.com
karimrashid.com

p.484

With over 3000 designs in production, Karim Rashid is one of the most prolific designers of his generation. A testament to Rashid's commitment to diversity and genuine design is the fact that he has worked in over 35 countries. His collection of work includes interior design projects, everyday objects, furniture, brand identities and high-tech products. Rashid's core design belief is based on 'the betterment of our lives poetically, aesthetically, experientially, sensorially and emotionally'.

Kinney Chan & Associates
11th Floor, Chung Nam Building
1 Lockhart Road
Wanchai, Hong Kong
Hong Kong
+852 2545 1322
info@kca.com.hk
kca.com.hk

p.300

Kinney Chan & Associates offers a full spectrum of interior design and project management services across multiple industries. Founded in 1995 by Kinney Chan, the key motivating words behind the studio's approach are creativity and originality. With its initiative-taking and innovative team of designers, KCA has a varied portfolio including hospitality, bar, restaurant, residential, commercial and corporate projects.

Koncept Stockholm
Grev Turegatan 29
11438 Stockholm
Sweden
+46 8 5458 7900
info@koncept.se
koncept.se

p.510

Koncept Stockholm is an architecture and design firm based in Sweden. The company has a creative team of 40 employees working in the areas of design, architecture and concept development, with a product portfolio including retail, hotels and offices. Koncept produces unique environments that create value and a competitive advantage for its clients.

LABOR13
Delnicka 13
170 00 Prague 7
Czech Republic
+420 220 511 129
info@labor13.cz
labor13.cz

p.466

LABOR13 was established in 2007 by Martin Vomastek, Albert Pražák and Jiří Bardoděj. The practice is based in Prague and has produced a number of projects, mostly in the Czech Republic, including public and private buildings, renovations of historical buildings, public and private interiors, museum expositions and the design of public urban spaces. A significant aspect of its work is that it devotes specific care and attention to landscape and urban context and keeps an open mind towards the needs of the client and the logic of building purpose.

Lieven Musschoot
Kopsdreef 2, Apt 3.1
8300 Knokke
Belgium
+32 475 685 537
lieven.musschoot@sk be
lievenmusschoot.be

p.058

Lieven Musschoot studied interior design at the Sint-Lucas Academy of Visual Arts and Architecture in Ghent, Belgium and founded his own studio in January 2008. The studio's portfolio covers projects which focus on restaurant, hotel, residential and retail design. In collaboration with Mathias Hennebel, the studio has also designed products for Wever & Ducré, Sywawa and Xala.

Little
17-3 SPBS Kamiyama-cho,
Shibuya
150-0047 Tokyo
Japan
+81 3 5465 0577
saorimiwa@gmail.com
little-inc.com

p.574

Saori Miwa is an experienced designer based in Japan. After working with Tonerico for over 10 years, she decided to establish her own interior design studio, Little, in Tokyo in 2010. The studio has already built up a portfolio that includes a range of interior design projects, including restaurants and cafés, offices and exhibition stands, and shops and retail spaces.

LOFF
Braga
Portugal
+351 966 562 449
loff@loff.pt
loff.pt

p.328

LOFF is a lighting design and architecture practice founded in 2009 by Cláudia Costa, which aims to create a dynamic approach to architecture by combining it with light, a fundamental element of creation as well as of human well-being. The ultimate goal is to show clients that by demanding quality, one can aspire to better spaces, better light and better living.

Luchetti Krelle
56 Cooper Street
Surry Hills NSW 2010
Australia
+61 2 9699 3425
studio@luchettikrelle.com
luchettikrelle.com

p.118, 380

Luchetti Krelle is an interior design firm established by partners Stuart Krelle and Rachel Luchetti in 2008. The studio has a diverse portfolio, with a primary focus on the hospitality sector. As the various disciplines of design often overlap and integrate, the firm endeavours to offer a total concept, from branding and identity design, to customized furniture and fitting design, to salvaging and appropriation and even sourcing site locations.

M+R interior architecture
Aalsterweg 230
5644 RK Eindhoven
the Netherlands
+31 40 213 7408
info@mplusr.nl
mplusr.nl

p.462

M+R interior architecture is an internationally operating office founded in 2000 by Hans Maréchal. Its fields of activity often involve complex assignments, such as converting and designing offices, airports, libraries, restaurants, hotels, theatres and shops. In addition to its design skills and core activities for building and interior architecture, it is also involved in revitalizing existing buildings and monuments. The power of a strong design and its realization is vision, innovation and quality.

mancini enterprises
17 Crescent Avenue,
Kesavaperumalpuram
600028 Chennai
India
+91 44 2461 4000
architects@
mancini-design.com
mancini-design.com

p.334

Founded in 2004, mancini enterprises offers comprehensive design services in the fields of urban planning, architecture, interiors, landscape and product design. With a base in Chennai, in the south of India, mancini's team – headed by J.T. Arima and Niels Schoenfelder – has a portfolio that covers hotels, resorts, schools, residential developments, urban landscapes, interiors, furniture and lighting.

Mansikkamäki+JOY
8 Beck Road
London E8 4RE
United Kingdom
+447894900360
studio@manandjoy.com
manandjoy.com

p.070

Mansikkamäki+JOY is a young practice operating in the realms of architecture and design, founded in 2010 by Taneli Mansikkamäki and Joy Sriyuksiri who both studied at the Architectural Association in London. The office sees design as a totality: unique concepts that continue through to physical spaces and structures, taking into consideration the image and individuality of the client and the context. With projects that vary in scale and location, the studio's portfolio ranges from a summer cottage in Finland, to a residential/work unit built using recycled shipping containers in Koh Samui, to an experimental timber pavilion that utilises local construction materials in southern Thailand.

Manuelle Gautrand Architecture
36 Boulevard De La Bastille
75012 Paris
France
+33 15 695 0646
contact@manuelle-gautrand.com
manuelle-gautrand.com

p.314

Manuelle Gautrand qualified as an architect in 1985. After working on several joint projects, she set up her own practice in Lyon in 1991, and moved it to Paris in 1994. Gautrand's portfolio includes a broad range of projects, from museums and theatres to office buildings, from shopping malls to the apartment buildings. She also teaches and works as a consultant.
photo Harixcalde

Marco Sousa Santos
Rua Latino Coelho
83, 5º esq
1050-134 Lisbon
Portugal
+351 933 036 840
marcoss@netcabo.pt
marcosousasantos.com

p.076

Marco Sousa Santos has developed numerous interior, product and exhibition design projects since he began his own studio in Lisbon in 1995. Commissioned to undertake projects around the world, Sousa Santos has also been involved as art director in a number of design shows and exhibitions in Portugal, Italy, Germany and Japan.

Maurice Mentjens
Martinusstraat 20
6123 BS Holtum
the Netherlands
+31 46 4811405
info@mauricementjens.com
mauricementjens.com

p.128

Based in the Netherlands, Maurice Mentjens is a designer of interiors, objects and furnishings. The studio focuses on intriguing, smaller-scale projects and almost exclusively creates interiors for shops, hotels, restaurants, offices and museums. The aim of this compact, talented and dynamic team is to deliver high-end design reflecting its passion. Quality and creativity are prioritized in all aspects of the design and implementation process.

Ministry of Design
20 Cross Street #03-01
048422 Singapore
Singapore
+65 6222 5780
studio@modonline.com
modonline.com

p.514

An integrated spatial design practice, Ministry of Design was founded by architect Colin Seah in Singapore in 2004. MOD's explorations are created amid a democratic studio-like atmosphere and progress seamlessly between form, site, object and space. The studio's portfolio includes projects in architectural, interior, product and experience design.

mode:lina
Concordia Design / CoOffice 01
Zwierzyniecka 3
60-813 Poznań
Poland
+48 66 715 6700
hello@modelina-architekci.com
modelina-architekci.com

p.498

In 2009 in Poznań, Poland, Paweł Garus and Jerzy Woźniak founded mode:lina: a group of designers specialized in the creation of space and design, whose passion is creating beautiful things that are also fully functional and environmentally friendly. When designing they strive to create a space that reflects individual lifestyle and ensures maximum impact. The studio is constantly in search of new technologies. The ambition is to implement the idea of an 'open studio' – based on the continuous exchange of experiences with various outside professionals and cooperation with universities and research centres – to be able to promote new technologies and use them in designs.

motorberlin.com
Engeldamm 68
10179 Berlin
Germany
+49 30 8573 1482
ingo.strobel@motor.com
motorberlin.com

p.234

Ingo Strobel founded the design office motorberlin.com in 1996. His work focuses on interior and brand design for premium bars and restaurants, as well as office spaces. He also works as a freelance designer and consultant for clients worldwide, and in 2006 he co-founded 'Hidden Fortress' in Los Angeles, an international network of creatives.
Photo Thomas Meyer

naumann.architektur
Robert Mayer Strasse 77
70191 Stuttgart
Germany
+49 711 305 8006
info@naumannnaumann.de
naumannnaumann.de

p.418

Stefanie and Martin Naumann founded naumann.architektur in Stuttgart in 2009. The studio's goal is to discover new strategies and the team works on various small and large projects, ranging from exhibitions to hotels and residential projects. The designers take time to sharpen their view, which is why they often find surprising solutions, solutions that are not only functional but offer so much more, revealing aspects of building that are very often forgotten.

nemaworkshop
49 Bleeker Street, Suite 401
New York, NY, 10012
United States
+1 212 645 0400
a@nemaworkshop.com
nemaworkshop.com

p.258

Led by founder Anurag Nema, nemaworkshop is an interior design and architecture firm based in New York. The studio's goal is the creation of innovative spaces that combine modern concepts with personality, cultural awareness and comfort. Current projects include a number of restaurants, hotels and spas.

Neri&Hu Design and Research Office
88 Yuqing Road
200030 Shanghai
China
+86 21 6082 3777
info@nhdro.com
nhdro.com

p.536

Founded in 2004 by partners Lyndon Neri and Rossana Hu, Neri&Hu Design and Research Office is a multidisciplinary architectural design practice based in Shanghai. NHDRO works internationally providing architecture, interior master planning, graphic and product design services. The studio boasts a multicultural staff and the diversity of the team reinforces a core vision for the practice: to respond to a global worldview incorporating overlapping design disciplines for a new paradigm in architecture. With Shanghai considered a new global frontier the city's cultural, urban, and historic contexts function as a point of departure for the architectural explorations involved in every project.

Note Design Studio
Heliosgatan 13
12030 Stockholm
Sweden
+46 8 656 8804
info@notedesignstudio.se
notedesignstudio.se

p.238

Note Design Studio is a Stockholm-based design company specializing in interior design, product design, architecture, branding and design management. Note Design Studio develops ideas, design concepts and branding strategies for brands. Their projects vary in scale from isolated design projects to long-term strategic brand reinforcing projects.

Nuca Studio
50-58 Nuferilor Street, Corp. A, 3rd Floor, Apt 14
013621 Bucharest
Romania
+40 722 237 678
robert@nuca-studio.ro
nuca-studio.ro

p.110, 134

Architect Robert Marin and set designer Ramona Macarie joined forces in 2008 to establish their Bucharest-based design firm, Nuca. The design team works on projects that range from architecture and interior design to product design and set design for theatre

Orbit Design Studio
Unit 2701a, 27th Floor, Thai Tower, All Seasons Place
87 Wireless Road
10330 Bangkok Thailand
+66 2 6543 6679
info@orbitdesignstudio
orbitdesignstudio.com

p.220

Orbit Design Studio is a creative multidisciplinary design agency with offices in Bangkok, Singapore and London. The company was established in 1996 and has become recognized internationally for innovative solutions that have a lasting impact. Notable projects include Bed Supperclub in Bangkok, Umami restaurant in Copenhagen and the Swatch restaurant in Shanghai, as well as office globally for Nike, PepsiCo and Diageo and retail design for Louis Vuitton and BMW.

Parolio & Euphoria Lab
Cruz 1, 5º p
28012 Madrid
Spain
+34 91 522 0309
info@euphorialab.com
euphorialab.com

p.250

Parolio & Euphoria Lab is an interior and communication design agency founded in 2003 by creative director and designer Parolio. The agency focuses on designing bars and clubs that include hip, dynamic and exciting new spaces. Parolio is also responsible for the naming, branding, image and creative direction of the projects. The agency also offers international trend consulting and market research for companies worldwide, especially in Asia and Latin America.

Patricia Urquiola
Piazzale Libia 5
20135 Milan
Italy
+39 028 738 1848
info@patriciaurquiola.com
patriciaurquiola.com

p.454

Spanish-born Patricia Urquiola opened her practice in Milan in 2001. Working in product design, architecture and concept creation, she crafts installations and designs for companies worldwide. Some of her products are on permanent display at the MoMA in New York and other museums, and exhibitions of her work have been held across the world.

Peter Kostelov
Bolshaya Serpuhouskaya 36, Apartment 24
115903 Moscow
Russia
pk71@ya.ru
kostelov.ru

p.304

Peter Kostelov started out as an art director for film and television studios in the early 1990s before deciding on a new career direction. He established his own design studio in 1995 and has been undertaking architectural projects ever since. His portfolio is varied and ranges from apartments and private houses to bars and clubs, often using cubic designs and natural materials in his projects.

plajer & franz studio
Erkelenzdamm 59-61
10999 Berlin
Germany
+49 30 616 5580
studio@plajer-franz.de
plajer-franz.de

p.064

Based in Berlin, plajer & franz studio is an international and interdisciplinary team of architects, interior architects and graphic designers. The company carries out all project stages, from concept to design as well as full-out supervision. Special project-based teams work on overall interior and building construction projects and on communication and graphic design.

Pubblik
Sassenheimstraat 51
1059 BC Amsterdam
the Netherlands
+31 6 2248 5046
info@pubblik.nl
pubblik.nl

p.212, 244

Pubblik is an Amsterdam-based design agency established by Marjolein Bangma in 2009. The expertise of the studio centres on hospitality projects, with a portfolio that already includes a number of bars, cafés and restaurants. The Pubblik ethos is to incorporate identity and purpose with entrepreneurial effects, inspired by back-to-basics concepts and an understanding of how service, selection, price, quality and interior can be mutually reinforcing.

Raëd Abillama Architects
Dbaye Street 66
2501-0923 Metn
Lebanon
+961 4 541 880
info@raarchitects.com
raarchitects.com

p.280

A staff of 20 architects, interior designers and structural engineers make up Raëd Abillama Architects. Since its founding in 1997, the Lebanon-based practice has completed many projects, including banks, offices, commercial and residential commissions, ranging in scale from complete buildings to interiors and architectural detailing. The studio has a team approach that facilitates the integration of technical, economic and management expertise into the planning and design of each project.

Ralf Gründer
Zittauerstrasse 2
03046 Cottbus
Germany
+49 355 383 2287
info@erides.de
erides.de

p.542

Ralf Gründer founded his own interior design company Erides in 1999. The company works on interior design projects, but their main work is producing tables, chairs, beds and other upholstered furniture. As they produce all the furniture themselves they can create almost any customer request.

Rashed Alfoudari
Khaldiya, Block 3, Al Naser Street, Avenue 39, House 33
72303 Khaldiya
Kuwait
+965 9793 6822
rashed@ubonkw.com

p.186

Rashed Alfoudari obtained his bachelor's degree in architecture from Kuwait University in 2010. He began his career as a freelancer, designing furniture pieces and small interior spaces for various clients. Having a passion for boutique restaurants, his first completed larger-scale project was Ubon. In 2012, he established his own design studio in Kuwait.

Raw Design
118 Hewlett Road
Cheltenham GL52 6AT
United Kingdom
+44 1242 227 342
design@matthewrawlinson.co.uk
raw-design.com

p.358

Set up by Matt Rawlinson in 1994, Raw Design is an individual creative practice specializing in the design of contemporary social environments, including cutting-edge bars, restaurants and nightclubs. UK-based Raw Design uses a creative approach to produce high-impact interiors to a wide variety of budgets. Raw's portfolio also includes residential projects, boutique hotels, retail spaces and corporate headquarters.

Rockwell Group
5 Union Square West,
8th Floor
New York, NY, 10003
United States
+1 212 463 0334
info@rockwellgroup.com
rockwellgroup.com

p.572

Founded in 1984 by David Rockwell, based in downtown New York with a satellite office in Madrid, the firm specializes in a wide array of project types, from hospitality, cultural and health care to educational, product and set design. With a desire to create immersive environments, Rockwell Group takes a cross-disciplinary approach to its inventive array of projects. Crafting a unique narrative and strategy for each client is fundamental to Rockwell Group's successful design approach. From the big picture to the last detail, the story informs and drives the design.
Photo Blandon Belushin

rojkind arquitectos
Tamaulipas 30 Piso 12, Col.
Hipódromo Condesa
06140 Mexico City
Mexico
+52 55 5280 8521
info@rojkindarquitectos.com
rojkindarquitectos.com

p.180

Founded by Michel Rojkind in 2002 in Mexico City, rojkind arquitectos is a firm with a portfolio that spans a diverse and global platform. The studio provides solutions for contemporary architectural and urban strategies, nurtured by a multinational team, bringing together experts from all fields involved in a highly collaborative, research and experimental-based design process.

Rooms
I. Chavchavadze
Avenue 75
0162 Tbilisi
Georgia
+995 57 755 3553
info@rooms.ge
rooms.ge

p.436

Rooms is a partnership between young Georgian designers Nata Janberidze and Keti Toloraia, recently joined by new business partner Baia Davitaia. Janberidze and Toloraia founded their design company after graduating from the Academy of Art in Tbilisi, Georgia in 2003. The studio focuses mainly on retail, restaurant, hotel and residential interior design projects but recently added product design to its portfolio. Since 2011, the team has collaborated with Moooi which now includes their Position Lamp in its collection. Rooms' work can also be found in Tbilisi, the capital city of Georgia.

SAQ architects
Arenbergstraat 44
1000 Brussels
Belgium
+32 2 500 6924
info@saq.eu
saq.eu

p.102

SAQ architects, managed by director Frederik Vaes, is a conceptual and interdisciplinary design agency specialized in developing spatial sceneries and concepts. It promotes working with artists, such as Arne Quinze, in order to ultimately give a project a unique and profound character. The subjects on which SAQ works is varied, ranging from master-planning, architecture and interiors, to creating concepts for marketing strategies, as well as for visual animations for public events. The studio's headquarters is in Brussels, with projects in Europe, the United States and Hong Kong.

SEHW Architektur
Wikingerufer 7
10555 Berlin
Germany
+49 30 3087 8510
info.berlin@sehw.de
sehw.de

p.410

SEHW was founded in 1996 and is now a registered trademark. Under the brand, several international companies of varying legal forms exist, currently employing about 40 people in several locations. Besides the original architecture activities, SEHW is also active in the areas of general planning and project development. Areas of focus are public-use buildings, mostly as the result of preliminary architect competitions, as well as offices, hotels and retail for private owners, investors and developers.

SHH
1 Vencourt Place
London W6 9NU
United Kingdom
+44 20 8600 4171
info@shh.co.uk
shh.co.uk

p.014, 122

SHH is an architecture practice and interior and branding design consultancy, formed in 1992 by chairman David Spence, managing director Graham Harris and creative director Neil Hogan. The company, based in its own West London studio, is a 55-strong practice and employs a cosmopolitan team of creative, technical and administrative staff. With a highly international workforce and portfolio, SHH initially made its name in ultra-high-end residential schemes, before extending its expertise to include leisure and offices. Clients include The Barbican, Liberty's, Teaspoon, Christie's and Savills.

Shop Around
2° Jacob van
Campenstraat 100hs
1073 XW Amsterdam
the Netherlands
+31 20 470 4727
info@shop-around.nl
shop-around.nl

p.286

Established in 1998 as a rep agency – mainly representing illustrators and graphic designers – Shop Around developed over the years into a creative production agency that specializes in contemporary illustration, graphic design, animation, motion graphics and interactive design. From their offices in Amsterdam, Rotterdam and New York they coordinate all their projects and hold strong contacts with their network of about 80 freelancers. Their aim is to give a broad overview of 'what is happening' to advertising agencies, publishers, TV and record companies and direct accounts.

Simone Micheli
Via Aretina 197/r
50136 Florence
Italy
+39 055 691 216
simone@simonemicheli.com
simonemicheli.com

p.546

Simone Micheli founded his eponymous Florence-based studio in 1990. Rather than limiting himself to one area of design, Micheli has built up a portfolio that includes architecture, interior design, exhibition design and graphic design. His strong commitment to the environment invariably leads to the creation of sustainable designs. When Micheli is not designing, he can be found teaching at the University of Florence's Department of Architecture or representing Italy at various international design exhibitions.
Photo Maurizio Marcato

Softroom
341 Oxford Street
London W1C 2JE
United Kingdom
+44 20 7408 0864
softroom@softroom.com
softroom.com

p.572

For over 15 years, award-winning London-based architecture firm Softroom has developed a reputation for design excellence and creative innovation. The firm has worked on a wide spectrum of projects for clients including The British Museum, Sony, Westfield Malls and the BBC. Softroom has also worked as creative consultant to YOTEL for several years, while its Clubhouse for Virgin Atlantic at Heathrow Airport has been repeatedly voted 'the best airline lounge in the world'.
Photo Joseph Burns

Space Architects & Designers
Hacı Emin Efendi Sok. 32/a, Nişantaşı
34365 Istanbul
Turkey
+90 212 231 5513
info@space.com.tr
space.com.tr

p.552

Founded in 1997 by Kaan Çetinkaya as Han Architectural Design, Space Architects & Designers, as the firm is now known, continues to produce numerous innovative projects. The architects, interior designers, landscape architects and project managers at Space serve their clients in professional teams in analysing situations and sites, setting up the correct concepts and planning, implementing the ideas of the projects, and carrying out project management.

Stephen Williams Associates
Admiralitätstrasse 71
20459 Hamburg
Germany
+49 40 8793 3400
mail@stephenwilliams.com
stephenwilliams.com

p.398

Hamburg-based Stephen Williams Associates was established in 2009 by architect Stephen Williams with Julia Erdmann as associate partner. It is an architecture and design office that aims to develop value-added concepts in the fields of society, property and brands. The 13-strong team sees architecture and design as a communications platform, as inspiration, experience and discovery. Its portfolio includes planning, architecture, and interior and furniture design.

Studio Gascoigne
19A Blake Street
Ponsonby
1011 Auckland
New Zealand
+64 9 378 8088
info@studiogascoigne.com
studiogascoigne.com

p.036

Studio Gascoigne is a multidisciplinary design and consultancy office that integrates architecture with interior and lighting design, as well as retail branding services. Gascoigne specializes in creating new retail brands and re-imaging existing ones. Design services are provided for a wide range of projects, such as retail chains, flagship stores, 'pop-up' stores, showrooms, shopping malls, retail and food precincts, cafés and restaurants, in New Zealand and overseas. Clients include many of the most successful retailers in Australasia, as well as several multinational corporations.

Studio Nitzan Cohen
Naupliastrasse 103a
81545 Munich
Germany
+49 89 2032 8681
mail@nitzan-cohen.com
nitzan-cohen.com

p.034, 096, 098

Nitzan Cohen has a research-oriented attitude towards conceptual design and the ability to translate this into a new visual language, objects and spaces. His studio has a multidisciplinary approach, with projects ranging from industrial products, furniture and spaces to art direction and strategic consultancy.
Photo Gerhardt Kellerman

Studio SKLIM
318C King George's Avenue,
King George's Building
208563 Singapore
Singapore
+65 6293 6275
info@sklim.com
sklim.com

p.172

Architect Kevin Lim, an alumnus of the Architectural Association, worked extensively in London, Singapore and Beijing with various renowned offices before establishing his own design practice, Studio SKLIM, in 2010. The Singapore-based studio believes that banality breeds creativity and each project stems from its own unique set of pragmatics and constraints. The studio strives to explore the complex relationship with the environment with the most basics of design solutions.
Photo Luca Gabino

Studio UP
Ulica Grada Mainza 18
10000 Zagreb
Croatia
+385 1378 9996
info@studioup.hr
studioup.hr

p.424

Studio UP was founded by Croatian architects Lea Pelivan and Toma Plejić at the end of 2003. The Zagreb-based firm concentrates on contemporary architecture and urbanism. The studio employs five to ten architects and designers at any one time to work on international projects that include the design of sports buildings, public spaces, corporate interiors and hotels.

SynergyHamburg
Eschenstieg 2
20259 Hamburg
Germany
+49 40 2351 8994
info@synergyhamburg.com
synergyhamburg.com

p.044

SynergyHamburg is a network of independent Hamburg-based designers cooperating on larger projects. The core group members – lighting designer Tom Schlotfeldt, Feng Shui expert Sabine von Waldersee, as well as photographer and designer Martin Zitzlaff – collaborate occasionally on projects such as exhibitions, hotel interiors, culinary concepts and health care design.

Takenouchi Webb
17 Woking Road, #03-05
Tangier
138696 Singapore
Singapore
+65 6475 4005
info@takenouchiwebb.com
takenouchiwebb.com

p.368

Established in 2007 in Singapore, Takenouchi Webb is a partnership between British architect Marc Webb and Japanese interior designer Naoko Takenouchi. It is an integrated design firm that develops architectural and interior environments, specializing in hotel, restaurant and bar projects. The duo believes in a holistic approach to design, developing the architecture, interior and furniture for each project, with rigorous detailing and complete involvement at every stage of the process.

The Metrics
195 Chrystie Street, #701D
New York, NY, 10002
United States
+1 646 379 7836
info@metricsdesigngroup.com
metricsdesigngroup.com

p.194

The Metrics is a New York design consultancy led by creative director and founder Elle Kunnos de Voss. Established in 2007, the studio is dedicated to creating social environments and hospitality experiences. From designing restaurants to experimental temporary installations, their work is always defined by a strong conceptual narrative. As creating experiences goes well beyond furniture, finishes and function, the team's design methodology is much like theatre; always starting with a plot that defines the process.
Photo Felix de Voss

Tomás Azevedo Neves, Arquitecto
Rua do Centro Cultural 7b, 1º f
1700-106 Lisbon
Portugal
+351 218 489 098
tomasaneves@mail.telepac.pt

p.076

Tomás Azevedo Neves opened his own architectural office in 2000 and since then has worked in the fields of architecture, interiors and design. Mastering the process and working to different scales, the studio offers insight at all stages of a project; starting on the design up to the planning and construction phases. Developing new projects as well as rehabilitations in historic centres, from single and multi-family dwellings to urban interventions, commerce, services and industry, Azevedo Neves works in Portugal, Spain, France, Poland and Brazil.

unit-berlin
Lobeckstrasse 30-35
10969 Berlin
Germany
+49 30 7871 1355
mail@unit-berlin.de
unit-berlin.de

p.012

Established in 2001, unit-berlin is a creative studio specializing in corporate design and architecture. It is run by managing director Hinnerk Dedecke together with Heike Dertmann, and the unit team works together to create, design and build identities. The studio's main focus is the creation of restaurants, shops, trade fair stands and temporary architecture projects.

Very Space
11th Floor No. 17, Sec.
Zhongxiao E. Road
Taipei 110
Taiwan
+886 2 2749 1238
id@very-space.com
very-space.com

p.050

Interior design company Very Space was founded in 2002 by Louis Liu, a designer with a strong background in the visual arts and an artist with vast experience in architectural, industrial, interior, stage and public art design. Always an active participant in the planning and creation of spaces for exhibitions and performances and the design of art installations, he has completed projects throughout the Taiwanese capital. The company specializes in residential interior design with projects ranging from sophisticated apartment buildings and spacious luxury residences to smaller customized homes.

VLS Interior Architecture
Gonsiori 5A-13
10117 Tallinn
Estonia
+372 507 8409
ville@vls.ee
vls.ee

p.230

VLS Interior Architecture was founded in 2007 by Ville Lausmäe. The small team now also includes Kadi Karmann and Peeter Klaas. The design office specializes in interior architecture and design at both the local and international level. The firm's portfolio includes projects ranging from work on the Art Museum of Estonia and Tallinn City Theatre to the interior design of cruise ships, offices, private houses and to other projects ranging from graphic work to furniture.

Vrtiška•Žák
Na Zderaze 3
12000 Prague
Czech Republic
+420 605 730 018
design@roman-vrtiska.com
design@vladimirzak.cz
roman-vrtiska.com
vladimirzak.cz

p.472

Vrtiška•Žák since 2008, Roman Vrtiška and Vladimir Žák have been friends since their studies at the Academy of Arts, Architecture and Design in Prague. The Czech designers have a wide-ranging portfolio that includes projects in the fields of architecture, product design and graphic design.

Wonderwall
3-4-10 Sendagaya,
Shibuya-ku
151-0051 Tokyo
Japan
+81 3 6438 1717
contact@wonder-wall.com
wonder-wall.com

p.342

Founded in 2000 by Masamichi Katayama, the interior design firm Wonderwall is best known for its retail concepts. Katayama's interest in design has always been broad, respecting conventional aspects of architecture while breaking traditional boundaries. The company portfolio includes projects that are distinctly unique in design and yet attentive to function.

Workshop of Wonders
Oudegracht 362
3511 PN Utrecht
the Netherlands
+31 30 231 8686
info@workshopofwonders.nl
workshopofwonders.nl

p.286

Founded in 1993, Workshop of Wonders is about creating memories and designing experiences. Their seasoned interior architecture studio, and them being a dealer of many design brands, allow them to create stimulating environments for living, working and relaxing. Their diverse hospitality projects, schools, private residences and working environments directly reflect the character of their clients and their companies, making every project unique. The Dutch team does everything from concept development via custom designs to managing the execution and supplying the furnishing and lighting.

Wunderteam
Wierzbowa 24/26/19
90-245 Łódź
Poland
+48 500 147 864
info@wunderteam.pl
wunderteam.pl

p.336

Wunderteam is an independent Polish interior design studio founded in 2008 by Magdalena Koziej and Paulina Stępień. The team designs interiors for public utility buildings, including historic structures, commercial spaces and offices. All the studio's projects combine functionalism, technical knowledge and creativity, and implement innovative space adaptation solutions. The team members approach the entire design process so that at every step they have total control, including analysis of ideas, concept and design, and supervision of the execution.

Zege Architects
6 Likiou Street
10674 Athens
Greece
+30 210 721 4706
zege@zege.gr
zege.gr

p.518

The Zeppos – Georgiadi + Associates architectural design office was founded by Tasos Zeppos and Eleni Georgiadi in 1981. After collaborating closely for over 20 years, the two architects created Zege Architects. The wide range of Zege architects' activities includes architectural, interior design and furnishing studies, landscape designs, tender packages-detail drawings and site monitoring. For the team, Leonardo da Vinci's maxim 'Simplicity is the ultimate sophistication' is the key to contemporary well-being and finds its perfect expression in the company's work.

VENUE ADDRESSES

...

.HBC → p.012
unit-berlin
Karl-Liebknecht-Strasse 9
10178 Berlin
Germany
hbc-berlin.de

25hours Hotel Zurich West → p.388
Alfredo Häberli
Pfingstweidstrasse 102
8005 Zurich
Switzerland
25hours-hotels.com

25hours Hotel Vienna → p.392
Dreimeta
Lerchenfelderstrasse 1–3
1070 Wien
Austria
25hours-hotels.com

25hours Hotel Hamburg Hafencity → p.398
Stephen Williams Associates
Ubersee Allee 5
20457 Hamburg
Germany
25hours-hotels.com

A

Allure by Cipriani → p.220
Orbit Design Studio
Yas Marina, Yas Island
Abu Dhabi
United Arab Emirates
nightcluballure.com

Arthouse Café → p.224
Joey Ho Design
Hangzhou
China

Atelier Mecanic → p.228
Corvin Cristian
12 Covaci Street
Bucharest
Romania

B

Barbican Foodhall & Lounge → p.014
SHH
Barbican Centre
Silk Street
London EC2Y 8DS
United Kingdom
barbican.org.uk

Bonbon Club → p.230
VLS Interior Architecture
Mere pst 6e
10111 Tallinn
Estonia
bonbon.ee

Bond & Brook → p.018
d-raw
Fenwick Department store
63 New Bond Street
London W1S 3BS
United Kingdom
fenwick.co.uk

Buck and Breck → p.234
motorberlin.com
Brunnenstrasse 177
10119 Berlin
Germany
buckandbreck.com

Bullerei → p.024
Giorgio Gullotta Architekten
Lagerstrasse 34b
20357 Hamburg
Germany
bullerei.com

Buon Grande Aria → p.026
brownbag lab.
2-1-3 Kitahama, Chuo-ku
541-0041 Osaka
Japan
buongrande.com

Burj Al Hamam → p.030
GM Architects
Pearl Island
Doha
Qatar

C

Café Foam → p.238
Note Design Studio
Karlavägen 75
11449 Stockholm
Sweden
cafefoam.se

Café Schilders → p.244
Pubblik
1e van der Helststraat 45
1073 AC Amsterdam
the Netherlands
cafeschilders.nl

Charlie → p.034
Studio Nitzan Cohen
Schyrenstrasse 8
81543 Munich
Germany
charl.ie

City Garden Hotel → p.406
IDA 14
Metallstrasse 20
6300 Zug
Switzerland
citygarden.ch

Club 69 → p.246
Glenn Sestig Architects
Oude Beestenmarkt 5
9000 Ghent
Belgium
club-69.be

Club Musée → p.250
Parolio & Euphoria Lab
C. Alberto Alcocer 33
28036 Madrid
Spain
musee.es

Cocoro → p.036
Studio Gascoigne
56a Brown Street, Ponsonby
1021 Auckland
New Zealand
cocoro.co.nz

Cornelia & Co → p.042
GCA arquitectes associats
C. Valencia 225
08007 Barcelona
Spain
corneliaandco.com

osmo Hotel → p.410
uka design and SEHW Architektur
pittelmarkt 13
0117 Berlin
ermany
osmo-hotel.de

ristini → p.254
ndrea Lupacchini Architetto
iazzale Aldo Moro 23
0041 Albano Laziale
aly
www.cristiniloungebar.it

'espresso → p.258
emaworkshop
17 Madison Avenue on 42nd Street
ew York, NY, 10017
nited States
espresso.com

a Re → p.260
ndrea Lupacchini Architetto
ia Bisagno 19
0199 Rome
aly

aCaio → p.044
ynergyHamburg
he George Hotel
arcastrasse 3
2087 Hamburg
ermany
hegeorge-hotel.de

Das Neue Kubitscheck → p.264
Designliga
Gollierstrasse 14
0339 Munich
ermany
as-neue-kubitscheck.de

De Gusto → p.046
C+L Studio and Costa Group
ia Bastia 16/1
8017 Lavezzola
aly

De Vorstin → p.268
Beers|Brickworks
Koninginneweg 44
211 AS Hilversum
he Netherlands
devorstin.nl

Dishoom Pop-Up Beach Bar → p.270
Honest Entertainment
Queen Elizabeth Hall Terrace,
Southbank Centre
Belvedere Road
London SE1 8XX
United Kingdom
dishoom.com (Temporary venue)

DN innovación → p.050
Very Space
93, Songren Road, Xinyi District
Taipei 110
Taiwan
dn-asia.com

Duycker Café → p.276
Beers|Brickworks
Raadhuisplein 5
2132 TZ Hoofddorp
the Netherlands
duycker.nl

Elbgold → p.278
Giorgio Gullotta Architekten
Lagerstrasse 34c
20357 Hamburg
Germany
elbgold.com

Empire Hotel → p.414
AS Design Service
33 Hennessy Road
Wanchai, Hong Kong
Hong Kong
empirehotel.com.hk

Eten bij Lieven → p.058
Lieven Musschoot
Philipstockstraat 45a
8000 Bruges
Belgium
etenbijlieven.be

Forsthaus am Eiswoog → p.418
naumann.architektur
Eiswoog 1
67305 Ramsen
Germany
haeckenhaus.de

Galoupet → p.060
Blacksheep
13 Beauchamp Place
London SW3 1NQ
United Kingdom
(Venue closed)

Giacomo → p.064
plajer & franz studio
Bleibtreustrasse 32
1070 Berlin
Germany

Ginette → p.280
Raëd Abillama Architects
Gemmayzeh Gouraud Street
Convivium 05 Project
Beirut
Lebanon
ginette-beirut.com

Goli±Bosi → p.424
Studio UP
Morpurgova poljana 2
21000 Split
Croatia
gollybossy.com

GRAB Thai Street Kitchen → p.070
Mansikkamäki+JOY
5 Leonard Street
London EC2A 4AQ
United Kingdom
grabfood.co.uk

Grand Café Pearl → p.072
Barzileye Concept & Design
Hilton Hotel
Zeestraat 35
2518 AA The Hague
the Netherlands
grandcafepearl.com

H3 → p.076
Marco Sousa Santos and
Tomás Azevedo Neves
Rua da Trindade 13
1200-467 Lisbon
Portugal
h3.com

Haiku → p.078
Imagine Native
IFC Mall
8 Shiji Da Dao
200000 Shanghai
China
haikushanghai.com

Happy VIP → p.284
CLOUD-9 interior design
Dutch Pavilion 'Happy Street'
World Expo Shanghai 2010
Shanghai
China
(Temporary venue)

Hi/Lo → p.286
Workshop of Wonders
Croeselaan 213
3521 BN Utrecht
the Netherlands
smokingclub-hi-lo.com

Hilton Pattaya → p.430
Department of Architecture
333/101 Moo 9 Nong Prue,
Banglamung, Pattaya
20260 Chonburi
Thailand
hilton.com

Holiday Inn → p.436
Rooms
1.26 May Square
0171 Tbilisi
Georgia
holidayinn.com

Holyfields → p.080
Ippolito Fleitz Group
Kaiserstrasse 19-21
60311 Frankfurt
Germany

Hotel Acta Mimic → p.440
Equip
C. Arc del Teatre 58
08001 Barcelona
Spain
hotel-mimic.com

Hotel da Vila → p.446
Duarte Caldeira
Rua Dr Joao Augusto Teixeira
9360-215 Ponta do Sol (Madeira)
Portugal

Hotel Missoni → p.450
Graven Images
Arabian Gulf Road, Salmiya
22012 Kuwait City
Kuwait
hotelmissoni.com

House of the Purple → p.292
...,staat creative agency
648-6 Sinsa Dong, Gangnam-gu
Seoul 135-896
South Korea
houseofthepurple.com

Hyde → p.300
Kinney Chan & Associates
Lyndhurst Tower, 2nd Floor
1 Lyndhurst Terrace
Central, Hong Kong
Hong Kong
hyde.hk

Jaffa\Tel Aviv → p.086
BK Architecture
98 Yigal Alon Street
67891 Tel Aviv
Israel

Kismet → p.302
Blacksheep
The Park Hotel
22 Raj Bhjavan Road
500082 Hyderabad
India

Kluchi → p.304
Anton Grechko, Peter Kostelov and Alexey Rozenberg
Moscow
Russia

Koozie → p.090
Beers|Brickworks
Burgwal 13
5341 CP Oss
the Netherlands
koozie-oss.nl

Kufra Lounge Bar → p.308
Collidanielarchitetto
Oasi di Kufra Hotel
Strada Lungomare, km. 29.800
04016 Sabaudia
Italy
oasidikufra.it

Künstlerhaus-Farm → p.096
Studio Nitzan Cohen
Lenbachplatz 8
80333 Munich
Germany

Künstlerhaus-Grill → p.098
Studio Nitzan Cohen
Lenbachplatz 8
80333 Munich
Germany
the-grill-munich.de

Kush → p.100
A00 Architecture
98 Yanping Road
200042 Shanghai
China
kush.sh

Kwint → p.102
SAQ architects
Kuntsberg 1
1000 Brussels
Belgium
kwintbrussels.com

La Gaîté lyrique → p.314
Manuelle Gautrand Architecture
3 Bis Rue Papin
75003 Paris
France
gaite-lyrique.net

Le Fonograf → p.320
Andrea Mantello Architetto
Rue de la Violette 32
1000 Brussels
Belgium
lefonograf.be

Les Cavistes → p.108
blazysgérard
4115 Saint Denis
Montreal QC H2W 2M7
Canada
restaurantlescavistes.com

oft → p.110
Nuca Studio
Metropolis Center
Strada Grigore Alexandrescu 89-96
010627 Bucharest
Romania
oftlounge.ro

Lookout Café → p.326
Design spirits
Niseko Village, Abuta-gun, Niseko-cho
048-1592 Hokkaido
Japan

Mandarin Oriental Hotel → p.454
Patricia Urquiola
Passeig de Gracia 38-40
08007 Barcelona
Spain
mandarinoriental.com

Maze → p.114
Bates Smart
Crown Metropol hotel
8 Whiteman Street
Melbourne VIC 3000
Australia

Meltino Bar & Lounge → p.328
LOFF
Shopping Center Braga Parque
4710-427 Braga
Portugal
meltino.com

Mint Hotel → p.462
(now DoubleTree by Hilton)
M+R interior architecture
Oosterdoksstraat 4
1011 DK Amsterdam
the Netherlands
doubletree.hilton.com

Miura → p.466
LABOR13
Celadna 887
739 12 Celadna
Czech Republic
miura.cz

Mocha Mojo → p.334
mancini enterprises
72, 1st Avenue, Indra Nagar, Adyar
600020 Chennai
India
mocha.co.in

Momofuku seiōbo → p.118
Luchetti Krelle
The Star, Level G
80 Pyrmont Street
Sydney NSW 2009
Australia
momofuku.com

Moods → p.472
Vrtiška•Žák
Klimentska 28
110 00 Prague
Czech Republic
www.hotelmoods.com

MOSI → p.122
SHH
Liverpool Road, Castlefield
Manchester M3 4FP
United Kingdom
mosi.org.uk

Motto am Fluss → p.124
BEHF Architects
Franz Josefs Kai
1010 Vienna
Austria
motto.at/mottoamfluss

MS Café → p.336
Wunderteam
Wieckowskiego 36
90-734 Łódź
Poland
mscafe.com.pl

New Hotel → p.478
Estudio Campana
Filellinon 16
10557 Athens
Greece
yeshotels.gr

nhow → p.484
Karim Rashid
Stralauer Allee 3
10245 Berlin
Germany
nhow-hotels.com

Opera 02 → p.490
Costa Group
Via Medusia 32
41014 Levizzano di Castelvetro
Italy
opera02.it

Ozone → p.342
Wonderwall
The Ritz-Carlton hotel
1 Austin Road West
Kowloon, Hong Kong
Hong Kong
ritzcarlton.com

Park Café → p.128
Maurice Mentjens
Schiphol Amsterdam Airport
Evert van de Beekstraat 202
1118 CP Schiphol
the Netherlands

Phill → p.134
Nuca Studio
120 Drumul Potcoavei Street
077191 Bucharest
Romania
phill.ro

Plaza → p.350
Aroma
Badenerstrasse 109
8004 Zurich
Switzerland
plaza-zurich.ch

Ponce et Cheese Bar → p.354
Gabriel Corchero Studio
C. José Abascal 61
28003 Madrid
Spain
ponceetcheesebar.es

Project → p.358
Raw Design
Unit 1b, Riverside Retail Park,
Wherry Road
Norwich NR1 1WX
United Kingdom

Prosopa → p.138
360id studio
4 Konstantinoupoleos Street
11855 Athens
Greece
prosopa.gr

Puro Hotel → p.494
Blacksheep
Wlodkowica 6
50-072 Wroclaw
Poland
purohotel.pl

Quotel → p.498
mode:lina
Sniadeckich 30/5
61-001 Poznań
Poland

Renaissance → p.140
Glenn Sestig Architects
Nationalestraat 28-32
2000 Antwerp
Belgium
renaissance-antwerp.com

SANA → p.504
Francesc Rifé Studio
Nürnbergerstrasse 33/34
1077 Berlin
Germany
berlin.sanahotels.com

Scandic Grand Central → p.510
Koncept Stockholm
Kungsgatan 70
11120 Stockholm
Sweden
scandic.se

Seerestaurant Olympiapark → p.146
Clemens Bachmann Architekten
Spiridon-Louis-Ring 7
80809 Munich
Germany
olympiapark.de

smith&hsu teahouse → p.364
Carsten Jörgensen
No. 21, Section 1, Nan Jing East Road
Taipei
Taiwan
smithandhsu.com

Spice Market → p.152
Concrete Architectural Associates
W London
10 Wardour Street
London W1 D6QF
United Kingdom
spicemarketlondon.co.uk

Starhill Tea Salon → p.366
design spirits
Starhill Gallery Shopping Center
183 Jalan Bukit Bintang
55100 Kuala Lumpur
Malaysia
starhillgallery.com

Studio East Dining → p.158
Carmody Groarke
Westfield Stratford City,
Olympic Park
London
United Kingdom
studioeastdining.com
(Temporary venue)

Sushi Abuse → p.162
A00 Architecture
98 Yanping Road
200042 Shanghai
China
sushiabuse.com

Tanjong Beach Club → p.368
Takenouchi Webb
120 Tanjong Beach Walk,
Sentosa Island
098942 Singapore
Singapore
tanjongbeachclub.com

The Club → p.514
Ministry of Design
28 Ann Siang Road
069708 Singapore
Singapore
theclub.com.sg

The Forge → p.168
FFD
432 41st Street
Miami, FL, 33140
United States
theforge.com

The Met Hotel → p.518
Zege Architects
48, 26th October Street
54627 Thessaloniki
Greece
themethotel.gr

The Mirror → p.524
GCA arquitectes associats
C. Córcega 255
08036 Barcelona
Spain
themirrorbarcelona.com

The Nolitan → p.530
Grzywinski+Pons
30 Kenmare Street
New York, NY, 10012
United States
nolitan.com

The Tastings Room → p.172
Studio SKLIM
6 Raffles Boulevard,
Marina Square, #01-08
039594 Singapore
Singapore
tastings.sg

The Waterhouse at South Bund → p.5
Neri&Hu Design and Research Office
Maojiayuan Road No. 1-3,
Huangpu District
200011 Shanghai
China
waterhouseshanghai.com

The Weinmeister → p.542
Ralf Gründer
Weinmeisterstrasse 2
10178 Berlin
Germany
the-weinmeister.com

...nello → p.178
...rinkworth
...7 Pimlico Road
...ondon SW1W 8PH
...nited Kingdom
...nello.co.uk

...ori Tori → p.180
...ojkind arquitectos and Esrawe Studio
...emistocles #61, Col. Polanco
...560 Mexico City
...exico
...oritori.com.mx

...own @ House Street → p.546
...imone Micheli
...ia Goldoni 33
...0129 Milan
...aly
...ownhousestreet.com

...ulip City → p.552
...pace Architects & Designers
...Mesrutiyet Caddesi No. 95, Beyoglu
...4430 Istanbul
...urkey
...ulipcitytaksim.com

...Ubon → p.186
...Rashed Alfoudari
...Al Salhiya, Al Jawahara Tower, Ali
...AlSalim Street, Block 11, Plot No. 5
...Kuwait City
...Kuwait
...ubonkw.com

...Udon → p.188
...Girbau Mateu
...Clavel 6
...28004 Madrid
...Spain
...udon.es

...Unplugged Bar → p.370
...C4ID interieurarchitecten
...World Trade Center
...Strawinskylaan 377
...1077 XX Amsterdam
...the Netherlands

Vue de Monde Rialto → p.190
Elenberg Fraser
Rialto Tower, Level 55
525 Collins Street
Melbourne VIC 3000
Australia
vuedemonde.com.au

W London → p.558
Concrete Architectural Associates
10 Wardour Street
London W1 D6QF
United Kingdom
wlondon.co.uk

W Retreat & Spa Bali → p.566
AB Concept
Jl. Petitenget
80361 Seminyak, Bali
Indonesia
whotels.com

What Happens When → p.194
The Metrics
25 Cleveland Place
New York, NY, 10012
United States
(Temporary venue)

Wienerwald → p.198
Ippolito Fleitz Group
Wasserburger Landstrasse 198
81827 Munich
Germany
wienerwald.de

Yoshinoya → p.204
AS Design Service
Trend Plaza, Shop 25,
Level 3, South Wing
Tuen Mun, Hong Kong
Hong Kong
yoshinoya-hk.com

YOTEL → p.572
Rockwell Group and Softroom
570 10th Avenue
New York, NY, 10036
United States
yotel.com

Youdo Stone Café → p.374
Little
1-5-18 Komachi Kamakura
248-0006 Kanagawa
Japan

Yucca → p.378
Dariel Studio
Sinan Mansions 26F, 3rd Floor,
Sinan Road
200025 Shanghai
China
yuccashanghai.com

Zizzi → p.208
d-raw
8 Central Street Giles Plaza
London WC2H 8LA
United Kingdom
zizzi.co.uk

Zuiders Proeflokaal → p.212
Pubblik
Markt 5
5401 GN Uden
the Netherlands
zuiders.nl

Zumbo → p.380
Luchetti Krelle
The Star, Café Court
80 Pyrmont Street
Sydney NSW 2009
Australia
adrianozumbo.com

Night Fever 3
Hospitality Design

Publisher
Frame Publishers

Production
Marlous van Rossum-Willems

Authors
Sarah Martín Pearson, Carmel McNamara and Marlous van Rossum-Willems

Translation and editing
InOtherWords
(D'Laine Camp and Pierre Bouvier)

Graphic design
Mariëlle van Genderen, Cathelijn Kruunenberg and Marieke Vonk

Prepress
Edward de Nijs

Printing
IPP Printers

Trade distribution USA and Canada
Consortium Book Sales & Distribution, LLC.
34 Thirteenth Avenue NE, Suite 101
Minneapolis, MN 55413-1007
T +1 612 746 2600
T +1 800 283 3572 (orders)
F +1 612 746 2606

Distribution rest of world
Frame Publishers
Laan der Hesperiden 68
1075 DX Amsterdam
the Netherlands
distribution@frameweb.com
frameweb.com

ISBN: 978-90-77174-63-0

© 2012 Frame Publishers, Amsterdam, 2012

All rights reserved. No part of this publication may be reproduced or transmitted in any form or by any means, electronic or mechanical, including photocopy or any storage and retrieval system, without permission in writing from the publisher.

Whilst every effort has been made to ensure accuracy, Frame Publishers does not under any circumstances accept responsibility for errors or omissions. Any mistakes or inaccuracies will be corrected in case of subsequent editions upon notification to the publisher.

The Koninklijke Bibliotheek lists this publication in the Nederlandse Bibliografie: detailed bibliographic information is available on the internet at http://picarta.pica.nl

Printed on acid-free paper produced from chlorine-free pulp. TCF ∞
Printed in Poland

987654321